LONDON

AND THE

17TH CENTURY

THE MAKING OF THE WORLD'S GREATEST CITY

Margarette Lincoln

T0003509

YALE UNIVERSITY PRESS
NEW HAVEN AND LONDON

For information about this and other Yale University Press publications, please contact:
U.S. Office: sales.press@yale.edu   yalebooks.com
Europe Office: sales@yaleup.co.uk   yalebooks.co.uk

Set in Adobe Garamond Pro by IDSUK (DataConnection) Ltd
Printed in Great Britain by Clays Ltd, Elcograf S.p.A

Library of Congress Control Number: 2020946723

ISBN 978-0-300-24878-4 (hbk)
ISBN 978-0-300-26474-6 (pbk)

A catalogue record for this book is available from the British Library.

10 9 8 7 6 5 4 3 2 1

For Annie and Sophie

CONTENTS

CONTENTS

ILLUSTRATIONS

MAPS

1. London *c.* 1600, when Westminster was still a separate city.
2. London and Westminster *c.* 1700, showing the extent of expansion.

PLATES

1. The funeral procession of Queen Elizabeth I to Westminster Abbey, 28 April 1603, by an anonymous artist, 1603. BL Add MS 35324 f. 37v.
2. A panoramic view of London from the south bank looking across the River Thames, showing London Bridge and the City of London, by C.J. Visscher, 1616. Library of Congress Prints and Photographs Online Catalogue, http://loc.gov/pictures/resource/pga.02965.
3. *King James I of England and VI of Scotland*, by Daniel Mytens, 1621. © National Portrait Gallery, London.
4. *King Charles I*, by Daniel Mytens, 1631. © National Portrait Gallery, London.
5. *Oliver Cromwell*, after Samuel Cooper, based on a work of 1656. © National Portrait Gallery, London.
6. *Charles II Giving Audience at Christ's Hospital*, by Antonio Verrio, *c.* 1680. P.2-1956. © Victoria and Albert Museum, London.
7. *London: The Great Fire*, by Rocío Espín Piñar, 2016. © Rocío Espín Piñar. https://www.artstation.com/rocioespin.
8. *The Great Fire of London (1666)*, by an anonymous artist, *c.* 1675.

ILLUSTRATIONS

9. Scenes in London during the Plague of 1665, from a contemporary print in the Pepysian Collection, Cambridge. © Wellcome Collection.

10. The interior of a London coffee house, by an anonymous artist, *c.* 1690–1700. Chronicle of World History/Alamy Stock Photo.

11. *Prospectus intra Cameram Stellatam* [*View inside the Star Room*], by Francis Place, 1712. The History Emporium/Alamy Stock Photo.

12. *Samuel Pepys, 1633–1703*, by Godfrey Kneller, 1689. BHC2947, Caird Collection, National Maritime Museum, Greenwich, London.

13. Beheading of the Duke of Monmouth, 1685, by Jan Luyken, Jan Claesz ten Hoorn, 1689. Artokoloro/Alamy Stock Photo.

14. *East India Company Ships at Deptford*, English School, *c.* 1683. BHC 1873, Caird Collection, National Maritime Museum, Greenwich, London.

15. *Greenwich and London from One Tree Hill*, by Johannes Vosterman, *c.* 1680. BHC1808, Greenwich Hospital Collection, National Maritime Museum, Greenwich, London.

NOTE ON CONVENTIONS

During the period covered by this book, England, Wales and Ireland followed the older Julian Calendar, which was ten days behind the new-style Gregorian Calendar that most European countries used. All dates in the text are given in the Old Style but, as in modern usage, the New Year has been taken to commence on 1 January. Although 25 March (Lady Day) remained the official start of the year, 1 January had been called New Year's Day from at least the thirteenth century.

In quotations, the original spelling, punctuation and capitalization have been retained throughout. And in this period, 'u' and 'v' were often used interchangeably.

The symbols £ s. d. denote the pre-decimal currency in Britain of pounds, shillings and pence. Under this system there were four farthings in a penny, twelve pennies in a shilling and twenty shillings in a pound.

The Bank of England calculates that goods and services costing £1 in 1600 would cost £1 9s. 8d. in 1700, and £224.60 in 2019: https://www.measuringworth.com/ukcompare.

Before decimalization, Britain used imperial units of weight. There were 16 ounces (ozs) to the pound (lb), 14 pounds to a stone, 2 stones to a quarter and 4 quarters to a hundredweight.

PREFACE AND ACKNOWLEDGEMENTS

The seventeenth century was a remarkable period in London's history, which saw the emergence of the capital as a modern city. This book seeks to chart that progress, steering a path between matters of high politics and the thoughts and deeds of ordinary people. It includes merchants and artisans, not just royalty and military figures, and traces the untold stories of everyday Londoners. It surveys the entire century, helping to put major events and reversals into perspective. It delivers a broad political, economic and religious context for everyday life in the capital, unusually placing the history of London as a port alongside its social and political history. And it explores the civic use of public spectacle, rituals and pageants throughout the century. Overall, the book offers fresh insights into a fascinating age. The seventeenth century was not simply a disastrous epoch of domestic ills, civil strife and defeat at the hands of the Dutch. London's dynamic population showed tremendous energy and resilience in adversity. An extended history of London in this period helps to explain how England could emerge from such a turbulent century poised to become a great maritime power. At a social and cultural level this book also shows how masculine and feminine identities in these years were in part forged through the making of a modern, cosmopolitan city and how, increasingly, London gathered significance as an imagined landscape. The distinctive developments that took place in Stuart London continue to influence our impressions of the city today.

In writing this book I have received help and encouragement from many friends and colleagues. I owe a special debt to my agent, Maggie Hanbury, who first suggested that I explore the subject, and to my editor, Julian Loose at Yale University Press, who has provided expert advice throughout. I am grateful to

Yale's anonymous specialists who reviewed both the book proposal and the manuscript; they gave helpful advice and saved me from several factual errors. Thanks are also due to the hard-working team at Yale who oversaw the production of the book, particularly to Rachael Lonsdale, Marika Lysandrou, Lucy Buchan, Katie Urquhart, and Tree Abraham who created the jacket design. I was fortunate to have Richard Mason as my copy-editor, and the text has benefited immensely from his helpful suggestions. I would also like to thank proofreader Robert Sargant and cartographer Martin Brown.

I would also like to thank my former colleague Liza Verity, who shared useful source material, Jenny Moseley who arranged access to the archives of the Sir John Cass Foundation, and Roger Knight and Timothy Walker for a valuable preliminary discussion about this fascinating century and the relevant archives. Goldsmiths, University of London, offered a stimulating intellectual environment, and my particular thanks go to Vivienne Richmond and John Price.

I owe a great practical debt to expert staff in various libraries, archives and museums: the British Library, the British Museum, the Courtauld Institute of Art's libraries, the Guildhall Library, Lambeth Palace Library, the London Metropolitan Archives, The National Archives, Kew, and the Caird Library at Royal Museums Greenwich. Special thanks to Melanie Johnson of the British Library for checking references when Covid-19 restrictions were in place. My understanding of daily life in seventeenth-century London owes much to museum collections as well as to archives and libraries.

Most of all I am indebted to my husband for generously taking time from his own work to read versions of all the chapters and for listening with patient enthusiasm to innumerable stories from the period. I may just have convinced him that the key to understanding London, and possibly Britain itself, is to be found in the seventeenth century.

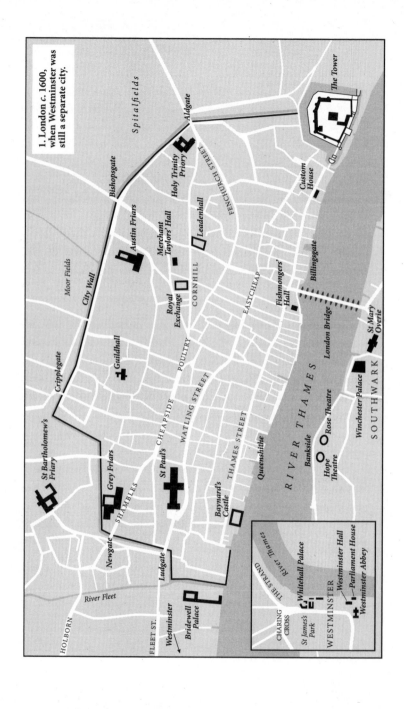

1. London c. 1600, when Westminster was still a separate city.

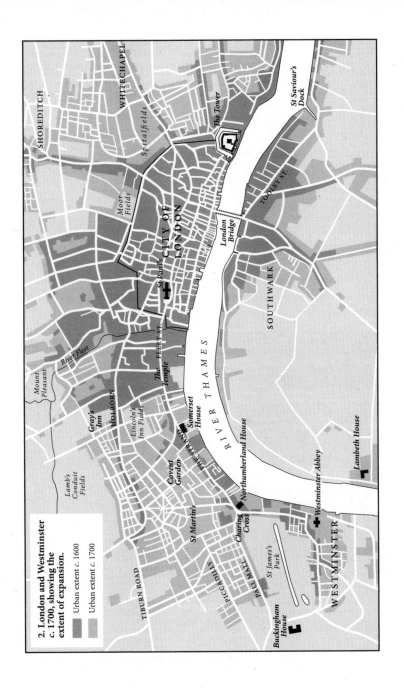

2. London and Westminster c. 1700, showing the extent of expansion.

Urban extent c. 1600

Urban extent c. 1700

SHOREDITCH

WHITECHAPEL

Spitalfields

The Tower

St Saviour's Dock

Moor Fields

CITY OF LONDON

TOOLEY ST.

London Bridge

St Paul's

SOUTHWARK

THE FLEET ST.

River Fleet

The Temple

RIVER THAMES

Mount Pleasant

Gray's Inn

HOLBORN

Lincoln's Inn Fields

Somerset House

Lamb's Conduit Fields

Northumberland House

Lambeth House

Covent Garden

THE STRAND

St Martin's

Westminster Abbey

Charing Cross

TIBURN ROAD

PICCADILLY

PALL MALL

St James's Park

WESTMINSTER

Buckingham House

1

'OH WHAT AN EARTH-QUAKE IS THE ALTERATION OF A STATE!'

Londoners opening their shutters at first light on Monday 28 April 1603 found the day promised to be dry and clear. Before the smoke from early-laid fires had spiralled up many chimneys, crowds were hurrying west, beyond the City and down the Strand to Whitehall, hoping for a good view of Queen Elizabeth's funeral procession to Westminster. The City of London and its neighbouring City of Westminster were already linked by a ribbon of development either side of the route. Most of these buildings were palaces or noble mansions with fine gardens behind, owned by courtiers and the elite. Here the air smelled sweeter and there was far less noise. The public road went through the palace complex at Whitehall, where the queen had been lying in state for three weeks. Pedestrians could make out shadowy movement behind upper windows as people took up the best positions to watch the show.

The mood was not particularly sombre. In the past decade, Elizabeth had lost much of her popularity as poverty and crime in England increased with disastrous harvests and a costly war with Spain. Some were glad to see her go. Yet the queen's officials had genuinely feared that her demise would cause violent disruption, even civil war. London had grown jittery during the queen's last illness; many predicted that the succession would not be smooth. A watch was placed on the City, its gates were closely guarded, and lanterns were kept burning all night. In this crisis, the Privy Council took extreme precautions: vagabonds who might cause trouble were deported to Holland on the pretext of sending them to serve the Dutch, suspects were incarcerated, and the navy was ordered to keep a close watch on the Channel.[1] There was more than one possible claimant to the throne and religious differences continued to plague the country. The queen herself had never named her successor for fear of inciting rebellion.

Elizabeth had died at about 2 a.m. on 24 March, the last day of the old year. This concurrence added to the general sense of unease. In those days, people recognized the New Year on 1 January; but the real New Year's Day was still held to be Lady Day (25 March), which for Christians marked Christ's Annunciation. The Privy Council and nobles acted swiftly to secure their preferred succession. They had an interval in which to orchestrate affairs: the winter had been severe and when Elizabeth grew ill she had retreated to Richmond, her warmest palace, about ten miles outside London. Within five hours of her death, Robert Cecil, Secretary of State, formally announced at the palace gate that her successor was King James VI of Scotland. A messenger was sent galloping up the North Road to bring James the news he was waiting for. Cecil then rode into the City with attendants and trumpeters, meeting the lord mayor on the way. In a show of unity, together they proclaimed James King of England, first at the great cross in Cheapside, and then at the Tower, carefully detailing to the crowd his lineage and legal claim to the throne. To the surprise of foreign ambassadors and other onlookers, people seemed to receive the news calmly. England had been ruled by women for fifty years, as long as most could remember. The thought of a king, still in his thirties and with heirs already, seemed a welcome novelty. People hoped for a more prosperous future and lit bonfires of joy in the streets.

Yet Cecil and the Council remained apprehensive. For them, the queen's funeral was a vital ritual that would reinforce public order and obedience. James, now making his slow progress south, had no intention of entering the City until Elizabeth was buried; he approved the Council's arrangements and the expenditure. Huge amounts were soon spent on expensive black cloth for the royal household. On the day of the funeral, it was this sea of black that subdued the crowd as the procession began. This was an age when proclamations and processions were still the chief means that rulers used to communicate with their subjects and Elizabeth's funeral was designed to strike awe. In London, a surprisingly high number of people could read, thanks to good schools and the demands of manufacturing and commerce. About 70 per cent of men and 20 per cent of women were literate, or at least could sign their names.[2] And as reading was taught before writing, perhaps many more could read, although illiteracy remained high among poorer craftsmen.[3] Yet if Londoners supported a flourishing publishing industry, with booksellers clustered in the area around St Paul's Cathedral formerly associated with manuscript production, they were also finely attuned to the rituals of public display. All eyes now turned on the mourners.

The procession was headed by Knight Marshals who cleared the way, pushing back the overcurious. Then came testimony to the queen's great charity: fifteen poor men of Westminster, wearing low-crowned hats as befitted their status, and 266 poor women, in heavy cowls. Members of various departments of the royal household followed, from Grooms of the Scullery to Chaplains of the Queen, punctuated at intervals by Sergeants at Arms, trumpeters, and peers carrying the banners of different parts of the kingdom. Towards the front of the procession was the queen's grey horse, draped in black and displaying the royal standard. People looked out for key figures, such as the Lord Chief Justice and members of the nobility. There were over a thousand mourners and it took time for the entire procession to cover the half mile from Whitehall Palace to Westminster Abbey, then called the Collegiate Church of St Peter. 'Never did the English nation behold so much black worn as there was at her funeral,' exclaimed the dramatist Thomas Dekker.[4] In the City, the first plague cases in the terrible outbreak of 1603–5 had been recorded at the beginning of March, but mourning for plague victims was not yet so familiar as to lessen the effect of this solemn pageant.

Certain details caught the crowd's interest. Cecil, a great political force, was a hunchback barely five feet tall. The French ambassador, Christophe de Harlay, with a train six yards long, walked earnestly alongside the Archbishop of Canterbury, John Whitgift. (The Venetian ambassador, Giovanni Carlo Scaramelli, had refused his invitation and gift of mourning cloth, unwilling to take part in a Protestant ceremony.)[5] The French envoy overcame his Catholic scruples sufficiently to attend Elizabeth's final rites in the church crypt. Was this a hopeful sign or an indication that Catholics would make dangerous inroads under James? Sir Walter Raleigh, as Captain of the Guard, led his men with their halberds respectfully pointing towards the ground. Would he transfer his allegiance readily to the new king? The queen's ceremonial sword, her helm and shield of office reminded onlookers of the martial aspects of sovereignty, but the greatest intake of breath was inspired by her coffin, towards the end of the procession. Draped in purple velvet and beneath a canopy, it was drawn by four horses in black trappings. Six barons marched on either side, each bearing aloft the royal standard. On the coffin itself lay a life-sized effigy of the queen. It had been carved in wood but the face, probably modelled on Elizabeth's death mask, was vividly painted, with orange hair, red lips and open eyes. The effigy had been dressed in a set of the queen's magnificent royal robes, and a ball and sceptre placed in either hand. The effect was unnervingly lifelike.

We are told that at the sight of the coffin there was 'such a general sighing, groning, and weeping as the like hath not been seene or knowne in the memory of man'.[6] This tribute, added afterwards to the description of the event, was probably an exaggeration. Yet the effigy was designed to produce a powerful reaction and succeeded in doing so. Flanked by billowing royal standards, never dipped because there is always a monarch, the effigy signalled to the mourning populace that England's body politic was healthy still. The queen's passing was perhaps more tenderly signalled by the sight of her riderless palfrey, a smooth-gaited horse favoured by women, which two grooms led in front of her coffin. The whole elaborate ritual underlined the unwavering stability of the state and emphasized the network of power supporting the monarchy; now a new ruler demanded obedience. The queen's funeral was a talking point for days and neatly filled the interval until James could enter the City and claim his own.

Yet Elizabeth had left unresolved on her death two major problems: religious division and the dovetailing of the monarch's powers with those of parliament. Both these issues helped to make the seventeenth century one of the most turbulent in London's history. Londoners would experience a series of revolutions: political, scientific and financial. They would struggle with unprecedented disasters: the Plague and the Great Fire. And they themselves would play a key part in the battle to establish the rights and liberties of citizens.

THE CITY OF LONDON

One of the key figures in Elizabeth I's funeral procession was London's lord mayor, carrying his heavy mace of office. The mayor was head of the City's governing body, the Corporation of London, with its Court of Aldermen and less important Court of Common Council. The Corporation's meetings and elections were held at Guildhall, a magnificent building which survives today on the site of a Roman amphitheatre. The City upheld a democratic form of self-government. It was divided into twenty-five wards, each sending one official to sit on the Court of Aldermen and several men to sit on the Court of Common Council, which comprised more than 200 members.[7] All aldermen served for life and belonged to one of the City's livery companies, so called because of the gowns worn on civic occasions, each company overseeing the membership and practice of a trade. The mayor was elected annually from aldermen who had served as sheriff and demonstrated powers of governance. The office was unsalaried and costly, since its holder was expected to keep an open table; mayors were therefore invariably rich.

London had a strong civic identity and jealously guarded the right to run its own affairs (its ancient privileges were said to pre-date the Norman Conquest of 1066). Periodically, there were tensions between the City and the Crown: London's size and importance meant that any public opposition to the political system tended to concentrate there. Opinion in the metropolis often divided along class lines. If the poor were fractious, City aldermen tended to support the monarch, who relied on civic wealth for loans to support policies at home and abroad. In return these wealthy men secured deals that enabled them to advance their status further. It was usually expedient for the Crown and City officials to work alongside one another and the mayor's annual inauguration ceremony was an opportunity for government to alert him to the tasks it wanted done.

If London's ward system provided a local basis for civic independence, there was localism at parish level, too. As in other English towns, officials such as churchwardens, overseers of the poor and the parish constable were elected to serve in rotation for a term of one or two years, as were lesser officials including beadles, night watchmen and scavengers in charge of removing refuse from streets. Some offices were unpopular, and it became usual for those elected to hire a substitute; many constables, for example, were almost waged professionals. But if London's network of small parishes helped to forge cohesion, in this rapidly growing city there were signs of social strain.

In 1600 the circuit of London's wall from the Tower in the east to Ludgate in the west extended some 2 miles and 200 yards. Some of the City's wards already extended beyond the walls and three were wholly outside: Farringdon

Without, abutting deep indentations in the line of the western wall; Portsoken, to the east; and Southwark, on the south bank of the Thames. London Bridge offered the only road across the river before 1750, so hundreds of watermen ferried people and goods to either bank. The road along the bridge was narrowed by houses and shops on each side. Some of its buildings, like Nonsuch House, were very fine; there was no way that powerful residents were going to allow any widening of the road. In any case, their rents paid for the upkeep of London Bridge. Above its gates on the Southwark side were impaled the heads of those who had been executed, sometimes as many as thirty, displayed as a warning and mark of shame.

This was the London that Shakespeare knew. Broadly, it comprised three entities: the City, housing London's commercial centre; Westminster, the seat of government; and Southwark, a site of pleasure. There, in an area just outside the jurisdiction of the City called Bankside, lay most of London's brothels. On days when plays were performed in the Bankside theatres, watermen estimated that 3,000 to 4,000 people crossed London Bridge. For those crossing by water, the most popular landing place on the south bank was Paris Garden Stairs, close to the Swan Theatre. Londoners also flocked to Southwark's bear gardens, where bears and bulls were baited by dogs. (In James's reign these gruesome matches took place on Monday afternoons.) The Hope Theatre, built on the site of the old bear garden in 1613–14, was used alternately for plays and animal sports. No wonder the playwright Ben Jonson described the Hope as dirty and stinking.[8]

We tend to think that all Shakespearean theatres were at Bankside because the iconic Globe Theatre is reconstructed there today, but others existed north of the river, outside the city walls: the Curtain in Shoreditch; the Fortune north of Cripplegate; and the Red Bull in Clerkenwell. There were also indoor theatres that relied on artificial lighting and allowed for more innovative staging: Whitefriars, south of Fleet Street; the Cockpit, near Drury Lane; and the larger Blackfriars Theatre. Blackfriars was within London's walls but outside the jurisdiction of the City because of its former monastic status. Such was the power of the theatre that, within weeks of his coronation, James I shrewdly patronized the leading company to which Shakespeare belonged, renaming it the King's Men. From 1609 the King's Men played at Blackfriars for seven months of the year and used the open-air Globe in summer. They could easily travel between the two theatres by crossing the Thames, getting a boat at Blackfriars and landing at Paris Garden Stairs, opposite.

Blackfriars was a fashionable area where aristocrats with no ambition to own a mansion in Westminster or to make a show at court were content to live privately. In this wealthy quarter the indoor theatre could charge high prices, so although it had fewer seats it netted more than twice the profits of the Globe. Residents in Blackfriars might complain that on performance days their roads were blocked to traffic from 2 p.m. to 6 p.m., making it impossible to get in bulk domestic goods such as beer, wood, coal and hay. But the theatre was too successful to close, except during bouts of the plague.

Shakespeare moved lodgings as his wealth increased, always within easy distance of his work. Early in his career he had lodged in edgy Bankside. From at least 1604 he was based in respectable Cripplegate, living on the corner of Silver and Monkwell Street (now under the Barbican Estate). He rented a room in the house of a Huguenot tiremaker, someone with both wig-making and artistic skills who specialized in elaborate hair ornamentations for women. From here, Shakespeare would have walked regularly to nearby Clerkenwell because new plays had to be rehearsed under the supervision of the Master of Revels or general censor, who was based in what had been St John's Priory, Clerkenwell. Towards the end of his career, in 1613, Shakespeare bought a gatehouse in wealthy Blackfriars, probably as an investment since he rented it out while semi-retired at Stratford.

By 1600 the population of London had risen to perhaps 200,000. In the tumultuous century that followed, it more than doubled, largely due to migration from the rest of England and an influx of refugees from France and the Netherlands fleeing religious persecution. Rapid growth transformed the metropolis and created problems of government. As London's suburbs expanded, largely housing the needy, the livery companies' ability to regulate trade and manufacture in those districts weakened. Houses were subdivided into tenements; poor sanitation grew worse, and disease was rife. By the 1690s, London was the largest city in Europe, with more than half a million inhabitants, and already fast evolving into a multicultural city. Aside from Huguenot and Flemish refugees, a Jewish community grew up in Bishopsgate, and international trade brought transient communities of seafarers and merchants from across the world. Growing numbers of African and Asian seamen swelled London's black population which, at the beginning of the century, had totalled just a few thousand black servants, musicians and dancers.

London was a city where most people walked. Less than two miles wide and one mile deep, it could be crossed in under an hour, but roads were so crowded it was often easier to go by river. In London's narrow streets three- and even four-storey buildings jutted out overhead, each storey larger than the one below to make the most of expensive street frontage. Thoroughfares could be dark and the air stale, but Londoners were only ever a short walk from open countryside. To the west, past Holborn where today's Shaftesbury Avenue lies, stretched pastures and fields where women spread out washing to dry. To the north of the City lay Finsbury Fields leading to rising countryside, and to the east, beyond riverside wharves and ribbons of development to Whitechapel and Ratcliff, lay marshes and more grassland for cows. Yet the transition from smoky city to open countryside was not without hazard. Despite proclamations to the contrary, heaps of waste and dung were dumped in stinking laystalls along roads leading out of London. The dung was used in the market gardens encircling the capital, which supplied citizens with fruit and vegetables; refuse collection and distribution were far from efficient. One inhabitant wrote with feeling to his friend in the Low Countries, 'Heere I am in a great, vast, durtie, stinking cittie, o that I had but a little of your Brabant ayre, howe greedily would I suck it in.'[9]

London householders dumped their filth in the streets. The pigs, allowed to roam freely, dealt with some of it but there had to be a system of street cleansing. In each parish the scavenger oversaw a team of rakers drawn from the poor who swept streets daily except on Sundays. The results were hardly satisfactory; blood and guts from slaughterhouses were a special problem. The River Fleet, running into the Thames at Blackfriars, was little better than an open sewer. Its four bridges had stone lanterns that held lights after dusk, to prevent travellers from falling into its filthy waters – a hundred years later the Fleet still overflowed with 'Sweepings from Butchers' Stalls, Dung, Guts, and Blood'.[10] In 1654 the City's Common Council contracted out street cleaning to the enterprising John Lanyon, who promised efficiency at no extra cost, but the arrangement broke down a decade later in the aftermath of the Plague and the Fire. A new system was then introduced whereby 'carmen' carted away refuse and swept City streets early in the morning. In outlying suburbs, improvements in street hygiene were more haphazard. One problem was that London had too many dogs. They fouled the streets, although their faeces were useful in the disgusting process of tanning leather, and strays kept people awake at night fighting.

The business of keeping bodies and houses dirt-free was a trial, even with servants to fetch and boil water. London drew a central supply from the Thames and its tributaries; it also had public conduits and cisterns, often built with charitable donations, and many of the conduits had been converted to pumps. From these places, poor labourers sold water on the streets in long, iron-hooped, wooden vessels, broader at the bottom than the top. Archaeologists have traced deformities produced by such back-breaking work in the skeletons of early Londoners.[11] Due to increasing pollution, piped water was better than well water and some houses had a piped water supply by 1600. Water wheels under London Bridge sent Thames water to the middle and west of the city but it was so tainted that people complained it left a stench even in clean linen. In 1613, Hugh Myddelton, a Welsh entrepreneur, opened a new waterway (the New River), bringing drinking water from the River Lea. But London's primitive sanitary systems continued to pollute its water supply, causing unpleasantness even for the middling sort. In 1660, Samuel Pepys famously entered his cellar to find his neighbour's cesspit overflowing: 'I put my foot into a great heap of turds, by which I find that Mr. Turners house of office is full and comes into my cellar, which doth trouble me.'[12]

London needed prodigious food supplies. By the middle of the century, food for residents travelled long distances: cattle were driven from Wales and Scotland, fattened near London, then sold at Smithfield outside the northwest gate of the City. Ducks and geese were walked from Lincolnshire and East Anglia. Corn came from the East Midlands, East Anglia, Kent and Surrey; dairy produce was brought from Suffolk and Cheshire; fish from around the coast; and fruit and vegetables from market gardens and orchards about London. Much came by water, with thousands of watermen in small boats using the twice-daily tide to get goods up the Thames. Little food could be preserved, and perishable goods filled London's markets. Most markets were specialized: Billingsgate sold fish and coal;

Leadenhall, meat, skins and bays; Queenhithe, meal and flour; Southwark, meat and hay. Some, like Cheapside and Gracechurch Street, were general markets. All were noisy, sociable places where women traders had a significant presence – particularly in Billingsgate where their foul language was legendary. The capital's growing population spawned more markets in the second half of the century, worsening congestion. The City resisted applications for new ones in the suburbs since they would threaten its exclusive rights, and there was friction when the king authorized them, as he did at Covent Garden, where fruit and vegetables were sold from 1670. London also supported thousands of street sellers. Lower-class women, for instance, hawked oysters, mussels, salted fish and cockles. The Crown was always careful to maintain London's food supplies to prevent discontent and rebellion.

London's greatest shopping street was Cheapside, running from St Paul's to Poultry, which pulsated with life. A famed meeting place was the Great Conduit, a public fountain in the middle of the street near Poultry, where servants and apprentices would stop to chat. Cheapside had been medieval London's chief market, reflected in the surviving names of nearby streets: Milk Street, Bread Street and Honey Lane. Eastcheap, its continuation from London Bridge, was lined with butchers' shops in the early part of the century, yet the clustering of certain occupations around a fixed location was breaking down. Goldsmiths, for example, who once occupied Goldsmiths Row between Bread Street and Bow Church, were moving north to the area around Cornhill, diminishing the glittering displays of Cheapside's handsome shop windows.[13] This important thoroughfare was also a site of public punishment: the pillory was in Cheapside and criminals might be tied to carts and whipped through the street. Shoddy goods that contravened the regulations of the livery companies were publicly burned there.

The emerging financial district in Cornhill, Lombard and Threadneedle Streets was enhanced by the nearby Royal Exchange, which wealthy merchant Thomas Gresham had built in 1571 as a centre of commerce for the City. But St Paul's also functioned as a central meeting place where deals could be struck, and news exchanged. The great tower of old St Paul's dominated the City, although its magnificent steeple had burned down after a lightning strike in 1561 and repairs were still outstanding. In its main aisle labourers sought work, servants were hired, and gossip circulated. St Paul's had a fine organ, and many would loiter for evening prayers, which were mostly sung, accompanied by the organ and other instruments. In its churchyard stood a pulpit on the site of Paul's Cross where weekly sermons were delivered. The mayor sometimes attended, sitting in a gallery with other wealthy members of the congregation, sheltered from the weather.

London's skyline was dominated by church towers; its streets rang with the sounds of manufacturing and trade. Its glamour defied urban problems of crime, disease and pollution. 'Come to London, to plaguy London, a place full of danger and vanity and vice,' wrote the poet John Donne, neatly encapsulating its horror and allure.[14] Migrants were attracted to the capital by wages, which could be as much as 50 per cent higher; some were driven there by poverty, as enclosures to boost the wool trade drove people off the land. Others just wished to experience life there: Shakespeare's London already had intense imaginative appeal. 'I hope to see London once ere I die,' says a poor country servant in *Henry IV, Part 2*.

The Mermaid Tavern in Bread Street, Cheapside, was a lively meeting place for poets, politicians and intellectuals. Ben Jonson and other dramatists went to a literary club there – an early recorded instance of such gatherings. The Boar's Head in Eastcheap, where the statue of William IV now stands, was another famous venue in an area full of taverns. Shakespeare depicts Sir John Falstaff holding forth in the Boar's Head, creating a powerful effect for a theatre audience familiar with the tavern, though it did not exist in Falstaff's time. London was also a magnet for courtiers. Lady Anne Clifford noted in 1616 that her extravagant husband 'went much abroad to Cocking, to Bowling Alleys, to Plays and Horse Races'.[15] Other social places included tennis courts, barber shops and gaming houses. Men still practised archery at the butts on Moorfields; the Tower of London's gunners discharged their guns weekly in Artillery Yard (near Artillery Passage, Bishopsgate), and the City's local militia assembled for drill on Mile End Common, where reviews of royal troops also took place.

London's population was predominantly young, and boisterous apprentices often threatened public order, especially on Shrove Tuesday when they had their holiday. In the suburbs as many as one in six houses was a drinking establishment, which increased disturbances.[16] A variety of brothels catered for a male population that outstripped that of females. Apprentices were forbidden to marry until they had completed their term, so marriage did not usually take place until men were in their late twenties. The Inns of Court, between the City and Westminster at Temple, Lincoln's Inn and Gray's Inn, added to London's young population. They trained men for the law but since there was no university in London, young gentlemen and members of the aristocracy attended for two years or so to study common law as part of a general education. By the 1610s the average student intake at the Inns of Court was 280 a year.[17] This intellectual community helped to link courtly and urban culture; the cross-fertilization helped to account for London's vibrant society, which had no rival in England.

Yet life in London was of course unequal. Poverty was on the increase and vagrancy was a problem. For most of the century, reformers failed to set up a workhouse system able to cope with these social issues; vagrants were periodically sent abroad to foreign wars and to new colonies in America. If the capital was partly orientated around symbols of wealth and power – palaces, stately mansions, Guildhall – its many prisons and places of execution served as potent reminders of human failure. There was a hierarchy in places of execution: traitors were beheaded on Tower Hill, pirates hanged at Execution Dock in Wapping, felons met their end at Tyburn gallows or Newgate, burnings took place in Smithfield. The Tower by this time was essentially a royal prison for those suspected of political crimes, although Londoners quailed at the sight of its well-armed battlements. Newgate was London's largest and most notorious prison, on the corner of Newgate Street and the Old Bailey, with a courthouse conveniently nearby. Overcrowded and unhealthy, Newgate held the most dangerous prisoners. And each of the City's two sheriffs were responsible for a compter (small prison), which housed debtors and other offenders. The oldest compter was at Poultry, and there was another in Wood Street. Debtors made up a sizeable proportion of the inmates at other prisons: in Ludgate, at the westernmost gate in London Wall; in Fleet Prison, off today's Farringdon Street, above Ludgate Hill; and in Southwark's prisons – the Clink, the White Lion, the Marshalsea and the King's Bench Prison, all around what is now Borough High Street.

Most prisons were administered by the royal household and run by private individuals, appointed for life, whose aim was to make a handsome profit.

Prisoners with money could obtain better treatment from guards who demanded exorbitant fees. The destitute, dependent on charity, were often left to starve or die of disease; typhus ('goal fever'), spread by lice and fleas, killed far more than the gallows. Prisons were not viewed as a form of punishment in themselves but were holding places for those awaiting trial or people in debt. The exception was the old royal palace of Bridewell, used as a house of correction where the disorderly poor were put to work and homeless children were taught a trade.

The scale of vagrancy and migration, given that new arrivals often faced language or dialect problems and could not easily keep in touch with distant families, helped to make London a bewildering and alienating place for many. Livery companies and religious observance were forces for stability, while Jews, Huguenots, the Irish and Welsh each built their own communities. Such ties were doubly vital when epidemic disease ravaged the capital.

KING JAMES

After Elizabeth's death, James reached the outskirts of London by May. He could not make the usual formal entrance to occupy the Tower because plague raged in the City. Instead, he cut through fields from Stamford Hill to the Charterhouse, where he was received by Admiral Lord Thomas Howard, a hero of the struggle against the Spanish Armada in 1588. Afterwards, James rode to Whitehall and looped back to the Tower by river. He was crowned on 25 July (St James's Day) 1603 but forced to issue a proclamation forbidding citizens to come to Westminster for fear of the plague, which had killed 857 that week alone.[18] Over 33,000 would die in the outbreak. Thinking that bad housing was a factor, James ordered the houses of the dead to be pulled down and not rebuilt. He followed this with more proclamations against building in the City, a policy which only contributed to overcrowding in the suburbs.

James's coronation procession through the City had to be delayed until 15 March 1604. This three-mile pageant was a rare and extravagant event. It started at the Tower, moved along a time-hallowed route through Cheapside to St Paul's, and then passed through Ludgate to Westminster. It was a visible statement of the power of the monarch, but also affirmed the values of the City which paid for it.

On the day of the procession railings kept the crowd back. The companies in their livery, their banners raised, lined one side of the route from Fleet Street to Park Street in Westminster. The City's water conduits ran with wine, and many Londoners were half-drunk by the time the king left the Tower around eleven o'clock. James was preceded in the procession by the magistrates of the City, court officials, the clergy, bishops and archbishops, and the nobility, all superbly dressed in gold silk with pearl embroideries. Prince Henry, his eldest son, was on horseback, ten paces ahead of the king, who rode a white horse under a canopy carried by eight Gentlemen of the Privy Chamber for the Barons of the Cinque Ports. The queen followed with her maids of honour and seventy ladies mounted. Shakespeare, now a courtier as well as an actor, walked in the procession with the eight other members of the 'King's Men', since by their royal patent they became Grooms of the Chamber; each had received four and a half yards of scarlet wool cloth with which to have their livery jacket and breeches made.

It was pure theatre. The procession passed through seven elaborate arches, built for the occasion. The first, at the east end of Fenchurch Street, supported a model of the whole City. The second and third had been paid for by the Italian and Dutch merchants, keen to stay on good terms with City authorities. The sixth, above the conduit in Fleet Street, featured a moving globe. All seven arches were so magnificent that they were engraved and published in a book called *The Arches of Triumph*. Not all spectators would have understood the allegories of the pageant, but everyone would have responded to the excitement. The procession was accompanied by drums and trumpets, and at key stages there were presentations, speeches composed by professional playwrights and anthems. The expense was enormous. With pardonable exaggeration, the Venetian ambassador estimated that 40,000 people had flocked to court for the coronation, hoping for advancement, and that in total London had 100,000 extra mouths to feed.[19]

King James made his first speech to parliament four days later. He expressed joy at being so heartily welcomed and declared himself a peacemaker, intent on creating conditions for trade and prosperity. He also set out his ambition to unite England and Scotland, pointing to the fact that he had heirs already, which gave hope that his aim would be realized. His audience was anxious to know his views on the difficult question of religion and on this point James was clear. He found three religions in his new realm: the 'true Religion', established by law, which he himself believed in; Catholicism, which might be suffered if Catholics kept the peace; and Puritanism, a tendency rather than a religion, which wanted radical reform of the Established Church and a 'purer' form of worship. Puritanism, James noted, did not differ greatly in points of religion from the Established Church but it had a political dimension. Puritans – whom he had long battled in Scotland – were 'ever discontented with the present government'; they disliked hierarchy, and for that reason could not be suffered in 'any well governed commonwealth'.[20]

James was delighted to find England so much wealthier than Scotland. He adopted the Palace of Whitehall, sprawling over some twenty-three acres, as his permanent residence. (Elizabeth I would be the last monarch to move the court in a stately progress around the country.) Initial reports of the new king were encouraging: he was 'prudent, able in negotiation, capable of dissimulating his feelings', said to be 'personally timid and averse from war'.[21] In the spring of 1604, James's ambassador to France promptly asked Henri IV to lift the embargo on English goods in French ports, now the plague was over, at least inducing the French king to seek advice on the matter from his own ambassador in London. And James made peace with Spain on 18 August. Yet he could not so easily resolve the chief issues of the day: his relationship with parliament and the difficult religious question. The wheels of discontent were already turning, and bitter social divisions would worsen in later reigns. Such would be the pace of change that before the century was out Stuart London would become a completely different world.

2

'THE MOST HORRIBLE TREASON'

On 26 October 1605 the Catholic peer, Lord Monteagle, was sitting down to dinner at home in Hoxton when a servant brought in a letter. He passed it to a gentleman in his service and asked him to read it aloud while he continued eating. The letter began:

My lord, out of the loue I beare to some of youere frends I haue a caer of youer preseruacion, therefor I wowld aduyse yowe as yowe tender youer lyf to deuyse some exscuse to shoft of youer attendance at this parleament . . . for thowghe theare be no appearance of anni stir yet I saye they shall receyue a terrible blowe this parleament and yet they shall not seie who hurts them.[1]

Monteagle did not know what to make of the cryptic warning, but in Elizabeth's time he had been uncomfortably close to people involved in treason and he wanted to avoid suspicion now. Instead of burning the letter, as it instructed, he hurried down to Whitehall and showed it to Secretary Robert Cecil, who was just sitting down to supper. Cecil, now made Earl of Salisbury for his services to the king, knew that conspiracy was afoot. Catholics who had fled to Europe were said to be planning an invasion; he thought the pro-Jesuit intelligencer in Brussels, Hugh Owen, was involved somehow. In the presence of Monteagle, Cecil appeared sceptical, but afterwards he showed the letter to other members of the Privy Council. They agreed to do nothing until the king returned from hunting in Royston. He did not like to be disturbed there and parliament was not due to meet until 5 November.

James returned to London on 31 October; the next day, Council members presented him with the letter. It was All Hallows Day, when saints and martyrs are honoured, adding to the solemnity of the moment. Salisbury allowed the king to think that he alone perceived the letter's meaning: the 'terrible blowe', James declared, could only refer to gunpowder. As a divinely appointed monarch, it made sense that James should receive providential warning and in later proclamations he duly claimed to be the first to decipher the obscure message. But there is no doubt that his councillors had already worked it out. Nothing would be done for the moment: any traitors would be left to incriminate themselves. In retrospect, the letter appeared so clumsy a mechanism, it was rumoured that Salisbury had known of the plot all along and devised the message himself to entrap the conspirators.

During Queen Elizabeth's last illness, leading Catholics had begged James for greater religious tolerance when he became king of England – after all, his mother, Mary Queen of Scots, had been a devout Catholic. Thomas Percy, cousin to the Earl of Northumberland who headed up one of England's foremost Catholic families, had made the journey to Scotland and extracted from James a promise of more lenient treatment for Catholics – or so he thought. But even if James's response had been sincere, once on the English throne his Privy Council urged him to allow Catholics no respite: Jesuits might lure English subjects to place their allegiance to the Pope above their allegiance to the king. In February 1604, faced with ongoing Catholic intrigue, James issued a proclamation banishing priests and Jesuits from the land. In July he gave his consent to a new Act enforcing Elizabeth's laws against Catholics: those refusing to attend services of the Church of England (recusants) were fined £20 a month. This heavy fine was to be collected every four weeks, so thirteen rather than twelve times a year; Catholics also had to settle fines owing, because payments had been lax since Elizabeth's death. As propertied Catholics ran into debt, two-thirds of their lands and their goods became forfeit.

Clearly, there was money to be made from Catholic persecution. Minor officials called 'pursuivants', who served warrants for the king, avidly tracked down suspected Catholics and brought them to trial for unpaid fines. In London, constables and pursuivants put a watch on certain houses, knocked on doors after dark and, if not given prompt entry, forced their way in. With swords drawn, they searched people's homes from attic to cellar for evidence of hidden priests and Catholic worship, maliciously destroying furnishings and sometimes taking valuables. It was claimed that these ruffians even disturbed married couples in bed and women in childbirth.

Meanwhile, the Scots dignitaries who had followed James to London were finding court life expensive. 'Hungry and ravenous', they looked to the king for support.[2] James advised these needy Scots to seek out substantial Catholics who owed fines for non-attendance at Protestant services. He then made these fines over to his countrymen and authorized them to proceed to law to recover the money. The French ambassador soon reported sympathetically that Catholic families were 'driven to despair'.[3] Only about 2 per cent of the population of England and Wales was openly Catholic, but thousands more kept the faith, outwardly conforming and attending services of the Established Church, or perhaps attending without being wholly won over to Anglican doctrines, conveniently retaining their wealth and position.[4] Now fervent Catholics were increasingly forced to abjure their faith before a court of law. In London, suspicion reigned, turning citizens against their neighbours. Catholics petitioned the king in 1604, complaining that unruly apprentices and workmen now taunted priests in the street, calling out 'Stop the traitor!' although they were innocent of treason.[5] The situation worsened: that year news reached London that a priest and two laymen had been hanged, drawn and quartered in the Midlands purely for their religion. In 1605, St Paul's Cross became a centre of anti-Catholic protest: Catholic books were symbolically burned there in the heart of London's book trade and, in August, the Bishop of London delivered a sermon denouncing papists.

Robert Catesby, a prominent and charismatic Catholic, had begun to think about blowing up parliament early in 1604, even before James's first speech to the House made it clear that there would be no religious toleration. Catholic attempts to get Philip III of Spain to invade England had proved fruitless. Catesby, who had been imprisoned for rebellion against Elizabeth, now believed that only desperate action could relieve the plight of Catholics in England. His plan was to massacre the king and his ministers at the next opening of parliament, stir up rebellion in the Midlands, and place James's young daughter Elizabeth on the throne as a puppet queen. He took trusted friends and kinsmen into his confidence, including Thomas Percy, who smarted under the belief that James had made a fool of him. They identified an English mercenary in Flanders who was an expert in explosives: Guy Fawkes, who liked to be known as Guido. A fanatic, he was a convert to Catholicism, as were several of the conspirators; other plotters had flirted with Protestantism, suggesting that they were using the Catholic religion as a badge of disaffection. Early meetings took place in a house behind St Clements in the Strand, often identified as the Duck and Drake tavern, and the plotters stockpiled gunpowder at Catesby's house in Lambeth. But their plans were delayed: first James postponed parliament until February 1605, then plague broke out and parliament was postponed until October.

In March 1605 the conspirators set to work again. Percy rented a cellar under the medieval House of Lords, and they began bringing the gunpowder across the Thames from Lambeth, concealing the barrels under piles of firewood. Fawkes, posing as Percy's servant and taking the name John Johnson, kept watch over the cellar. When the time came, he was to light a fuse, then escape to the Continent while the others raised rebellion in the Midlands. But as plague still raged in London, the opening of parliament was again postponed until 5 November. These delays made it difficult to keep the plot a secret, although conspirators had sworn an oath to do so. Newer recruits began to worry that Catholic Members of Parliament would be unfairly killed in the explosion. Seemingly it was one newcomer, Francis Tresham, who warned his brother-in-law, Lord Monteagle, not to attend the opening ceremony.

Although Robert Cecil, Earl of Salisbury, had been put on guard, he delayed any search of the buildings around parliament until the afternoon of 4 November. Even then, to allay fears, the search party gave out that it was just looking for missing goods belonging to the court. It found nothing, only a stockpile of firewood in one of the cellars that a servant (Fawkes) explained was the property of Thomas Percy. But when the searchers reported back, someone recalled that Percy was a Catholic and a second inspection was ordered, although it was nearly midnight. This time, Thomas Knyvet, Gentleman of the Privy Chamber and Justice of the Peace, found Fawkes, dressed and booted at the door of the cellar, and arrested him. There was no street lighting in London – anyone venturing out after dark had to carry their own torch or lantern and their own weapon – so his mere presence was suspicious. A thorough search revealed the gunpowder, and Fawkes was found to be carrying matches and touchwood. Denial was impossible. Hauled before the king and members of the Privy Council before daylight, he allegedly swore that he had meant to blow the beggarly Scots back to their native mountains but would not name his accomplices.[6]

Most of the conspirators had galloped north from London on 5 November as soon as they heard that Fawkes had been arrested, throwing their heavy cloaks into a hedge to gain speed. The City was soon aflame with rumours. Crowds gathered at alehouses and conduits; anyone in foreign dress prompted suspicion, but Spaniards were the most obvious target. In Westminster, the guard at the palace gates was strengthened and soldiers began stopping people at major roads. The king issued his first proclamation for the arrest of Thomas Percy that day, 'a tall man, with a great broad beard, a good face, the colour of his beard and head mingled with white haires'.[7] He was to be captured alive so that his fellow conspirators might be discovered. That evening, church bells were ordered to be rung in London and bonfires blazed in every main street to mark the king's providential escape.

On 6 November, James approved the use of torture on Fawkes, stipulating only that 'gentler tortures' be used first.[8] The very next day James was able to release a second proclamation naming the seven confederates to be arrested with Percy who, 'cloaked with zeale of Superstitious Religion', had plotted 'the most horrible treason that ever entered into the hearts of men'.[9] Anyone who harboured these traitors, or did not do their utmost to apprehend them, would themselves be judged traitors. The mood in London can be sensed by the fact that this proclamation refuted rumours that the plot had been incited by religion (rather than rebellion) and specifically denied that any foreign ruler had supported it. Already, there were murmurings against the Spanish ambassador and James had no desire to antagonize foreign powers. Nor did he wish to encourage disaffected subjects to expect help from abroad.

Fawkes was now brutally tortured on the rack to reveal all he knew and to try to force him to implicate Catholic priests in the plot. He could barely sign his confession on 8 November; his juddering signature is graphic evidence of terrible suffering. The final, printed version of his confession, implicating Jesuits and naming the intelligencer Hugh Owen, is suspiciously well crafted; Salisbury most likely had a hand in shaping it. The first Sunday after the discovery of the plot, a sermon was preached at St Paul's Cross giving thanks for the king's deliverance and condemning the cruelty and 'Hyperdiabolicall deuilishnesse' that had made religion a stalking horse for treason.[10]

Salisbury's henchmen questioned Londoners to find out which Catholics had left the capital in a hurry. The new Venetian ambassador, Nicolò Molino, took the opportunity to stress the difficulty of his mission, 'The city is in great uncertainty; Catholics fear heretics, and vice-versa; both are armed; foreigners live in terror of their houses being sacked by the mob that is convinced that some, if not all, foreign Princes are at the bottom of the plot.'[11] Meanwhile, Catesby's plans for rebellion in the Midlands came to nothing. When the surviving conspirators were caught, their confessions were rushed into print as the king and his advisors aimed to control the narrative of events. Official publications were adapted to counter the questions and rumours current in London. Not until December did one of the conspirators, Thomas Bate, reveal that he had confessed the plot to his priest. At once, James issued another proclamation calling for the arrest of three named Jesuit priests, describing them individually. Two managed to escape overseas, but on 27 January 1606, Father Henry Garnet, leader of the Jesuit order in England, was taken at a manor in Worcestershire after weeks of hiding and brought to London for interrogation.

On 30 January four of the conspirators were hanged, drawn and quartered in St Paul's Churchyard. This was not the normal place of execution and the choice of venue illustrates the power of association residing in key locations within the capital. St Paul's, where Elizabeth had given thanks for the defeat of the Spanish Armada, was a potent symbol of the Protestant faith. The location was intended to counteract any tendency to make Catholic martyrs of the conspirators. Yet, as the plotters all met their deaths bravely, many sympathizers in the crowd returned from the bloody executions full of pity. The next day, the remaining four, including Fawkes, were dragged ignominiously on hurdles from the Tower to their scaffold. They were hauled down the Strand, lined on both sides with hostile crowds, to be executed near the Houses of Parliament in the Palace of Westminster. The choice of this site emphasized the point that the conspirators were punished for treason not heresy. Fawkes, weakened by torture and sickness, could barely climb the scaffold but jumped off vigorously enough, breaking his neck and sparing himself the pain of disembowelment.

Father Garnet's trial was carefully prepared for 28 March and took place at the Guildhall, where state trials were held. It lasted from eight in the morning until seven at night. The power of the Pope was so dreaded that the hall was packed with spectators keen to see a Catholic priest in the dock. Although Garnet swore that he had never heard of the plot except in confession, the verdict was never in any doubt. Garnet was a firm believer in the Jesuit doctrine of equivocation, which made a fine distinction between what a speaker intended, and the actual words spoken, so that in extreme circumstances Catholics might lie under oath. This dangerous doctrine further predisposed the jury against Garnet. He was executed for treason on 3 May, the king mercifully allowing him to be hanged until he was dead before the rest of the punishment. Again, the authorities took the risky decision to stage the execution at St Paul's, in a display of government power and to underscore James's providential escape. Gruesome prints of the conspirators' executions, liable to be interpreted as examples of James's tyranny, were not printed in England; they were produced in Germany and the Netherlands. English authorities chose to issue a broadsheet portrait of Garnet as 'the Popes Darling' with a text claiming he had connived at every plot in England for the past thirty years.[12] An official account of his trial and execution was also printed. But if the authorities hoped to avoid Catholic appropriation of Garnet as a martyr, their plan backfired.

After Garnet was beheaded, Catholics in the crowd rushed forward to get a drop of what they believed was martyr's blood. One man later testified that a straw from the basket prepared to receive Garnet's head and limbs rose up and sprang into his hand. He kept it as a relic and took it to a tailor's house. After three or four days he was astounded to find that the blood on one of the husks had congealed to resemble Garnet's dead face, by then displayed on a pike at London Bridge. Afterwards, the straw was credited with miraculous cures, proof that God was on the side of the Catholics. The authorities were so worried that the Archbishop of Canterbury himself interrogated the tailor and other witnesses, hoping to retrieve the straw; allegedly it ended up with the Spanish ambassador for safekeeping.

The details of this horrifying treason, with its many points of interest, gripped London for months. Key locations in the City featured in the narrative of events and helped to shape it. Aspects of the plot are also reflected in popular literature of the time. No author dared to treat it directly, but readers and playgoers would have been attuned to passing references. Most famously, Shakespeare alluded to Garnet's support for the doctrine of equivocation in *Macbeth*, written in late 1606 or early 1607. The drunken porter of Macbeth's castle, answering impatient knocking at the door, imagines himself to be the keeper of hell's gate:

Faith, here's an equivocator that could swear in both the scales against either scale, who committed treason enough for God's sake, yet could not equivocate to heaven. O, come in, equivocator.[13]

Shakespeare, who came from a Catholic family, is careful to link equivocation and treason. He also echoes the black humour directed at Garnet in the official account, who was advised on the scaffold to confess all he knew and not to waste his last breath on equivocation.

Thomas Dekker's *The Seven Deadly Sinnes of London* (1606) obsessively alludes to the recent intrigue. He substitutes contemporary failings for the seven cardinal sins identified by the Church, describing such transgressions as lying, intrigue by candlelight and cruelty. When denouncing falsehood, Dekker addresses London outright and asks, 'Is it possible that . . . so many bonfires of mens bodies should be made before thee in the good quarrel of *Trueth*? And that now thou shouldst take part with her enemy?' Rulers, he continues, have suffered the '*Triple-pointed* darts of *Treason*', because men were deaf to the true religion. Can London now be 'in *League* with false Witches' that bring only death?[14] Dekker's most vivid image of cruelty is the plague pit into which the dead were often tumbled indiscriminately. Yet his work also makes clear that recent treason trials were indelibly etched on the public consciousness. When he condemns foreign fashions, as was routine at the time, he compares an Englishman's suit, incongruously aping different continental styles, to a traitor's body that had been hanged, drawn, quartered and set up in various places. The traumatic executions, the fearful atmosphere created by government spies, the suspicions encouraged within small communities about neighbours' religious beliefs, created a deeply destabilizing environment.

MAGIC

Supernatural powers lurked in London streets. The irrepressible Dekker gives us one of the liveliest contemporary descriptions of London:

> In euery street carts and Coaches make such a thundering as if the world ranne vpon wheels: at euerie corner, men, women, and children meete in such shoales, that postes are sette vp of purpose to strengthen the houses, least with iusling one another they should shoulder them downe. Besides, hammers are beating in one place, Tubs hooping in another, Pots clincking in a third, water-tankards running at tilt in a fourth: here are Porters sweating vnder burdens, there Marchants-men bearing bags of money, Chapmen (as if they were at Leape frog) skippe out of one shop into another: Tradesmen (as if they were dauncing Galliards) are lusts at legges and neuer stand still: all are as busie as countrie Atturneyes at an Assises.[15]

But although Dekker revels in the physical detail of his home town, he just as readily refers to supernatural beings and domestic goblins, joking that kitchen maids and apprentices are frightened into feverish shivering when caught together after dark, as if the mischievous fairy Robin Goodfellow had been conjured up among them. He seems to accept that unseen powers inhabited London as much as any remote rural area.

James I was himself interested in witches. He had led witch hunts in Scotland and authored a book about witchcraft which was republished in England in 1603 when he came to the throne. In 1604 he passed a harsh statute against witchcraft, reaffirming its existence in law. England was more sceptical about evil spirits than Scotland and James gradually became less insistent about his expertise on the subject. He did, though, perform one magic ritual himself: he touched for the King's Evil or scrofula, a tubercular inflammation of the lymph glands in the neck. He may have taken part in this healing rite because it cemented popular belief in his right to reign. But even if he rationalized that he was merely interceding with God on the victims' behalf, he would have known that others, so-called 'cunning folk' who included charms and conjurations in the practice of medicine, could be hanged for asserting they cured by stroking, even if in London folk healers were now rarely harassed.[16]

Given the ineffectiveness of most medicine and the limited understanding of natural phenomena, it is not surprising that belief in magical forces persisted.[17] Magic was part of everyday life and helped people deal with difficult situations such as childbirth, sickness, lost objects and falling in love. It was a response to insecurity and offered people the consolation of actively doing something to prevent ill-luck. Even in fashionable west London, towards the end of the century, most houses had horseshoes nailed to the threshold to foil the power of witches.[18] Offerings like old shoes might be concealed in chimneys or placed under thresholds as charms to ward off evil spirits. Protective ritual signs to entrap demons were commonly placed at these entry points. And if evil forces had already struck, a common remedy was to create a witch bottle.

Dozens of witch bottles have been found in London from the period, and the phenomenon extended to elsewhere in the country. People liked to use a small German stoneware jug or bottle called a bellarmine. It was decorated with a bearded mask, which may have encouraged their belief that it would prove useful in influencing human affairs. When bellarmines were no longer made, people used glass bottles instead. Common ingredients were nail clippings, hair, a cloth heart pierced with pins, sulphur matches and crooked nails – but the essential ingredient was the victim's urine. The reasoning behind this was that in infecting someone, witches had to leave some of their own blood in the victim. By including urine in the witch bottle and exploiting this magical link with the victim, the spell was cast back at the witch and the victim would be relieved. The bottle had to be heated in the fire to the point of explosion or buried (upside down) in the earth; some witch bottles have also been found in the Thames.[19]

The Gunpowder Plot was itself presented as the work of devilish heretics and linked to witchcraft: the conspirators were said to have been under the influence of the Pope and Satan, used to destroying 'by charmes and sorceries'; they had been 'bewitched' by the Devil.[20] Fear of the occult helps to explain why Catholics were charged with encouraging the use of magic and accused of mistaking superstition for religion:

If a man would but a little looke into their Idolatries, hee should see a worlde of such mockeries, as would make him both laugh at their fooleries, and abhor their villanies. The kissing of babies, their kneeling to wodden Ladies, their calling to Saintes that cannot heare them, their praying by the dozen, their taking of penance, their pilgrimages to Idols, their shauings and their washings, their confessions and their crossings, and their deuelish deuises to deceiue the simple of their comfort.[21]

The authorities could be sceptical of accusations of witchcraft: in 1605 the Bishop of London asked physicians to examine a girl who claimed she had been bewitched by an old woman, Elizabeth Jackson. He suspected the girl was lying and not suffering from magic spells at all. But in 1621 another old woman, Elizabeth Sawyer, was tried at the Old Bailey and executed at Tyburn for bewitching her neighbour to death. Women tasked with searching Sawyer for witch's marks in Newgate found she had an extra teat through which she nourished her familiar, who took the shape of a dog. Sawyer denied killing her neighbour but confessed to a relationship with the Devil, who, she said, came to her when she was cursing and blaspheming.[22]

The Witch of Edmonton, a play by John Ford, William Rowley and Thomas Dekker, exploited the notoriety of this case, which inspired several street ballads and a cheap pamphlet by the Newgate chaplain, Henry Goodcole. Unlike the pamphlet, which claims to be factual and condemns Sawyer in her own words, *The Witch of Edmonton* offers no consistent portrayal of witchcraft – probably reflecting different opinions within the audience. Sawyer complains:

And why on me? Why should the envious world
Throw all their scandalous malice upon me?
'Cause I am poor, deformed and ignorant,
And like a bow buckled and bent together,
By some more strong in mischiefs than myself,
Must I for that be made a common sink,
For all the filth and rubbish of men's tongues
To fall and run into? Some call me witch;

And being ignorant of myself, they go
About to teach me how to be one.[23]

On the one hand, it seems that witchcraft can be socially constructed and easily targeted at the lower classes. On the other, Sawyer seems to internalize witchcraft, arguing that to be counted a witch is the same as being one, and inviting the Devil to help her punish uncharitable neighbours. Witchcraft was a nationwide issue, but London's vibrant culture meant that it could be openly debated and sceptical views aired in dramatic form.

RELIGIOUS POLICIES AND LONDON

Religion was inseparable from public and private life, and nowhere was this more obvious than in London, the centre of government. There were no fewer than 110 parishes in London, half of them small, few of which paid tithes of more than £50 a year.[24] These tiny parishes helped to build a strong sense of community, given that worshippers could be migrants or teenagers apprenticed away from home. In an age without regular newspapers or a police force, the pulpit was a key means of influencing opinion and policing conduct. James therefore took enormous care to propagate what he saw as the true religion, as he was bound to do anyway for the welfare of his subjects. This meant both purging it of the taint of extreme Puritanism, which could tip into sedition, and protecting it from Catholicism. Both religious positions would be caught by the laws against recusancy, but much depended on local clergymen. In February 1605, for example, Secretary of State Robert Cecil replied to the Archbishop of York that if Catholics were on the increase in the north he had only himself to blame: as archbishop, he should be taking strong action against those who failed to attend services of the Established Church.[25]

James came to England prepared to be tolerant but found it difficult to be even-handed. Nor could he ignore pressure for church reform. The Protestant religion, unlike Catholicism, was not rooted in centuries of tradition; many demanded clarity about the tenets of Protestant belief. Yet Protestants were divided: some were happy with the form of worship that Elizabeth had established, others wished to purify it further. Some were content with the ceremonies prescribed in the Book of Common Prayer of 1559, including kneeling for communion and making the sign of the cross at baptism; others wanted more emphasis on the scriptures and preaching. James recognized that there were genuine points of confusion and agreed to the Puritan suggestion of a conference to debate them.

In January 1604, James invited representatives of the Church of England and four moderate Puritans to Hampton Court Palace, outside London, where they conferred in bitterly cold weather over three days. James enjoyed showing off his learning and reported that he had soundly 'peppered' the Puritans and shot down their arguments.[26] There was no way that he was going to lessen his support for bishops, as Puritans hoped. Yet he did make concessions and supported their wish for greater emphasis on the sermon in church services. A revised prayer book was published in February, differing little from the old one but officially sanctioned by the Church. The conference also resulted in a new, authorized translation of the Bible, the King James Version, which today is regarded as one of the greatest achievements in the English of the time, but which caused little stir when it appeared in 1611.

In return for his concessions, James wanted Puritan ministers to subscribe to a revised definition of the laws and beliefs of the Church. As these urged kneeling at communion and condemned private fasts and other Puritan practices, many Puritan groups protested. In London, thirteen ministers refused to subscribe and lost their livings. The number of refusals in the capital was second only to Peterborough, which had sixteen. After this initial crackdown on Puritans, James seems to have been content to balance different Protestant views. For example, most of his bishops were Calvinists who followed the theologian John Calvin, believing that the fate of the human soul was predestined by God and decided at birth. But he also promoted clergymen liable to be called Arminians, who believed that all Christians could be redeemed.

Probably only a minority of Londoners were absorbed by the finer points of religion. It was easier to associate different attitudes to the Church with conflicting views about politics and social behaviour. London was at the centre of much public discontent. Puritan reformers objected to the behaviour of courtiers, to their duelling and use of brothels. They complained vociferously, as others did, that monopolies on trade had been granted to wealthy individuals, thereby restricting the economic activity of lesser tradesmen. Merchants holding monopolies were liable to charge others for a licence to trade, effectively imposing another tax on top of the taxes Londoners paid to maintain the court. Puritans were easily mocked for hypocrisy: Dekker typically described a Puritan as 'wrapping his crafty serpents body in the cloake of Religion'.[27] Other writers, including Shakespeare and Ben Jonson, staged anti-Puritan stereotypes. But insofar as Puritan values seemed opposed to a corrupt court and to wealthy merchants who monopolized trade, they were popular in London.

James made clear in his 1604 speech to parliament that he did not wish to be known as a persecutor and would negotiate with Catholics if they could meet him halfway, though he would never allow them to cherish hopes that they could increase in number and bring the country back to Catholicism. Yet he could not take action against Puritans without even-handedly repressing Catholics, and inevitably after the Gunpowder Plot life for Catholics got much worse. Parliament passed a law in 1606 that allowed the king to seize two-thirds of the lands of Catholic recusants instead of the monthly fine, a measure designed to prevent wealthy Catholics turning their homes into centres of Catholic worship. This legislation also introduced an oath of allegiance. Catholics had to recognize James as their lawful king, deny the power of the Pope to topple a king, and repudiate the doctrine that the Pope could pardon the assassin of a Protestant monarch since to overthrow one was no sin. Catholics who refused the oath were imprisoned; recusants were barred from public office and the professions, including the military.

After a Catholic fanatic, François Ravaillac, assassinated Henri IV of France in May 1610, there was such an outcry in London that to satisfy public opinion the Privy Council ordered a search of all recusant houses and inns in the capital to identify suspicious persons. In June, at parliament's request, James issued a proclamation banning all recusants from court and within ten miles of London without special licence. Priests were again banished and the oath of allegiance once more upheld, suggesting that neither had been strictly enforced before. Parliament's call for action against recusants was probably a delaying tactic as James had just requested parliament for an annual contribution towards his maintenance. Still, over time, the ban contributed to an increase of Catholics and Dissenters living in the outskirts of London.

Puritan dissent was an internal issue, whereas the Catholic question had complex links with James's foreign policy. Puritans were against having bishops in the hierarchy of church government, and in parliament they were prominent opponents of the king. Catholics were suspected of seeking help from European Catholic powers, possibly for an invasion to set a rival on the throne who would be sympathetic to Catholic interests. But England could not afford a foreign war and James, perhaps with little choice, took pride in being a peacemaker who encouraged trade to prosper in peacetime. In dealing with religion, James was determined to oppose any limitation to his power as monarch.

Although an experienced king, used to temporizing between different factions, James soon lost some of the lustre he seemed to have on accession. There were reports that his court lacked dignity – when King Christian IV of Denmark was entertained in July 1606 courtly celebrations degenerated into drunken chaos; personal hygiene at court was not what it had been in Queen Elizabeth's time, one aristocrat complaining 'we were all lousy by sitting in the chamber of Sir Thomas Erskine'.[28] James had to support households for his consort and children, unlike Elizabeth, so royal expenses were greater than before. His extreme love of 'the hunting life' also raised eyebrows. The Venetian Secretary in England reported that 'the new King . . . seems to have almost forgotten that he is a King except in his kingly pursuit of stags, to which he is quite foolishly devoted'.[29] James spent long periods at Royston and left government in his absence to the Privy Council, which grew in power.[30] When the king was absent, London tradesmen grumbled that they got less from court expenditure. His bounty to fellow Scots was another irritation. Their building projects were changing London: Scottish nobles 'nestled themselves about the Court', building great houses along the Strand to replace mud walls and thatched dwellings, helping to join the cities of London and Westminster.[31]

Effectively a foreigner, James did not have the same intuition about popular feeling in England that had helped Elizabeth to rule. In religion, he wanted 'to have all come to conformity', because he thought it essential to the smooth running of government and believed people needed to be taught obedience.[32] Yet the bishops themselves were unsure about excluding so many worshippers who were in other respects loyal subjects. Crucially, the effect of the Gunpowder Plot cemented negative policies towards Catholics for the rest of the century.

James ordered his subjects to attend an anniversary service of thanksgiving each year to mark his deliverance. The annual event on 5 November became a popular celebration, which Londoners helped to shape, later burning effigies of the Pope and Devil. Ironically, the Catholic plot helped to ensure that England remained a Protestant country.

3

FORGING CIVIC IDENTITY

'Turn again, Whittington!' The tale of Dick Whittington has been used for generations to encourage young people to work hard and persevere. Allegedly, Whittington, a poor boy from the country, despaired of ever making his fortune in London and left the city with his cat. On Highgate Hill he heard church bells, which he took to be a sure sign he would be mayor one day; he returned and duly became rich and famous. The story is largely folklore. A Richard Whittington served London three times as lord mayor, but he came from a wealthy family; there is no record of his cat. The myth was cherished because it helped to create the belief that London was a place of opportunity. It encouraged migrants to the capital and contributed to its reputation as a centre for good apprenticeships.

Apprentices were bound to a master for seven years to learn a craft or trade. They paid him a fee for their training and lived in his household, though the cost of their board and clothing might be met by parents or sponsors. Apprentices worked for little or no wages and were not allowed to marry until they had served their time. Then they could become a citizen or freeman of London and might be admitted into a guild or livery company. Youths were usually apprenticed aged seventeen and, given the substantial fee to be paid (easily more than a year's agricultural wages for a sought-after trade), most had middling or well-to-do backgrounds.[1] Hundreds of young people travelled long distances each year to be apprenticed in the capital. Some families and sponsors used kinship ties to match apprentices to suitable masters, but most resorted to wider networks or to middlemen.

Part of the experience of living in London was the loud presence of thousands of young apprentices from across England. In the seventeenth century between 5 and 10 per cent of teenaged males in England entered apprenticeships in London. As the capital became more populous, so did the number of apprentices, who always counted for some 10 per cent of its population and totalled 3,800 by 1700.[2] Some were London-born, but a minority of these Londoners would be under the eye of their fathers; usually they were apprenticed in a different workshop. Few young women entered skilled apprenticeships in London until the 1650s, when modest numbers were assigned to women milliners and seamstresses (although registered with their husbands). The capital therefore had to cope with a body of young men, mostly new to its streets, living in unfamiliar households rather than under parental supervision, and generally getting up to mischief. They committed crimes and visited brothels; their annual holiday on Shrove Tuesday often ended in a riot. John Chamberlain, a man of leisure and wide correspondence, recorded in 1617 that apprentices, or unruly people from the suburbs imitating them, broke into the Cockpit theatre near Drury Lane on Shrove Tuesday; they destroyed costumes and burnt playbooks. Indignant actors managed to shoot three of them dead, but the disorder escalated:

> In Finsbury they brake the prison and let out all the prisoners, spoiled the house by untiling and breaking down the roof and all the windows, and at Wapping they pulled down seven or eight houses and defaced five times as many, besides many other outrages, as beating the Sheriff from his horse with stones and doing much other hurt too long to write. There be diverse of them taken since and clapt up, and I make no question but we shall see some of them hanged this next week, as it is more than time they were.[3]

Apprentices could be used to stir up political mischief too. In July 1618 they joined thousands of protestors who attacked the house of the Spanish ambassador after one of his men accidentally rode over a child in Chancery Lane. King James, anxious to preserve good relations with Spain, insisted that the mayor punish the rioters. Seven were found guilty, imprisoned and fined more money than they could ever pay. Spaniards in London had cause to fear the rabble. The Venetian chaplain Orazio Busino explained:

Foreigners are ill regarded not to say detested in London, so sensible people dress in the English fashion, or that of France, which is adopted by nearly the whole court, and thus mishaps are avoided or passed over in silence. The Spaniards alone maintain the prerogative of wearing their own costume, so they are easily recognised and most mortally hated.[4]

In April 1621 the Spanish ambassador was insulted by three apprentices; they were sentenced to whipping but freed by a crowd some 300 strong. At this, James came to Guildhall and threatened to garrison the City at its own expense unless order was kept. He issued a proclamation to suppress all abuse from disorderly apprentices and so-called 'base people' against ambassadors, other foreigners and English people of quality. Citizens were urged to arrest offenders themselves if they could not find a constable, in case disorder spread to the suburbs. But anti-Spanish feeling was deep-seated; the Spanish ambassador remained a target. In 1628, during the reign of James's son, Charles I, an Act was passed requiring aldermen to knock on doors and tell householders to keep children, servants and apprentices under control. Londoners had to respect the ambassadors and nobles in their streets 'and do neither throw nor shoote anything at them'. Nor were they to play rowdy sports 'as Trap, Squibs, Foote-ball, or the like' upon pain of severe punishment.[5] The emphasis on the disciplinary role of the head of the family helps to explain Samuel Pepys's embarrassment when he was too drunk one Sunday to lead household prayers.[6]

Much official time was taken up by London's apprentices. Some cases were exceptional: in 1623 a brazen apprentice clothworker seduced a young heiress, tricked her into a sham marriage sworn on the Book of Common Prayer, and embezzled her inheritance.[7] But everyday cases of poor training and ill-treatment also offer bizarre details. Edward Green, a surgeon's apprentice, took his case to the Middlesex Sessions of the Peace. His master did not teach him but 'forced him to daunce on the Ropes, to Tumble & to play' in 'diverse public places . . . at the hazard of his life' – presumably to drum up a crowd for the sale of quack medicines.[8] Thomas Hotchkin protested that his master, also a surgeon, gave him no instruction but sent him to practise at sea. He had been forced to buy his own medicines, but his master still pocketed his wages.[9] Apprentices often sought protection from violent masters. Daniel Hecktoll, apprenticed to a ropemaker in Shadwell, was 'barbarously beate'.[10] His master tied him up, whipped him with a rope until he bled, rubbed salt into the open wounds, then left him to hang by his wrists for five hours. William Masters, apprenticed to a gardener in Stepney, complained that because he had fallen ill, his master turned him out of doors and left him to the care of friends. His only option was to join the navy and he wanted formal release from his indentures before fitting himself out for sea. Luckily, his master had not formally registered or 'enrolled' the apprenticeship with the City's chamberlain, so it could be cancelled on this technicality.[11] Non-enrolment was so common it seems that both parties connived at the omission to ensure that apprenticeships were easily dissolved if they did not work out.[12]

Indentures could be cancelled in the Lord Mayor's Court in the City, in other courts, or by private agreement. The disputes give insights into the lives of the London poor. In 1691, Richard Atkinson went to court to be quit of his apprentice, Eve Salmon, who had 'severall times Deserted his service, purloynt his goods [and] frequented debauch't houses'.[13] She had already attended a charity hospital to be cured of the pox. Neighbours feared she would rob them, and Atkinson was afraid to be away from home in case she ruined him in his absence. In her defence, Salmon claimed she had been apprenticed to Atkinson and his wife 'for the space of eight years to learn the Art of Houswifery' but had suffered repeated abuse. She said that only lack of food and clothes had caused her to keep bad company. Now she begged to be discharged since she could provide for herself.[14] London held many temptations for vulnerable apprentices. In 1695, Edward Furse, an apprentice tailor, went on Sundays to a coffee house in Drury Lane. He was seduced by the owner, Mary Hambleton, who kept a small brothel in a back room, and later claimed that she had incited him to steal from his master.[15] The apprenticeship system demanded vigilance, but livery companies valued it as a powerful means of controlling their trades.

LIVERY COMPANIES

London was a hive for fortune-seekers, but London's merchants and tradesmen did their best to conserve the honey. At the beginning of the century they were organized into fifty-five livery companies, which, under the City of London, regulated trade and looked after the well-being of their members. The companies got most of their income from rents or by fining members for breaching trade rules; they flourished in the first half of the century, growing in economic importance and reaching out to the nation through education, regulation, charity and patronage. Collectively, these companies were the wealthiest and most powerful institutions in the realm. The twelve foremost, known as the Great Twelve, were ranked by their economic and political power, starting with Richard Whittington's company of general merchants, the Mercers.

Livery companies laid the foundations of Britain's global wealth and were responsible for the City's importance as a financial centre. Their halls in the City, some dating back to the fourteenth century, were as lavishly decorated as a company's resources allowed. Here members kept up traditions of corporate feasting and drinking that helped to bind them together. On such occasions the gold and silver plate winking in candlelight demonstrated a company's wealth. But the commercial experience of companies also ensured that assets were carefully managed for the benefit of members, especially in sickness and old age.

The dress of London's richest merchants exhibited judicious opulence; their houses, in fashionable Bishopsgate and around the Royal Exchange and Cheapside, offered stunning displays of imported luxury goods. Merchants bridged the gulf between their wealth and the poverty of others by supporting their company's charitable activities. Using legacies and investment income, the companies ran schools, awarded regular pensions or one-off grants to members who had fallen on hard times, and lodged elderly members in their almshouses. The Catholic religion had underpinned this charity until Henry VIII broke with Rome; afterwards, companies refashioned their rituals in a Protestant context. The change came easily: international merchants had early contact with the Protestant Reformation on the Continent and soon recognized that aspects of Protestantism, including the acceptance of moneylending, were good for business. Under Catholicism, companies had organized masses for the souls of departed brothers; under Protestantism they encouraged bequests – endowments, plate or tapestries – to perpetuate the status and civic reputation of the deceased. Companies retained their patron saints but increasingly emphasized charity, brotherly love and the well-being of their members.

In 1614, Andrew Willet, Chaplain to Prince Henry, the king's eldest son, used company records to show that charitable works had increased, not declined, since the Reformation – a key feature in the depiction of London as a godly city.[16] But if the livery companies were enthusiastically Protestant, the nature of their religious and political allegiances did shift over time. Under James I officials in the Haberdashers Company tended to be consistently Puritan, while in the Merchant Taylors, they were somewhat divided. As senior officials in the Merchant Taylors were replaced, its government became more tolerant of High Church rituals. By the 1630s, the Merchant Taylors were well placed to secure the support of the ruling elite, notably that of the Archbishop of Canterbury, William Laud, who favoured ceremony in church services – a clear example of how a shift in religious views might gain political and financial advantage.[17]

Most members gained the 'freedom' of a livery company by completing an apprenticeship, but it could also be obtained through patrimony (if a parent was a member), marriage (a widow carried on her husband's business), or by paying a fine. Membership of a company qualified a person to receive the freedom of London, rightly prized because no one could run a trade or business in the City without it. This rule was policed but subject to evasion, as when Thomas Fryer was caught trading illegally in the 1670s. He had been apprenticed to a distiller, but his master had died after only five years; for the remainder of his apprenticeship he was turned over to Mary Laundy, a widow who practised the trade. At the time of transfer, Fryer married the daughter of a Mr Withins of Red Cross Street, near St Giles Cripplegate, who fitted up part of his house as a shop selling spirits (Londoners often worked where they lived). The newly married Fryer now distilled for his own benefit; no money went to Mrs Laundy. He was trading before he had served his time or gained the freedom of the City, so his company had him arrested. When his case was heard, Fryer was ordered to return to his mistress for the rest of his apprenticeship and Mr Withins, his father-in-law, was told to shut up his shop. Both men seemed to accept the verdict but, within a week, Fryer reopened the shop. He claimed that he had served his seven years and he petitioned the Court of Aldermen to be made a freeman on payment of a fine. Withins, for his part, swore that the shop was his, since Fryer was not even twenty-one years of age. Clearly there were ways of bending the rules.[18]

The freedom of London maintained its popularity. There were around 30,000 citizens in 1640 and 50,000 in 1675 – some three-quarters of London's adult males. They could take part in ward meetings to elect aldermen and common councillors, so by the standards of the day the proportion of citizens involved in city government was high. This gave Londoners a sense of being able to direct their own affairs and was a force for stability, alongside overlapping memberships of close-knit wards and parishes. Within the livery companies, those with a higher category of membership had more political privileges. Senior liverymen could elect important City officials – the mayor, sheriffs and chamberlain – and vote in general elections. Liverymen were fewer in number than freemen of the City, about 2,500 in 1600 rising to around 8,200 by 1700, but their ranks still included artisans and petty retailers, who served as liverymen in the smaller companies.[19] As the City returned four representatives to parliament, citizens also had considerable political force. And the parliamentary voting rights that came with membership of a livery company became more important as party politics evolved.

Freedom of the City offered other advantages in an era when epidemics could bring sudden death. If a freeman died leaving children who were underage, his executor was bound to report the death at Guildhall; the London Court of Orphans then protected the children's inheritance until they came of age. The dead man's wealth was calculated, his bequests paid, and the remainder divided between his widow and legitimate children. The court appointed guardians for the orphans and monitored these custodians to make sure they did not cheat orphans of their money. It was an admirable system, which only began to fail towards the end of the century. By then, inheritances were often deposited with the chamberlain and used for temporary loans within the City's economic structure. In the 1680s and 1690s the City got into severe financial difficulties; it could not pay the inheritances due and orphans had to petition parliament for their money.

Livery companies liked to restrict the number of apprentices a member could take at any one time to limit competition from the newly trained. They also maintained quality control over members' work, examining businesses for defective goods and fining those who put them on sale. In 1624, for instance, the wardens of the Goldsmiths' Company swooped on the Royal Exchange, where they spotted 'suspicious-looking' chains and bracelets of beads linked together with gold in the shop of Thomas Clowse, a milliner. Clowse became abusive and refused to let them examine his goods; meanwhile, he slyly dispatched his man to the Poultry Compter to enter a lawsuit against the wardens for £500. The man returned with a sergeant from the prison to arrest the wardens, who were jailed amid 'great tumult and uproar' until they could arrange bail; meanwhile, the jewellery they had seized proved to be bad and 'deceptive'.[20] Clowse was committed to the Fleet prison and made to apologize to the Goldsmiths' Company. He had to sign a bond for £500 guaranteeing that he would not sell similar false wares, pay a fine of £40, and sign another bond for £200 certifying that he would no longer mix the Goldsmiths' craft with another trade. But when Clowse apologized in writing, his fine was reduced to £10. This was common practice because above all companies valued submission to their rules and they had no wish to antagonize members. And for tradesmen, operating within complex systems of debt and credit, any fine was bad enough. It could seriously disrupt business – especially if made public.

At the beginning of the century companies were expected to monitor City apprentices to make sure that they did not dress above their station, even though King James had repealed most sumptuary laws restricting what people could wear. In 1611 the mayor proclaimed a royal decree that apprentices should wear only clothes provided by masters or friends. None was to wear a hat expensively lined, faced or stuffed with velvet, silk or taffeta; none should wear breeches or doublet of silk or silk-mix. Apprentices should not sport elaborate hairstyles or wear shoes of soft Spanish leather, or shoes with heels – which signalled privilege and refinement. If they did, they could be imprisoned in 'Little Ease' – a gated hole in the wall for wayward apprentices in the Guildhall, aptly named because it was so small that inmates attempting to escape were trapped in a crouch position. The same punishment awaited any apprentice found taking dancing or fencing lessons, cock fighting, frequenting bowling alleys or brothels, or keeping 'any horse, gelding, or mare, dog, or bitch, or fighting cock', confirmation that apprentices often came from well-to-do families.[21]

Livery companies took their civic duties seriously. And one crucial fact bolstered their authority: the greatest official in any company would himself have experienced an apprenticeship. As the Venetian chaplain, Busino, noted, 'those who aspire to the mayoralty must have served bare-headed for seven years in their youth in some workshop for the sake of obtaining the mere title of apprentice'.[22] The system encouraged stable government: the most powerful aldermen reached their position through service in the ranks of lesser officials – in which ranks modest tradesmen also served.

But the status of livery companies was as much about exclusion as inclusion. Mere labourers, journeymen who had not completed an apprenticeship, servants, transients and 'aliens' from overseas did not qualify for membership. Women rarely feature in company records: they might be admitted as independent masters if they were the widows of freemen, but few entered apprenticeships. (The wives of important members could, for a fee, be buried with great pomp and receive a lavish funeral dinner.) Although the power of companies barely extended to the evolving suburbs, merchants, especially those in foreign trade, found it useful to seek membership. They prized all clubs and memberships that offered opportunities for networking and exchanging commercial information:

> Merchants, by these clubs or meetings, have intelligence of ships going out, and coming in; and also of the rates and prices of commodities, and meet with customers by accident, which possibly might never make inquiry at their houses or warehouses.[23]

The relationship between a livery company and a trade could be loose: not all members of the Grocers Company were grocers, although within smaller companies – such as the clockworkers and apothecaries – there remained a high correlation between a particular trade and company membership. Wealthy merchants had a choice of companies and either opted for the most prestigious or clustered within those boasting a specific interest. Many overseas merchants joined the Shipwrights; the Huguenot community favoured the Dyers.

Individual livery companies worked to protect their status, which helped them to build loyalty, enforce rules, and gain a hearing whenever they petitioned higher powers. A powerful image was fundamental to their influence, prompting them to circulate their coats of arms as broadsheets and to print company histories. Their feasts and rituals were an important means of emphasizing their permanence, and festivities brought courtiers into the heart of the City. After all, much of the companies' power depended on patronage and contacts in high places. It was for this reason that the Merchant Taylors feasted James I in 1607 at a cost of over £1,000, entertaining him with songs and speeches composed for the occasion. During the festivities they presented him with a purse of gold and invited him to become a member. The king graciously accepted the gold but said that he already belonged to the Clothworkers' Company and that Prince Henry would join the Merchant Taylors instead.[24] A special relationship between the Crown and the Company ensued. Only the twelve great companies could invite sovereigns to become members and, for the most part, only they could entertain foreign princes and ambassadors.

The companies' concern with lavish display was nowhere more evident than in the Lord Mayor's Show. It took place on 29 October (the 30th if it fell on Sunday), when the new mayor took his oath of office at Westminster. His company had to foot the bill. Typically, the mayor travelled up the Thames in the morning, catching the incoming tide, escorted by representatives of the Great Twelve in resplendent company barges, each with its own musicians. The journey was marked by cannon fire and fireworks from the banks of the river. The barges, often hired, were freshly painted and decorated with streamers and flags. Among them was a 'galley-foist', a small version of a fully rigged warship that could be rowed if there was little wind. It carried drummers and trumpeters, and as many as twenty cannon, which were fired incessantly, creating noise and smoke all the way. On return, the cavalcade came ashore at Paul's Stairs, joined a procession to the cathedral, and paraded slowly up Cheapside. The liverymen wore their best fur-faced gowns; lesser officials wore budge, or lambskin dressed outwards. Each company held aloft banners and their coat of arms. There were musicians, dancers, 'giants' on stilts, with outlying 'devils' and 'wild men' to clear the way. At stations along the route performers acted theatrical set pieces based on mythology, history or morality, the props including exotic beasts: dragons, lions and camels. Afterwards, there was a banquet at Guildhall and usually a sermon in St Paul's, at the end of which the mayor was escorted by torchlight back to his house.

By the time of James I, the show had deepened its assault on the senses and served multiple purposes. Most importantly, the procession was a statement of the power and permanence of the livery companies, demonstrating to any haughty monarch that the citizens of London had their own strong power base. It also manifested the power of the companies to their own members, helping to enforce discipline, legitimate social inequality, and underline the value of their apprenticeships. Each company had a fixed station within the hierarchy of the parade but still competed in the opulence of their displays. They flaunted not only their trade skills but also their honour, patriotism and charity – qualities which might attract the wealthiest merchants to their number. The show itself helped powerful merchants to manage their community image as caretakers of public charity. The procession, which generally included characters symbolizing London, transmitted city culture to successive generations and helped to create civic pride. For migrants, the pageants staged at key locations added layers of meaning to a city that was new to them, helping to bind newcomers into what was deemed to be the essential nature of London and the spirit of Londoners. During the Civil Wars in the 1640s this emotional connection would have a powerful effect when citizens were asked to take up arms in their city's defence.

While these shows were street events, established dramatists often wrote about them, including Anthony Munday, Thomas Dekker, John Middleton and John Webster, all of whom were members of livery companies. The work was well paid and high-profile, so talented writers competed eagerly for the role. It also presented unique challenges: pageants were performed in the open air, subjects were mostly confined to traditional topics, and the performance had to engage all levels. In 1617 the Grocers paid Middleton £282 for writing the show, devising the pageants and costumes, rehearsing the chief players and charity children, organizing porterage by land and water, and getting the fireworks. Munday and Dekker received £5 and £4 respectively, just for bidding to do the work. Typically, the sponsoring company afterwards printed 300 to 500 copies of the text of the speeches for private distribution.[25]

The role of the artificer who created the props and special effects was as important as that of the writer, since the display of power and civic culture had to run smoothly. In some years, companies had to pay for trade signs and parts of shop buildings along the route to be taken down before the procession could pass through narrow streets, then replace them afterwards. One of the ships from the river display was often carried ashore to become a prop in one of the pageants. There were also complicated structures to build: the Goldsmiths' 1611 show called for 'The chariot of the two kings drawn with two leopards' and 'Two Moors, riding upon unicorns, casting abroad the air'.[26] One hundred porters carried models of beasts in the show and a new blue coat was needed for each porter. At the last minute organizers learnt that the queen, Anne of Denmark, would attend, so they enlisted the help of a hundred foreign goldsmiths working in the City to enlarge the performance. The expense could be eyewatering: in 1617, Busino considered that the cost of the show 'exceeded the means of a petty or medium duke'.[27] In 1624 the Merchant Taylors spent over £1,000 on a pageant by Webster. Then, as now, the Lord Mayor's Show was often marred by bad autumn weather and as it was partly staged on the Thames, strong winds produced dangerous conditions, scattering barges. In 1605, due to 'greate rayne and fowle weather', the show was called off, but such was its importance that costumes were dried out and it was rerun at additional expense on All Saints' Day on 1 November.[28]

In James's time, the show easily carried a political message of national significance. Munday's 1605 work, *The Triumph of Re-United Britannia*, celebrated James for uniting England, Wales and Scotland under one crown, though it also praised the Merchant Taylors for promoting overseas trade. In 1620, when merchants feared that England might be dragged into an expensive war on the Continent, the Haberdashers commissioned *The Tryumphs of Peace*, which pointedly celebrated James as a peacemaker. The annual procession could include foreign dignitaries and ambassadors, stressing the City's link with overseas trade and diplomacy. After all, London had a prime role in paying for national defence in wartime and the merchant community had potential influence on foreign affairs.

Not all Londoners would have understood the symbolism of the show or registered its lofty political messages. And it was hardly a staid affair. In 1617, Busino witnessed the surging mass of people, young and old. The women of the lower classes carried children; all jostled for a good view or tried to catch the sugar pieces, nutmegs, dates or ginger that performers riding in the cars threw to the crowd. Any nobles stupid enough to attend in carriages were immediate targets for the rabble:

They cling behind the coaches and should the coachmen use his whip, they jump down and pelt him with mud. In this way we saw them bedaub the smart livery of one coachman, who was obliged to put up with it. In these great uproars no sword is ever unsheathed, everything ends in kicks, fisty cuffs and muddy faces.[29]

There is some evidence of the shows 'dumbing down', perhaps to appeal to recent migrants. In 1660, Pepys was watching from a linen draper's window in Cheapside as the mayoral pageant drew near the Nag's Head tavern. He was treated to a performance in rustic dialect, followed by acrobatics, which he dismissed as 'good for such kind of things but in themselfs but poor and absurd'.[30] Yet the Lord Mayor's Show remained an important celebration of the civic virtue rooted in livery companies. As the metropolis expanded, the proportion of male Londoners belonging to a company decreased, but by the end of the century one-half at least were still members.[31]

ULSTER PLANTATION

Membership privileges of a livery company came at a price because the companies had to provide money for civic use. They maintained London's Trained Bands, or citizen militia: the Court of Aldermen paid professional soldiers to train the Honourable Artillery Company which, in turn, provided officers for the militia. Companies also covered exceptional military expenditure if, for example, the city gates needed an emergency guard. They contributed to public works such as widening streets and digging sewers. They were required to buy a quota of corn each autumn, when prices were low, and store it in the City's granaries to help the poor during months of scarcity. Later in the century they were also expected to buy supplies of coal on the same basis, thwarting any joint action by coal merchants to raise prices.

The Crown was dependent on the City to make up shortfalls in royal finances; in return, the City was relatively free from royal interference. But this would change: the livery companies' great wealth attracted the notice of James I, who urged them to help finance the founding of the Virginia colony in 1609. Their response was mixed: just as companies compared expenditure on Lord

Mayor's Day, so now they cautiously measured each other's outlay. Some merchants invested in a private capacity, but the new colony got off to a poor start; there would be no quick return on investment. In 1612 the Virginia Company took to raising funds through a lottery, which the Privy Council encouraged the companies to support. In 1614 a second lottery was put to them, the mayor writing positively that the new colony would be a means of removing idle vagrants from the City and nation as a whole: 'soe honourable and Christian a work, and by wch means wee may bee disburdened of many idle and vagrant persons, wch otherwise are and wilbe more and more chargeable, dangerous, and troublesome to the state'.[32] But although companies helped impoverished members to emigrate to Virginia, company interest in the new colony swiftly declined from 1616. This was because James was making heavy demands on them to finance his vision for Ireland, and this took precedence.

James wanted to prevent Ireland becoming a back door for invasion by Catholic powers, so in 1607 he determined to 'plant' or settle Ulster (the most Gaelic part of Ireland) with people loyal to the Crown. The philosopher and statesman Francis Bacon is most famous today for his ambition to promote 'the advancement of learning' by documenting the natural world using first-hand observation. But as solicitor general, he influenced Crown policy in Ireland from the start. He was a keen advocate of the union of the British Isles and supported an imperial civilizing mission in Ireland. He told James that the Ulster Plantation would be a 'second brother' to the union with Scotland and help to build a British state.[33] Bacon did not think of Ireland as a colony to be exploited like Virginia, but as a kingdom to be brought into James's vision of a 'Greater' or 'Great Britain'. But events did not go to plan.

Immigrants from England and Scotland were markedly reluctant to settle in the County of Coleraine, where there was a large and resentful native population, so in May 1609 James 'invited' the London companies for 'their present honour and future commodity' to finance a plantation in that part of Ulster. The project was a commercial venture but at the same time James was cynically putting to the test the companies' much-vaunted civic spirit. 'Civility' was a core element in London's urban identity, so the companies could underwrite the same spirit in Ulster, 'the Planting of Religion and Civility (the Seeds of Peace and Plenty)'.[34] From James's perspective in Whitehall, the project was easily envisioned. He had inherited great royal hunting parks from St James's to Hyde Park, tangible examples of what might be done in Ireland where thick woodland, hide-outs for rebel forces, stalled English attempts to subjugate local populations. The symbolism of wild woods in much contemporary drama (including the menace of Birnam Wood in *Macbeth*) worked to reinforce in the public imagination the benefits of controlling Irish woodland and encouraging people to live civilly in towns. The Ulster Plantation would be a means of achieving prosperity, community, civil manners and security.

The merchants of London were reluctant to underwrite the colonizing project, an area in which most of them had no experience. The Fishmongers observed, 'it were best never to entermeddle at al in this busynesse . . . for that it is thought it will be exceeding chargeable'.[35] They were not alone in the thought. Only when James threatened, fined and jailed key officials did the City bow to pressure. It sent commissioners to Ireland to assess the prospects of the scheme. They returned with a surprisingly positive report, so a new county of Londonderry was formally drawn up to include Coleraine and chunks of neighbouring counties rich in timber for building. Late in 1609 the companies offered to invest £15,000 in developing this county. At once, the Privy Council pressed for more until the companies agreed to an initial sum of £20,000. They had great difficulty in raising this money, even by instalment. Prosperous members of the Merchant Taylors were unwilling to contribute, despite intimidation; the smaller companies naturally found it hard to raise their share and had to band together as associates. In the end most of the compulsory levies for the new plantation were obtained by dipping into company reserves.

The project proved to be an unprecedented drain on the companies' resources. Companies were responsible for jointly building a fortified city (Londonderry) and a fortified town (Coleraine). They set up a governing body with wide-ranging powers to direct their operations in Ireland, which came to be known as the Irish Society. At the end of 1613, after difficult negotiations, the rest of the County of Londonderry was divided between the Great Twelve, who drew lots. The smaller companies were associated with them, again by lot. Individual companies were liable for the development and peopling of their estates – at an estimated additional cost of £22,000. By 1616 the companies had paid up to £60,000, an immense sum in relation to the usual level of taxation. Pressure was unrelenting: the king wrote personally to his Lord Deputy in Ireland, urging greater zeal in the business of building houses, castles and churches. Bullied by the Privy Council, the Irish Society worked to complete the new, fortified towns in Ulster. Given the distance from London, the Londoners made reasonable progress, thanks to their practical skills in management and logistics. But there was one great problem: state map-makers had failed to take correct measurements. Company lands were supposed to total 34,187 acres but turned out to be 307,278 acres.[36] Puzzled Londoners found they owned huge estates when they expected modest holdings. Their agents were supposed to displace the native Irish from Londonderry and settle the land with migrants from England and Scotland, but these enormous tracts of land could not be managed without the native Irish. Most were allowed to remain, if only for the time being, because they were needed for construction work. Remarkably, although company settlements were slow to finish and tenants hard to find, by 1630 an estimated 37,000 British people, mostly Scots, had migrated to Ulster.[37]

Yet all the while, the Ulster Plantation was storing up trouble that would erupt in the reign of Charles I, just when it seemed that the companies might finally see some return on their huge, compulsory investment. The Crown's alienation of London's powerful livery companies would prove a great error.

4
'FORRAIGN TRADE ... THE MEANS OF OUR TREASURE'[1]

On the morning of 26 October 1654 the *Mary*, laden with coals from Newcastle, was slowly making its way up the Thames, heading for the Port of London, while the *Freeman* was sailing more quickly down the Thames with a fair wind. The master of the collier, Robert Yaxley, later gave evidence that as he approached Gallions Reach, John Whitty, master of the *Freeman*, rammed the *Mary* 'violently and wilfully', though there was plenty of room to pass. Richard Cockett, a member of Yaxley's crew, confirmed that Whitty had crashed into their ship through 'willfull and obstinate miscarriage' and indignantly added that at the moment of impact Whitty shouted out, 'You Collierly dogs, would I had sunk you!'[2] The *Freeman* was a 400-ton vessel, the *Mary* barely 100 tons, and the larger ship caused extensive damage to the collier's hull, sails, masts and rigging: the estimated cost of repair was £200.

By mid-century, collisions in the Thames were common: coastal and foreign trade had risen steeply; the Thames was often crowded with vessels.[3] But this incident, and its aftermath, points to several things. First, growing international trade now called for larger, more impressive ships, and those who sailed them looked down on mere coastal vessels. Second, there was growing literacy among labouring classes, as is clear from witness statements in the legal case that followed: the *Mary*'s younger sailors could sign their names whereas those in their fifties could only make their mark. Third, England's growing trade was partly linked to the expansion of London itself: after all, most Newcastle coal was destined for London householders and manufacturers. The coal trade increased rapidly in the early decades of the century as national timber supplies dwindled: 73,984 tons of coal were shipped to London from Tyneside in 1605–6; by the 1640s, Londoners were burning over 300,000 tons a year.[4] The coal trade involved over 400 coastal vessels in thousands of voyages. Its growth rate had moderated by mid-century, but it was still described in 1671 as 'the greatest nursery of seamen we have in England', partly because coal was also exported across the North Sea to Europe.[5]

Already, by mid-century, the English liked to look back on the glory days of Sir Francis Drake and Walter Raleigh, and to think of themselves as a great seafaring nation. In fact, England had made a slow start in oceanic trade. By 1600 it had neither founded colonies nor discovered the wealth that South American silver was bringing to Spain and Asian spices to Portugal. English attempts to find a route to the East by sailing into Arctic waters were proving futile. All the same, English ships were routinely sailing to the Americas and the Mediterranean, and merchants were intent on breaking into the lucrative spice trade with Asia. Together with English politicians, they had become increasingly worried that the Dutch would monopolize the supply of spices to Europe; in 1600 the English East India Company was founded as a direct response to Dutch initiatives. A year later the Company's first fleet – four vessels, each only about the length of two double-decker buses – sailed around the Cape of Good Hope to the spice islands in Indonesia. The fleet returned with valuable cargoes of pepper in 1603 and its commander, John Lancaster, was knighted by the newly crowned James I.

London was England's largest port by far. In 1607 the Venetian ambassador, Nicolo Molin, described the advantages that London gained from the River Thames, which was both beautiful and 'of the highest service for the large number of ships from 300 to 400 tons burden, which come in upon the tide from all parts of the world, although the city lies upwards of sixty miles from the sea'.[6] Molin would have had ample opportunity to assess these benefits: the Thames was the usual route into London for foreign dignitaries, who left narrow, robber-infested roads at Gravesend or Greenwich and proceeded to Westminster by water. The river offered Londoners a continual spectacle of merchant ships coming and going with the tide, and bulk goods transported to yards and manufacturing sites along its banks. From such activity they could judge the prosperity of their city and even form an opinion about the state of the national economy.

Much of the traffic on the River Thames was internal as coastal shipping brought in supplies to sustain the capital. Grain came from Essex, East Anglia and Kent to make bread and beer. Much was landed at Billingsgate, the oldest wharf on the Thames and the chief place in the City for landing fish, corn, malt and salt. Hay was always in demand and oats helped to meet London's need for fodder, since by the 1620s the capital had more than 3,000 carthorses alone.[7]

Foreign trade was flourishing when James I came to the throne. England, still an agricultural country, chiefly exported heavy woollen textiles, traded to northern, central and eastern Europe. After 1615 demand for these goods slumped. The immediate cause was the scheme devised by William Cockayne, a merchant and alderman, who thought more money could be made if all English cloth was dyed and dressed before export. He persuaded James to grant him a monopoly, but the project failed and helped to depress the cloth trade for decades. This catastrophe was partly offset by the English production of 'new draperies', lighter woollen-mix cloth mainly exported to southern Europe. This expanding trade helped to pay for imports from Spain and Portugal: wine, olive oil and fruit – chiefly raisins, consumed by all classes and without which, it was said, the English could 'hardly digest bread, pastries, broths and bag-puddings'.[8] Since England exported woollens almost exclusively, markets for them were a source of constant anxiety. The growing Spanish market for England's lighter woollen textiles, which did not peak until 1620, was one reason why relations with Spain slowly grew more cordial.

The costs and risks of trying to establish new trade routes led to the founding of trading companies, which were granted monopolies by the Crown. Some were 'regulated', meaning that their members engaged in trade either individually or in groups; among these were the Merchant Adventurers, controlling the cloth trade, and the Levant Company, trading to the eastern Mediterranean. Others became joint-stock companies, like the East India Company and the Royal African Company, which traded as corporate bodies on behalf of shareholders who invested their capital. Trading companies obviously benefited merchants, and potentially their shareholders, by spreading risk. They were also attractive propositions to successive monarchs who awarded them royal charters. Chartered companies could be tapped for loans, providing cash-strapped rulers with a source of revenue without resource to parliament. Companies could also be expected to exert some control over their members, lessening the risk that their trade would upset diplomatic relations with other nations.

The London-based trading companies were dominated by a small group of merchants who jealously guarded their monopoly rights. In the reign of James I only the Eastland Company, trading with the Baltic and Scandinavia, lacked a full monopoly. Naturally, these chartered companies attracted growing hostility from other merchants, especially those in the provinces, who complained as early as 1604 that 'the Whole Trade of all the Realm is in the Hands of some Two Hundred Persons at most'.[9] The result, they claimed, was complacency and inefficiency. The business of the Muscovy Company was thought to be shouldered by just fifteen members in 1604 and their unwillingness to expand was said to have let the Dutch into trade with Russia. Within a single company, power might be further contracted to an inner coterie of the most affluent. Many in the Levant Company were additionally linked by birth or marriage, which helps to explain how they could keep such a tight control on membership to exploit their position and regulate their trade. By 1621 parliament contained many members who were openly hostile to the companies and wanted free trade. Yet when Charles I imposed customs duties without consent of parliament after 1625, the companies joined in strong protest, and for a while company merchants and MPs seemed to be on the same side. The alliance was brief: merchant opposition to the king soon fragmented because powerful trading companies gained so much from their royal privilege. Still, it showed how commercial ambition would play a part in the complex political divisions opening within the country.

In the first half of the century long-distance trade fired merchants with genuine excitement, but its logistics were in development. In 1615 an estimated two-thirds of English seamen were still employed in the coal trade and the fisheries. The latter hardly impacted on London: West Country ports serviced the Newfoundland fishery and Yarmouth exported red herring to Spain and the Mediterranean.[10] Still, London's East India trade – which had moved forward as an extension of trade in the Levant – was becoming hugely profitable, despite Portuguese opposition in the Indian Ocean and the disapproval of the Dutch. James I gave the country two decades of peace, during which foreign trade prospered.[11] The East India Company's most profitable 1612 voyage gave investors their money back and a staggering 220 per cent profit.[12] Within twenty years of its foundation the Company had more than ten trading bases in Asia and, until the troubled 1630s under Charles I, its gains exceeded all expectations.

Valuable cargoes of spices (nutmeg, cloves, cinnamon, black pepper), medicinal drugs, perfumes, silks, and aromatic woods such as sandalwood, poured into London from the East, although pepper and saltpetre (needed for gunpowder) formed the greatest volume of every ship's cargo. Merchants began to re-export large quantities of pepper and other eastern goods through the Straits of Gibraltar to the Mediterranean. The re-export market revolutionized English trade with Italy which, by the 1630s, centred on the port of Leghorn (Livorno) where goods were traded duty-free. City merchants also extended their networks in the Far East, often sending out trusted family members as agents. Their letters show how merchants built up a knowledge of what goods would sell and at what price. In the 1630s, for example, Thomas Rogers wrote to his uncle, a merchant in Bishopsgate, from Madagascar, the Gulf and Surat. The death toll of English merchants in the region was high, he reported, and accidents common, but he was making progress. He asked if his mother could send out more paper for making into ledgers, and he specified the goods his uncle should ship out. Both were employees of the East India Company, but the letters are about private business ventures.[13]

London's trade with the American colonies, and with West Indian islands settled between 1622 and 1632, was also fast growing, but of modest significance until mid-century. The Virginia Company's first fleet to America had sailed from Blackwall in 1606. At first colonizers had to focus on growing food to support themselves, but the colony in Virginia soon found an export staple in tobacco and the West Indian islands followed suit. (The Barbados planters turned to cultivating sugar cane only around 1640.) Crop production in Barbados and Jamaica then increased mid-century as ailing white labourers were largely replaced by enslaved Africans. England's trade in colonial produce was dominated by London merchants, but not by those operating within chartered companies. The Virginia Company was dissolved in 1624 because it failed to attract enough investment. Instead, it was mostly individual merchants, excluded from the powerful companies, who contracted with colonial planters, advancing them money and shipping people out to work on the land. Trade was uncertain to begin with, and London merchants relied on being able to sell return cargoes quickly because they lacked capital.

England's growing commerce pushed up the demand for shipping. This, in turn, increased the demand for materials with which to build ships: timber (chiefly for masts), imported hemp for ropes, flax for sails, and pitch and tar for waterproofing. These vital naval stores, from Norway, the Baltic and northern Russia, were all high-volume cargoes that further boosted the shipping industry. England had almost no exports for ships doing business with these northern countries or trading long-distance to the American colonies and the East Indies. English woollens were certainly not wanted in the Far East; there great men only made initial use of them to cover their elephants and make saddles for their horses. Ships for these destinations sailed from London almost empty, except for the silver bullion needed to purchase Asian goods; some cargoes might be picked up during the voyage out, but as a rule the freights brought back had to cover the cost of any imbalance. London's growing re-export trade therefore proved vital.

There were signs that London was becoming an entrepot as early as 1600: it had warehouses along the riverfront holding quantities of merchandise for re-export rather than distribution within England. By the 1640s re-exports were five times greater in volume than they had been at the end of Elizabeth's reign.[14] This increase had a marked effect on London, which had always handled the bulk of the nation's foreign trade. Merchants began shipping East Indian goods to Russia, the Netherlands, Germany, Italy and even the Levant. Virginia tobacco was sent to Hamburg, and European manufactures to Africa and the American colonies. There was an increasing amount of invisible exports, too, as goods were traded between foreign countries without ever being shipped to England. London merchants began to see that fortunes could be made from colonial expansion if the produce of English colonies could be promptly sold elsewhere, although this angered the Dutch who had the same idea.

The expansion of London's trade led to the growth of distinct seafaring and shipbuilding communities, east of the City in rural Stepney and south of the river where private shipyards complemented the royal dockyard at Deptford. Stepney was a large parish stretching from the City and Bishopsgate to the River Lea. It had several distinct areas and before 1700 Shadwell and Wapping were made separate parishes. Mariners had long used Ratcliff Cross, on the north shore of the Thames, as a landing point. Before the riverside was banked at Wapping and its marshes drained, Ratcliff Cross, located on higher gravel, was one of the few places below London Bridge where wharves could be built. Inland, Ratcliff Highway, a narrow, unpaved road, ran directly west to Wapping, then towards the Tower of London. Elm trees had once lined the route, but by the beginning of the century trees had been replaced by tenements. Haphazard building also advanced along the riverside east of the Tower: behind the Wapping embankment a narrow road, running parallel to the river, was raised above the marshland. It sprouted small alleys, dotted with the hovels and cottages of sailors and the shopkeepers who supplied them. Ropewalks and other maritime trades also took root. Before 1620, Hermitage Dock was constructed, half a mile east of the Tower on the Wapping foreshore. Houses and work buildings soon multiplied along the riverfront at Wapping; several builders were former shipwrights who constructed a variety of large, strong houses for the well-off and smaller ones for sailors.

Shadwell, between Wapping and Ratcliff Cross, next saw rapid growth, especially in the 1630s and 1640s. Barely inhabited when Elizabeth was on the throne, by 1650 it had 700 houses, numerous shops and taverns, and a dock where ships could be built and repaired. It was an established commercial centre by the end of the century with manufacturing sites, shipping, and a densely housed population. Further east, the hamlet of Blackwall began to expand when the East India Company built a dock there in 1614, employing hundreds of men and boosting London's reputation for shipbuilding. Residential development took off in the 1620s and 1630s; inns were built to serve travellers, and Blackwall became a victualling point for outward-bound vessels. By 1650 almost all the riverside from the Tower to Poplar had been wharved, providing storage for goods from Hertfordshire that had come down the River Lea and which, unlike foreign goods, did not need to be landed at the Legal Quays in the Port of London to pay customs duties. Ship chandlers along the riverbank needed ready access to a range of provisions: they had to supply merchant vessels on demand, or they would lose contracts. Their task was exacting because many so vessels sailed at once: the heavily armed fleet for the East Indies, for example, was always prepared in March. Behind this noisy belt of riverside activity there developed massed accommodation for sailors and other workers.

In sum, the population of these eastern districts exploded: in 1600 it had been around 21,000, but it exceeded 91,000 by the end of the century; in the 1630s, Thames boatmen alone were said to number some 20,000.[15] By 1700 well over 50 per cent of Stepney's mariners and boatmen were living in Wapping, although it also had more shore-based workers than the other maritime districts. These included skilled map-makers, scientific instrument makers who might specialize in navigational aids, tailors, smiths, shoemakers, bricklayers and brewers.[16] The two most populous districts were Limehouse and Ratcliff, where newcomers included Irish, Dutch and Scandinavians. The maritime districts also held transient communities of polyglot seamen. Indian sailors, mostly from Bengal where the East India Company had a base, helped to increase London's ethnic diversity. It was growing anyway since peace with Spain in 1604 meant that black people reached England through Anglo-Spanish trading networks. Refugees also settled: Flemish and French Protestants fleeing religious persecution, their numbers increasing in the second half of the century, though French Huguenots mostly clustered in Spitalfields.

New housing advanced steadily over the riverside pastureland. But despite pockets of very poor areas, where tenements were shoddily built and closely packed, there was not yet general overcrowding in these eastern suburbs. And residents had opportunities: a charity school, founded in 1531 on Ratcliff Highway, offered boys the chance to learn mathematics; others learnt to read and write at sea. Yet Poplar and Limehouse, where the population had grown more slowly, had more people who were comfortably off than Wapping and Ratcliff.[17] That said, all maritime districts housed some wealthy residents whose business interests required them to live near the river. They included merchant-captains, timber merchants, shipbuilders, dealers in ballast, and tradesmen who provisioned ships. Several brewers, taking their water from the Thames, built up large complexes in St Katharine's and East Smithfield. In Shadwell, although most were relatively poor and lived in narrow houses with one or two storeys, there were rich merchants who built houses with frontages of 30 feet and more, often with business premises attached and sometimes three storeys high. Most of these larger houses were in Lower Shadwell, close to the river, although some were on Ratcliff Highway. Generally, houses were built of wood, but brick became more popular in the closing decades of the century, and after fires wooden houses were usually replaced by brick. In Limehouse, terraced housing of the late seventeenth and early eighteenth centuries can be seen in Narrow Street today.

By 1700 probably more than a quarter of London's population depended on the River Thames, if the dependants of seafarers, shipbuilders, victuallers, watermen and lightermen, warehousemen and porters are included.[18] The work of those who laboured on the river itself was weather-dependent: adverse winds and severe frosts disrupted trade. When the Thames completely froze over, as it did several times in the century, these workers and their families suffered great hardship. All London's suburbs were less well-regulated than the City, but the indications are that crime was high in London's maritime districts, despite the presence of established Dissenting communities. There was much domestic irregularity arising from the absence of menfolk at sea, and casual violence fuelled by alcohol, although the hard-drinking elite set no great example in this respect. Traces of disorderly lives remain in parish records: in Shadwell a Mary Gregory asked for maintenance as her husband, a lighterman, had thrown her out of the house and taken another woman whose husband was at sea; John Stringer, a tobacconist in Ratcliff Highway, was accused of killing with a rapier a seaman who had been drinking in his house.[19] The perils of seafaring impacted heavily on vulnerable women: seamen's wives whose husbands had been captured by French privateers or north African corsairs applied for licences to beg, hoping to raise the ransom money for their release. Records of prosecutions in these districts, then in the county of Middlesex, are sparse for the period, but the archives certainly indicate concern for maintaining law and order at a local level.[20] Residents requested stocks, whipping posts, cages, night watchmen, watch houses and lock-ups.

LONDON SHIPBUILDING

By the early seventeenth century, the south bank of the River Thames was England's foremost centre for shipbuilding – the north bank focused mainly on ship repair and ship fitting. At Deptford, the royal dockyard built and repaired warships whereas the private shipyards nearby built both naval and merchant ships. The period up to 1650 saw important technological advances and an increase in the size of vessels. *Susan Constant*, the lead ship in the expedition to found Virginia in 1607, was barely the length of one and a half London buses, but long-distance trade and rampant privateering (when the government licensed merchant ships to harass the enemy in wartime) soon produced larger vessels.[21] Powerful merchant ships were useful for national defence in wartime and, to the end of the century, government liked to see a reserve of merchant vessels for this purpose. Their engagement in battle was also a matter of civic pride: in 1633, Thomas Dekker celebrated the use of merchantmen against Spanish and French navies in his Lord Mayor's Show. Only after 1700 did warships and merchant ships become so different that the latter were no longer useful in naval battles.

Since the days when Elizabethan Sea Dogs harassed Spanish shipping as privateers, English merchant captains had employed aggressive tactics in distant oceans. Most foreign trade was armed trade: East Indiamen carried twice the number of men needed to work the ship in case they were required to defend cargoes. The Venetian ambassador gave a detailed picture of England's naval force in 1635 to inform policy-making in his own country: the king had just four warships in service but another thirty-six ready for commission and he could make use of up to 1,000 merchant ships that might be fitted out for war. The impressive galleons of the East India Company were 'moving sea fortresses', capable of serving a double purpose, for war and trade. The English, he explained, 'assume the title of lords of the Ocean as far as the Canary Islands', adding tartly, 'at present they exercise possession more by pretensions than by force'.[22] Charles I aspired to create a powerful navy both for national defence and to protect commerce from piracy; his navy was better than his father's. Early in James's reign the Venetian ambassador in post reported that many English warships were rotten and barely fit for service, while only three were armed.[23] Charles signalled his naval ambition by attending the launch of two warships at Deptford dockyard in 1633, his visit helping to raise the prestige of London's maritime districts.

In the early decades of the century London shipbuilding did not have much of a reputation. The *Susan Constant* seems to have been widest below the water-line, which would have made the ship inherently unstable. Sir Henry Mainwaring, a former pirate who was pardoned and honoured by James I because he was useful to the state, noted bluntly in 1618 that English sea rovers generally preferred Flemish ships, because 'they go well, are roomy Ships, floaty [draw little water] and of small charge'.[24] English ships, he explained, commonly had to be widened after launch to make them sail better:

> I think in all the world there are not so many ships furred [widened] as are in England, and it is pity that there is no order taken either for the punishing of those who build such ships or the preventing of it, for it is an infinite loss to the owners and an utter spoiling and disgrace to all ships that are so handled.[25]

Mainwaring even thought that English ship cables were poor; the Mediterranean peoples, the Flemish and Russians, all made better ones.

But Thames shipbuilding progressed as merchants opened new, fast-growing trading routes. The East India Company built the largest merchant ships. After purchasing vessels for its early voyages, it decided to build and repair its own and, in 1607, leased a shipyard in Deptford. Some of its East Indiamen were the largest sailing ships ever built in England: the *Trade's Increase*, which James I launched in 1609, was nearly 1,000 tons. But if merchants expected to ship cargoes home at cheaper rates, they soon learnt a lesson. The *Trade's Increase* was wrecked off Java on its first voyage. The Company saw that losses on this scale would be unsustainable. As a result, it standardized on ships of 500 to 800 tons. Even by 1614 its scale of operation had outstripped the facilities it had for shipbuilding and repair at Deptford, so it decided to build ships at Blackwall on the eastern side of the Isle of Dogs. Blackwall was further downriver with a greater depth of water so there was less risk that heavily laden vessels would damage their hulls. After 1618 the enterprise slowly moved its operations from Deptford to Blackwall. By 1620 the Company had built an astonishing seventy-six ships on the Thames, but years of crisis followed.[26] At home, there was criticism of its export of silver bullion, which some felt impoverished the country; overseas, there was increasing friction with the Dutch. Then in 1635, Charles I allowed a rival company, the Courteen Association, to trade with the East. Partly as a response, the East India Company decided to sell its Blackwall Yard and hire ships rather than build them. It eventually did this in 1656, but its investment in Blackwall had a lasting effect: the shipyard went on to become the largest in London.

If the English specialized in building armed ships for long-distance trade, Dutch merchant vessels – cheaper, lighter and roomier – were better suited to European waters. The English themselves realized this by mid-century, but because they were to capture so many enemy vessels during the Dutch wars and because English shipwrights were reluctant to adopt new methods, the industry responded to new demands only towards the close of the century. Even then, the response was strongest in the northeast and East Anglia, where coastal trades called for bulk carriers. Meanwhile, shipbuilding on the Thames prospered because the colonial, Levant and East Indies trades needed strongly built, armed ships. East Indiamen tended to have fine lines, for speed. The Venetian ambassador enthused in 1635, 'They are so skilfully built and so carefully provided with everything that can possibly be required that they excite universal admiration.'[27] But, despite appearances, many East Indiamen were 'crank': long, deep and narrow, they keeled over in the wind, making a long, slow roll before coming back to the vertical. Shipbuilding was a practical skill, based on trial and error, and there were few opportunities to test hull shapes before construction. The beautiful wooden ship models that are seen in museums today were not necessarily a means of designing better hulls. Often they were created to honour the recipient, or to attract support and investment.

Still, for some, the requirement to produce better ships and better aids to navigation carried the same intellectual excitement as the challenges of space travel today. Shipbuilding became linked with the mathematical practice in the early part of the century. Matthew Baker, the greatest shipwright in Queen Elizabeth's reign, devised a method of laying down a ship's lines on paper rather than working exclusively with full-sized wooden templates on the site of construction. He worked out mathematical principles for drawing the curved lines of a ship's hull, without relying wholly on traditional rules of proportion to give him a ship's dimensions. Traditional practices could be dismissed as mere rules of thumb, although Baker probably used them more than he cared to admit; he himself suggested that a ship's breadth should be between a half and a third of the length of its keel.[28] But once Baker had a ship's lines on paper, the design could be discussed with mathematicians and other experts. When he died, in 1613, he left his notebook to John Wells, Keeper of the Naval Stores at Deptford, Chatham and Portsmouth, who added more insights of his own. Their joint papers were preserved by Samuel Pepys, who bound them into a book, still in the Pepys Library at Magdalene College, Cambridge.

Wells had been well tutored in mathematics and used his dockyard position to get to know the master shipwrights, discussing with them such issues as weight distribution and other technical aspects of ship design. His mathematical interests led him to associate with professors at Gresham College, endowed by the merchant and royal advisor Sir Thomas Gresham and established in Bishopsgate in 1597. Its professors gave free weekly lectures to the public in Divinity, Astronomy, Music, Geometry, Law, Physic and Rhetoric. Wells helped Gresham's geometry professor, Henry Briggs, to construct tables of logarithms, which he then applied to ship design. He was responsible for linking Gresham experts with naval officials at the Deptford dockyard and this group later worked on methods to calculate the tonnage of ships more accurately. Baker's legacy was taken up by others attracted to ship design, including Thomas Herriot, probably the most expert practical mathematician of the early seventeenth century, who is believed to have been the first to draw the Moon from observations made through a telescope. Although master shipwrights guarded their secrets – making available the results of their calculations to subordinates and trainees but never revealing the formulae they used to produce them – English shipbuilding soon became the most mathematically advanced of any country in Europe.

The lecturers at Gresham were also interested in navigation and Wells worked with Henry Gellibrand, the Professor of Astronomy, to prove that magnetic compass needles are subject to change over time. The discovery that Earth's magnetic field changes slowly over time was made in the garden of Wells's house in Deptford in 1634. Gellibrand repeated a reading made twelve years earlier and found that magnetic variation near London had been gradually decreasing, a hugely important discovery for navigation.

This spirit of inquiry which Londoners applied to ship design, sails and rigging, and questions of navigation, in time gave the English an edge over competitors in building vessels that could carry out combined tasks of shipping and warfare.

RIOTOUS CONSUMPTION

Luxury consumption at home was a spur to international trade. The demand for lavish goods from Europe and Asia had been growing since the 1540s, but under James I it expanded dramatically. The clearest sign of expensive tastes in contemporary account books is the purchase of exquisite clothing, which signalled wealth and status. Fine gowns required many yards of coloured silk or velvet. Each garment was a small project that had to be carefully thought through: silk thread, hooks and eyes, silk points or laces, trimmings, ribbons and bindings all had to be considered, and tailors or dressmakers engaged for complex items.[29] Silk imports grew once English merchants could trade directly with the Far East. In 1621, England imported 120,000 pounds of raw silk, much of it still brought from eastern Mediterranean countries by way of northern Europe. By the late 1620s, 90 per cent of England's silk was imported directly from source by Levant and East India merchants; 170,000 pounds in 1630; 200,000 in 1634; and 220,000 in 1640.[30] In the same period fewer silk fabrics were imported from Italy and other continental weaving and dyeing centres as the Crown encouraged domestic production. Expert silk throwers, dyers and weavers were enticed to London from the Continent and later on refugee Huguenot craftsmen swelled their numbers.

Much domestic expenditure was still spent on bulk goods: flour, beer – if not brewed at home – tubs of soap, fodder, wood and candles. Running a home was labour-intensive, and by our standards, rooms were sparsely furnished, with wooden stools and chairs, and rush matting on the floor. But the wealthy classes increasingly advertised their status and creditworthiness through material goods as well as expensive clothes. They bought hangings and padded furniture to make homes comfortable, carpets so precious they were displayed as table coverings, and pewter and Venetian glassware; they travelled in richly upholstered coaches. Sir John Coke's household accounts for 1627–30, when he was a commissioner of the navy, show the level of spending the elite might devote to an aspirational project. When furnishing Melbourne Hall in Derbyshire for his retirement, Coke commissioned two sets of rich hangings, each of five pieces, ten feet deep, one telling the story of Abraham and the other of Joseph. He purchased low, feather-upholstered stools covered in fringed silk, a couch of 'Turkey work', an elaborate bedstead, and featherbeds, bolsters and silk cushions.[31] In his London house, expenditure was more modest, but clothes for himself and his family cost significant amounts and his coach had to be expensively oiled and blacked to maintain its sleek appearance.

Novelty imports from China soon influenced the design of domestic items. No one in the West could make porcelain, but by the late 1620s English potters were imitating Chinese blue and white porcelain designs in earthenware. Inventories suggest that the number of people owning Chinese items by mid-century was increasing – although porcelain seems to have been kept for display and to indicate the owner's taste and knowledge of different cultures; the Coke family certainly ate off pewter plates and dishes. Coke also amassed silver and gilt plate for show. He received many items as New Year's gifts due to the network of court patronage and he kept careful inventories of their weight and value. Most trading companies gave Coke plate each year, but the East India Company presented him with pepper, cloves, mace and nutmegs, so reducing his housekeeping bills.

Londoners could purchase luxury goods in the Royal Exchange, which had two floors of small shops. In 1609, Robert Cecil, Earl of Salisbury, opened a New Exchange outside the City in the Strand; milliners, haberdashers, perfumers and other luxury tradesmen and women leased shops there, which was well placed for attracting courtiers. Luxury shopping became a leisure activity, protected from the dirt of the streets and the weather, and soon this pursuit began to affect expectations of London's social spaces. Shopping arcades were places where well-to-do women could congregate, as well as men, show off new clothes, learn about the latest fashions and exchange gossip in a safe space. In the 1630s more than 10 per cent of the shops in the New Exchange were leased by women.[32] The increasing visibility of women associated with luxury trades, whether as purchasers or shopowners, exposed them to criticism: aspersions were cast on their morality and willingness to break gender norms. But nothing could reverse the tide of consumption because this form of social display so enticingly advertised a person's elite connections and knowledge of the latest trends.

The consumption of tobacco also skyrocketed in the 1620s and 1630s at all social levels because it dropped in price: in the late 1630s, 4 oz of tobacco cost 1s.[33] Since it was so affordable, thousands of tobacconists opened in London; James I had already granted the Company of Tobacco Pipe Makers a royal charter in 1619. As London's commerce expanded, City institutions flourished. In 1641, Sir Thomas Roe, a clear-sighted diplomat who had led embassies to India and Turkey, firmly defended the direct and re-export trades as essential to the English economy:

> Nothing exported of our owne grouth hath ballanced our Riotous consumption at home, but those forraign commodities, which I call naturalized, that is that surplus of our East-India trade, which being brought home in greater quantity, then are spent, within the kingdom, are exported again and become in Value and use as naturall commodities.[34]

Trends in foreign trade naturally affected power relations within the City. Increasing trade with the Mediterranean and the East led to a decline in the reputation of the Merchant Adventurers, who exported cloth, and a rise in the prestige of the Levant and East India Companies. By 1640 almost half of the twenty-six aldermanic offices in the City were in the hands of these two organizations. Both did all they could to prevent shopkeepers, ship captains and small producers from participating in their trades, fearing that they might be able to undersell them by eliminating middlemen. Their policy exacerbated political divisions: international commerce became intricately linked to politics and affected the course of political debate in the lead-up to civil war. At the same time new imported luxuries were not only changing the quality of life in the capital but also impacting on London's built environment, producing new social spaces. In just a few decades, trade had changed England's place in the world and was affecting the fabric of London itself. The outcome would be very different for rich and poor.

5

A CITY OF EXTREMES

On 16 June 1625, Queen Henrietta Maria, Charles I's new bride, made her first public appearance in London. Only fifteen and brought up a staunch Roman Catholic in the French court, she had refused to marry Charles I, aged twenty-four, in a Protestant service; a proxy marriage had taken place before she left Paris, when Charles was represented by a French kinsman. Now their union was marked by a water procession: the couple journeyed in the royal barge from Gravesend to Whitehall, entering the City at London Bridge. They were accompanied by thousands of other boats; crowds waved and shouted from the shore and fifty ships along the route discharged their cannon. The king and queen wore green outfits to symbolize youth and renewal. Equally symbolically, perhaps, the procession met with a sharp shower of rain. London's bells rang until midnight and its streets were full of bonfires. Charles's court would go on to reach new heights of elegance and artistic prestige. Influenced by the court, the affluent western parts of London would flourish. But in the City overcrowding would get worse and the suburbs would sink further into poverty and disorder. Only medical ignorance, if not disease, afflicted all ranks indiscriminately.

The sumptuous river procession of Charles and his queen, less than three months after the death of James I on 27 March, substituted for Henrietta Maria's coronation: she would not consent to the Protestant ceremony. Much to Charles's annoyance she refused even to enter Westminster Abbey the following year to see him crowned, though a screen had been prepared for her so that she could watch unobserved. Charles deferred his royal entry into the City due to public health concerns after a recent outbreak of the plague and, unlike his father, never made the entry. These incomplete rituals would long be remembered by an uneasy public not only deprived of their royal spectacles but also of the money-making opportunities that came with them. A Catholic queen caused anxiety in London. In 1623, James had sought a Spanish match for Charles to help cement peace in Europe. But Londoners still loathed Spain so much that there were spontaneous celebrations when negotiations fell through and Charles returned from Madrid empty-handed. A French Catholic queen was little better: some hoped she might convert to Protestantism, but it was not to be.

Stunted by childhood rickets, Charles was barely 5 feet 4 inches tall. He was diffident and never quite able to fill the place of his much-admired older brother, Henry, who had died of a fever aged eighteen. Charles was also plagued by a stammer, which meant that he did not care for public speaking and never addressed parliament at length. Perhaps in compensation, he adopted a high moral tone and followed a strict daily routine. He could be very stubborn, and he subscribed utterly to his father's view that a king was appointed by God and ruled by divine right. Perceptive enough to see that his wife's Catholic retinue was not only causing dissension in his household but also alienating Londoners, especially after she made an ill-advised pilgrimage to Tyburn where Catholics had been executed, Charles sent her attendants packing back to France. His queen reportedly punched through a glass window in her frustration but, for a while, he was visibly master in his own home. This was important for his sense of himself as a ruler because, like many of his contemporaries, he viewed the royal household as a microcosm of the nation.[1]

Charles imposed more formality on the court than his father had done. This protected his privacy and allowed him to assert the power of his monarchy through outward symbols. The Spanish court had made a deep impression on him, many of his courtiers had also travelled to the Continent, and Charles meant to create around him the aura of an important European monarchy that nobles and foreign ambassadors would admire. He spent a staggering £30,000 on art in the first five years of his reign. He had to rely on agents in Europe to select masterpieces for his collection and certainly struck lucky in 1627–8, when his go-between in Mantua seized on the circumstance that the Gonzaga family needed money and acquired its famous collection of Italian Renaissance art. The Gonzaga Collection included works by Titian and Correggio, and

Andrea Mantegna's nine monumental canvases titled *The Triumph of Caesar*. These works came to England in stages, after months of negotiation, in 1628 and 1630.

The Italian style in architecture already had its devotees in London. In 1616, King James had commissioned the architect Inigo Jones to build the Queen's House at Greenwich in the classical style, and in 1619 he asked Jones to design a new Banqueting House in Whitehall that would be a statement of his royal authority. Completed in 1622, it was the first classical building in England. Jones had visited Italy twice, was utterly captivated by the buildings of the sixteenth-century architect Antonio Palladio and aimed to reproduce their classical proportions at home. James had meant the Banqueting House to be just the first phase in a remodelling of the entire palace at Whitehall, a plan that Charles revived in the 1630s, but neither monarch had the money to complete such a vast project.

Charles's fashionable courtiers were keen to demonstrate their understanding of art and architecture as well. The royal favourite, George Villiers, Duke of Buckingham, rebuilt and modernized York House, his mansion on the Strand, using it for elaborate receptions to advertise his status. He commissioned a water gate in Portland stone, which would give access to the Thames from his gardens and advertise his Italianate taste to everybody on the river. Built by Nicholas Stone in 1626, the classical design has been attributed to Stone himself, to Inigo Jones and to Sir Balthazar Gerbier, the Anglo-Dutch courtier and designer who carried out the alterations to Buckingham's house. York Water Gate survives but, thanks to the Victoria Embankment, now stands 137 metres from the river.

These costly artistic projects were taking place at a time of military disaster for England. War had broken out between England and Spain in 1625. France became Spain's ally in 1627 and English forces, commanded by the Duke of Buckingham, were ignominiously defeated by the French at La Rochelle. Buckingham was loathed by the populace. He had allegedly been James I's lover, swiftly ennobled and promoted to high office (James's reputation subsequently suffered from homophobic as well as anti-Scots prejudice), and now Buckingham retained supreme influence at court under Charles. Londoners complained that the flamboyant duke was an incompetent commander, careless of the lives of his sailors and soldiers, oblivious to both the tax burden of war and the need to conserve resources; worst of all, he failed to uphold the honour of the nation by winning a victory. He was soon judged the manifest cause of all that was wrong in the state. When in June 1628, John Lambe, a physician and astrologer under Buckingham's patronage, was spotted in the streets of London, he was battered to death by a mob. Londoners believed that Lambe had some kind of supernatural hold over Buckingham, helping him to resist parliament and win royal favour. They called him a wizard and a devil: a note was placed near the site of his attack, which read 'Who rules the kingdom? – The king. Who rules the king? – The duke. Who rules the duke? The devil'.[2]

That August, Buckingham was himself assassinated in Portsmouth. His killer was John Felton, a disappointed soldier who believed he was doing his country a service; the weapon, a cheap knife purchased from an ordinary cutler. Felton was hailed in London as a hero who had triumphed over Lambe's wizardry. But Henrietta Maria comforted her husband on the death of his friend, and their difficult relationship blossomed into mutual love. In the years that followed, as their union produced welcome heirs to the throne, Charles was no longer able, perhaps not even inclined, to kerb his wife's overt Catholicism; as a result, Londoners' suspicion of the queen's grip on royal power increased.

Charles wanted a display of magnificence in his palaces that would emblazon his authority and help to enforce obedience by conveying strong messages about his kingship. Buckingham had encouraged the artist Orazio Gentileschi to seek patronage in England in 1626, to work on York House. In the 1630s, Charles tried to entice other European artists to court with some success: Sir Antony Van Dyck, the Flemish artist, became the official court painter in 1632. The king's patronage of foreigners was unpopular with native artists: members of the Painter-Stainers' Company, clustered in their studios around Blackfriars, grumbled that they were not being given commissions. To them Charles's policy seemed almost unpatriotic. In early Stuart London the connoisseurship of paintings was still largely confined to the elite. A Puritan pamphlet probably spoke for many in the 1650s when it satirized 'None-Such Charles' as a prince without equal for wasting money on art in wartime: 'great summes were squandred away on braveries and vanyties. On old rotten pictures, on broken nosed

Marble.'³ Puritans were naturally suspicious of any overindulgence or ornament that might distract attention from God, but the king's expenditure had
many other detractors.

Charles's artistic projects celebrated his view of divinely ordained kingship
as a harmonizing power that brought order to the nation. When Peter Paul
Rubens visited London as a diplomat in 1629, Charles commissioned him to
decorate the ceiling of the Banqueting House with a stupendous work that
would support the cult of royal divinity and celebrate his father's role as peacemaker. A key panel portrayed James as Christ, ascending to heaven and
bequeathing the gift of peace to his people. For his part, Van Dyck, in many
of his portraits, depicted Charles as a chivalric ruler, bringing order to his
kingdom. His first major commission in 1632, known at the time as 'The Great
Peece', shows Charles and Henrietta Maria with their two eldest children.
A work of skilful propaganda, it presents the couple seated so that their small
stature is disguised. The Houses of Parliament in the background suggest that
Charles runs the country with the same effortless harmony with which he
manages his growing family. Ordinary people could view the ceiling in the
Banqueting House, fully installed in 1637. Although the building was reserved
for diplomatic receptions and court entertainments, tickets were issued for
people to watch the royal family dine there in public. But Charles's other
new portraits, destined for palace locations, would have been viewed only by
courtiers.

The element of theatre that graced Van Dyck's paintings of the royal family
was taken much further in the performance of court masques. These lavish
entertainments involved music, dancing, singing and acting. The queen was an
eager patron of these masques, which reached unheard-of levels of expense;
ladies at court took them very seriously indeed, spending hours in rehearsal.
The playwright Ben Jonson wrote several, collaborating with Inigo Jones who
designed the costumes, scenery and stage effects in a stunning display of technical virtuosity. Jonson was at ease with this art form, subscribing to the classic
view that poetry and painting were parallel arts since both imitated nature and,
in the process, heightened it. The masques of Charles's court celebrated beauty
and order in the world with as much magnificence as possible. But as the flamboyant spectacle encouraged extremes, the masques edged towards an eroticized

presentation of the royal couple's marital chastity, identifying Charles's regal power with sexual potency and fertility.

Puritans were scandalized, not least because however faithful to each other the royal couple might be, their court contained notable rakes. In 1632 the Puritan lawyer, William Prynne, mounted a bitter attack on court ritual and other recreations, adding critical remarks about the growing use of ceremony in the services of the Established Church. In his work, *Histrio Matrix; or, the Players Scourge*, he accused any woman who took part in masques as acting like a whore. As Henrietta Maria was an avid performer, often taking lead roles, the outcome was only a matter of time. Prynne was clapped in the pillory in Westminster then Cheapside, where his ears were cropped; copies of his book were burnt so close to the stocks that he almost suffocated; he was fined £5,000 and sentenced to life imprisonment. Since Prynne was a lawyer, Charles also demanded that London's Inns of Court stage a grand masque at Whitehall Palace to demonstrate their loyalty to the Crown. *The Triumph of Peace*, staged in February 1634, was preceded by a torch-lit procession from Holborn, down the Strand to Whitehall, and cost more than £21,000. The expenditure, during a period of poor harvests and increasing food prices, did little to heal the growing tension between courtiers and Puritan Londoners.

Henrietta Maria spent immense sums herself on decorative projects. Inigo Jones's initial foray into classical architecture had been the Queen's House at Greenwich, begun in 1616 for James's queen, Anne of Denmark. It was unfinished on her death in 1619, and in 1629 Charles gave the house to his queen. Schooled in the early baroque style emerging in France, Henrietta Maria set about completing and decorating the rooms with verve and enthusiasm, displaying a taste that more than matched her husband's. The building was finished in 1636 and most of the interiors by 1639. She engaged Gentileschi to paint canvases for the ceiling of its Great Hall, possibly helped by his daughter Artemisia, who followed him to England in 1638. The interior decoration of the house involved a bevy of upholsterers, sculptors, woodcarvers and furniture-makers. The queen's taste also extended to gardens, which were fast becoming a status symbol for those who could afford to grow flowers, pay for the cultivation of plants brought to England from distant parts, and spend time at leisure in private grounds. Hyde Park, reserved for hunting in James's time, now became a parade area for the wealthy in their coaches. Spring Gardens, near Whitehall, turned into a public pleasure ground with a bowling green, food and drink; it soon became linked with scandalous behaviour.

Given the increasing contact between the Stuart court and European powers, Charles wanted to impress foreigners with the wealth of his capital city. He called for the renovation of Goldsmiths Row in Cheapside, so that the route to St Paul's would be flanked by glittering displays of gold in shop windows, and he aimed to impose greater order on London's slipshod development. James I had boasted in 1615, 'Wee found our Citie and Suburbs of London of stickes, and left them of Bricke, being a Materiall farre more durable, safe from fire, beautifull and magnificent.'[4] But London's classical facades and brick houses were the exception not the rule. James's boast was just the start of a trend that Charles was anxious to continue because his capital lacked the fine vistas and public spaces that graced Antwerp, Rome and Paris. The streets of London were narrow and often dangerous, and although sixty-three parish churches had been refurbished in James's reign, many were still in disrepair; housing was irregular.[5] Less than six weeks after succeeding to the throne, Charles issued a proclamation giving the most detailed specification to date of acceptable building standards. Largely devised by Inigo Jones, these measures ranged from the height of doors to proportions of windows and depth of cellars, advocating regular, classical symmetry.

The clarity and proportion of Jones's architecture had the most immediate impact on the Covent Garden estate, a large tract of ground to the west of the City owned by Francis Russell, fourth Earl of Bedford. The earl agreed with the king that he would construct a high-quality development in brick and stone there, which Jones designed. Begun in 1631 with the church of St Paul's in Covent Garden, Jones's arcaded scheme and Italian-style 'piazza' became one of the models for London's squares. By 1639 almost all the buildings were occupied. Early residents in the grand houses on the piazza included at least three earls, each paying an annual rent of £150, although houses had no water supply until 1633 and were not linked up to sewers until 1635.[6]

Other developers sought to make a profit in the west of London. In 1638 the speculative builder, William Newton, purchased the lease of Lincoln's Inn Fields and obtained a licence to build. The scheme, in brick and stone, took its inspiration from Covent Garden and again the buildings were mostly leased by noblemen. Lindsey House, which later became two dwellings, now 59 and 60 Lincoln's Inn Fields, is accepted as the work of Inigo Jones, and his influence was also behind the terraced houses, built on the south side of nearby Queen Street from about 1635 to 1640. The central house in the terrace was adorned with a bust of Henrietta Maria, and Newton placed another bust to honour the queen on the central house in Lincoln's Inn Fields. The formal layouts and relative uniformity of these developments were a complete contrast to building in the City, not to mention London's manufacturing and maritime suburbs. One notable sign of gentrification in the west was the absence of incessant manufacturing noise. Yet the shopping and marketing district around the Strand soon expanded in a ragged way; superior buildings were interspersed with the irregular housing of shopkeepers, artisans and labourers who pursued trades such as coach making and tailoring for a courtly clientele.

Prynne, the Puritan pamphleteer, later implied that Catholics financed these genteel developments, that Newton, for one, had no capital for building projects of his own; he was merely their agent:

> All her Majesties servants, who doe suck the marrow of our estate, doe buy whole streets of houses in *Paris* & *Lordships* in the Country, and when they first came hither they were but poore beggers, & now they keep Coaches: What houses have they built in the Covent-garden, and what faire houses do they built [*sic*] in Lincoln In-fields? And the City must lend money to build them in other mens name.[7]

Prynne, writing as Parliament was gearing up to fight the First Civil War to the finish, was hardly an independent witness. Yet some Londoners had long regarded the Italianate squares to the west of the City with deep suspicion as visible signs of usurped power and privilege.

Overt Catholics at court had naturally formed a faction around Henrietta Maria. They often worshipped together: the queen had been guaranteed the free practice of her religion on her marriage and had places to worship at all royal palaces. In 1632, Inigo Jones started work on a splendid new Catholic chapel at Denmark (now Somerset) House, the London residence for queens consort. When Henrietta Maria laid the chapel's foundation stone, 2,000 Catholics attended. On completion, in 1636, it became the focus of worship for London Catholics: daily masses could be held there with impunity. And the new chapel was put to other uses: serviced by Capuchins, who had a strong missionary bent, it offered lectures about the Catholic faith, prompting several high-profile conversions. A cosmopolitan, minority religion had great appeal for an increasingly cosmopolitan court, eager to be fashionable. Catholics now seemed dangerously close to the seat of power and Protestant onlookers feared a papist plot. The queen became a despised figure to zealots, her coterie at Somerset House labelled 'Antichristian vermine' and the king criticized for being too lenient towards Catholicism.[8]

OVERCROWDING

London was a city of enormous contrasts. If spacious squares and streets were being built in the west, in the City rampant overcrowding was fast becoming the norm. Then, as now, there was continual new building to cope with population growth. In 1631, Charles endorsed earlier proclamations that had tried to curb London's expansion by forbidding building construction on new foundations; he extended the ban for two miles beyond its gates and included the city of Westminster. The reasoning was simple: fear of plague (over 35,000 Londoners had been swept away by an epidemic in the year of his accession), fear of fire among timber buildings, and increasing air and water pollution. The suburbs, especially to the east, were notoriously unhealthy and becoming more so: the large parish of Stepney even had its own pesthouse for plague victims. In 1636, City authorities petitioned that Stepney's high number of plague deaths might not be included in London's Bills of Mortality, so as not to give a worse impression of sickness in the City than was the case. They feared that country people would stop coming to London to trade and also refuse London's goods.

Within the City, rich and poor might live cheek by jowl; alleyways intersected with more prosperous streets. It was an effort even to keep wheeled traffic moving. In 1631 the Court of Common Council took issue with stallholders causing obstructions by selling fruit, tripe, bread and fish in the streets against regulations. London had long suffered from traffic jams: officials had introduced a one-way system for carting in 1617. Hackney or hired coaches came into use in 1605, but people of fashion aspired to their own coach so congestion increased. In 1634, Charles noted that streets were so full of coaches that pedestrians were in danger and carts carrying provisions could not pass. He licensed sedan chairs – even though when Buckingham had adopted one in the 1620s, people objected to chair men being used like horses, and even though, in narrow streets, they were just another nuisance. Charles banned hackney coaches the following year.

Wealthy merchants and retailers still lived comfortably in the City, in well-appointed houses with servants and perhaps high-status lodgers. At the east end of Cheapside there were large houses rising to five storeys; despite high-density accommodation, they offered luxury and comfort. Such houses were clean, well-aired and perfumed with dried herbs, cedar wood and flowers. Yet the most fashionable parish seems to have been St Botolph's, Aldersgate, where there was still room for orchards and gardens, and where several members of the nobility lived.[9]

Elsewhere, makeshifts were adopted to cope with population increase. Families with a dwelling to themselves took in tenants, buildings were partitioned into tenements, cellars were dug, and storeys added to houses, further overhanging narrow streets and obstructing light. Every kind of shed and outhouse was converted into a dwelling place, and there was much infilling of yards and gardens.[10] Developers could make profits from rents even on jerry-built accommodation. Some of the poorest clusters of squalid housing lay between the City and Westminster, around Holborn and the area of the Fleet River, which discharged sewage into the Thames, unfortunately a major source for the supply of water to London. Haphazard development and shared living spaces led to numerous boundary disputes with neighbours, mostly affecting shared chimney stacks, water drainage, light obstruction, the location of privies, and whose turn it was to clean them.[11]

Some parts of London became infamous. The area of the old Whitefriars Monastery, between Fleet Street and the Thames, was a base for criminals and others engaged in various kinds of marginal activity. Known as 'Alsatia', debtors and sharpers enjoyed a form of sanctuary there because it was outside the jurisdiction of the City. There was intermittent lawlessness in the suburbs: poor workers in Southwark, clustered in alleys and yards behind their wealthier neighbours in the High Street, were often unruly; Southwark's prisons were the focal point for riots.[12] And London's maritime parishes erupted during the war with Spain, after the mismanaged expedition against Cadiz in 1625 when over half the seamen died. Survivors who returned were left destitute in the streets without pay. Angry sailors continued to riot into the 1630s.

The biographer Donald Lupton ruefully noted London's variety in 1632: 'She's certainly a great World, there are so many little Worlds in her.'[13] His wonder is mixed with traces of disgust: London, he said, was like a glutton that desired always to be full, or a great beehive that swarmed four times a year with people of all ages and callings. Life in London might be a daily struggle to find food, shelter and kindling. The poor often had no means of cooking food at home, although chafing dishes, heated with coals in a portable brazier, were good for light meals and hot drinks. Many found it difficult to keep clean. The New River Company opened its artificial waterway in 1613 and within five years was supplying water to over 1,000 houses, but the poor could not afford connection to a private supply, whether from the New River or the Thames; they fetched their water from public conduits or pumps standing in yards.

Those barely able to pay their rent moved frequently from one ramshackle dwelling to another. Boarding houses for the poor were associated with debt, violence and petty theft; the shortage of lodgings and sharing of beds encouraged immoral relationships and even abuse. Between 1610 and 1618, George Wilkins, a lodging-house keeper known to Shakespeare, appeared in court twelve times, accused of stealing from his tenants, harbouring thieves, beating one woman, kicking another in the belly when she was pregnant, and standing bail for a man who had committed assault with a meat hook. Wilkins, in turn, accused lodgers of pulling down 'a great part' of his boarding house.[14] Yet such conditions offered women ways to earn a living, especially widows with experience of childbirth or tending the sick, who might specialize in lodgings that offered nursing, childbed and deathbed facilities.[15] Even billets like this were so much better than the fate of the destitute, who died in the streets, or ended their days in a constable's lock-up or cage.

Overcrowding produced foul odours. Lupton singled out the 'scavengers' who cleared the streets of animal excrement by day, and the 'goldfinders' who cleaned out privies at night, as being happily liberated from any sense of smell. But crowded Londoners often found their neighbours' behaviour offensive. The keeping of pigs caused frequent complaints of stench and noise, especially if owners slaughtered them close to home. The livestock market at Smithfield and the abattoirs in nearby streets yielded nightmarish scenes. Even vegetable markets left filth and rotting produce, although officials tried to enforce a system of sweeping and debris collection at the end of each market day. The coal-fired furnaces of glasshouses, soap boilers and breweries produced thick, acrid smoke. Other noxious trades near the river included tallow melting, alum yards and vinegar yards. Londoners knew the benefits of fresh air; they often complained about dung and detritus of all kinds blocking street gutters. To those living in pestilential slum dwellings, a glimpse of the open squares going up in districts to the west would have seemed like another world.

POLLUTION AND HEALTH

In 1662, Sir William Petty, an early statistician, wrote that it was natural for London to expand westwards. For three-quarters of the year the prevailing winds blew from the west, so its houses were 'so much more free from the fumes, steams, and stinks of the whole Easterly Pyle'.[16] Petty did not exaggerate. When the Dutchman, Lodewijck Huygens, looked back at the City as he journeyed to Hampton Court in 1652, he was amazed to find that St Paul's and its tower 'were too much obscured by smoke' to pick out.[17] Londoners were burning ever more 'sea coal' shipped from the River Tyne. Consumption increased as much as twentyfold in the hundred years up to 1680, creating such a smog that the diarist John Evelyn compared the city to the suburbs of hell, or Troy after the Greeks had left.[18] His *Fumifugium* was a troubled tirade against the 'Clowds of Smoake and Sulphur, so full of Stink and Darknesse' polluting London.[19] He believed it was damaging people's lungs. Was there ever such '*Coughing* and *Snuffing*', he asked, as was heard in London churches, 'where the Barking and Spitting is uncessant'?[20] Smoke from commercial ovens and domestic fireplaces in the capital turned clothes and even rain black. People thought it healthier to bathe in running water (if at all), and most found it easier to dip in the Thames than organize a bath at home, yet Evelyn noted that even if they bathed outside the City, the river water was coated in 'a thin Web, or *pellicule* of dust', which they carried home on their bodies.[21] The fastidious noted that coal smoke impregnated vegetables in the field, affecting the taste.

The link between pollution and ill-health was imperfectly understood. People complained about smoke, smells and filth, and some merchants who could afford it moved their families out to western suburbs, where the air was cleaner. But others willingly put up with discomfort because London was the place to earn money. Pipe smoking added to the general fug. Tobacco and snuff helped to mask body smells, and tobacco was widely recommended as a prophylactic and fumigant. The chief problem with 'piping', some argued, was not the health issue but its adverse effect on national valour:

> For, whilst we leave our wonted honourable exercises and studies, following our pleasures, and of late years besotting our selves with pipe and pot, in a beastly manner, sucking smoak, and drinking healths, until death stares many in the face; the said Dutch have well-neer left this swinish vice, and taken up our wonted valour.[22]

Excessive smoking and drinking was bad because it dampened England's martial spirit; the two vices allowed the Dutch to gain the upper hand in bravery and, in consequence, trade.

Illness struck rich and poor alike, and doctors had limited notions of what to do about it. In 1612, when Prince Henry contracted a fatal fever, the disorder seemed worse in his head, so they shaved it and applied 'warm cocks and pigeons newly killed', but with no success.[23] An autopsy could help to absolve physicians of blame. In 1617, Secretary Sir Ralph Winwood died despite all the remedies that physicians could give. Yet they were not overly criticized:

> Seeing that it appears upon the opening of the body that he could not possibly last long, having his heart withered almost to nothing, his spleen utterly rotten, one of his kidneys clean gone, the other perished, his liver full of black spots, his lungs not sound, besides diverse other defects.[24]

The writer noted, perhaps with some irony, that it was a wonder how Sir Ralph had held out so long and looked so well.

The poor were, of course, most vulnerable: rising prices in years of poor harvests led to malnutrition, weakening their resistance. In 1630 the harvest failed, causing much hardship, and high grain prices in 1637–8 prompted another surge in mortality. Some occupations were more unhealthy than others: the noxious substances that painters used withered their limbs and blackened teeth; potters could become cadaverous and pale due to lead poisoning; water carriers and porters suffered physical deformity; sawyers, starch-makers and scavengers, working in clouds of dust, were subject to eye infections; unwashed chimney sweeps got cancers from carcinogenic soot.[25] But even the rich suffered disfigurement and skin diseases: itchy or pustular patches aggravated by harsh cosmetics or poor hygiene. A person's face and hands were on show, so a clear complexion was much prized, partly because blemishes could be symptoms of sexual diseases and therefore of moral decay. Thomas Tryon, who wrote several self-help guides, warned the rich that stinking feather beds were especially dangerous to health and painted a vivid image of lice, fleas and small worms feeding off the putrid detritus trapped in unaired mattresses.[26] A straw bed, he declared, was healthier.

Those who could afford medicines took an active role in their own health. A course of physic comprised an expensive cocktail of vomits, laxatives and enemas, administered over several days under the supervision of an attendant. When, in 1630, Sir John Coke decided such a regime would restore him to full health, the cost over four days amounted to £2 13s. 8d.[27] The most expensive item in the medical bill was a 'Cordiall Electiary', or strengthening syrup, costing 5s. And after the long list of purges and powders he had ingested, a cordial would have been sorely needed. The purchase of expensive drugs, merely to attain a sense of equilibrium and well-being, was just another form of lavish consumption. The letter writer John Chamberlain learnt from experience that physic did more harm than good, 'so that now I am resolved to commit myself to good order and government and let physic alone, and if I had done so from the beginning I make no doubt but I had been a sound man by this time'.[28] The use of extreme purges owes much to contemporary understanding of the body as driven by four fluids or 'humours' which had to be in balance. These were blood, choler (or yellow bile), phlegm and black bile. Illness resulted if one of these fluids diminished or built up to cause an obstruction, which then needed vigorous expulsion. Unfortunately, dosages were hard to regulate for laxatives and emetics. Bloodletting, a standard resource to relieve excess humours if the body seemed overheated and feverish, was another treatment liable to weaken the constitution.

London had numerous charlatans willing to play on people's fears or hopes for a cure. Dr William Butler enjoyed tobacco so much that he invented a medicinal drink to accompany it called 'Butler's Ale', commemorated today by a pub in Masons Avenue, Moorgate, named the Old Doctor Butler's Head. His other treatments were controversial – he heaved one patient suffering from an ague, or fever, into the Thames from a balcony at his lodgings in the Savoy; the shock allegedly cured him. The College of Physicians tried to regulate medical practice in London, licensing those who were qualified and punishing those who were not. In 1627, Thomas Winche, a tailor, was hauled before the College accused of practising magic. He had cured the lord mayor's kitchen servant of an ague at the cost of a shilling by collecting his nail parings. When questioned, he said he gave no medicine but cured by reading in a book and taking nail clippings. The physicians were unable to decide whether this was medicine or magic.[29] In 1627 the College also tried John Lambe, Buckingham's doctor, as a mountebank and imposter who charged up to £50 for 'cures', but he was murdered before the case concluded. Some quacks inadvertently killed patients, for instance by giving them vomits that contained poisons. Humfrye Beven, an apothecary in St Giles, administered a potion to a young woman in 1633 'on a knife's point, whereupon she voided bloodclots upward. Next day her gums were black; she died "spitting and spawling".'[30]

The controversial Dr Robert Fludd, who lived in Coleman Street, advocated a chemical approach to medicine based on observation rather than traditional theories about the four humours, still accepted by most of the medical profession. But Fludd was also drawn to the occult and the mystical Rosicrucian sect. His enthusiastic piety won admirers, and the sublime, unintelligible cant he spoke inspired some patients with great faith in his skill, possibly contributing to their cure. In his later career, Fludd became an accepted figure. He supported William Harvey's findings about the circulatory system of blood in 1628, but then he also defended the 'weapon salve' in the 1630s, said to cure at a distance by treating the weapon that made the wound. The idea was that the blood on the weapon and in the wound would 'sympathize' with each other due to the interrelation or sympathy that people believed existed between humans and external objects having some similarity or like quality. The salve contained outlandish ingredients: bear grease, boar fat, blood, wine, the moss that grew on exposed skulls, and the powdered remains of Egyptian mummies. Although 'sympathetic' cures had detractors, they were used for decades. Later in the century, wonder pills said to cure scurvy, syphilis and other chronic distempers had many advocates. Less dangerous, homely remedies may have afforded some relief: Henrietta Maria made great use of clove pills – presumably for toothache.[31]

London had the only major hospitals in England. Religious institutions had once provided hospitals, but when Henry VIII dissolved the monasteries this medical care was lost. Londoners petitioned the Crown for St Bartholomew's, St Thomas's and St Mary Bethlem (Bedlam) to continue, and these hospitals became centres of expertise that indirectly benefited the nation. For example, Harvey, encouraged by Charles I, carried out his experiments on blood circulation at St Bartholomew's. In Stuart times the only surgical operation to gain widespread acceptance, apart from amputation, was the removal of bladder stones. Pepys was successfully 'cut for the stone' and recorded the event in his *Diary*, but a more eye-watering description of the procedure, inflicted without anaesthetic, is to be found in a letter of 1605. The writer explained that when the barber surgeon cut open the man's bladder and inserted his probe, the tormented patient ripped off both his trusses in agony before the surgeon pulled out 'a stone as bigg as my palm'. Despite having borne the operation 'with great impatience', the man seemed likely to recover.[32]

Pain and insecurity were so common, living conditions resulting from rapid expansion were so precarious, it is not surprising that swathes of Londoners continued to be susceptible to superstition, portents and unfounded rumour. Nor is it surprising that the ruling classes feared the volatility of the population and the threat that the poor might pose to social stability. King Charles's unwillingness to communicate policy to his subjects partly stemmed from a fear of stoking popular debate.[33] Despite London's deadly epidemics, migrants still poured in, contributing to a view that it was plagued by idle vagrants whom it would struggle to support. Chamberlain had rejoiced in 1618 that the City was shipping out to Virginia a hundred young boys and girls who lay starving in the streets, 'which is one of the best deeds that could be done with so little charge, not rising to above £500'.[34] Certain segments of the population were clearly regarded as expendable. Under Charles I the tenor of life in the capital became even edgier. His actions increasingly reflected a new form of absolute power that only unsettled his subjects, while the state was ruthless in punishing Protestant controversialists thought to be sowing sedition: Prynne, who lost his ears for 'insulting' the queen, was to suffer a second, more savage, mutilation in 1637.

By the 1640s, Charles I had an art collection that exceeded in quality those of any European competitor; new trends in architecture offered an exciting glimpse of how London might develop. But in the narrow, fetid alleys of London's poorest areas, where filth and disease were rife, and even in wealthier, upright households, these aesthetic achievements were badges of a repressive royal power and targets for resentment.

6

THE PATH TO CIVIL WAR

Was Charles deluded about his role and personality? When aged twelve, on the death of his brother Henry, he inherited the position of 'warrior prince' and appeared in public in the armour Henry had worn. When king, he was surrounded by images of himself in power poses that made him look taller than he was. He had to live up to this magnificent image of kingship. The narrative he constructed about his life was one of mastery and decisiveness, and he kept strong men about him to do his bidding. Soon, however, king and parliament would be on a collision course.

London was the stage for this political battle that finally led to civil war. Under Charles, it was a hotbed of discontent but also of ambition where men, thwarted in their vision for foreign trade or blocked in their path to powerful ranks in the Church or politics, stoked dissent and fear. Opposing armies would fight no pitched battles in London but, as the nation's political, economic and cultural centre, and its chief port, London played a key role in the bitter disputes leading up to the crisis and in the conflict itself.

Charles had dismissed his last parliament in 1629: his inept conduct of hostilities against Spain, and then France, made MPs unwilling to give him the money to wage war. His parliament had insisted on debating religious grievances and did not pass the financial settlement he needed. Since medieval times, parliament had voted the sovereign customs duties called Tonnage and Poundage for life, but in 1625 MPs voted these duties to Charles for just one year. From the king's viewpoint, parliament had therefore encouraged him to pursue war against Catholic powers in Europe only to thwart his prospects of winning military glory. Angry and frustrated, he extracted loans from wealthier subjects to finance warfare, imprisoning those who refused to pay. He kept on collecting Tonnage and Poundage, without sanction of parliament; he had men press-ganged and he billeted soldiers in private residences by force. Soon he had sparked a fierce debate about the limits of a king's powers. In London, sailors who had not been paid wages, labourers, and even City merchants joined a wave of protest about unparliamentary taxation. When, in 1629, Charles dissolved parliament, he sent dissident ringleaders to the Tower: 'some few Vipers', as he explained, intent on anarchy.[1] But the word on London's streets was that the king would destroy the people's liberties and that the Protestant religion was under threat.

Charles now embarked on a period of personal rule that lasted eleven years. Without money, he was forced to come to terms with France and Spain. The 1630s were therefore years of peace and relatively benign rule that might be considered strong leadership. Charles set out to establish an order in his kingdom consistent with his elevated view of monarchy, but while he never lacked moral self-righteousness, he was always short of funds. Many of his decrees were as much about increasing royal revenues as stimulating the economy. And all the while, he resented having to devise ways of raising money to support his court and growing family: deference and ceremony were his due. These anxieties left him little room to consider the common lot of Londoners, still scarred by the plague epidemic in 1625 that had left 35,000 dead, and now adjusting to his arbitrary decrees. Between 1629 and 1640 the king issued 297 proclamations on matters as diverse as the punishment of vagabonds, the better ordering of coastal fishing, the manufacture of soap, the use of brass buckles on men's belts, the sale of cards and dice, and the wearing of counterfeit jewels. Without parliament, there was no forum for debating such measures and, in an atmosphere of growing distrust intensified by religious differences, deep grievances festered.

To get the money he needed, Charles sold patents and monopolies on various manufacturing processes and trading ventures. This policy angered merchants who were excluded from a trade or forced to pay for a licence. Syndicates holding monopolies reduced the lower classes to despair since they often dealt in essential household goods and tended to increase prices. It was a time of economic recession – in 1629 there were food riots even in London.[2] Already, the absence of parliaments was beginning to hit London tradesmen in the pocket because fewer gentry came to the capital. In June 1632, Charles sanctioned their absence, reissuing his father's proclamation that the gentry must fulfil their duties in the provinces. In this context new monopolies and patents caused misery and oppression. Nehemiah Wallington, a Puritan wood-turner living in a house and shop in Eastcheap, just north of old London Bridge, described how monopoly-holders 'did get all into the lion's paws to the undoing of many thousands of the poor'.[3] The politician, Sir John Colepeper, who before the Civil Wars supported the popular cause, compared monopoly-holders to 'a Nest of Wasps, or Swarm of Vermine' that had got their suckers into all parts of the household, 'in the Dye-Fat, Wash-Bowl . . . and Powdring-Tub. . . . We may not buy our own Cloaths without their Brokage: These are the Leeches, that have suckt the Common-wealth'.[4]

One of the most controversial monopolies was for the manufacture of soap, issued in 1632 to a syndicate with Catholic affiliations. Charles may have hoped it would stimulate domestic production, since it used domestic ingredients, not imported whale or fish oil, but London washerwomen denounced the 'Papist soap' as inferior and claimed that it blistered their hands. The government was reduced to staging a public trial in 1633: two washerwomen set up their tubs in the Guildhall to compare products. It was claimed that the new soap lathered better and got clothes cleaner, but the old soap was still preferred. It was sold under the counter at higher prices, a source of grievance that affected every household.

Charles's efforts to curb London's expansion provided other opportunities to fill royal coffers. His proclamations of 1625 and 1630 restricted new building, but whenever the poorer contractors were caught building unlawfully, their houses were demolished, whereas rich developers paid fines and their buildings were often allowed to stand. The legality of destroying property on the basis of royal proclamation was a moot point, justified at the time by saying that the new buildings were a public nuisance and punishable by common law. Yet shrewd developers were making sizeable profits. John Moore, a government official on £200 to £300 a year, doubled his annual income through construction projects, mostly on land between Covent Garden and St Martin-in-the-Fields. He was targeted in 1634: three-quarters of his houses were torn down by court order and he was fined £1,000. Afterwards, there was a trend of making developers pay dearly for development rather than preventing building altogether. Most builders in the west of London were substantial gentlemen who could afford the fines. The culmination of prosecutions for illegal construction was a decree in February 1637 against dividing tenements. Landlords who had partitioned their buildings within the last seven years had to restore them to their original state within a year or pay fines and legal costs. Although fears about the medical and social consequences of overcrowding were real, this policy hit pauper tenants and was felt to be another oppression of the king's subjects.

Charles's most controversial fiscal measure was Ship Money. In 1634 he ordered all maritime counties to provide a ship at their own expense. There were precedents for asking port towns to do this in times of emergency, but Ship Money had never been raised in peacetime. In 1635, Charles extended it to inland counties and it soon became clear that he meant it to be an annual tax. In theory the counties had to provide ships, but the levy was mostly accounted for in cash. There was some justification for it: the navy was in disrepair. European pirates attacked English shipping, North African corsairs threatened western coasts and held thousands of English seamen for ransom, and Dutch, Spanish and French warships flouted the Crown's claim to sovereignty over 'British Seas'. These seas were said to encompass the whole of the English Channel to the shores of France, and the North Sea to the shores of Flanders and Holland. A strong navy would protect trade, which was expanding. Seamen had been badly treated in the 1620s but people now appreciated them more; ballads of the period, such as *In Praise of Sailors* and *Saylors for my Money*, applauded seamen's industry, bravery and the luxury goods they brought back from long voyages to the East.

Charles's ship tax was a modest success: £800,000 was paid to the Treasurer of the Navy between 1634 and 1640.[5] The tax did not cover all naval costs but by the standards of the day it was paid swiftly and efficiently, at least in the early years. Charles's shipbuilding programme culminated in the iconic *Sovereign of the Seas*, a vessel designed at his personal initiative to impress European powers, project the splendour of his kingship, and revive his claims to sovereignty over British Seas. Completed in 1637, it carried 102 bronze guns on three decks, outstripping French and Dutch rivals. The ship prompted much controversy. It cost £65,587, fully ten times the price of the usual forty- to fifty-gun warship, plunging the king deeper into debt. The ornamental carving alone cost £6,691, a level of embellishment that was exceptional – ironically much of it had to be removed in service to improve the ship's stability.[6]

People grew suspicious about how Charles meant to employ his new fleet, especially after he used it to help Spain in 1635. Leading opponents of rule without parliament chose Ship Money as an issue on which to oppose his rule: the Buckinghamshire landowner John Hampden refused to pay the tax, although when his test case came to court in 1637, the legality of Ship Money was narrowly upheld. Paradoxically this ruling made the tax more unpopular. The City had to raise £32,163 in Ship Money after its attempt to claim exemption failed in December 1634, so it resorted to strong-arm tactics. Citizens who delayed making payments might be jailed in Newgate; or their goods might be confiscated and sold. Even so, there was a shortfall that the City had to make up with loans from its reserves. London's last attempt to raise Ship Money was in June 1640. The lord mayor and his sheriffs went from house to house, knocking on doors, to show their willingness to comply with the king's orders, but they still failed to get the full sum. Obdurate citizens only escaped punishment because the political crisis worsened that summer.

Sir John Coke, who became one of the two Secretaries of State chiefly responsible for domestic affairs, was determined to squeeze money from the City at every opportunity. In 1630 and 1631 he pursued measures to confiscate the lands belonging to the City's Irish Society. The king accused the Society of violating the terms of the Ulster agreement: the native Irish still inhabited Ulster; fortifications were inadequate, forests had been decimated. The livery companies were forced to defend themselves in court at huge legal cost, but in vain. In 1635 the City was ordered to pay a fine of £70,000, the Irish Society's charter was cancelled, its lands in Ireland confiscated. In the negotiations that followed about Ulster and other issues, officials pushed the price of settlement ever higher until the City was asked to pay the eye-watering sum of £125,000 or lose their Irish lands. In 1637 the City decided to sacrifice the lands rather than pay the fine; it also agreed to pay £12,000 in settlement of other claims. Such huge losses would not be forgotten. Charles recalled parliament in 1640; when, that November, parliament asked the companies for a loan to pay the king's army, Simon Vassall, one of the MPs for London, reminded the House that the business of Londonderry 'stickes heavie upon them to one hundred and sixtie thousand pounds'.[7] London's livery companies saw that their enormous and unwilling investment in the Ulster Plantation had simply gone to the king. Surely this was tyranny?

Although Charles extracted much wealth from the City, its powerful officials remained his natural allies. Yet there was a cohort of independent merchants in the Atlantic trades increasingly ready to side with the parliamentary opposition. These men were aligned with the Puritan Earl of Warwick and other opposition peers who, like him, were involved in colonizing schemes. They found the king's foreign policy most unhelpful. Peace might benefit the East India and Levant Companies by reducing lawlessness on the seas, but merchants trading with New England and the West Indies preferred war with France and Spain: under its cloak they could attack Spanish shipping in the Caribbean. With profits from tobacco and now sugar, some financed ventures in the East and so resented the monopolies of chartered companies. Even within the East India Company there were dissenting voices who wished to make its governing body more accountable. These men grew ever more hostile to the governing City elite.

RELIGIOUS REFORM

Meanwhile, Charles sought to bring order to the Protestant Church. In an age when newspapers were just starting up, the Crown depended on Sunday sermons to influence public opinion. Clergymen who reliably preached obedience to the king tended to want strong measures to curb Puritans. Charles himself lent towards Arminian forms of worship, prizing ceremony and church ritual. In 1628 he made William Laud Bishop of London. Laud passionately supported the authority and privileges of the Crown. He shared Charles's view that the Church should be governed by bishops, and upheld uniformity of worship according to the Book of Common Prayer. This was not surprising: Laud came from a relatively humble background – his father was a master tailor. He had risen up the ranks as a career churchman through intelligence and hard work; his own power depended on the status of bishops.

Laud was a small, red-faced man with piercing dark eyes. At just 5 feet tall he was extremely sensitive about his height, and his opponents took every opportunity to taunt him about it. Even at court, the king's fool once quipped, 'Give great praise to the Lord and little Laud to the devil.' He may have meant to warn Charles. Derision made Laud more determined to push through his reforms. He believed that church buildings and the divine service should impress parishioners, reinforcing the concept that divine sacraments are a means to secure grace and salvation. In 1633, Charles finally made him Archbishop of Canterbury. Laud was nearing sixty and felt he had no time to lose. He removed Puritans from church posts, persecuted Nonconformists in the church Court of High Commission, which he revived, and pursued them in the infamous Court of Star Chamber, which could order torture and inflict any punishment but death. This court became a byword for the abuse of power. Judges there passed swift sentence on Dissenters and opponents of royal policy. People were outraged. Judith, wife of the Puritan MP Sir Thomas Barrington, complained to her mother-in-law in 1632 that Laud had sent 'some 40ty honest People' to prison for being at a 'Conventicle in Black Fryers', although they were merely found at prayers.[8] Such attacks helped to polarize society; soon even moderates within the Church of England were labelled 'Puritan'.

London's suburbs had a reputation for Puritanism and, after 1640, for radicalism. Magistrates in the outskirts were less well organized than City aldermen and less likely to report subversive preaching. In Southwark, tanners, glovers and brewery workers were notorious for their lawlessness and sedition. Shadwell did not have even a chapel until 1656, and it was not made a parish church until 1671. True, wealthy royalists might live in the suburbs as well as in newly fashionable areas to the west of the City, but notable parliamentary Puritan leaders made the suburbs their home. A powerful group dwelt in Holborn, not far from the Earl of Warwick; Oliver Cromwell was based there from 1637 to 1643, living in Long Acre. Other prominent Puritans lived in Hackney.

Within the City itself, the parish of St Stephen Coleman Street was a hotbed of dissent. Wealthy merchants had houses in the parish but overcrowding to the north and east created conditions for discord. In Coleman Street and Swan Alley, which extended eastwards, intellectual opposition to the Crown took active shape. Printers secretly produced radical material and, by the mid-1630s, fiery preaching in St Stephen's whipped up support for strict Protestantism, with ministers inciting their congregations to react angrily to each new 'affront'.

In the heated, mistrustful atmosphere of the 1630s, social bonds seemed to be breaking down. There was a notable spate of violent domestic crimes, and people anxiously mulled over the significance of unnatural offences and cruel punishments. One wife gave her husband a potion containing melted lead because he came home drunk. Another woman was burned in Smithfield for poisoning her husband, a sentence so severe it upset people, 'sence thear was so much cause of mercy to her'.[9]

Church ritual became a battleground. Puritans refurbished several of their London churches, but objected to treating church fabric as if it were sacred. They placed weight on the sermon and the biblical word, rejecting any form of worship that emphasized the priest's intermediary role. But Laud was intent on restoring to church services something of their pre-Reformation character. Communion tables had to be treated like altars, placed at the east end of the chancel and railed off from parishioners so that they were compelled to receive the sacrament on their knees. Clergymen had to wear surplices and conform to the use of the Prayer Book. Some Puritan objections to Laud's reforms were practical – the view of the most holy part of the communion was obstructed if the priest before the altar had his back to the congregation and the altar itself was no longer in a central position. Only the rich in the front pews could see. But Laud's reforms affronted people at a much deeper level.

Why did worshippers attach such importance to details of church services? For one thing, dreadful visitations of the plague were attributed to the collective guilt of a sinful city. *The Cities Safetie*, published in 1630, insisted that God sent the plague to punish popery and sin, so people wanted the comfort of knowing that their collective worship was the purest religion. The diaries of Nehemiah Wallington make clear that plague caused unimaginable terror:

> Oh this is terrible and fearefull to those that be living: when we consider how the infection is derived from one to another by waies and meanes neither visible nor sencible that no man knows where he shal be safe.[10]

Whole households were swept away; sixty children died in one alley alone. Wallington found himself thinking who, in his own family, he could most easily part with. The maid was an easy first choice, but after that? His young son? His daughter? He recorded in his diary how his daughter fell sick one evening. Her last words as she said goodnight were, 'Father I goe abroode tomorrow and bye you a Plomee [plum] pie.'[11] But within a day she was dead. Nehemiah was inconsolable. After an interval, his wife tried to rally him, but he angrily accused her of not loving the child. She humbled him by replying that no, she did not grieve, but willingly gave the child back to the Lord from whom she had received it. Religion enabled families to cope with tragedy; it governed the way that people treated their kin and those they employed: when Wallington caught his journeyman stealing from him, he made the fellow confess and came to an agreement but did not go to court; and religion kept Wallington hard at work at a job he did not particularly enjoy for the good of his family, rising at four in the morning or even earlier. Puritan belief was linked to prosperity; Wallington wrote, 'Hee then that would be prosperous and speed well: let him be religious and pray well.'[12] This was why Laud's reforms were insufferable to many, and why they feared lest he bring popery in through the back door.

There seemed to be no avenue for peaceful protest. If parishioners turned to their local clergyman, either he sided with Laud, who was filling many parishes with Arminian ministers, or he would be too afraid to complain; and if he did, he would be silenced. If parishioners turned to the law, the magistrate would say it was a church matter and would be fearful of meddling with it. Laud believed in persuasion but was assiduous in pursuing his cause and meted out vindictive punishment to protestors. In 1637, Prynne – who had been writing seditious pamphlets in the Tower exaggerating the tyranny of Laud and his allies – was sentenced to have the rest of his ears sliced off, and to be branded on the cheeks with SL for 'seditious libeller'. He was pilloried with independent minister Henry Burton and physician John Bastwick, who also lost their ears. It was a very bloody affair and all three became public heroes. Even Laud saw the blunder of putting the men in the pillory, then allowing them to harangue a crowd of applauding friends with seditious and treasonable utterances during the whole time of their supposed punishment. When the offenders were taken from the City towards separate prisons in the provinces, admiring crowds followed. But punishment could fall on lesser figures: Wallington was hauled up before the Star Chamber in 1638, accused of possessing and distributing seditious books. In trepidation, he explained that he had only bought pamphlets from those hawking them from door to door. He was released, but it was a terrifying experience.

Others were less timid than Wallington. In an era when neighbours kept close watch on each other's behaviour and even reported to officials such misdemeanours as repeated use of the wrong church pew, it was easy to raise the level of suspicion and tension in the capital to fever pitch. Then, as now, aggression could simmer just below the surface, and even in church: when one woman nudged her 'pewfellow' awake during the sermon at St Katherine Cree in Leadenhall Street, the sleeper accused her of being a 'drunken sow', adding, 'O you bould drunken slutt doe you kicke me'?[13] The curate of Stepney, Mr Edgeworth, was reviled by parishioners for using the Book of Common Prayer. Rachel Weaburne of Limehouse was indicted for saying that Edgeworth 'was a damned dogg and [tha]t shee would rather goe to heare a cart wheele creake and a dogge barke then to hear him preach'.[14] Francis Bourne ranted that Stepney's vicar, Timothy Stampe, 'deserves to stand in the pillory and hopes to see him hanged'.[15] The outward, visible signs of Laud's reforms became easy targets for people who were not to be reasoned with.

Laud supported the Divine Right of Kings, so his reforms represented another facet of Charles I's absolutism. They had the effect of radicalizing even moderate Protestants who then pursued Laud on political as well as religious grounds. In contrast, City aldermen, who had been largely Puritan before 1630, opted to back the king, following their long-standing political stance at the expense of any religious preference they might have. Their support for Puritanism dried up and they donated handsomely to Laud's scheme for rebuilding City churches and carrying out much-needed repairs to St Paul's. But in London's hectic state, political and religious allegiances did not always hold. The MP, Christopher Clitherow, who had lobbied parliament on behalf of trade and sometimes supported Secretary of State Coke, appeared to sympathize with Arminians yet came to distrust the king. In 1638 the news was that Charles had promised the Eastland Company a favour if it admitted his nominee. When Clitherow heard this he is said to have retorted, slightingly, 'that they all knew well enough what the King's good turns were when they came to seek them'.[16] Some Londoners fed their discontent with anti-Laudian pamphlets, others had more indirect ways of signalling their political opposition, including circulating manuscript poetry hostile to the king. Clitherow's collection included verses on the pretensions of the king's favourite architect, Inigo Jones; a poem sympathizing with the Queen of Bohemia, Charles's sister, deposed by Catholics; and a regretful poem about the death of Prince Henry.[17] In iconography, Henry had been strongly linked to the battle to preserve European Protestantism; Charles had signally failed in this respect, even when his own sister fell victim to Catholic aggression. People were fast losing faith in the king's authority and judgement.

The turning point was war with Scotland. In 1637, Charles and Laud tried to impose the Book of Common Prayer on the national Church of Scotland. The Scots rejected this interference and rioted in Edinburgh. Fearing to appear weak, Charles assembled an army and marched north in 1638 to deal with rebellion. In London, Henrietta Maria backed him by raising money from her Catholic following. Naturally, this increased popular suspicion about popery at court and the threat it posed to Protestantism and parliament.[18] Would Catholics take advantage of the trouble in Scotland to better their position? In fact, Charles's patchwork approach to royal revenues could not sustain the administrative and financial burden of waging war; his inexperienced, badly equipped army failed to defeat the Scots. Back in London, there was a scare that Frenchmen were about to land on English soil and that 50,000 French already lurked in the suburbs. To halt rumours, the Privy Council ordered Middlesex Justices of the Peace to carry out a census of foreigners dwelling in London's periphery, but the crisis dampened business, aggravating the discontent caused by royal taxes and religious reforms.

Charles needed money to form an effective army if he were not to witness the foundations of his monarchy crumble. In 1639 he tried to mollify the City, cancelling some unpopular charters given without the assent of the mayor and aldermen to new companies such as the Tobacco-pipe makers, Spectacle makers and Comb-makers. To appease East India Company merchants, he cancelled the right of the Courteen Association to trade with the East. Yet London businessmen remained cautious about risking their fortunes in this confused situation. The livery companies' elite did support Charles, but aldermen in the Court of Common Council were not so compliant. For the first time ever, the Council drew up a petition of grievances. It was moderate in tone, pointing out the burdens that afflicted poor householders, but Charles refused to receive it.

In the spring of 1640, Charles called his first parliament in eleven years, but it still failed to agree on the king's finances. Again, he asked the City for money but with no better result, so he opted for a forced loan and told aldermen to list the richest men in their wards. Only seven refused for fear of reprisals. Four of them made a courageous, public refusal at the Court of King's Bench. Thomas Soame boldly told the judges that he would not be an informer, for he had been 'an honest man before he was an alderman, and desired to be an honest man still'.[19] His words echoed around the city. Thomas Wentworth, the king's ruthless Lord Deputy in Ireland, recalled the previous September to help in this emergency and made Earl of Strafford, advised Charles to hang the men as an example but they were merely imprisoned. On 5 May the king dissolved the 'Short Parliament' on Wentworth's recommendation, blaming the stalemate on 'some few cunning and ill affectioned men'.[20]

London's underground press, meanwhile, was busy issuing radical Puritan material, some of it sympathetic to the Scottish revolt. On the night of 11 May hundreds of armed youths marched on Laud's residence in Lambeth to the beat of drums in a huge torchlit demonstration. It included sailors with no work due to the slump in trade, apparently brought together by the Earl of Warwick; radical workers from Southwark; and, as usual, apprentices. Laud escaped but punishment for the demonstrators was swift: one supposed ringleader was racked to extort a confession, then executed; another was hanged, drawn and quartered for treason. Public disaffection was expressing itself in religious terms because Laud's reforms increasingly stood for a regime that was hated.

Few trusted Charles in a war; some even feared that he was prepared to turn an army on his English subjects, but with money wrung from the City, the king rallied his troops and marched north again. This time, advancing Scots thrashed his rag-tag army at Newburn on 28 August and occupied Newcastle, strangling London's coal supply. Charles had to seek a truce and, as the Scottish army demanded daily expenses until a peace treaty was agreed, he was forced to reconvene a parliament in November; this 'Long Parliament' would sit from 1640 until 1660.

THE EXECUTION OF STRAFFORD

Puritans in the City government made sure that Charles got no money to pay off the Scots before parliament opened in November. Months of intrigue ensued. Militant Puritans had already organized a 'root and branch' petition calling for bishops to be abolished. Some 15,000 citizens signed it and counties across England followed their example. Naturally, London was at the centre of news: the first newspapers, 'corantos', were already popular, and because the licensing laws faltered during this crisis, conditions permitted a pamphlet war. Much content was 'fake news' but it engaged citizens in events at all levels. Once parliament was in session, events moved swiftly. Judges were purged; some courtiers fled. In November the Commons approved the release of Puritan 'martyrs', including Prynne, Burton and Bastwick. Prynne and Burton reached London on the 28th, entering in a great procession – there were 100 coaches and 2,000 on horseback – and church bells rang out as they passed. Crowds of jubilant spectators gave the men rosemary (for remembrance) and bays (for victory), in an obvious rebuke to those who had sentenced them to mutilation and imprisonment. Archbishop Laud would be impeached for treason on 18 December and sent to the Tower the following March. Laudian clergy were ejected from their churches.

For the moment, parliament reached no agreement on further religious reform, but opposition MPs easily united against the king's strongman, the Earl of Strafford. They feared he would stage a coup and dispatch them with the same single-minded ruthlessness he had displayed in Ireland, so they acted first: on 11 November they impeached him for treason. Word on the street was that Strafford was the enemy of all goodness; a man 'full of cruelty and blood' out to damage Church and Commonwealth.[21] High treason was hard to pin on him, but John Pym, the dissident parliamentary leader, drew up a long list of charges. Chief among them were that Strafford had tried to introduce tyrannical government by force of arms, embezzled funds, encouraged papists, and wilfully led the English army to defeat at Newburn. All popular grievances against Charles were heaped on Strafford, who had worked closely with Laud and was accused of giving the king evil counsel. Even the queen warned Strafford not to place his trust in the king's protection, but he left it too late to escape punishment.

Strafford's trial began on 22 March 1641. In a dramatic masterstroke it was held in the vast Westminster Hall, before both the Commons and the Lords; Strafford was placed at a desk at one end. When he heard the charges, which Pym set out with great heat and passion, Strafford saw at once that the case against him was weak. Pym had to explain that Strafford was not guilty of simple treason but 'Accumulative Treason'.[22] Despite being ill with gout and dysentery, Strafford defended himself with great skill and intelligence, deliberately countering Pym's passion with moderation. Puritan Londoners receiving progress reports concluded that Strafford was 'very cunning and very tough in the handling', as if Pym were wrestling with the Devil.[23]

The trial lasted a month. Every day a hundred soldiers in barges escorted Strafford up the Thames from the Tower to Westminster; on landing, 200 men from London's Trained Bands escorted him to the Hall at great expense and trouble, lest he escape. Constables guarded nearby streets to keep miscreants and loafers at bay. The king, queen and ten-year-old Prince Charles attended the trial but were screened off – although the king's very presence was taken to be a threat or a ruse to thwart the progress of justice. MPs feared that they would never convict Strafford of treason, and in this crisis the London crowd lent them support. On 21 April the Lords and Commons were presented with 'The Petition of the Citizens of London', signed by some 20,000, blaming Strafford, among other things, for loss of trade in the City.[24] That same day, in order to secure the verdict they wanted, MPs passed an Act of Attainder, which simply declared Strafford guilty of the offences of which he was accused. The king determined never to sign it.

London was soon at fever pitch. On 1 May the king appealed to the Lords, saying that although Strafford had offended, he did not deserve to die but would lose his position. If Charles hoped for calm, the mood in the city was for execution. False rumours circulated that papists had overtaken the House of Commons and that parliament was on fire. Many citizens took up swords or other weapons and rushed to its defence. At this point the king seems to have agreed to an attempt by a body of soldiers to spring Strafford from the Tower. 'The Army Plot' was botched and on 3 May an intimidating crowd, some 15,000-strong, marched to the entrance to the House of Lords. As the Lords arrived, it made a narrow lane for their carriages to pass and called out, 'Justice! Justice!' The tumults kept the king in his barge at private landing stairs at Whitehall; he did not dare come to Westminster but sent word that he would soon attend to the people's desires.

London waited for the king's verdict on Strafford. On Sunday 9 May people fancied they heard rebel drumming and trumpets all day. Late that evening the king tearfully signed the Bill of Attainder, and men started to build a scaffold on Tower Hill. On 12 May, after Archbishop Laud had given Strafford a last blessing, the earl met his end with characteristic bravery, taunted by thousands of spectators. The royalist, Sir Humphrey Mildmay, said that he 'died like a saint, to the shame of his enemies'.[25] Yet even those largely sympathetic to him were struck by the contradictions of his life in politics: one epitaph writer summed him up as 'The Enemie and Martyr of the State,/Thy Nations Glory yet thy Nations Hate'.[26] In his last speech, Strafford thanked Charles for his mercy in sparing him disembowelment and prayed that Charles too might 'find mercie when he stands most in need of it'.[27] It was an ominous wish.

Parliament now pressed its advantage. Charles agreed to a bill taking away his right to dissolve parliament without its own consent; he had already agreed it would be called every three years. The Star Chamber was abolished; Ship Money was declared unlawful. On 10 August, Charles left London to attend the Scottish Parliament; some feared his aim was to seek supporters there. Meanwhile, that September, parliament passed laws reversing Laud's innovations in worship. In most London parishes moderate Protestants were slow to make changes, but avid Puritans reacted with zeal: images of the Virgin Mary were taken down, altar rails removed. Already, towards the end of August, a Puritan mob had shattered 'scandalous pictures' in the stained-glass windows of St Margaret's in New Fish Street. In October it targeted St Leonard, Eastcheap; Nehemiah Wallington kept some pieces of stained glass to show future generations what prayer might achieve.[28] There was a real sense of shared power after so long a period of tyranny, although anxious onlookers wrote 'the times are so perplexed, that there is no resolving of any thing'.[29]

The tactician Pym set about compiling a 'Grand Remonstrance', or list of grievances against the king that parliament might agree and publicize to keep its grip on power. But while the king was in Scotland, rebellion broke out in Ireland: the Irish had found no redress for their many complaints and could see what the Scots had achieved by firm resistance. The news of terrible slaughter inflicted on the Protestants in Ireland reached London on 1 November. Many MPs now thought that this was no moment to present Pym's Remonstrance to parliament or declare that the nation had no confidence in the king. In any case, many of their grievances had been dealt with. On 22 November it was passed by only eleven votes and MPs decided not to print it, as proposed.

When Charles returned to London on 25 November, the mayor and aldermen gave him the customary welcome, preserving this outward sign of civic stability. They met him on horseback at Moorfields and, in an exchange of speeches, a grateful Charles promised to restore the City's charter to Londonderry – once he had tamed Ireland. Livery companies assembled in the streets with their banners, and the king rode in procession to Guildhall where he was feasted. City conduits ran with wine, and many citizens made themselves sick by drinking the king's health. Clearly, he still had many supporters. Perhaps this display forced Pym to make his move against Charles. In the deadly power struggle that followed, the king lost control of London in a matter of months.

In December some 20,000 Londoners signed a petition for bishops to be removed from the House of Lords. They had been spooked by rumours of papist plots and bloody rebellion in Ireland. When the petition was to be presented to the Commons, Charles sent 200 halberdiers to keep the peace against expected crowds in Westminster: it was taken as a sign that he was willing to use force against the Commons. Charles had received Pym's Remonstrance on his return and expressly forbade the Lower House to print it before he had given his answer; but on 15 December the Commons disobeyed him and ordered the petition and Remonstrance to be printed and distributed. Clamorous mobs now paraded through London's streets. The mayor and aldermen found that London's Trained Bands could not quell the disturbance: men would not arrest their neighbours.

On 21 December, Pym's allies won a majority in elections to the Common Council – a decisive factor in the struggle for supremacy. The next day, Charles further alienated Londoners by installing Colonel Lunsford, a godless henchman, as Lieutenant of the Tower. The king wanted an officer there he could trust, but citizens saw at once that Lunsford might train the Tower's guns on London itself. Realizing his mistake, Charles reversed his appointment on 26 December, but armed crowds were already preparing to march on parliament demanding the removal of bishops. There were violent clashes over the next two days. Two thousand apprentices, with clubs, swords and halberds, gathered in Cheapside and could hardly be dispersed. On the 28th a group of apprentices attacked St Paul's, threatening to take down the organs and other popish relics, before being stopped by church officials. The bishops were thoroughly alarmed and petitioned the king for a guard or else they feared to take their seats in parliament. Their letter reached the Commons, who at once turned it against the bishops, accused them of being traitors, and sent twelve to the Tower. London was almost out of control and Charles was losing the battle for public opinion. Military men talked of civil war.

7
'I SEE ALL THE BIRDS ARE FLOWN'

As dusk was gathering on 4 January 1642, Charles I arrived at the House of Commons with about 400 armed men, determined to arrest John Pym and four other MPs for treason. Violent street demonstrations were now almost daily events and he feared for the safety of his family; there were even rumours that parliament intended to impeach his queen. He threw open the doors of the chamber, leaving the soldiers in the lobby where they could still be seen, and took possession of the Speaker's chair. Where were the five Members? The Speaker, William Lenthall, respectfully explained that he was first and foremost a servant of the House and could give no answer; his reply marked the end of the Crown's influence on his office. Charles scanned the faces of the MPs as they stood before him, hats off, and strained to pick out the familiar features of Pym. Two snippets of dialogue reveal the tension of the moment: 'I am a good Marksman, I can hit right, I warrant you,' said a soldier from the door, his pistols cocked, strengthening MPs' fears of an armed attack; then Charles's low, dispirited aside, 'I see all the birds are flown.'[1] The colloquial expression betrayed deep embarrassment: for a man who set such store by protocol, the king was appalled to realize, too late, that he had committed a major breach himself.

Pym and his supporters, forewarned, had escaped by river to the City and taken refuge in Coleman Street. The next day the king travelled to Guildhall and demanded that the Common Council take steps to hand over the five Members (with one peer, also charged with treason). As he left Guildhall, angry crowds pressed about his coach shouting, 'Privileges of Parliament!'[2] His design to arrest the MPs had been taken as an attack on the institution itself; it was the worst day Charles had ever spent in the City. The queen was blamed for having egged him on, but he was rapidly losing popular support. Lord Mayor

Sir Richard Gurney escorted the king homewards past Temple Bar, but once he had taken his leave, angry protestors, including women, pulled Gurney from his horse and denounced him as a traitor.

On the night of 6 January there was panic: rumours flew across London – royalist mercenaries were about to take it by storm; the artillery in the Tower was to be turned on citizens themselves. In the absence of proof, Gurney refused to call out the militia but, contrary to his orders, men ran from door to door, rousing citizens and warning them to arm themselves. The City portcullises were lowered, chains were put across streets, barricades of tubs and benches were erected to obstruct cavalry, and women boiled water to pour over attackers. Many families imagined that the same bloody outrages being inflicted on Protestants in Ireland were about to happen in London. (The queen was suspected of encouraging the Irish rebels and exerting a malign influence among Catholics in London.) Pregnant women miscarried and at least one woman died of fright. Bloody confrontation seemed imminent but, after a few hours, calm was restored; people went back to bed.

Over the next few days, activists and popular fears kept London in a state of high tension. Thousands of demonstrators crowded into Whitehall calling for bishops to be removed from the House of Lords. They included apprentices who had signed petitions before Christmas in their tens of thousands complaining about the state of trade. Political uncertainty had helped to cause a slump, but apprentices blamed Catholics for it and demanded action against the rebels in Ireland, where their masters had invested so much money; they targeted bishops and denounced foreigners for taking their work. These tumults fuelled concern about social stability and order. Even men of substance took to the streets. Opposition leaders had placards secretly printed inviting people to march; they encouraged masters to arm their apprentices and send them to demonstrate in order to put pressure on parliament; zealous ministers preached resistance from the pulpit.

Charles dreaded the embarrassment of Pym's expected return to Westminster: elaborate preparations were under way to bring him back in triumph. The king also feared that he had lost control of the militia and could not keep his family safe. Parliament had tried to take over the appointment of army and navy officers before Christmas; he had resisted but the illegal mobilization of London's militia on the night of 6 January showed the direction events were taking. In any case, many serving in the militia were masters of the very apprentices protesting on the streets. London's Trained Bands, 6,000-strong, were impressive: permanent officers were regularly paid and, evenings and weekends, troops drilled and fired weapons in Finsbury's Artillery Ground. The militia had popular support: Londoners benefited from its supply contracts, and military parades offered free entertainment. At Whitehall Palace, unable to shut out the noise of nearby street protests, Charles made a difficult decision: late on 10 January as the incoming tide flowed upriver, he and his family slipped away by water, heading first to Hampton Court and then to Windsor. It was a strategic error: he left the Tower's armoury, the mint and the militia in the hands of parliament. His enemies would gain national and international status from the symbolic importance of London, while he lost his capital before the war even started. He would not see London for another seven years, and then it would be as a prisoner awaiting trial.

On 11 January, Pym and the four other MPs emerged from hiding. Escorted by the militia and 2,000 seamen, they travelled up the Thames from Grocers' Hall to Westminster in a jubilant procession, with colours flying, drumming and cannon fire. Radical propaganda now swamped London, and the power of unregulated print was exploited for political ends, just as social media would be nearly 400 years later. Parliamentarians rushed to publish their version of the king's attempt to arrest the five Members; scandalous rumours of the royal family's supposed involvement in the Irish rebellion were not just whispered behind closed doors but openly published. Nehemiah Wallington recalled the seductiveness of this material, 'I finding so many of these littel pamflets of weekly news about my house I thought they were so many theeves that had stole away my mony before I was aware of them'.[3] He worried that God might judge he was wasting his earnings, but consoled himself with the thought that he would copy out key passages to show future generations what the Godly might achieve through prayer.

Political change was being driven by ambitious aristocrats as well as by religious resolve; the Puritan earls of Bedford and Warwick were Pym's patrons and Pym was heavily involved in Warwick's colonizing activities. Yet ordinary people were engaged in political debate: sea captains, for example, offered support when Pym and the four other MPs were escorted back to Westminster. Sailors often rioted for pay, but *The Seamen's Protestation*, published that January, was not just a list of economic grievances. It was a pledge to support parliament and the Protestant religion, although since it was printed by order of the Earl of Warwick it may have been an intended contribution to the propaganda war. Parliament boldly thanked all groups involved in escorting the five Members back to Westminster, creating an impression of transparency rather than underhand manoeuvring. Yet the street procession had been a display of power as radicals tightened their grip on popular opinion.

In the war of words that followed, women took an active part. On 31 January they delivered a petition to the House of Lords, complaining that political turmoil damaged trade, that the Lords obstructed useful measures approved by the Commons, and that Protestants in Ireland needed urgent help. Exaggerated reports of Irish atrocities fuelled calls for reform in the capital, as women claimed they lived in fear of rape, of infant blood running in the streets and homes on fire over their heads. On 4 February, 400 well-to-do women and wives of tradesmen led by Mrs Anne Stagg, a brewer's wife, delivered another petition to the Lords, demanding an answer. Pym spoke to them in person and their petition was later printed for maximum effect. This new opportunity for ordinary people to make their voices heard was intoxicating.

Some were uneasy: parliament's calculated appeal to the people and the mobilization of popular sentiment against the Crown might backfire. Thomas Warmstry, a royalist minister, addressed the protesting mobs directly. They were, he wrote, an important part of society but not the whole; activists could not claim that they represented all people, who 'have not committed their cause to your vote, but to the parliament, whom they have made their Vicars and proxies'.[4] The protestors should return to their trades and stop the disorder at Westminster to avoid claims that the country's laws had been made under pressure of mob rule. But the people responded more readily to slogans than to rational argument. Moderate parliamentarians began to defect to the royalist camp, fearful of spy networks in London. Those who stayed tended to be zealots, but even radical thinkers would be split by fear of the popular multitude. It was time to take sides. In January 1642, Henry Oxinden, letter writer and poet, reported from London that people were utterly divided about who should have control of the army needed to put down rebellion in Ireland:

'I have heard foule languig and desperarat quarellings even between old and intire frends'.[5]

The terms 'roundhead' and 'cavalier' were already current on London's streets. 'Roundheads' (after a brief craze for round haircuts) were marked by their zeal for the Protestant religion. For them, obedience to what they took to be God's Will was more important than the king's bidding. They easily positioned themselves as defenders of historic English freedoms in the face of royal tyranny, a stand which appealed strongly to the nobility and gentry inclined to their cause. Their officers, as men of rank, wore their hair long. 'Cavaliers', contemptuously named after Spanish 'caballeros' (troopers), tended to be conservative in outlook. They were members of the Established Church, recognized the king as its head, supported bishops and the Book of Common Prayer, and ardently upheld the sacredness of the king's majesty. Their stance demonstrated the deep hold that 'middle-way' Anglicanism had over much of the population, although their ranks also included Catholics and those sympathetic to Laud's ceremonial forms of Protestant worship.

Some of the king's supporters were heavily swayed by family tradition, concepts of honourable service, and sworn loyalty to the king. They had difficult choices to make if, from morality or religion, they were also inclined to support parliament. This explains how the conflict came to divide families. There was popular support for the monarchy among the lower orders, too. Essentially, the two sides bought into competing myths, and for some young men the initial excitement of war left no room for deeper thought. Swashbuckling Cavaliers quickly earned a reputation for immorality. Nehemiah Wallington accused them of 'drunkonnes, inventing of new oths and blasphemies', and of committing rape and defilement wherever they went.[6] Even the sympathetic James Howell, an Anglican minister whom parliament imprisoned in the Fleet, noted the swaggering superficiality of lace-adorned Cavalier dress. 'Arms are come to be Legs,' he joked, 'for Bishops' Lawn-sleeves are worn for Boot-house tops', while boots and shoes 'are so long-snouted, that one can hardly kneel in God's House, where all Genuflection and Postures of devotion and decency are quite out of use'.[7]

Divided loyalties fractured the capital and the nation. Yet people's motives for going to war were not always principled. Some who had never enjoyed the right to vote were possibly energized by the chance to take sides in politics, but the controversial philosopher Thomas Hobbes, reflecting on the causes of the Civil Wars, surmised that 'there were very few of the common people that cared much for either of the *Causes*, but would have taken any side for pay and Plunder'.[8] Unfortunately for Charles, he lacked funds to pay an army and had left the resources of London's wealthy merchants and tradesmen at the disposal of parliament. In mid-February the queen left London for Holland, ostensibly to conduct their eldest daughter Princess Mary to the Prince of Orange after an arranged marriage, but really to raise arms and equipment for her husband – on the security of her jewels. In exile she would repeatedly urge her husband to stand firm.

THE FORTIFICATION OF LONDON

The City was slowly secured for parliament. In March 1642 parliament passed the Militia Ordnance in defiance of the king, giving itself power over the armed forces. Charles was raising an army, allegedly to quash rebellion in Ireland, which justified London increasing its own defences. In June parliament issued a general call for loans of money, plate and horse, to be repaid at 8 per cent. In November these 'voluntary' contributions became obligatory, with everybody expected to contribute according to their means. Collectors were appointed at parish level and those who defaulted were liable to have their goods seized. Parliament also issued warrants for house-to-house searches, which flushed out secret caches of royalist arms.

The City was asked to provide 6,000 muskets and 4,000 pikes; livery companies also had to contribute the weapons and armour they held to help defend London. At the end of April the mayor was told to ask each company to list its arms and ammunition, and to provide an engine for fighting fire. The quantities involved can be judged from the Goldsmiths' records. The company had fewer weapons than others in the Great Twelve but agreed to provide 40 pikes, helmets and corslets (breast and back pieces); 140 swords and belts; 100 muskets, bandoliers (shoulder belts) and rests; 14 halberds; 7 black bills; 318 pounds of matches; 24 barrels of powder; and 1,000 pounds of shot. It spent £71 on extra swords and muskets in July and ordered a fire engine for

£20 in November.[9] Parliament also ruled that company halls should be used to store gunpowder. The goldsmiths thought it most dangerous to stockpile gunpowder in their hall, presumably because of its expensive decoration, and offered free space in their granary instead; nevertheless, fifty barrels of gunpowder were rolled into their hall.

The Goldsmiths' finances were not in a healthy state. The company had earlier contributed £7,000 towards the relief of Ireland, although to get this sum it was forced to borrow and take out more loans to pay the interest on its debts. Company officials could not collect the quarterly fees from members: some had enlisted, many shops were shut, and the court's absence had hit their trade badly. Yet goldsmiths were too intimidated by parliament to disobey its orders. The Puritan underworld in London was increasingly powerful and not to be antagonized. When Henrietta Maria wrote to the Company in her own hand, offering to present them with a buck for a great feast to reward their service, the liverymen prudently determined to refuse the gift. Parliament's officers now imprisoned even substantial merchants if they refused to contribute to the war effort, confiscating their plate and goods. Men who merely delayed sending horses and money were harshly interrogated and threatened until they complied.

London's militia was increased to 8,000 men, organized into six regiments distinguished by their colours: Red, White, Yellow, Green, Blue and Orange. In addition, Southwark, Tower Hamlets and Westminster had their own regiments. Many apprentices enlisted, including Nehemiah Wallington's, who joined after listening to an emotional appeal from the pulpit. All this activity at local level gave officials insights into the allegiances of individuals, and it became increasingly hard to stay neutral. But everyone was exposed to conflicting proclamations: parliament demanded funds for war; Charles commanded that no one should give parliament money or plate. The Venetian ambassador, Giovanni Giustinian, noted that many Londoners simply made their choice according to existing prejudices:

> And so these unhappy people, attacked by the frequent appearance of these numerous documents, so mutually contradictory, set about to adopt the opinions which best square with their own disposition.[10]

The country edged to the brink of war, as both sides defined their position in terms calculated to win popular support. Parliament compiled a set of proposals for the king to consider called the Nineteen Propositions and sent it to York where he had set up his court. If moderates thought the document was a basis for discussion, they were quickly disabused. Among other things, Charles was being asked to accept that parliament should control the army and foreign policy; that all his ministers should also be answerable to parliament, and that no new peers should be appointed to the House of Lords without the approval of the Commons. He was appalled: the king would have no power over military forces or over national government. He would be nothing 'but the outside, but the picture, but the sign, of a king'. On 8 June he sent a firm refusal.

Both sides spent the summer in raising supplies for war. The royalist mayor, Gurney, worked hard behind the scenes to protect the power of elite aldermen, but in July he was impeached, removed from office and imprisoned in the Tower. Parliament replaced him with the radical Isaac Penington. In the navy, there had been opposition to the king since April 1641; in July 1642 it finally declared for parliament. The Earl of Warwick became Lord High Admiral, ousting the royalist officer, which was somewhat ironic as Warwick had been a notable defaulter in the payment of Ship Money. Any warships that remained royalist were boarded and overpowered. This was a blow for the king as Roundheads would use the navy to protect London's trade and supply other port towns that declared for parliament. Yet there were still cautious voices. That July the moderate MP and lawyer, Bulstrode Whitelocke, tried to dissuade parliament from raising an army: war would bring misery; people were sleep-walking to disaster. 'It is strange to note,' he said, 'how we have insensibly slid into this beginning of a Civil War by one unexpected Accident after another, as Waves of the Sea which hath brought us thus far, and we scarce know how.'[11] It was artful naivety; powerful men were intent on deposing the king. When negotiations failed, Charles raised his standard in Nottingham on 22 August, which allowed parliament to claim that he had started the war. The conflict that would devastate his kingdom had officially begun.

London became a garrison town. Parliament summoned men and horses from nearby counties, and ordered the renovation of city gates and portcullises. Chains and posts were set up across all routes into the capital unprotected by its walls, and the most dangerous routes had artillery positioned nearby. Travellers needed a pass to go in and out of the city. Although parliament now controlled London, not all citizens supported its policies and suspicion built up between different communities. The influx of Protestant refugees from Ireland, bringing tales of Catholic atrocities, increased fears of popish plots. MPs also suspected London's royalists of treachery and placed the most active under house arrest; later they were transferred to hulks on the river. Already Pym had been subject to the seventeenth-century equivalent of biological warfare: an enemy had sent him a letter containing a rag covered in the suppuration of a plague sore, wishing him a speedy death. In this climate there was a wave of oath-taking. Men over eighteen years of age had been required to take oaths of loyalty to the Protestant religion since May 1641; soon they would have to swear loyalty to parliament or be imprisoned.

Having encouraged street demonstrations, the authorities now worked hard to stamp out unhelpful disorder. There was a crackdown on all sorts of 'night-walkers'; quick action was taken whenever fighting broke out between armed groups of soldiers. Sedition was curbed including, for the moment, vilifying the king: in March 1642, William Berry, a mariner of Wapping, was charged with saying 'he cared not a fart for the kings army', while in August, Sara Linge, a Stepney widow, was accused of saying, 'If some of her neighbors would joyne with her, she would cutt the throats of a thousand Roundheads.'[12] Fortunately, the need to defend London from attack brought people together. After the indecisive Battle of Edgehill in Warwickshire, in October 1642, parliament's regiments failed to stop the king marching south, and Londoners began frantic work on new fortifications. The Venetian ambassador witnessed the great number employed, 'including the women and little children'.[13] By the beginning of November a wide arc of earthworks had been constructed in London's northern and western approaches, and a fort was being built in Hyde Park (the remains can be seen today). A river patrol was also set up on the Thames.

In this emergency Puritan lords worked hard to win City support. At a meeting in Guildhall the Earl of Holland, Warwick's younger brother, told aldermen that the king's troops had London in their sights: 'Your City is the strength of the Kingdom indeed; it is not only the life, but the soule of it; if they can destroy you here, the rest of the Kingdom must all submit and yield.'

The politician and colonist William Fiennes, Viscount Saye and Sele, warned what would happen if London fell: 'Your lives should satisfie their malice, your wives, your daughters their lust, and religion itself the dearest thing of all others to us, should be made merchandise of, to invite Papists, to invite foreigners.' Every man should therefore shut his shop, take up his musket, and trust the state to make reparation for financial losses when danger was past.[14]

On 12 November royalist troops sacked Brentford, west of London, and the king advanced on his capital. Given the crisis, the main parliamentary army under the Earl of Essex was reinforced by London's Trained Bands and other citizens, making a force 24,000-strong. On the 13th it marched westwards, expecting a decisive battle. The militia had never been required to operate outside London before and the new Venetian ambassador, Gerolamo Agostini, reported that some bands had to be threatened with severe punishment before they obeyed. Men could be trained to fire a musket in a few weeks, compared to the years of practice needed to become a good bowman, but as musketeers they no longer had the comfort of fighting in close formation. Regular drill helped to compensate, but London's citizens were understandably nervous as the force marched out of the city. The city's defenders included non-parliamentarians: even royalist householders were appalled at the damage done to property in Brentford. Families cheered them on, and women sent cartloads of food and wine to sustain them on the way. Whitelocke, who rode out with the militia, admiringly recorded how their commander, Major-General Philip Skippon, encouraged his troops, riding up and down the line, speaking to each company in turn, and saying, 'Come my boyes my brave boyes, lett us pray heartily & fight heartily.'[15] Yet Whitelocke also observed that some men slinked home as battle seemed to draw near.

The two armies met at Turnham Green, six miles from Westminster, where there was a tense standoff. Essex did not quite trust his untrained troops; the king doubted his army had the strength to win a victory over a larger force. Abruptly, Charles retreated, perhaps losing the best opportunity he would have to regain his capital. For relieved Londoners, the day turned into a cheerful picnic once the food arrived. Agostini, who watched the parliamentary soldiers return, scoffed that nothing had been achieved, but the militia had received an enormous boost to its morale. And it had undoubtedly saved London from royalist capture.

Work on London's defences continued. The diarist John Evelyn, who briefly served in the royalist army, visited 'the Lines of Communication' that December. They were already impressive but the push to complete them came in 1643. The ground was surveyed, plans were drawn, and a Committee of Fortification appointed. London had long since expanded beyond its city walls and extended nearly four miles from Westminster to Wapping. Now a ring of over twenty small forts joined by a rampart and ditch would be thrown right around it, north and south of the river. The word 'mount' in a street name today sometimes indicates where a fort stood; for example, there was one on the site of the Mount Pleasant Post Office building. Two were built at the Elephant and Castle, and one where the Imperial War Museum now stands. When finished, the defences extended over eleven miles from Wapping in the east, north to Whitechapel, west via Clerkenwell and Tottenham Court to Hyde Park, then southeast to Vauxhall before looping back south of the river to Rotherhithe, opposite Wapping. Archaeological evidence confirms the great labour involved: ramparts were 3.35 metres high and 7 metres wide, while the ditches, a mixture of wet and dry, were 5.5 metres wide and 2 metres deep.

Construction was a two-stage process. The expert work of building forts and bulwarks to take the weight of cannon began in March 1643. By April, Londoners could start digging and carrying earth for ramparts and ditches, although skilled bricklayers and stonemasons were needed to build entrances. Speed was essential, so parliament sent people through the City with drums and flags to enlist volunteers, some 20,000 in total. They were not paid but did get one meal a day from local innkeepers. Each morning, even on Sundays, crowds marched from the City to the suburbs with spades and baskets. Some saw it as pious work; others just wanted to protect their homes and families. Women and girls worked alongside men, carrying baskets two by two; in May 1,000 oyster women were said to be toiling on the earthworks. Livery companies marched out to help, carrying their colours: the tailors mustered 8,000 men, the watermen 7,000 and shoemakers 5,000. Parliament ordered that individual trades should dig on given days, when their shops would shut so that no trader would benefit from the absence of a competitor.

Ambassador Agostini, whose incisive analysis of London politics tended to favour the elite, tartly observed that the fortifications seemed to be turned on

Londoners themselves: 'The shape they take betrays that they are not only for defence against the royal armies, but also against tumults of the citizens, and to ensure a prompt obedience on all occasions.'[16] It was true that the ramparts would not resist a siege, but they did free up some Trained Bands to operate outside London. Guarded entrances in the lines of defence allowed Londoners to control who entered and left the city, helping to enforce parliament's trade restrictions with the enemy. But the earthworks also ruined good pastureland for years to come.

The militia, who helped to build the defences, afterwards manned them – one trained band was taken from other duties in rotation. Later in the war, volunteers were substituted as pressure on the militia increased. Despite volunteer labour, these defences cost a fortune; the City paid £8,000 and then an enforced monthly charge of £5,482 (charges on Westminster, Southwark and Tower Hamlets increased London's total monthly contribution to £6,962).[17] Money was also raised by sequestering property within the line of fortification. Yet timber merchants and artificers, carriage makers, smiths and carpenters who worked on the project were still petitioning for payment years later.

WAR'S IMPACT ON LONDON

Inevitably, war changed the tenor of life in London. As early as October 1642, Nehemiah Wallington was complaining that he often shut his shop because people spent less in uncertain times. Thousands neglected their businesses to build London's fortifications; luxury trades were hit by the departure of the court. There had been no Lord Mayor's Show since 1639, which meant a loss of business as well as pageantry, and in September 1642 parliament closed theatres. By 1645, Wallington was noting a fall in living standards, 'for our ware is deare because workmen are gon and trayding is dead and costomers hard and taxes grate'.[18]

To pay for its army, parliament imposed an unprecedently high level of taxation on London, collected with the help of soldiers. From September 1643 it also levied an excise on imports, soon extended to domestic produce like meat and beer, when price increases hit the poor hard. Butchers were among the most violent objectors: in 1647 a crowd demonstrated in Smithfield, burnt down the excise office and destroyed its records. Meanwhile, the City became increasingly reluctant to lend to parliament, which had failed its early creditors; it was obvious that loans would not be repaid for years. Even so, parliament managed to squeeze much money from London – a resource unavailable to the king.

Londoners experienced privation. There was a severe fuel shortage by summer 1643; Newcastle was in royalist hands and parliament banned coal-bearing ships from sailing there unless Newcastle declared for parliament. The price of coal rocketed from 20s. to 46s. a chaldron, so posts, gates and fences disappeared at an alarming rate as people burnt wood to keep warm.[19] In October 1643 parliament ordered that trees for 60 miles around London could be felled, especially those in the king's parks and forests. But the faithful could always find cause for optimism; that November, Wallington praised God's will in saving him from being squashed by a cart with a double load of wood and faggots as it overturned at the corner of Bread Street Hill. And by November 1644 trade with Newcastle had reopened.

War also affected medical provision in the capital. The College of Physicians was firmly behind parliament, long resenting the power that bishops had to censure medical books, thanks to ancient links between the Church and medical practice. When war broke out, MPs passed a bill that, for the first time, recognized parliament had a duty of care towards those wounded in its service. Nurses were recruited from the widows of soldiers and London's first dedicated military hospitals opened at the Savoy in the Strand and at Ely House in Holborn. They were run according to freshly drafted regulations that insisted on strict hygiene: linen and towels were to be changed weekly; wards deep cleaned. The surplices that clergymen were forbidden to wear after September 1643 were torn into bandages.

Londoners, however accustomed to plague pits, were shocked by the sight of the war injured, so to begin with they were carted in under cover of night. By May 1643, Agostini noted:

The hospitals are already full of wounded and sick and never a day passes that a considerable number does not arrive, to the universal horror, as the people here are quite unaccustomed to the horrible aspects of war, especially civil war.[20]

Hospitals had some success, because only the strongest patients survived the journey along rutted roads back to London. Injury to a limb typically resulted in amputation; the most dangerous wounds involved penetration, when fragments of dirty clothing might be driven deep into the body and cause infection. Many survived operations only to die a lingering death from blood poisoning. Thousands more, herded in unhygienic camps without proper food or shelter, succumbed to infectious diseases. Fewer than half of those who died in the wars are estimated to have been killed in battle. Sympathetic citizens did what they could. In December 1643, Wallington recorded, 'I went with my wife unto the Savey [sic] and there did I [behold] very sad specticles of misery of our own souldiers which moved my heart to much pety and to pray for them.'[21]

There were other disturbing sights. Refugees poured into London from embattled provinces and maimed soldiers begged on the streets: parliament had set up a graduated system of pensions for the wounded, widows and orphans, but pensions were not always paid and did not extend to those who had fought for the king. Serving soldiers, due 12d. a day, often went unpaid. One officer warned that his militiamen would pawn their weapons if they did not get their money on time.[22] In this climate, warrants for house searches were abused and there were complaints that soldiers were pillaging goods. Roving bands of religious enthusiasts caused more trouble; on Sunday 24 October 1642 moderate Protestants fought zealous Puritans in St Paul's after they tried to destroy the organ. Houses stood eerily empty as Londoners who refused to contribute to parliament's war effort fled the capital. Parliament eventually ordered that these dwellings could be leased or sold off, but the entire process disrupted business circles.

London traders who equipped parliament's troops did well. There was a large pool of craftsmen and women who could produce ready-made uniforms; Londoners also owned many of the gunpowder mills in Surrey and the Lea Valley. Parliament spent at least £450,000 on arms during the war and most contracts for personal weapons went to Londoners – fulfilled at first by imports and then by stepping up production.[23] The capital's arms industry expanded, but there was little innovation in manufacturing processes; most weapons were still made in small workshops. After all, a blacksmith could manufacture a musket and livery companies knew how to monitor quality control.

Yet war had a negative impact on London's economy overall. Internal trade suffered, particularly during the months from summer 1643 to summer 1644, when royalist blockades disrupted long-distance trading networks. Its cloth, cattle and coal trades were all curtailed, although in the long term London's dominance of internal trade was secure. Foreign trade survived because parliament's navy could protect commerce against royalist privateers, but it was badly hit during a second crisis, 1648–50, when bad harvests contributed to recession and a general dearth made the poor desperate.

There were waves of peace protests. In December 1642, Protestant leaders, mostly conservative, prosperous men, petitioned parliament for an honourable peace with the king. Their opponents judged them to be Cavaliers and a serious fight broke out, in which Puritans came off better as they were armed. In the new year, apprentices changed sides to join the peace campaign; on 2 January they assembled in Covent Garden before marching unarmed on parliament. Crucially, this movement failed to get the support of seamen, although they too were suffering from the slump in trade, so parliament was able to stamp out the protests.

Frustration at this failure spurred royalist plots in 1643. One involved the MP and poet Edmund Waller, but the conspirators did not get far before a servant betrayed them. Two alleged ringleaders, Richard Challoner and Nathaniel Tomkins, were hanged in June at the Holborn end of Fetter Lane where they lived; Waller ignominiously got off by telling all he knew and paying a huge fine. Pym was able to use the plot to whip up fear among his supporters and he would paint future peace proposals as covert, royalist conspiracies.

That summer, fresh from a string of victories, King Charles renewed overtures for peace. Mayor Penington assembled 5,000 militants on 7 August to pressurize parliament into dismissing the king's offer. Next day a moderate crowd, mostly women with children in their arms, took up the call for an end to the war. On the 9th thousands of women, wearing white ribbons in their hats, assembled in Whitehall. They refused to disperse and were reportedly joined by men disguised in women's clothes. A bloody fracas ensued in which several women (and men) were killed and more than a hundred injured. Although parliament dismissed the women as whores and fishwives, most seem to have been the wives of respectable tradesmen. Agostini, annoyed at having had his own horses briefly requisitioned, wrote, 'Every effort, not omitting violence, is used to purge this city of the pacific Royalists and neutrals. Many of the women who went to implore peace have been imprisoned, as well as their husbands.'[24]

Yet there was still fun to be had in the metropolis. Some royalist gentry escaped plundering troops in the counties and sought the safety of London, among them Sir Humphrey Mildmay, who arrived in March 1643 and stayed a year, resuming his former pleasures. He spent much of his time in taverns and on at least one occasion took his family to watch rope dancing. The gentry brought less business to the capital than formerly; they were not sending bulk goods like wine and candles back to their estates. Mildmay, a staunch Anglican, managed to cope with the capital's religious fervour. When parliament introduced a monthly fast, usually the last Wednesday of the month, he pointedly marked 'the damned fast' by eating well and kept to 'his Majesty's fast' on a Friday. He was put off by Puritan church services that insisted on parliament's cause, 'the Covenant being hot and I none of the tribe'.[25] Instead, he went to the French Protestant theologian, Jean D'Espagne, at Durham House in the Strand, or to private houses like Lord Petre's in Aldersgate Street that sheltered royalist divines. Parliament had removed their livings and placed them under house arrest, but they were still free to receive visitors.

Why didn't London descend into anarchy? Parliament controlled troops, imposed curfews, created a climate of fear, and some wealthy citizens – like the queen's physician – were simply unwilling to lose their fortunes by opposing parliament. Pym was also adept at retaining core support from the middle and lower end of the social scale, appealing to religious enthusiasm and offering intermittent opportunities for celebration. In March 1643, for example, parliament ordered the Queen's Chapel in Somerset House to be defaced and plundered. On 2 May, after parliament's army took Reading, it was emboldened to give thanks by destroying the Cheapside Cross. The old monument had its defenders, so militia companies of horse and foot stood guard to prevent disorder. There was a beating of drums as it fell, trumpets blew, and the crowd threw their caps in the air with a great shout. The site was given a new symbolic significance: on 10 May the 'popish' *Book of Sports* was ceremoniously burned by the hangman there, and afterwards at the Exchange. London churches sustained a new wave of iconoclasm: cherubs and angels were defaced, organs removed, altar rails burned, and even the skyline changed as crosses were taken from steeples.

Pym's death, from cancer of the lower bowel in December 1643, was a blow to the cause. As war dragged on, parliament finally put Archbishop Laud on trial in March 1644, possibly as a distraction or to obtain God's blessing by bringing the guilty to justice. It was hard to make the charge of treason stick, but on 10 January 1645, an overcast day, Laud was executed at Tower Hill; the sun emerged at the precise moment that he lost his head, which the crowd took as a sign that God would favour the parliamentary cause. Wallington praised God's mercy in seeing justice done to 'his littel grace the Bishop of Canterbury'. And yet Wallington was seized with new fears for the future of London. He was disillusioned by 'our sinfull and wicked Armies which are almost as vile as the cavalers'; he despised Puritan leaders who enriched themselves, 'now they be put in place and office they are proud and selfe seekers'; worse still, God's people had divided into factions, 'ready to devour one another'.[26]

8

'THE MEMORY OF THE WICKED
SHALL ROT'

The writer and London waterman, John Taylor, mostly self-educated, was in his element in the welter of dissent, disruption and drama that rocked London in the mid-1640s. Dubbed 'the water-poet', his writing extended to biting political pamphlets with a range of reference and topicality you might expect from this seventeenth-century equivalent of a London taxi driver, who met people from all walks of life. That a sometime labourer published at all in this century is rare; that his work survives today perhaps more so. But Taylor was a born self-publicist: he once claimed that he had rowed a brown paper boat from London Bridge to Queenborough, Kent, using dried fish strapped to canes for oars. He was a royalist and staunch member of the Established Church, proving that not all royalists were dashing Cavaliers in ribbons and lace, men who fidgeted through a good sermon. His witty attacks on Puritan groups hit home because he straddled social worlds.

As a 'media celebrity' and aggressive pamphleteer, the ageing Taylor was dangerous to parliamentarians because he appealed to a wide readership. In just two years from the beginning of 1642, over sixty of his works tumbled from the press. He fearlessly condemned the swarming Puritan sects as 'a rabble of ignorant *Mechanicks*', mere 'Coblers, Tinkers, Pedlers, Weavers, Sowgelders, and Chymney-Sweepers' who had usurped the Church and dared to preach.[1] They suffered from blind delusion or conceited fantasy to imagine they were Christ's spokesmen and able to save souls. Taylor also grumbled about the thousands of impoverished idlers who had flocked to London, where they set up as booksellers without serving any apprenticeship and sold unlicensed scandal. They published lies, speeches attributed to men without their knowledge, news made up overnight in an alehouse and passed off as fact. And in no time at all, this false news circulated across the country 'to the great abuse of true Writers, the scandall of this Honourable Citie of *London*, and the universall injury to the whole Kingdome'.[2]

Taylor was arrested for sedition in 1642 but released after interrogation. By now he had brutal enemies and he was set upon in a tavern near the Guildhall. Lucky to escape alive, he joined the king in Oxford where he continued to produce a stream of jaunty squibs attacking Roundheads. He also wrote for the royalist 'newsbook', *Mercurius Aulicus*, or 'News from the Court'. Newsbooks were overtaking *corantos*, which mostly published foreign news, and *Mercurius Aulicus* was the most hard-hitting. It was printed weekly from January 1643 to the end of 1645, by which time its appearance was sporadic as the royalist cause faltered. Its editor, John Birkenhead, can claim to be England's first journalist, and used many of the manipulative tricks familiar in news reporting today. He even had a mole in parliament who leaked to him the business of the House.

The *Aulicus* was printed at Oxford and smuggled into London, where copies were also secretly printed, producing an estimated one copy for every five Londoners. Readers were mostly of the middling sort and above, prepared to pay 1d. a copy (the price rose to 18d. as royalist finances worsened). Birkenhead's spirited commentary worried Pym and his colleagues. On 26 August 1643, for instance, he claimed to have intercepted 'rebel' letters from the capital which proved that people were deserting London, that no fuel was to be had there, and that 'Tumults there doe daily increase, occasioned chiefly by their daily *pressing* men to serve in their Rebellious Army, seizing poore men many times in their beds, and taking them from their wives and children, to fight in spight of their hearts they know not why.'[3] He also mocked parliamentary army officers, calling the Earl of Manchester 'that Honourable horse stealer' because he was so swift to requisition mounts.[4] Roundheads did not produce their own newsbook until August 1643, calling it *Mercurius Britannicus* to imply that it was aimed at all readers. Birkenhead quipped that his rivals could not spell good English and mocked their pretensions. So, when the Roundhead paper vouchsafed that at the Battle of Newbury in Berkshire, 'Parliament lost no man of eminency', he swiftly retorted that it was 'the onely true thing you printed'.[5]

Women were active in this war of words. If some positioned themselves as respectable housewives to get their peace petitions heard, several Puritan women flouted convention by preaching in radical sects around Aldgate and elsewhere. On the royalist side, women smuggled propaganda into London hidden in their skirts. Women who preached and, in 1645, organized weekly public lectures in Coleman Street, stoking religious debate, trod a difficult path because at this time Puritans were accusing Queen Henrietta Maria of wearing the breeches in her marriage, and denouncing her as 'the Supreme Petticoate', who conducted herself 'so meritoriously manfull'.[6] Yet women continued to swell the number of separatist meetings in taverns and private homes. London's apparent descent into social and moral confusion was partly caused by parliament itself, which had initiated debate about how best to reform the English Church. An assembly of divines met near Westminster for the first time on 1 July 1643 and continued to pray, fast and debate the best way forward for the next five years.

The explosion of publications in London owed much to the abolition of the Star Chamber in July 1641; as Charles I lost power, state censorship declined. In the 1630s an average of 630 new works were published each year but in 1641 that number more than doubled. It stayed at a high level for the rest of the decade. The publisher and bookseller, George Thomason, who had premises within the churchyard of St Paul's, collected 22,000 different publications during the civil war period, perhaps just three-quarters of all pamphlets and tracts produced. The taverns, inns and bookstalls around St Paul's and the Exchange were brimming with newsbooks, broadsides and ballads, each reaching many more than one person because posted on tavern walls, sung or read aloud.

The printing trade was one of the few businesses to expand in wartime. Turmoil across the country meant that people everywhere were avid for news, although much of it was unreliable. Trade networks of different commodities between London and the regions allowed bundles of pamphlets to travel with other goods as an informal postal service. Sir Humphrey Mildmay talked dismissively of the 'pamphlets of fooleries' that easily reached his estate in Essex.[7] Londoners aimed to pick up reliable news at the Exchange and other social venues so that they could keep their extended families informed. There was also a regular exchange of letters between London housewives and their husbands in the parliamentary army: when the army was in Northampton, for instance, postmen collected letters for soldiers at the Saracen's Head in Carter Lane once a week and carried replies back in saddle bags. This correspondence gave the royalist *Aulicus* a propaganda opportunity. In September 1643 it printed a letter allegedly written by Susan Owen to her husband serving outside London in the militia:

> Most tender and deare heart, my kind affection remembred unto you. I am like never to see thee more I feare, and if you ask the reason why, the reason is this, either I am afraid the Cavaleers will kill thee or death will deprive thee of me, being full of grief for you, which I fear will cost me my life.[8]

In fact, that September the militia had helped to force Cavaliers to lift their siege of Gloucester and then fought bravely at the Battle of Newbury. There was no prospect now that the king could easily recapture London.

Parliament reacted quickly to the storm of propaganda. In June 1643 it issued an order requiring censorship before publication to suppress the 'many false, forged, scandalous, seditious, libellous, and unlicensed Papers, Pamphlets, and Books' that it claimed were harming 'Religion and Government'. Newsbooks, already part of London life, were not easily suppressed, but parliament had wider targets in its sights. Parliament's champion, William Prynne, once a firebrand opponent of the Established Church, now found himself defending a reformed, Protestant Church against even more radical Independents, who emphasized individual conscience rather than rules imposed by a church hierarchy. Prynne heaped vitriol on London's multiplying sects, but also levelled his anger at recent tracts by John Milton, otherwise a respected poet and advocate of the parliamentary cause. These tracts, published from 1643, called for divorce to be made legal if husband and wife turned out to be incompatible, but to Prynne such 'divorce at will' was ungodly.

Milton's first wife Mary had deserted him a few weeks after their marriage in May 1642, returning to her parents. The cause of the rift is unknown and may have been a fall-out of the war rather than based on personal differences (her family was royalist, Milton anti-royalist), but after more than a year of appealing for her return, Milton determined to resolve his unhappiness by getting a divorce. He was already experiencing a loss of sight that would lead to blindness and he wanted a stable marriage.

Prynne's attack on the divorce tracts and parliament's clamp-down on unlicensed publishing sparked Milton into writing a vehement defence of free speech and liberty of thought. His *Areopagitica*, named after the rock on which the council of classical Athens debated serious crimes and points of religion, has become a cornerstone in the liberal defence of people's right to express opinions without censorship. When the book was published on 23 November 1644, Milton bravely put his name on the title page, although the printer and bookseller thought it too dangerous to do so. He made a passionate case for the unfettered circulation of ideas being essential to the development of a free people: 'Give me the liberty to know, to utter, and to argue freely according to conscience, above all liberties.'[9] Citizens, he argued, must learn to sift ideas, test morals and weigh up conflicting sources, if they are to identify truth from fake news. There is nothing admirable in 'a fugitive and cloister'd vertue', and censorship is likely to produce 'a grosse conforming stupidity'.[10] Although the details of Milton's argument are faintly remembered today, his soaring prose and vision of London as a haven of liberty remain powerful:

> Behold now this vast City; a City of refuge, the mansion-house of liberty . . . there be pens and heads there, sitting by their studious lamps . . . others as fast reading, trying all things, assenting to the force of reason and convincement.[11]

His toleration had limits: he denied the rights of Catholics to publish works in defence of their religion. Yet *Areopagitica*, sharpened by a context of religious and political upheaval, still stands as a fundamental defence of free speech.

King Charles had effectively lost the war by 1646, defeated by parliament's New Model Army, set up in February 1645 as a professional force equipped to serve across the country. He gave himself up to the Scots but since he refused to establish Presbyterianism in England, they handed him over to parliament on payment of the £400,000 owed them for war expenses. Parliament gained the support of the Scots by agreeing to align the English Church with the Presbyterian Kirk of Scotland, which was governed by elected assemblies not bishops. Powerful men in the City, conservative in outlook, strongly favoured a national Presbyterian Church as a means of imposing social order and preventing a much-feared descent into religious licence. Presbyterian MPs became an influential force within parliament, and significant pressure was applied to promote Presbyterian worship in London, from city pulpits and through the circulation of handbills and petitions. Ironically, having defeated the king and his Cavaliers, the Puritan victors now began to fall out with each other.

THE PUTNEY DEBATES

A pamphlet war soon raged between Presbyterians and Independents; a key figure was the energetic radical, John Lilburne. As a youth, Lilburne had been inspired by John Foxe's *Book of Martyrs* (1563), one of the most influential books ever published in the history of the Christian world, which described the torments Protestants endured during the reign of Catholic Mary I. Lilburne became active in the Puritan cause and fought with distinction in the parliamentary army, accompanied by his wife who took lodgings close to wherever the troops were quartered. But he fell out with his general, the Earl of Manchester, a leading Presbyterian, and afterwards put his talent for activism to the service of the Independents, writing and distributing radical literature. After a long ordeal in the Tower, imprisoned on a charge of illegally printing scandalous material, Lilburne emerged as a leader of the Leveller movement. As he was keen to point out, the term 'Leveller' did not mean that the movement wished to ban titles or do away with property rights. It was no early form of Communism. But Levellers did encourage fundamental debate about the rights of freeborn Englishmen and equality under the law, prompted by religious and political turmoil in the capital. They demanded religious toleration and a widening of the franchise. They used the City's ancient charters to validate their arguments, even misrepresenting the charters to advance their claim that all government must be by consent.[12] Their writings helped to create a more radical public, increasingly adept at comparing the works of different authors, despite parliament's steps to rein in unlicensed printing.

By September 1647 the New Model Army, under the influence of the Independents, had snatched King Charles from the control of the largely

Presbyterian parliament and was holding him an honourable prisoner in Hampton Court. The aldermen and common councillors of the City had been keen to fund the Army when it was set up, but they now became anxious about its religious principles, which seemed likely to boost religious extremism in London. With the king defeated, parliament planned a large-scale reduction of its military forces, not least because Londoners were sinking under the weight of taxation needed to sustain them, but parliament needed money to pay off the Army. Because trade had declined and London's economy was doing badly, it did not dare to raise taxes. Instead, it asked the City for a loan. In return, the City wanted its old power over the militia returned. Would it, in time, use the militia against the Army?

The moderate, Presbyterian element in London was pushing for a settlement with the king and lasting peace. Among the lower classes its ranks included the watermen, whose trade had been affected by the absence of the court, butchers who loathed the excise, and sailors. Presbyterians now used their influence over the London masses: on 26 July a mob of apprentices, mostly bound to watermen and respectable tradesmen, invaded parliament to force them to take measures against the Army, which City authorities did not dare to demand in their own name. The mob succeeded in driving Independent members of both Houses to seek refuge with the Army. London and the Army now squared up to each other.

The Army, under General Thomas Fairfax and his deputy, Oliver Cromwell, battle-hardened and pivotal in winning the war for the Roundheads, was angered by parliament's plans to reduce its numbers. For one thing, soldiers had not been paid. For another, parliament seemed about to send the men it retained to fight in Ireland. Soldiers, who had endured years of deprivation and faced countless dangers, were beginning to wonder what they had been fighting for; the king was going to be reinstated and they would be denied their just rewards. Although moderates in the City were now united against the Army and pushing for a resolution with the king, the Army could still count on the support of artisans and tradesmen in the suburbs and in Southwark, usually at odds with the City. There were also some disaffected people in the City causing trouble – destitute disbanded soldiers from old armies, refugees and hangers-on.

On 4 August the Army began to occupy fortifications on the outskirts of London, starting with Southwark; Fairfax and Cromwell were soon in complete control of all garrisons. Londoners panicked. Would the soldiers plunder and set fire to their houses? Some hid their goods, tradesmen shut up their shops, others fled into the country or overseas. On 7 August, ostensibly to restore order, some 18,000 troops under Fairfax and Cromwell marched through London's streets in a blatant show of strength, escorting the Independent MPs back in triumph and reseating them in parliament. Citizens were greatly relieved that the troops were under control; their weapons glinted, their uniforms were impressive, and some onlookers gave them a warm reception. It was testimony, if any were needed, that the capital was deeply divided, though moderate Presbyterians might be in the majority. Bowing to pressure, the mayor and aldermen had formally welcomed Fairfax at Hyde Park and put up a brave show, but military occupation was a defeat for the Presbyterian elite. The mayor would soon be imprisoned. The Army's committee of officers insisted that London could no longer have its own defences; a submissive parliament agreed. By the end of September its citizens, aided by soldiers, had been compelled to destroy the surrounding earthworks constructed with so much labour. The balance of power in the capital had changed, and events in London would again determine the direction of the war.

Even so, the City refused to pay parliament's taxes. There was no money for soldiers' wages and their families suffered; meanwhile, the troops were camped at Putney, about six miles upstream of London Bridge. Discontent within the ranks led to wide-ranging discussion about the way forward. The arguments soon extended to the nature of the constitution, the powers of the Crown and the rights of man. The cavalry was the most radical group. Regiments elected agents to represent their views and, with Leveller input, drew up a political manifesto, *The Case of the Armie Truly Stated*. This document listed soldiers' grievances but also called for political reforms, including biennial parliaments, wider male suffrage, and the rights and freedoms soldiers had fought for. At the end of October the Army's General Council permitted a formal debate of these issues, cutting across the settlement that senior army officers and parliamentary allies were trying to get with the king. A series of meetings began in the Church of St Mary the Virgin, Putney.

Today these debates are hailed as a milestone in the expression of demo-cratic and republican thought. For libertarians, who value liberty and personal autonomy above all else, the famous words that Colonel Thomas Rainsborough uttered at Putney epitomize all they stand for: 'For really I thinke that the poorest hee that is in England hath a life to live, as the greatest hee; and therfore ... every Man that is to live under a Governement ought first by his own Consent to putt himself under that Governement.'[13] Yet the debates went unreported at the time; we would know nothing of the cut and thrust of the arguments if a shorthand account of the proceedings had not come to light at the end of the nineteenth century. Captain William Clarke, secretary to the General Council, had been instructed to take notes, which were published at last in 1891.

Clarke's account shows that Cromwell, who chaired the debates, and his son-in-law, Henry Ireton, however sympathetic to Leveller ideas, disagreed on how to bring about reform. They insisted that political authority had to remain with landowners and men of wealth and estate if stable government were to be preserved. But the soldiers argued that legitimate political authority resided, as a birthright, with the collective people alone (although they excluded women, beggars and servants from the franchise). Their proposals were redrafted, with Leveller input, to form *An Agreement of the People*, printed and on London bookstalls by 3 November 1647. This paper went further, calling for a more equal redrawing of parliamentary constituencies, liberty of conscience and equality before the law. Soldiers were now mixing with radicals in taverns where religious meetings were often held, notably in the Mouth, Aldersgate, and in the Windmill near Coleman Street. London activists helped to shape the troops' demands but, in the short term, the Putney Debates did nothing but exacerbate disunity in the Army.

Women were among the activists. They claimed spiritual equality with men in radical sects. They took part in the Leveller movement even if their domestic situation meant they were ill-placed to challenge patriarchal society: Lilburne's wife, Elizabeth, would give birth to ten children. The House of Lords thought the Levellers dangerous and targeted them, but although some leaders were impris-oned, their radical pamphlets still circulated, largely thanks to Leveller wives who continued to produce and distribute these works. Elizabeth, for example, acted as a courier, distributing tracts her husband wrote in prison. Wives also produced petitions, which were usually published afterwards, demanding the release of Leveller leaders and relief from taxes. The women endured hardships and loss of income in their husband's absence and were harassed and imprisoned themselves. Mary Overton, a printer's wife, was dragged on a hurdle to Bridewell with a six-month baby in her arms (the child died in prison); Ellen Larner, another printer's wife, suffered a miscarriage when officials ransacked their home looking for seditious writings and arrested her husband.

Yet women had no political rights; they were legally represented by their husbands (apart from the very few who could vote as householders). Nor did Leveller women demand the vote. Even so, with other women, they certainly took part in political life. Most of these activists are lost to history, but Katherine Chidley gained recognition as a formidable woman. She wrote and preached on behalf of independent churches and was an active supporter of the Leveller movement. This did not seem to harm her prospects in the longer term: after her husband's death, she took over his haberdashery business and even won lucrative government contracts, supplying stockings for the army.

For a brief, exciting period, radical groups engaged in passionate discussion about the entire system under which people lived. But harvest failure led to food shortages and hunger; the wars had thrown society into upheaval, wrecked towns and estates, damaged the economy and caused catastrophic loss (the death toll across the kingdom was proportionately greater than in the First World War). Many just wanted peace.

KILLING THE KING

Soldiers at Putney, debating the fate of the king, were the first to describe him as 'that man of blood'. Charles was the cause of all the bloodletting, and he deserved punishment as a matter of justice, separate from any desire to manage the political situation. These fiery debates within the New Model Army spooked Charles into escaping from Hampton Court on 11 November. He headed for the relative safety of Carisbrooke Castle on the Isle of Wight and was soon taken prisoner there. Undaunted, he continued to scheme with the Scots to regain his kingdom. Another civil war threatened and different factions within the New Model Army closed ranks.

By 1648, London had become a hotbed of royalist intrigue, unsettled by the high taxation needed to maintain parliament's war effort, and the confrontation between Army and City. Women were again active on both sides: as couriers for royalists, as informers and spies for parliament. In March there were royalist demonstrations calling for the king's reinstatement. Troops were used to disperse the crowds and arrest ringleaders, but more demonstrations followed, as usual involving apprentices. On 9 April some 4,000 marched down Fleet Street to the Strand, heading for Whitehall. A cavalry detachment thundered into the protestors, dispersing them around Charing Cross and killing two. Undeterred, royalist sympathizers regrouped next day and assaulted the lord mayor's house, beating back his guards and seizing a cannon. They took a magazine at Leadenhall, then marched along the Thames with drums, inviting seamen and watermen to fight 'for God and King Charles'.[14] The lord mayor took refuge in the Tower. For some hours, it seemed as if London might remain in royalist hands, but at dawn the following day parliamentary troops managed to enter London at Aldersgate. They attacked the rioters at Leadenhall and restored order.

When the Second Civil War followed in May, London did not declare openly for the king (events had shown that Londoners were no match for the New Model Army), but apprentices, watermen and others did support revolts elsewhere in England. And the fighting did get alarmingly close to the capital, with royalist forces advancing to Deptford, Blackheath and Bow Bridge before they were repulsed. Major-General Philip Skippon, in charge of all forces within London, played a key role in suppressing loyalist support there. He had the money to create an intelligence network and rooted out stockpiles of arms, horses and men prepared for the royalist cause. The war was short-lived: Cromwell dealt a crushing blow to the royalists and Scots at the Battle of Preston in Lancashire in August, but had Skippon lost control of London the outcome might have been very different. The victors now expected King Charles to agree to a constitutional monarchy but, devious to the end, he played off parliament, the Scots and the Army, seeking a better deal. Cromwell saw that it would be impossible to come to a settlement with him. Reluctantly, he now sided with the group supporting revolution. These men argued that as the king stubbornly refused any pact that abolished bishops, could not be trusted to keep the peace, and seemed ready to grasp any opportunity to renew war, they would have to execute him.

Prominent Cavaliers had already fled the capital. Senior army officers clamped down on remaining pockets of resistance, rounded up royalist, Presbyterian conspirators and imprisoned them in Windsor Castle. Meanwhile, Independent preachers called for the king's trial and the overthrow of monarchy. Radicals in the suburbs were especially outraged that parliament seemed to be under the control of conservative Presbyterian forces, enemies of religious toleration and unwilling to take a hard line with the king. The tone of radical opinion in the suburbs can be gauged from criminal court records: one spinster was ready to label Queen Henrietta Maria a whore and all the king's children bastards.[15]

That December, Fairfax ordered his soldiers to be billeted within London's walls, using churches and livery halls; soldiers of the New Model Army had still not been paid and Fairfax insisted that his men would stay put until the City fathers settled the taxes they owed. The Goldsmiths' Company duly boarded up the windows of their hall and nearby houses in case soldiers tried to enter. London was so unruly that beggars, pretending to be maimed soldiers, accosted members of the Company on their way to meetings and demanded money before they would leave. Soldiers billeted in St Paul's combated the winter cold by tearing down its ornamental carvings and making fires on the cathedral floor.

Early on the morning of 6 December, Colonel Thomas Pride and his regiment took up positions at the approach to the House of Commons. As MPs tried to enter, he checked them against a list, turning back all those who supported the king and arresting hardliners. 'Pride's Purge' left a submissive 'Rump Parliament', which finally sided with the Army and ruled out a negotiated settlement with the king. Cromwell, who now overshadowed Fairfax, being more prepared to take radical action, was conveniently out of London; the military coup took place on the orders of his son-in-law Henry Ireton, but Cromwell certainly approved of it. The way was now clear for the trial of the king.

While it might seem bizarre today that a populace would go along with a trial likely to end in their king's execution, the idea of killing Charles had long been given popular voice and not just in the Army. For instance, in 1644 Joan Sherrard, a spinster from the Strand area, was recorded as saying, 'His Majestye is a stuttering foole', adding, 'If I were a man, as I am a woman, I would helpe to pull him to pieces.'[16] Yet the Army did not dare bring Charles to London from Windsor until 19 January 1649, fearing the effect his presence might have on public opinion.

The Rump Parliament set up a High Court of Justice to try the king for 'high treason and other high crimes' and on 20 January his trial began in Westminster Hall.[17] Lord President Bradshaw, prosecuting, was dressed wholly in black and wore a bullet-proof hat, lined with sheet iron. He sat in a crimson velvet chair, a desk before him, while lawyers sat either side on benches decked for the occasion in scarlet cloth. A crimson velvet chair had been placed opposite Bradshaw, for the king. Soldiers and privileged people filled the body of the hall and spectators packed the galleries. Among them was General Fairfax's wife. When her husband's name was called out, she retorted spontaneously, 'He has too much wit to be here.'[18] Once silence had been ordered, the king was allowed to enter, visibly older, thinner, with grey streaks in his hair. He stood to survey the court, then took his seat when the Lord President addressed him. Yet his haughty dignity was undercut dramatically at the outset: as the Commonwealth's solicitor was about to speak, Charles thrust his white staff against the solicitor's shoulder two or three times to gain his attention. The silver knob fell from his staff and rolled a short distance on the floor. There was a pause; the king waited. At last, he understood that no one would pick it up for him. There was a moment of throttling tension, until he slowly stooped and reached for it himself. The symbolic meaning of the episode was lost on no one.

It is by no means certain that all the court officials intended to execute the king; some may just have wanted Charles to recognize the people as sovereign. Charles understood that if he acknowledged the court's power to try him, it would be an admission that power resided with the people. This he would not do, although given repeated opportunities. Instead, he warned, 'Remember, I am your King, your lawful King and what sin you bring upon your heads; besides those other judgements you bring upon the land. Think well upon it, I say, think well upon it, before you go from one sin to a greater.'[19] Every day of his trial he kept his hat firmly on his head in defiance of the court's authority and refused to answer any questions, claiming that no earthly court had authority over a divinely appointed sovereign answerable only to God. In his own way he was as deft as the Earl of Strafford had been in parrying the prosecutor's charges.

Charles even claimed to be upholding the rights of Englishmen by insisting on his right to be tried by lawful means: 'It was the Liberty, Freedom, and Laws of the subject, that ever I took – defended myself with arms; I never took up arms against the people, but for the laws.'[20] It was an argument liable to provoke derision. One of his judges, John Hewson, became so exasperated that he crossed the intervening space and spat in the king's face, calling for justice upon the traitor. The king drew out his handkerchief, wiped his face, and calmly replied, 'Well sir! God hath justice in store, both for you and me.'[21]

Between 20 and 27 January, when Charles was sentenced, he was brought four times to the bar. As he did not recognize the court, he was never allowed to speak at length in his defence. Finally, it was announced that the sentence would be read in the name of the people of England, at which point Lady Fairfax and another woman, wearing masks, caused uproar in the gallery by denying it was the will of the people, calling out, 'It is a lie . . . Not half or a quarter of them!'[22] Charles now realized the mortal danger he was in and tried to make himself heard, but it was too late. He was found guilty as charged: a 'tyrant, traitor and murtherer' and a 'public enemy to the Commonwealth of England'.[23] His panicky attempts to speak up were rebuffed. 'I am not suffered for to speak,' he shouted. 'Expect what Justice other People will have.' But he was led away, mocked by soldiers.

Charles was executed in the public street at Whitehall on 30 January 1649. A scaffold, draped in black, was built outside the Banqueting House, deliberately tarnishing an iconic site firmly associated with royal power. In an ironic twist, to reach the window that opened onto the scaffold, Charles had to pass under the glorious painted ceiling he had commissioned from Rubens to celebrate majesty. Cowardice was not one of his faults. It was a bitterly cold afternoon and he had asked for an extra shirt so that no one would think he shivered with fear when he took off his doublet for the executioner. He had a speech prepared, but a strong guard of several regiments of horse and foot encircled the scaffold to hold back the people; there was no chance that he would be heard when he firmly declared his innocence. London's hangman, Richard Brandon, had allegedly refused to behead the king and another had to be hired. The man's identity was never proved since both he and his assistant were disguised and wore black visors. Whether by design or because Brandon had withheld his equipment, the block was lower than usual and Charles had to lie prone, arms spread. Staples had been put into the scaffold to tie him down if he struggled, but there was no need to use them.

Charles gave the signal and the executioner swung his axe. As the king's blood spurted out, the crowd uttered a 'dismal universal groan'.[24] It was an unexpected reaction. Many pushed forward to dip handkerchiefs in the royal blood; soldiers saw a way to make money and set about selling relics of the king's hair and bits of blood-soaked wood. At the very point of his execution, the king became a martyr. But Samuel Pepys, who as a teenager was a sturdy Roundhead and had skipped school to see the execution, loudly quipped that were he to preach about the event, his text would be 'the memory of the wicked shall rot'. Later he would agonize that someone would remember his bravado and use it against him. The execution over, a troop of horse was ordered to proceed from Charing Cross to King Street, and another in the opposite direction, to scatter the people and prevent unrest.

Doubtless the king had hoped to live, but he had prepared for death. And, reasoning that the best way to secure sovereign power for his son was to die a martyr, he had already set about fashioning this image of himself. Just ten days after his execution, a book appeared that cemented the myth of his martyrdom: *Eikon Basilike*, or 'image of the king', evoked sympathy for the royal victim and outrage against his killers. Ostensibly the reflections of Charles awaiting trial and execution, it was in fact written by his chaplain. It was an astounding piece of propaganda that seemed to offer a glimpse into the king's private thoughts; all could relate to the fears he expressed for his children. It presented the dead king as a second Christ, a martyr holding fast to his beliefs, and contained his final prayers. It also included noble advice to his eldest son, which may even have been a factor in bringing about his son's restoration. The book went through fifty editions in just twelve months. Parliament's Council of State worried that it might subvert the new Commonwealth and turned to Milton to write a suitable riposte. With the monarchy and House of Lords abolished, Milton was proving a useful tool for the new republic: during the trial of Charles I he wrote *Tenure of Kings and Magistrates*, arguing on the title page that, 'It is lawful . . . for any who have the power, to call to account a Tyrant or wicked King and after due conviction, to depose, and put him to death.' The work was published on 13 February 1649 and a month later the Council of State appointed Milton Secretary for Foreign Tongues with accommodation at the Scotland Yard end of Whitehall.

Milton's efforts in the service of the republic were heroic in view of his failing eyesight. He had resorted to frantic measures to stave off blindness – including 'seatoning', recommended for chronic headaches and inflammation of the eyes, which involved piercing the skin just below the hairline and passing a hot cautery with a diamond point through holes, then a needle with thread dipped in egg white and rose oil. This and other standard remedies, including bloodletting and violent laxative purges, left him utterly miserable.[25] Even so, he published his answer to *Eikon Basilike* in October. Its title, *Eikonoklastes*, or 'image breaker', is meant to suggest the destruction of superstitious belief. Milton tried to show that the carefully crafted self-portrait of Charles as sainted martyr was hypocrisy, and that readers who allowed themselves to be moved by the picture of the king at his prayers were just a credulous herd. His book incensed royalists. By 1650, Goldsmiths Company officials making routine searches to ensure members sold no defective goods were finding 'pictures of the late King Charles' alongside small heart boxes, thimbles and napkin hooks.[26] The image of his martyrdom would endure.

9

CROMWELL
A KILLJOY REGIME?

The months after the execution of the king offered Londoners nothing but confusion and disappointment. Parliament voted to abolish the House of Lords and proceeded to do away with the monarchy altogether, passing legislation to make England a republic. Common soldiers were billeted in mansions confiscated from royalists. Women were still demanding a political voice. To use a phrase much repeated at the time, London was 'the world turned upside down'.[1]

In the spring of 1649, Cromwell smashed the Leveller contingent in the Army: he was no believer in wholesale social revolution. 'You must cut these people in pieces,' he is reported to have said, 'or they will cut you in pieces.'[2] When a regiment of dragoons sympathetic to the Levellers' cause mutinied in London, their ringleader Robert Lockyer was court-martialled and shot outside St Paul's. His funeral provoked a mass demonstration: thousands followed the coffin to Bethlem Burial Ground, their hats decked with ribbons of sea-green, the colour of the Levellers. But their support was now confined to a small section of the London populace. Royalist newsbooks gloated that London had merely exchanged one kind of tyrannical rule for another, but City merchants welcomed this clear signal from Cromwell that he would be a protector of property. In gratitude they gave him and Fairfax a splendid feast. Yet both men remained wary, always travelling with an escort of some 300 troops. Fairfax did not lift his guard on London's gates until October.

Cromwell spent the next eighteen months quashing rebellion in Ireland and Scotland. The Scots had recognized the Prince of Wales as their king and Cromwell's military campaigns culminated in the defeat of the 'King of the Scots' at Worcester on 3 September 1651. Charles's escape by hiding in an oak tree after the battle, then travelling to the coast in disguise, became the stuff of legend. He joined his mother, Henrietta Maria, at the Château de Saint-Germain-en-Laye west of Paris, where she kept a royalist court in exile. Cromwell's triumphant re-entry into London on 12 September seemed to mark a new beginning. He avoided the flamboyant display associated with monarchy – he rode in a coach, for example, rather than on horseback. But in his own mind he surely linked his proud return, marked by volleys of gunfire from troops at Hyde Park Corner, with the victory processions of Roman emperors. Charles I's great art collection had already been put up for sale to help meet parliamentary expenses, but Andrea Mantegna's nine canvases known as *The Triumph of Caesar*, showing Julius Caesar entering Rome in a chariot after a victorious campaign, were among the works Cromwell kept for his own use.

London was central to how the Roundheads projected the new republic. One of parliament's early diktats was the removal of the king's arms from all public buildings and their replacement with the Commonwealth arms. European powers had reacted with horror at the execution of a king, but pragmatism prevailed and foreign ambassadors soon fell over themselves to be received in London, struggling with the new forms of address that the 'Parliament of the Republic of England' demanded, and reconciling themselves to having all statements translated into English since the new parliamentarians were unfamiliar with diplomatic niceties and understood few languages. (The blind Milton was much in demand for Latin translation.) Rival ambassadors, anxious to make a fine display when entering the capital, noted with regret that their processions were much truncated under the new regime as noblemen chose to stay away.

Cromwell with his army now held a central position between the Levellers on the one hand and conservative Presbyterians on the other. The man of the moment, he still had to work through the Rump Parliament in session, which now began a programme of reforming measures to underpin the regime and deter revolt. But war with the Dutch – long bitter trade rivals – broke out in May 1652 and the extra cost and administration took a heavy toll on the Rump, already accused of corruption. Tensions increased between MPs and the army, which was calling for faster reform; Cromwell saw that if he was to keep his vital military support he would have to act against an unpopular parliament. On 20 April 1653 he dissolved the Rump and later installed a chosen assembly. Horse and foot regiments were marched towards London to maintain calm.

The parallel with Charles I's attempt to imprison Pym and bend parliament to his will was not lost on Londoners. Still, most seemed to welcome the prospect of more efficient government and, if they did not, they had no force to match the army. Meanwhile, Cromwell curried favour with the masses by visiting churches with a large Bible under his arm. The Venetian ambassador reported that Cromwell had declared publicly that God, who had granted all his victories in battle, had directed him to make this change in government.[3]

According to the moderate lawyer, Bulstrode Whitelocke, Cromwell had long despaired of the Rump ever doing God's great reforming work. The previous November, while the two were walking in St James's Park, Cromwell had burst out, 'What if a man should take uppon him to be King?'[4] Whitelocke was against the idea, reminding Cromwell that he already had as much honour and power as a king, and risked alienating the army. In 1653, with the Rump gone, Cromwell reassured people that he intended no military dictatorship. But when his new assembly tried to push through reforms, it only spooked conservatives into thinking it was about to introduce a social revolution that would destroy all privilege and property rights. The assembly and its supporters also proved intolerant of fellow Protestants, the Presbyterians. Some members were equally anti-army. Reluctantly, Cromwell saw that he would never achieve his aims for the Commonwealth with this group. The assembly jumped before it was pushed and handed power to Cromwell in December, just five months after it had been set up.

On 16 December, Cromwell was installed in London as Lord Protector. It was a curiously lacklustre ceremony, invented for the occasion. Cromwell, who deliberately wore a sober black suit and cloak, travelled from Whitehall to Westminster in his coach, accompanied by dignitaries and a military escort. He took his oath of office in the Court of Chancery, where he received the Great Seal for authenticating state documents, and the lord mayor presented him with the City Sword. He then returned it, gesturing towards some form of partnership. The Protector had a council of twenty-one and ruled in accordance with a constitution, the 'Instrument of Government', drawn up by Major-General John Lambert, commander of the army in the north. Yet Cromwell's power was based on the rights of a conqueror: while the basis of the new constitution was rule by a single person with a parliament, it contained clauses that showed a distrust of parliaments and plainly infringed parliamentary liberties. Notably, the new Council of State had the right to exclude elected MPs at the beginning of each session, and the Protector and Council could legislate in intervals when parliament was not sitting. Cromwell was no longer called 'Your Excellency' but 'Your Highness'.

Some Londoners now consciously saw their city leading the nation to greatness. Attitudes towards the new republic were naturally influenced by two contemporary republics: cosmopolitan Venice, a byword for wealth and magnificence, although its power was waning, and the Dutch republic, growing ever more powerful through trade. Even the writer James Howell, a conservative royalist, was captivated by the commercial ambitions of Cromwellian rule. He published *Londinopolis* in 1657, drawing parallels between London and other world trading centres. Referring to Venice, he declared, '*London* may claim as much interest in the *Sea* as she, if regard be had to *Maritime* Dominion and Naval power.'[5] As for the Dutch, he cheerfully noted that although Amsterdam had perhaps tripled in size thanks to trade with the Indies, London must be more populous: Bills of Mortality indicated that about 300 died there every week. Those not born to landed wealth or high office saw opportunities to grow rich in a thriving commercial society; an emerging national myth of maritime domination would in time help to bring together a fractured populace. Meanwhile, London's rituals were adapted to grease the wheels of the republic's new political system.

There were continuing debates about the power of the City. One contemporary assertion, which Howell did not explicitly deny, was that the independence of London's powerful livery companies had undermined royal power. 'And though there be some, who hold such Corporations, and little *Body politiques*, of this kind, to be prejudicial to *Monarchy*,' he wrote, 'yet they may be said to be one of the *Glories of London*, and wherein she surpasseth all other Cities.'[6] London's pageant dramas had long carried the message that the privileges of the City complemented royal power for the benefit of all citizens. During the Civil Wars, when civil administration had been infiltrated by radical elements, the Lord Mayor's Show and other civic displays had not been held. Now Levellers continued to attack livery companies. Was election to civic office fair? Should not all citizens vote, rather than just privileged liverymen, who had risen by wealth not merit? Why did companies admit foreigners prepared to work for lower wages? But powerful companies could charge immigrants a hefty admission fee and were not inclined to listen. The tide was in any case receding from further social upheaval; with the connivance of the Protectoral government, the traditional City elite recovered much of its former power. In this climate the livery companies dared to resume their pageantry and again take their benevolent civic message to the masses. First, they invited Cromwell to a banquet at Grocers' Hall.

Cromwell took up the invitation weeks after his investiture, deliberately choosing Ash Wednesday for his entrance into the City to show his disapproval of the traditional fast day, which for Puritans was a relic of the Catholic faith. He orchestrated the event to imply that, as Protector, he humbly represented the people he served, the source of his legitimacy. He again wore subdued civilian clothes, travelling to Temple Bar in a convoy of coaches for another ceremonial exchange of the City Sword. Then he mounted a superb horse and, with the lord mayor riding before him, sword in hand, rode in procession to Cheapside. There were no triumphal arches. Official reports stressed the approval of enthusiastic crowds lining the streets; private accounts indicate that spectators were either aghast or hostile. John Evelyn noted in his *Diary* for 8 February 1654, 'Ash Wednesday. In contradiction to all costome and decency, the Usurper Cromwell feasted at the Lord Maior's, riding in triumph thro' the Citty.' The Venetian ambassador later claimed that a great stone had been thrown from a window, smashing the roof of Cromwell's coach, narrowly missing his head. It was the reason, he said, why the Protector had never shown himself in London since.

The Lord Mayor's Shows duly resumed – their symbolism toned down to indicate a forward-looking change in the political state and in City governance. In 1655 the Mercers staged a pageant featuring a young woman wearing luxurious materials, drawn in a chariot by six white horses. Musicians played fifes and drums, but there was no spoken drama.[7] The pageant was well received, so in 1656 the Skinners revived the full communal performance, reasserting the independent power of the City within the state and representing its officials as the champions of prosperity. These civic performances signalled London's increasing stability and confidence, but disaffected observers sneered at a City that courted a usurper. Lucy, wife of Colonel Hutchinson, one of the regicides who had signed Charles I's death warrant only to lose favour with the Protectorate, claimed that hypocrisy had become an 'epidemicall disease'.[8]

Cromwell's London homes matched his rise to power. In 1651 he moved his family from Drury Lane to the Cockpit near the palace of Whitehall, where he was given rooms after victory at Worcester. As Protector, he lived in Whitehall Palace itself, spending weekends at Hampton Court, where he occupied the splendid apartments that had been decorated for Henrietta Maria. This gave him the option of adopting the formal French court etiquette she favoured, although he shared rooms with his wife Elizabeth, departing from the royal custom of maintaining separate suites. In this retreat he played bowls and hunted, on one occasion even entertaining the Swedish ambassador, who spoke fluent English.[9]

The rich tapestries of Charles I went to Hampton Court, as did the Diana Fountain at Somerset House, commissioned by Charles for his queen. Cromwell also kept Charles's classical (pagan) statues for the gardens at Whitehall and Hampton Court, much to the disgust of strict Puritans who would not recognize that he had to match the prestige of international courts. Works of art not sold in the auction of the king's pictures now decorated Cromwell's palaces, and he retained other items for personal use, including the king's padded, red velvet close-stool.

In January 1657, Cromwell's supporters begged him to take the crown. There is evidence that he rather wished to do so, but soon realized that, if he did, he would lose the support of the army on whom his power depended. He already enjoyed greater powers than any English king had ever possessed, so he rejected the royal title while accepting a new constitution prepared for him. Even so, his investiture as Lord Protector at Westminster on 17 July 1657 was blatantly monarchical in tone: he sat in a sumptuous chair raised on a dais beneath a rich canopy; he wore ermine and was given a sword and sceptre (although not a crown). Royal symbols helped to define and legitimize his rule; the military aspects of his first installation were toned down. Still, the Venetian ambassador judged that most Londoners disapproved. 'It all went off rather sadly,' he noted, 'without spontaneous shouts of joy.'[10] Cromwell's new status was proclaimed throughout the City and suburbs, just as new sovereigns had been under the monarchy, but the customary slick organization was lacking.

As Protector, Cromwell ruled three kingdoms (England and Wales long having been regarded as one), but he never again left the environs of the capital. At Whitehall and Hampton Court he echoed royal ritual, and soon court spending was at least as high as in the time of Charles I.[11] The court continued to set fashions: the more prominent members of the new regime, like Major-General Lambert, even adopted the cultured lifestyle of the nobility. But committed royalists derided what they considered to be the bourgeois house-keeping of Cromwell's wife, never comfortable in her new role. Lucy Hutchinson also mocked the Cromwells for aspiring to the dignity of a royal family. Riches suited them no better, she claimed, 'than scarlett on the Ape'. Yet she was honest enough to add that Cromwell 'had much natural greatness in him and well became the place he usurp'd'.[12]

LONDON UNDER CROMWELL

The Venetian ambassador considered Cromwell's rule was military despotism. In 1652 he reported that the grandeur of the Stuart court had vanished utterly, while Cromwell had the first and last word. London was perfectly tranquil, he wrote, because the army was paid on time and tightly disciplined. He omitted to mention clashes between soldiers and civilians, inevitable when troops were used to collect taxes and enforce reform, closing alehouses on Sunday. Still, army officers were quick to reassure Londoners by making a public example of disobedient soldiers. Typically, in 1654, two were nailed by their ears to the whipping post at Charing Cross for taking bribes.

Security arrangements in London tightened whenever there was a royalist threat. In August 1651 householders were ordered to detail the weapons they held and give the names of their lodgers. Lists were made of horses owned. Soldiers often collected this information and were ready to seize disaffected people speaking ill of the regime. In 1656, Robert Plumstead, a victualler in Fulham, was accused of assault and of alleging that both his victim and the army were 'murthering rogues, that they had murdered their King, and that theire hands were soe dipt in blood they could not wash it off'.[13] In this atmosphere of suspicion many lived in fear. Letters were intercepted and read, passports were needed for foreign travel, and even female travellers might be searched for treasonous letters.

Puritans had long pushed for moral reform. Already, in 1644, parliament had banned maypoles and fairs, the remnants of folk culture associated with immorality. It advised citizens to spend Christmas in contemplation not feasting. It banned theatres in 1647, because plays inflamed the emotions and could sway public opinion. In 1650 the Rump enacted a law against cursing and swearing, a law enforcing strict observance of the Sabbath, and a Toleration Act repealing compulsory attendance at a national church, so Dissenters could worship freely. It also approved a Blasphemy Act, aimed at suppressing radical sects, and the infamous Adultery Act, which punished an adulterous woman and her lover with death. But contemporary double standards meant that a married man who committed adultery with a single woman faced just three months' imprisonment, the offence being equated with fornication. In practice, the death penalty was rarely carried out and the Act was mostly used to coerce reform. Inevitably, it proved a tool for disgruntled spouses and suspicious neighbours. If some thought the Act would help to clean up their neighbourhood, many more resented it as a snooping, repressive measure used to terrorize people.

Cromwell sincerely believed that he was an instrument of God, called to establish a 'godly reformation' in England that would bring the full benefits of God's mercy. His thinking was influenced by the Old Testament story of the Israelites who, by taking God as their guide and purging their sins, escaped Egyptian bondage and emerged from the wilderness into the promised land. Once made Protector, Cromwell banned crowd events such as cockfighting and bear-baiting, and re-enforced laws against drunkenness. Whenever there were national setbacks and military defeats, he blamed them on England's sinfulness and immorality, offensive to God. At such times the number of alehouses in London was more rigorously controlled, while gaming houses and brothels were suppressed with renewed rigour. Cromwell genuinely wanted moral reform but restrictions on public assembly were also useful security measures.

Women faced new constraints. Many had been radicalized by the Civil Wars: they had shouldered the responsibility of nursing the wounded, seen their menfolk die, been left to run households. They had joined marches and petitioned for peace; many continued to protest during the Interregnum. On 27 October 1651 they presented 'The Women's Petition' to Cromwell on behalf of 'many thousands of the poor, enslaved, oppressed and distressed men and women in this Land', calling for an end to imprisonment for debt and bluntly claiming that the king's death had not ended tyranny. The response was typically dismissive. But Quaker women turned the concept of the weaker sex on its head, claiming in 1659 that women's status made them fitter handmaids of God when they petitioned against church taxes. Leveller wives seeking their husbands' release from prison organized petitions signed by thousands. The spiritual equality preached by sects emboldened some women. Levellers' wives never claimed to be inspired by God but did believe that they played a part in the struggle for liberty. In their 1653 petition to get the charismatic John Lilburne released, they reminded parliament of women's contribution, 'who did think neither their lives, nor their husbands and servants lives and estates to be too dear a price for the gaining of yours and the Nations ancient Rights and Liberties out of the hands of incroachers and oppressors'.[14] But in standing up to Cromwell, they alarmed the ruling classes.

A counter-movement tried to put women in their place. Gender hierarchy dictated that men had rights over women's bodies and some men were outraged by the way women dressed and wore make-up. In 1650 parliament debated whether to pass an Act against 'the Vice of Painting and wearing black Patches, and immodest Dresses of Women'.[15] The bill did not make it into law but had some popular support. In 1654, John Evelyn noted rather belatedly that women had started to paint their faces, 'formerly a most ignominious thing & used only by prostitutes'.[16] The Puritan obsession with sexual promiscuity was also reflected in a crackdown on all forms of 'nightwalking' – aimed at removing prostitutes from the streets and shutting down brothels as well as reducing crime. This clean-up benefited from curfews imposed whenever there were security alerts. The 1650 Adultery Act also targeted prostitution: bawds and brothel-keepers were to be whipped, branded on the forehead with a 'B', and imprisoned for three years. Re-offenders could be hanged. In London, action against prostitutes increased during the years 1651–3, but magistrates tended to impose the traditional sentences, whipping offenders and imprisoning repeat offenders for short periods. In 1656 a new tactic was tried: soldiers rounded up over 400 prostitutes from London's brothels and shipped them out to Barbados.[17]

Cromwell's rule became more authoritarian after January 1655, when he dismissed his second parliament, which had also proved intolerant and averse to the army. Now Cromwell ruled alone, although he still took advice. He strengthened measures against Christmas celebrations, adamant that excess prompted immorality. From 1656 people were told to work on 25 December; shops and markets were to stay open and soldiers patrolled the City streets, seizing any festive food being prepared. Churches were ordered to close, so people had to observe the day at home. These measures were deeply unpopular: the Venetian ambassador reported in 1657 that Londoners closed their shops as usual. Clerics conducted services according to the Book of Common Prayer in private houses. On Christmas Day 1658, John Evelyn and his wife attended a service in the chapel of Exeter House on the north side of the Strand. Members of the royalist elite met there regularly in a form of dignified political protest, so it was an obvious place for soldiers to check out. As the vicar began to administer the Holy Sacrament, troops surrounded the chapel and arrested the congregation. That afternoon, high-ranking army officers came from Whitehall to interrogate individuals, but after making threats, they allowed the communion to proceed and released the worshippers, unwilling perhaps to ignite popular protest. Although anxiety clouded Christmas celebrations, New Year's Day and Candlemas Day on 2 February were resoundingly kept as festive seasons.

The regime enforced censorship in the battle to win wholesale public support, but royalists had access to the printing presses, daring to circulate bawdy songs that mocked Cromwell's efforts at moral reform. Much nonsense was presented as 'news' to suggest a surreal world that had lost its grip on reality under Cromwell. But Cromwell made sure that communication from the pulpit was tightly controlled. In a diary entry for 14 March 1652, Evelyn noted angrily that it was 'now a rare thing to find a priest of the Church of England in a parish pulpit, most of which were fill'd with Independents and Phanatics'. Cromwell issued ordinances to ensure that the regime oversaw appointments to church livings, with the result that most ministers were Puritans.

Cromwell vowed that he worked for nothing but 'liberty of religion & freedom of trade'.[18] But he never championed wholesale religious toleration.

Catholics were still persecuted: ambassadors from Catholic countries were told not to allow Catholic Londoners to attend mass in their houses. The multiplying sects were also regarded as a threat to public order: in October 1653 a riot broke out in St Paul's when Presbyterian apprentices tried to eject rival worshippers. Troops quelled the fighting but there were deaths and injuries. Afterwards guards were posted to prevent such scenes. The Venetian ambassador reckoned in 1656 that there were 246 different Protestant religions in London, all incompatible, so none were powerful enough to threaten Cromwell's rule. Nehemiah Wallington was staggered by their number and thought they would prompt God to destroy England. Cromwell had no wish to alienate those with conservative, Presbyterian sympathies and so welcomed the curb on religious freedom introduced in the constitution that he accepted as Lord Protector in 1657.

There were almost constant royalist plots. Most were badly planned, as if none of the king's supporters dared to commit wholeheartedly, but this intrigue created an atmosphere of tension and instability. Cromwell travelled in a heavily armoured carriage with a military guard whenever he went by land to Hampton Court. On more than one occasion assassins lay in wait; others planned to kill him when he took the air in Hyde Park. But either Cromwell chose an unexpected route or other circumstances forced conspirators to abandon each attempt. The year 1654 saw an eruption of royalist plots, the work of a powerful group called the Sealed Knot, but it failed to keep its plans secret. In July 1655 royalists were banished from living within twenty miles of London. Most obeyed, but typically some bragged that 'a London jayle with frinds and drinke' was a better prospect than life in the country.[19] Cromwell faced more danger in 1657 when a disgruntled soldier conspired with others to set fire to the Chapel Royal under his chamber in Whitehall. A would-be assassin confessed before the materials ignited. Cromwell's spymaster, John Thurloe, controlled an efficient secret service that easily foiled most plots, and some Londoners suspected that plots were fabricated as an excuse for sudden arrests and harsher security.

Troops were always out in force on state occasions but also for parliamentary elections. In 1656 passions ran high at the Westminster hustings; Cromwell tried to get his preferred candidate elected by intimidation, posting soldiers at voting places. Two people were killed and many injured. Londoners were also appalled at high-profile cases of arbitrary justice. When the royalist minister Dr John Hewett was convicted of treason in 1658, Evelyn recorded that Hewett was 'condemned to die, without Law, Jury, or Justice, but by a mock Council of State as they calld it. A dangrous, tretchrous time.'[20] Evelyn himself had reason to be fearful: a firm royalist, he continued to correspond with Prince Charles in exile.

But the Interregnum also brought positive reforms. Parliament sanctioned an overhaul of London's poor relief as part of an initiative to clean up the capital. The sick and elderly were housed in charitable institutions, soldiers' widows and orphans were supported, able-bodied vagrants were put to work. The education of children was made a priority so that they could contribute to the Commonwealth as adults. London's infrastructure received attention: the postal service was improved, highways repaired, and action was taken against polluting the Thames. Apprentices and servants were given one day off a month to compensate for the loss of religious holidays, and Jews were more openly tolerated. This last measure may have been stimulated by the common belief that the conversion of the Jews would herald Christ's second coming, or else encouraged by the evident prosperity Jewish magnates had brought to rival Holland. That said, a community of Jews had lived in London for many years, outwardly conforming to Christian worship.

London was still a magnet for luxury consumers and the war was followed by a spending spree. The royalist Henry Oxinden, for example, came up from Kent to buy dress fabrics, a watch in a silver case for his sister, and a pearl necklace for his wife. In the early 1650s the Venetian ambassador complained that wealth was now in the hands of a class of men more used to hoard than to spend, so that shopkeepers suffered, but by the end of the decade people were spending more freely. Despite Puritan abhorrence of sumptuous fashions and long hair for men, the ruling classes continued to dress stylishly and many – including Cromwell – wore their hair long as a mark of rank. Wigs for men became increasingly fashionable in the 1650s. Perukes allowed men to disguise baldness, grey hair or symptoms of venereal disease. Hair was also easier to keep lice-free if cut short beneath a wig. One indication of London's regeneration was traffic congestion, which became so bad that in 1654 Cromwell passed an ordinance restricting hackney coaches to 300 in number.

The fashionable social round in London continued alongside military occupation; there was still fun to be had. In 1654, Evelyn reported that Mulberry Garden (near Buckingham Palace) was 'the onely place of refreshment about the Towne for persons of the best quality'.[21] It had a bowling alley, fruit trees and pleasant walks. Yet the wealthy flocked to Hyde Park during good weather, parading in their best clothes, and on May Day there was a profusion of coaches to be admired in the park, status symbols in themselves. Coach races took place there by 1658 and horse races also drew crowds. Young people enjoyed open-air suppers in London's parks, though such pleasures drew moral censure from some. Cromwell's court was never closely associated with these activities and parks were closed during security scares, but his daughters rode in a coach in Hyde Park.

How much impact did Cromwell's godly reforms have on daily life? Londoners remained strongly attached to traditional festivals, sports and drinking. The capital's great fairs were still held, and 5 November was celebrated enthusiastically: in 1652, Evelyn stayed with friends as it was too dangerous to travel home that evening, 'the insolensies there were so greate in the streetes'.[22] Wrestling matches in Moorfields and Lincoln's Inn Fields were still popular, and in town there were bowling alleys, tennis courts and shuffle boards. Alehouse culture was so engrained, so interwoven with trading practices, and beer so important in the diet of the poor, that reform of alcohol consumption was at best patchy. There were prosecutions for cockfights, indicating that the sport went underground. Cromwell was more successful in enforcing the Sabbath, which many observed anyway; parish constables readily fined people for working or travelling without licence on the Sabbath, both of which were banned. But Cromwell himself enjoyed a drink with close advisors, and sometimes smoked tobacco. He took pleasure in music, which was a feature of his court. Puritans may have abhorred church music, but paid music gatherings emerged in London, livery companies continued to have music at events, and there were private performances in people's houses.

Ironically, the Commonwealth edict for the sale and dispersal of the king's pictures stimulated the arts. The cash-strapped parliament gave some masterpieces to creditors and servants in lieu of wages, and this brought ordinary people closer to great art; those who received pictures often sold them on, contributing to a growing art market. Lucy Hutchinson recorded how her husband visited London to buy up choice works. The king's embroiderer, Mr Harrison, was noted for having several of the king's paintings at his home by the Thames, at a wharf near Landsel House.[23] Continental artists were soon attracted to the capital and copyists reproduced great paintings, increasing patronage of the arts. Artists also experimented with print techniques, which attracted the interest of amateurs. There were growing numbers of print sellers and proof printers in London, so a print market developed alongside the art market and increasing numbers of prints were exported.

Many royalists, exiled on the Continent, had visited artists, palaces and architectural sites they might not otherwise have seen, taking notes and sketching. On their return, this experience influenced the decoration and furnishing of their houses, and their collecting of precious objects, books, prints, manuscripts and curiosities. As John Evelyn's *Diary* shows, in London and its environs, the elite enjoyed visiting private collections to see objects as various as fine porcelain and rare monkeys from the East Indies.

The Interregnum is noted for its closure of London's theatres. And the interiors of the Fortune, Cockpit and Salisbury Court were demolished in 1649, leaving only the Red Bull in St John's Street, Clerkenwell, offering low-brow performances. But acting persisted. Despite intermittent raids, the Red Bull staged 'drolls' or simple pieces, and even the comic scenes of existing plays. There was acting at fairs and taverns, often alongside entertainments such as rope dancing. Evelyn marvelled at one performer in 1657 who danced on a high rope blindfold, with a twelve-year-old boy tied to one of his feet some twenty feet below him, 'dangling as he daunced, & yet moved as nimbly, as it had ben but a feather'.[24] Acting companies also continued to stage plays in private houses. And if popular drama was feared for its ability to stir passions or mask subversive activity, operas exploited a loophole in the law. The playwright and poet William Davenant is credited with devising the first English opera, which he got past the censors by claiming that its moral representations would lift the public mood and turn minds from possible sedition. His *Siege of Rhodes*, first acted in a private house in 1656, even included a female actor, Catherine Coleman. In 1658 the piece was staged at the Cockpit, now refurbished, a truly lavish spectacle that delighted the eye and ear.

Some classes of tradesmen still found life hard, even if luxury shopping at the New Exchange had revived and overseas commerce was taking off. Nehemiah Wallington complained in 1653 about oppressive taxation and 'dead trayding in this citie'.[25] Wages for labourers certainly increased in the 1650s but were eroded towards the end of the decade when poor harvests led to inflated food prices. And all Londoners suffered during the winter of 1658–9, the coldest in living memory, when Evelyn was shocked to see crows' feet frozen to their prey and dead fish and fowl enclosed in islands of ice on the Thames. In the battle for daily survival most Londoners adjusted to political reality and made the best of such security as the Commonwealth offered. For some, too, the negative effect of repression at home was counterbalanced by admiration for Cromwell's military achievements: his quelling of rebellion in Ireland and his victories against European powers.

CHANGES TO THE FABRIC OF LONDON

Key sites in London were marked by recent, terrible events, helping to preserve the memory of the king. The place of Charles's execution outside the Banqueting House excited a frisson of superstitious fear; there was a vacant space where the Cheapside Cross once stood, 'utterly destroyed by the fury of the *long Parliament*', as one royalist put it.[26] Scarred walls in livery company halls showed where, under pressure, their members had removed the royal arms. Some Londoners continued to frequent taverns where radical discussions had taken place, nursing their memories of Leveller demonstrations.

As Cromwell applied himself to public office, he and his advisors developed protocols to enact the new republic. The fabric of London was essential to this process: in its search for legitimacy the regime made ceremonial use of London's public spaces and buildings. Cromwell used the Banqueting House to receive foreign ambassadors in ceremonies that became increasingly royal. There was a suite for ambassadors at Somerset House; other dignitaries were lodged in the houses of royalist noblemen that had fallen vacant and been taken over by the state. In July 1658, for example, the Dutch ambassador was lodged in Derby House, which stood in today's Canon Row near Parliament Square. Westminster Abbey was early appropriated by republic and Protectorate for ceremonial use, including state funerals, usually with a more martial aspect than under the monarchy. In consequence, St Paul's was deliberately neglected, used for stabling horses and quartering troops, though churches were not desecrated as part of a regular programme. Its south transept vault collapsed in 1654, killing several people. John Evelyn exclaimed, '*England* is the sole spot in all the world, where, among *Christians*, their *Churches* are made jakes, and stables, markets and Tipling-houses.'[27]

The character of Westminster changed. It became more central to government than under the Stuarts simply because parliament sat for longer. There were more government committees, and as town houses close to parliament came under state control they were used to accommodate them; most of these large houses had once been owned by royalists. Along the Strand, too, the state confiscated numerous royalist mansions. Some were handed over to parliamentarian peers whose country properties might have been plundered. Others provided space for official business: William Lenthall, Speaker of the Commons, was lodged in a succession of furnished town houses. Large residences were needed for soldiers, and might even be seized for that purpose, their noble gardens soon overrun and neglected. At least most Londoners were spared the ordeal of having troops forcibly billeted in their homes.

Westminster became more militarized. After Sir Thomas Fairfax entered London in 1649, the army quartered a garrison in Whitehall and another in the royal Mews at Charing Cross. Parliament and Whitehall were a greater security risk than the City, which had walls and gates that could be defended. A disproportionate number of royalists lived in Westminster, where they had once been near the Stuart court, so it was natural to think that it was a hotbed of conspiracy. The army was therefore a major presence and source of harassment at Westminster, especially when plots were detected. A semi-permanent standing battery, together with an artillery train, defended Whitehall, and after an attempt to assassinate Cromwell in 1654, ten pieces of ordnance were installed near his Whitehall residence. Westminster was full of the noise of troops being drilled. The Venetian ambassador complained in 1656 of 'the ceaseless noise of drums and trumpets, and numerous companies of officers and soldiers at their various posts'.[28] At the same time the Royal Menagerie in St James's Park fell into disuse; instead Cromwell's wife kept a dairy there. Yet because Cromwell had appropriated

Whitehall Palace, it survived with little change. In 1656, John Evelyn was relieved to find it 'very glorious & well furnish'd, as far as I could safely go'.[29]

Almost no aristocratic mansions were built during the Interregnum, but London's expansion did not totally cease. The Earl of Salisbury acquired houses in Newport Street and leased them to an entrepreneur who rebuilt them in brick for the well-to-do. The Earl of Clare continued building around popular Clare Market, which met three times a week to sell meat and vegetables. Royal parks were sold off to help fund the Commonwealth, and ramshackle housing mushroomed in these open spaces. Given assassination fears for Cromwell, this unwelcome development prompted an official order in 1654 to repurchase the royal parks and clear them for Cromwell's use. In 1657 a law was passed prohibiting new building within ten miles of London, but some developers obtained exemptions. A fashionable new scheme began at Lincoln's Inn, and a development in Hatton Garden took shape. In 1659, Evelyn went there to see the foundations for a long street and buildings, inspired by fashionable Covent Garden. The Earl of Southampton also began to build himself a new mansion in Bloomsbury to replace one damaged by the building of London's defences during the Civil Wars.

The strain of keeping a lid on the various factions within the capital took a heavy toll on Cromwell. His power depended on the army, which had to be kept occupied, yet people associated the army with radicalism and resented the heavy taxation needed to pay for it. As early as 1655 the Venetian ambassador reported that Cromwell looked ill and drawn: 'I noticed that as he stood uncovered the hand holding his hat trembled.'[30] But if Cromwell's health was failing, he did not lose his firm sense of purpose.

10

THE UNCERTAINTIES OF WAR
AND COMMERCE

Robert Blake, Cromwell's heroic General at Sea, destroyed the Spanish treasure fleet at Tenerife in 1657 only to die on the voyage home as his flagship entered Plymouth Sound. Blake had never recovered from a thigh wound received years earlier and, in this last campaign, had lived for months on broths and jellies as his fleet kept a dreary winter blockade off the Spanish coast.

The general's body was embalmed and carried to London by sea after the bowels had been buried separately in the Plymouth parish church of St Andrew. The body reached the Thames on 17 August and lay in state in the great hall of the Queen's House in Greenwich until 4 September. Then it was taken by barge upriver to Westminster in a stately procession, accompanied by trumpet fanfares and cannon fire. Finally, it was carried into the Abbey, ranks of soldiers keeping back crowds of spectators. Cromwell attended the funeral, alongside government and military leaders, and members of Blake's family. Soldiers fired three volleys in salute as the body was lowered into a vault beneath the Henry VII Chapel; a year later it would be joined by Cromwell's corpse.

Victory at Tenerife meant that the English fleet was now feared far and wide. The extravagant ceremony of Blake's funeral was a public symbol of the navy's new-found status. Soon the maritime identity of London's eastern districts, on both sides of the river, would become strongly identified with English sea power and the future of the nation on the world stage. The dramatic growth of London's suburbs eastwards was already a talking point: Shadwell, mostly wasteland in 1600, boasted some 3,500 residents by 1650 and continued to expand into neighbouring pastureland. The maritime districts were susceptible to fires. In 1657, John Evelyn reported an explosion in Wapping, across the river from his home in Deptford, that 'shooke my whole house, & the chaire I was sitting & reading in [in] my study'.[1] He thought a ship had deto-nated, but the explosion proved to be caused by a single barrel of gunpowder in a chandler's shop in Ratcliff. Maritime industries and warehouses rose phoenix-like from the ashes, with wider streets and substantial buildings replacing tangled alleyways.

These riverside parishes were places of distinct odours, sounds and experi-ences. The smell of tar hung on the wind, the sound of water slapping against wood was never far away, and roads were deeply rutted by straining teams of horses carting loads of massive timber. A sense of movement was at the heart of maritime London, as ships sailed upriver with the tide to unload goods, then departed downriver again. The mental horizons of its inhabitants also stretched across oceans – to the New World, where increasing numbers of kinsfolk lived; and to the East, where seafarers searched out cargoes of spices, indigo and luxury fabrics on a seasonal cycle of trading voyages.

After Charles I was executed, the Rump Parliament immediately set about expanding the navy. The army may have secured victory for the Roundheads but only a loyal navy could defend the new republican regime. Warships were needed to defend the country from the invasion of hostile continental powers and to convoy merchant ships, threatened by royalist and other privateers. To help pay for naval expansion, parliament raised taxes, which in 1649 stood at a staggering eighteen times the pre-war level.[2] By June 1651 the Venetian ambas-sador was reporting that England had eighty fine warships and that the fleet could be increased to 200 sail by taking over merchant ships.[3] Parliament ordered warships and naval dockyards to fly the new Commonwealth flag; a similar order was put in place for merchant vessels. Sensing that the navy was a key propaganda tool for the regime, it also renamed warships: the *Charles*, for example, became the *Liberty*.

The Commonwealth's naval strategy brought some prosperity to the welter of ropeworks, cooperages, breweries, shipyards and warehouses along the Thames waterfront. It also meant new hardships for poor labourers, working to tight deadlines on government naval contracts or enduring wartime shortages. The river offered exciting spectacle but also glimpses of cruelty: Scots prisoners, captured at the Battle of Worcester, were kept in hulks before being shipped to New England or the West Indies; convicts were now routinely transported to the colonies where labour was in short supply. For seafarers, just passing through, London's waterfront was a place of transit to be compared with wharves and quays in other towns and cities; they offset feelings of rootlessness by performing the same rituals of carousing and wenching whenever they set foot ashore. Their labour was ruthlessly and often violently harnessed by merchants and the state. Market forces also meant that increasing numbers of seamen were used to enslave Africans in the transatlantic slave trade, although many sailors were reluctant to voyage to Africa, fearing the climate.

London had mostly financed the plantations and had a population large enough to set trends in the consumption of novel products from the colonies; it took the greatest share of England's colonial trade. London merchants might even own land and slaves in Virginia, as did Arthur Bailey, a major importer of sugar and tobacco who lived just north of Wapping.[4] Many Puritans, targeted for their religious beliefs, had emigrated to the New World, so hundreds of Stepney families had links there. These connections greatly benefited long-distance trade, which depended on bonds of trust, not least to obtain credit; colonial trade ended up in the hands of a few powerful families, many of them Dissenters.

Merchant and shipowning families in the eastern suburbs exploited their connections to gain influence. They worshipped in the same independent churches and intermarried. For example, Thomas Rainsborough, who played a prominent part in the Putney Debates, came from a shipping family in Wapping and was connected by marriage to Nehemiah Bourne, a merchant and shipowner whom Cromwell later employed as a naval administrator. Bourne had emigrated to Massachusetts but returned during the Civil Wars to serve in Rainsborough's regiment. Prominent merchant families also sought power through the Corporation of Trinity House, responsible for pilotage on the Thames. It was independent of the City, being governed by a court of Elder Brethren under a Master, and at this period had its headquarters in Ratcliff.

The Civil Wars caused a dip in London's maritime trade, but the underlying trend was healthy: between 1640 and 1663 England's exports doubled.[5] London's privateers, expensive to fit out, did not make huge profits in the wars but at least kept seamen in work. Even so, in the aftermath of war, merchants were troubled: the East India Company found it hard to raise money, obtain ships and sell luxury imports, though religious fervour hardly affected luxury consumption in the longer term. Royalist privateers still attacked English shipping, which also faced competition from the Dutch. The Dutch had made peace with Spain in 1648 and were set to dominate the carrying trade: their roomy, lightly crewed ships transported goods more cheaply than heavily armed English cargo vessels. Some London merchants happily used Dutch carriers themselves; all they cared about was the bottom line. Others were affronted that the Dutch prospered at the expense of English interests and lobbied government to protect trade.

Parliament could see that London shipping was vital to the nation's economy and that seamen and merchant ships were needed to support the navy. It passed Navigation laws in the early 1650s to confine the colonial trade to English and colonial ships, and to funnel all trade to and from the colonies through England. In this period the English mercantile system became entrenched: all agreed that the role of government was to protect trade from rival nations and to maximize the value of exports, thereby increasing national wealth. But in May 1652, just as London's overseas trade was beginning to pick up, a minor altercation with a Dutch warship in the Channel tipped parliament into declaring war on the Netherlands. Ministers hoped to strike a blow that would damage England's main trading rival. Strangely enough, given that the Netherlands was a Protestant country, some diehard Puritans even regarded the war as the beginning of a godly campaign to defeat the Catholic powers of Europe.

The First Dutch War impacted heavily on London's merchants: taxes were already high, and war disrupted trade. In August 1653, for instance, merchant ships were forbidden to leave the Thames without permit for fear they would be captured by the Dutch (and to ensure they were available for naval use). Imported provisions became scarce as the Dutch patrolled the sea lanes; cloth exports faltered. Cromwell inherited an impressive force of 160 warships when he was made Lord Protector that December but saw that trade was suffering and wanted peace. His view did not endear him to religious extremists, but he brought the war to an end in April 1654. Fortunately, London merchants had been able to buy an enormous number of captured Dutch ships from English privateer and warship captains. The English merchant fleet was now more balanced than ever before, comprising both heavily armed ships and carriers for bulk cargo.

Cromwell continued the Rump's policy of building a powerful naval force because it was essential to the security of the Commonwealth. The Navy Commission was responsible for building and supplying ships; it replaced the Navy Board during the Civil Wars and operated from headquarters in Mincing Lane, near the Tower. Cromwell proclaimed that all men who served in the military for one or two years would be free afterwards to exercise any trade in London or elsewhere. This attracted apprentices into the navy who were unwilling to be bound for seven years and liked the idea of joining any company they pleased.[6] Next Cromwell had to find something for the navy to do. In December 1654 he ordered an attack on Spanish possessions in the West Indies. The venture suffered major setbacks, although his forces did manage to capture Jamaica. War with Spain followed, in which English shipping suffered heavy losses, especially from privateers operating out of Dunkirk and Ostend – two ports under Spanish control. Other factors reduced the tonnage available for trade: the English captured few enemy vessels in this new war to compensate for losses; the navy absorbed seamen and merchant vessels; shipyards along the Thames were building warships not merchant ships. Unsurprisingly, both freight rates and the cost of insurance shot up.

The letters of London merchant John Paige, who during the Interregnum dispatched ships to five continents and often advised government on trade, show the mindset that enabled men to weather such turbulent times. He was intentionally reticent: 'In these dangerous times,' he wrote, 'it's good for men to be circumspect and cautious of what they say.'[7] Paige dealt in 'old trades', as an importer of wines and exporter of fish, but he also did business in new colonial trades, which took off mid-century despite England's troubles. Involved in the sugar trade, he was also an East India merchant and a broker of American fish, sugars, hides and dyestuffs. The range of his business interests reflects London's position at the centre of an expanding shipping industry.

By 1656 a new Venetian ambassador was astounded by the activity in the port of London: 'Ships frequent it in such numbers that on my arrival more than 2,000 were counted up and down the famous River Thames,' he wrote.[8] Aside from oceanic trades, merchants imported heavy silks and currants from Turkey; rice, brimstone, oil and silk from Italy; wine, fruit, oil, salt, tobacco, wool and hides from Spain; iron and wools from the Bay of Biscay; and sugar, salt and cinnamon from Portugal.[9] Most ships were still smaller than 200 tons, but Londoners would have noticed a striking increase in large ocean-going ships, particularly for the East Indies trade. Vessels bringing timber from Norway and the Baltic also towered above others in the river. The re-export trade mushroomed: in fifty years from 1638 to 1688 England's combined export and re-export trade grew three or four times in value despite several wars.[10] The leading re-export was sugar, and the sugar trade centred on London.

Chartered companies had monopolies, but private traders did their best to ignore these rights; during the Interregnum, parliament did not protect monopolies, so interlopers had a field day and their numbers grew. The masters of London's merchant ships were often owners or part-owners of ships (it was usual to spread risk by dividing the property of a ship into sixteen or thirty-two shares). In international trades, masters earned 120 shillings a month but could supplement wages by private trade and became expert at doing so.[11] Later in life, ship masters came ashore and often set up as merchants or shipowners themselves, trading to ports where they had trusted agents. This was true of Captain Thomas Bowrey, who spent eighteen years criss-crossing the Indian Ocean before marrying a London apothecary's daughter and setting up house in Well Close Square, Wapping, a location popular with sea officers. Afterwards, he managed the affairs of a group of ships that he part-owned, exploiting his knowledge of the Indies, and ran a profitable china shop in Mansell Street near Goodman's Fields, buying stock from importers of ceramics. Parts of Wapping were improving: the area around Cato Street would be paved in the 1690s. But many merchants and sea captains preferred Clapham, where the air was cleaner and housing cheaper.

London's poor and vulnerable reaped the negative effects of global trade. Many were kidnapped or lured on board ship and 'spirited' away to the colonies where plantation owners were desperate for labour. In 1655 a woman called Christian Chacrett was accused of being 'a spirit', someone who took up men, women and children and sold them on board ship to be taken overseas.[12] She had lured a young family to the riverside and put them on a ship called the *Planter* sailing for Virginia. London kidnappers could make a tidy sum because they had no overheads. Convict labour gives a sense of the money to be made: convicts sentenced to eight years in the plantations were reckoned on average to be worth £13 15s. each, but merchants who bought them had to bribe prison officials and pay £100 surety that convicts would not escape.[13] There were never enough convicts, so it is not surprising that merchants and ship captains encouraged kidnappers. There were related crimes: rogues caught people and just threatened to ship them overseas, extorting payment for a release. In 1656, Judith Danie accused a seaman of 'Violently assaulting and beateing of her and for impresting her for Jamegoe [Jamaica] with a pretended warrant and then takeing 12d. to discharge her'.[14] In the 1680s the Lord Chief Justice finally cracked down on the practice of snatching young people from the streets. Those down on their luck, emigrating from choice, afterwards signed a contract with ship captains or merchants to prove they were leaving voluntarily.

Colonial crops demanded intense physical labour and, from mid-century, created a profitable market for enslaved Africans. Slavery was soon central to the economies of Barbados and Jamaica; tobacco planters in Virginia depended on enslaved Africans from the 1680s, although other English colonies in America had few until the early eighteenth century. London merchants were quick to enter the transatlantic slave trade and during the seventeenth century they controlled England's involvement in it. The Guinea Company (founded in 1618) engaged in slaving after about 1640 to provide Barbados with cheap labour. Numerous private traders were also drawn to the trade in the hope of large profits. We find John Paige and his partner planning to ship 300 Africans from Guinea to sugar-cane plantations in Tenerife in 1651. Their captain, William Pyle, flatly refused to go, complaining that had he known the destination he would never have signed up, that Guinea was too dangerous, that enslaved Africans might rise up and slit crewmen's throats, and that anyway most of his thirty-strong crew had already absconded. When Pyle's wife also appealed against the 'unhealthy' voyage, Paige found another captain, but the voyage ended in disaster. Having obtained a cargo of Africans, all his senior officers died before reaching the Bight of Biafra; the ship then ran aground and was lost. Most of the Africans survived and thirty were sent to Tenerife; the remainder were sold to other English ships at a loss. Paige was left to sort out complicated costs and threats from the widows of fourteen dead seamen who swore they would come with their children to his doorstep to appeal for their husbands' wages. His letters show that he cared more about personal embarrassment and the dent to his reputation at the Exchange than about the terrible human cost of the failed voyage.[15]

The Guinea Company folded in 1657, unable to contend with pirates, Dutch rivals and private traders. But London's role in the slave trade gathered momentum and even gained royal backing. Charles II would boost the trade at the Restoration in 1660, granting a royal charter to the Company of Royal Adventurers of England trading into Africa (later the Royal African Company). Guinea gold was the initial attraction, but the Company's trade in captive Africans was formally recognized by 1663. Interlopers who broke into the trade were also mostly based in London. The brutality of slaving captains was such that about 25 per cent of Africans chained below deck died on the voyage, even though the Company ordered great care and only paid for those delivered alive.

Meanwhile, London's black population increased as foreign trade expanded. Merchants, particularly those engaged in privateering, had kept black servants in their households since Tudor times. Wealthy residents in Westminster now set a fashion for them. To the east, in riverside districts, there were more African seamen working in English ships; south of the river in Deptford, where the East India Company kept a shipyard until 1644, there was a sizeable Asian community: Lascars, sailors from Asia, helped to bring East Indiamen home when their original crews were struck by high mortality rates but were not allowed to crew on the outward passage. If the Company neglected to repatriate Lascars, they settled and married local women.[16]

It is no surprise to find some merchants suffering from depression. Directions for brewing a tonic to guarantee mirth were carefully preserved among the accounts of the merchant Thomas Wood, who dealt in the West and East Indies trades: 'If sorrel be infused in whey & then boyled a little it becometh good phisicke against melancholy clenseth ye braine & purgeth it.' The remedy also worked, he noted, against old fevers and all diseases caused by melancholy.[17] Wood placed his agent, John Pack, in a property he owned off Thames Street. Pack's duties included managing the family account at the local apothecary, whom Wood may have helped to supply with foreign drugs. Anxieties apart, Wood enjoyed a comfortable lifestyle: his domestic accounts show that he kept a carriage, commissioned portraits of his children, bought fine wainscot for his drawing room, and ordered four periwigs at a time.

Overseas trade created thousands of jobs along the Thames, changed the contours of riverside building, transformed streets and squares further inland, and promoted London's greatness. Foreign trade also began to create new, visible centres of power in the capital. In 1648 the East India Company moved to Craven House, a mansion in Leadenhall Street. By 1661 its governing board had the confidence to install a wooden structure across the facade of the building to show paintings of Company ships. Above this towered a large, wooden sculpture of a seaman. The headquarters of the Royal African Company, Africa House, were first established on Broad Street; both buildings became hubs for extensive national and international networks of agents and outposts. The two companies also loomed large in the public consciousness. The East India Company gained a reputation for bringing strange animals to London. John Evelyn was one of many to be captivated by these arrivals. He went to see 'a sort of Catt' (actually a type of lemur): 'It was of a wolly haire as a lamb, exceedingly nimble, & yet gentle, & purr'd as dos the Cat,' he wrote.[18] In time, menageries sprang up over London, just one facet of a spirit of enquiry spurred by foreign trade that served to enhance its prestige.

SAILORS AND SHIPWRIGHTS

East of the Tower, thriving shopkeepers and wealthy merchants lived close to the desperately poor because maritime businessmen valued access to the river more than a fashionable address. Sometimes elite locals were troubled by signs of poverty. John Evelyn noted that it was all very well for his father-in-law to give Trinity House some of his land in Deptford to erect almshouses (where seamen's widows would be lodged and receive 5s. a month) but he would have done better to relieve the poor already in the parish.[19] Evelyn had settled in Sayes Court on his father-in-law's Deptford estate in 1652 to protect it from parliamentary encroachments. It was close to the naval dockyard and swathes of its timber had already been surveyed for naval purposes in 1650. But Evelyn was interested in the navy and came to see the planting of trees for building warships as a patriotic duty; he published *Sylva, or a Discourse of Forest-Trees*, which encouraged many landowners to start planting. He also had sympathy for seafarers.

At the outset of war with the Dutch in 1652, parliament issued warrants for the impressment of seamen. At once, sailors went into hiding. To get warships to sea in that summer, the Privy Council authorized Trinity House to summon sailors from riverside hamlets 'by beate of Drum' and then impress 300 when they appeared.[20] A census was also taken of Thames watermen and many were forced into warships. In Deptford any well-dressed stranger was soon suspected of being a 'press master'. When a Mr Penny enlisted two local constables to help him impress sailors, the constables, being poor men and unwilling to displease their neighbours, secretly gave local seamen warning so that they could not be found.[21]

In January 1653 the government introduced a new naval pay scale, raising the wages of able seamen from 19 to 24 shillings a month. This failed to attract men into the navy: the money was less than they could earn in merchant ships and naval pay was generally late. By February the Venetian ambassador was reporting that sailors deserted at the first opportunity 'and the whole navy displays a mutinous spirit'.[22] As national security now depended on the fleet, parliament approved increasingly brutal measures to bring it up to strength. One mutineer who refused to serve and threatened to set fire to his ship was executed immediately. This so infuriated others that many seamen deserted overnight to the Dutch, who at least paid crews on time. The morale of men who stayed loyal was hardly improved when in 1653 one of parliament's new thirty-gun frigates went to sea in a stiff breeze and promptly keeled over, drowning all 200 on board. In this manning crisis 1,500 sailors were pressed along the Thames at the beginning of March, leaving maritime communities angry and frightened. These communities were further disrupted by the arrival of impressed men from other ports. In February 1653, for instance, officials in Yarmouth sent eighty pressed men to Deptford, needing to be fed and housed.[23]

By April 1653 the government was impressing seamen as they came into port, giving them no chance to see their families. Such was the need for experienced sailors that press gangs also seized men from colliers coming into London. The government lacked funds, so sailors were kept at sea all year to avoid paying them off; they began to lack clothes as well as provisions. When the wives of unpaid seamen – who lived by borrowing and other makeshift activities while their menfolk were away – reached the limit of their credit, families faced destitution. Wartime prices did not help. In April 1653 when the Dutch and Danish blockaded the collier fleet in Newcastle, the price of coal tripled in London. Such was the state of government finances that, after the Battle of Scheveningen in July 1653, an appeal was made in churches for donations of linen for bandages, needed for wounded seamen just landed.[24] Whenever crews were paid off, they were mostly given tickets – effectively government IOUs – to be drawn on the treasurer of the navy. Sailors who needed cash in hand were forced to sell their tickets to dealers at ruinous discounts. Discontent grew.

In October 1653 sailors at Chatham mutinied, demanding their pay and prize money. They deserted their ships and, armed with swords and pikes (some even with firearms), they assembled at Tower Hill and marched on Westminster. A party of them happened to chance upon Cromwell, out walking with General Monck near Whitehall. Monck drew his sword and fought them off, wounding a few. The following day the mutineers came out in force. The Council of State feared insurrection and, according to the Venetian ambassador, sent 1,000 foot and some troops of cavalry against them. There were clashes at Charing Cross: one seaman was killed and many wounded. The ringleaders were caught, and the boldest was accused of attempting to kill Cromwell with a firearm and promptly hanged. A proclamation was made at the Exchange and at other prominent places in Wapping and Ratcliff, warning that if seamen persisted in the mutiny they would be put to death. The hanging took effect and sailors returned to their duty. In parallel, the Council put in place measures to relieve the widows and orphans of seamen, employing both carrot and stick.[25]

Yet disturbances continued as seamen fought impressment, and worse followed. After war with Spain was declared in October 1655, unpaid seamen were sent to fight leaving families starving at home. Many dreaded the voyage to the Spanish West Indies and had to be dragged from their houses by soldiers. In this tense atmosphere popular belief in witchcraft, still entrenched, was put to blatant political use. Elizabeth Newman of Whitechapel, whose husband had been impressed by soldiers, was accused of taking revenge on the captain of the Tower Hamlets' Trained Band by bewitching his wife and children. Brought to trial, she was found not guilty, but the captain was a prominent lay preacher of the Independent faction and loyal to Cromwell. She was retried, found guilty and hanged early in 1654.[26] Women were particularly fierce in resisting press gangs. In Shadwell, Alice Bent, a seaman's wife, struck Captain Valentine Jowles in the face, drawing blood, calling him 'a rogue and a horse-turd' for serving the Protectorate.[27] Her abuse shows how alienated from Cromwell some communities now were, and how badly let down they felt by a government that had promised liberty.

Seamen could hope that prize money or plunder might augment their meagre pay. When they made their wills before a long voyage, as they often did, they had little to leave their families beyond wages owing and any share of prize money that might come to them. Warrant officers, such as gunners and carpenters who stayed with the ship when it was out of commission, had better opportunities and pilfered goods. Gunners might try to keep back barrels of gunpowder, which they could sell in London at the end of a voyage. When the *Marmaduke* docked at Deptford in June 1657, the naval storekeeper found five barrels of gunpowder on board, which the gunner had hidden for his own benefit but been unable to get ashore.

War with the Dutch meant that the eye of government turned firmly on London's maritime districts. Here, outside the City, law enforcement was notoriously loose, and several authorities now tried to address the morals of seafaring communities. In July 1655 the vestry of St Dunstan's in Stepney enforced stricter observation of the Sabbath. It set up a cage and stocks in the churchyard and warned 'idle & disorderly persons' who spent Sunday loitering in the streets or lolling about in churchyard grounds that prompt retribution would follow.[28] Constables in Wapping tried to prevent seamen visiting prostitutes, but with little success.[29] Aware that many in these radical districts hankered after the republican regime that Cromwell's Protectorate had replaced, officials took measures to prevent disorder. They encouraged informers, taking swift action against sedition and even loose talk. One Whitechapel resident was prosecuted for possessing 'a scandalous and trayterous paper of verses against his Highnesse the Lord Protector' and being the suspected author, while a mariner was indicted for speaking 'scandalous and abusive words' about Cromwell.[30] While the murder rate was high in maritime parishes, some godly folk were outraged by the severe sentences meted out for lesser offences.[31]

War, almost continuous in the 1650s, impacted directly on Thameside dockyard workers and their families because the building of warships advanced at a breakneck pace, Sundays included. Large warships had to be built in the naval dockyards since they were too big for private yards. During the Interregnum forty-five ships over 500 tons were ordered, ten of them from Deptford dockyard.[32] Naval shipwrights and caulkers, who had the dirty job of sealing a ship's hull with old rope and tar, could be 'pressed' to work away from home in another dockyard, depending on pressure of work. As encouragement, in 1652, shipwrights' pay was temporarily increased from 2s. to 2s. 2d. a day, while by the end of that year caulkers were being offered 3s. a day.[33] But pay rates had little meaning if, as in 1657, wages were six months in arrears. In dockyards injuries were common and men toiled in all weathers. In January 1665, Jonas Shish, assistant master shipwright at Deptford, explained to the naval commissioners that the ice was so thick in the wet dock, no ship could be launched; in the summer old canvas was rigged up as protection from the sun.[34]

All master shipwrights in naval dockyards had their own private shipyards, where they might build small-sized warships for the state. There was a glaring conflict of interest: often they were charging the state for ships built with materials and even labour appropriated from naval dockyards, which the state had already paid for. Whenever naval expenditure was high, senior dockyard employees rose to affluence. The extended Pett family of shipwrights, who at various times ran Deptford, Woolwich and Chatham dockyards, had a powerful network of patrons and cronies that enabled them to brush off accusations of corruption. Christopher Pett, who became master shipwright of Deptford and Woolwich, would even complain about the meanness of his salary at £103 8s. 4d. a year.[35] Doubtless he felt justified in making money on the side. But if the Petts excited fear and envy, Jonas Shish, who took over at Deptford on Christopher Pett's death in 1668, was down to earth and liked. He served in the vestry at the local church, St Nicholas, willingly helped with the work of an ordinary shipwright in the dockyard, and spent his evenings in the tavern, smoking and drinking with his assistants. John Evelyn noted that Shish could barely read and could give no lucid explanation of his methods, although he was able to build good warships. But if, in Evelyn's terms, Shish was 'illiterate altogether', he signed his name with a flourish in the vestry minutes.[36]

Naval expansion during the Interregnum brought work to Deptford, as it did to other dockyard towns, while along the Thames waterfront shipyards were busy with small vessels and refits. Deptford dockyard was enlarged and improved under Cromwell: it was paved, a mast dock and three wharves were added, and a wooden crane house was ordered in 1655. The dockyards were England's biggest industrial sites, although workforces fluctuated with peace and war. In 1660, Deptford dockyard had 278 workers and a weekly pay bill of nearly £115, pumping the modern equivalent of many thousands of pounds annually into the local economy.[37] The dockyard underpinned much of the business activity in the area, including timber merchants, ironmongers and sailcloth suppliers; it also sustained the shopkeepers and craftsmen who furnished dock workers with food and clothing. Several businesses with naval contracts were run by women. In 1661, for example, we find a Mrs Browne, 'plumberess to the yards at Deptford and Woolwich', demanding payment.[38] The community also profited illegally: theft in the dockyards was endemic, partly because wages were paid so late. Wood, iron, cables and even anchors were all embezzled from the stores; a black market in stolen goods helped to sustain the local economy. Between the 1630s and 1660s, Deptford's population doubled to 5,000 but, because the prosperity of the town depended on naval work, whenever the fleet was scaled back, deprivation followed.[39]

ENGLISH SEA POWER

The warship building programme in the 1650s was an important step towards developing a navy that could give battle without the support of merchant ships. England's naval infrastructure also became more efficient, as did the operations of Trinity House. Some outstanding naval commissioners emerged, like Nehemiah Bourne, but if such men were driven by Puritan zeal, they happily used their personal connections and standing in the community to line their own pockets. Bourne, for example, championed the use of mooring chains in the Thames, which were newly invented and used to secure vessels three-deep. Shipowners paid different rates for various anchorages, with Blackwall being the most expensive at 15s. a week – a sign of its growing importance as a victualling point for outbound vessels. In 1658, Cromwell granted Bourne and two colleagues the right to levy mooring charges for twenty-one years, in return for maintaining the chains.[40] It was a profitable sideline: there might be no money to pay seamen but while government credit held good, naval administrators thrived.

Ship launches became regular events that helped to raise the profile of maritime districts. When one of parliament's early frigates was launched at Deptford in 1650, MPs came downriver in five barges to watch. John Evelyn was a grudging spectator at these events, writing in 1652, 'I saw the *Diamond* & *Ruby* Launch'd in the Dock at *Deptford*, carrying 48 Brasse Cannon Each; Cromwell & his Grandees present.'[41] Under the Protectorate, new warships were named after parliamentarian victories: *Marston Moor, Dunbar, Naseby*, linking the regime to England's growing command of the seas. Evelyn went to the launch of the *Naseby* at Woolwich in 1655. The ship was a large first-rate with 80–86 guns, and he noted that the ship's figurehead was a clear propaganda statement: 'In the *Prow* was *Oliver* on horseback, trampling 6 nations under foote.'[42]

Cromwell's Commonwealth owed its international reputation to naval power. Naval victories against Spain also revived English ambitions for naval dominance, overtly encouraged by the elaborate funeral given to Robert Blake. This spirit of regeneration was captured by Andrew Marvell, whose celebratory poems helped to bolster Cromwell's regime. In a tribute to the first year of the Protectorate, he applauded English seafarers, 'Theirs are not ships, but rather arks of war', and he portrayed Cromwell as an expert helmsman steering the ship of state to safety.[43] English sea power was celebrated in popular art forms: the satirist Ned Ward would note that 'scarce can a Royal Ship be sooner built and launch'd from the Stocks, but straight we have ten thousand Pictures of her, drawn and dispers'd around the Island by some or other topping Dawber of Sign-Posts'.[44]

If growing sea power raised the national importance of London's maritime districts and encouraged regulation there (Shadwell residents would soon be prosecuted for throwing rubbish into the Thames), seamen themselves prompted a mixed public reaction.[45] On the one hand they were national treasures; on the other they were berated as unreliable marriage partners. The ballad *A Mad Marriage; or, the Female Fancy of Debtford* offers a cautionary tale that would have helped to colour perceptions of life in maritime parishes: a servant girl is abandoned by her sailor lover who sailed to the Indies after he had promised marriage and 'by consent rummidgd her hold', leaving her pregnant.[46] She needed a marriage certificate to convince the man's mother to take her in, and begged her mistress to dress as a man and marry her to get one. The cheat worked, the priest taking a bribe to antedate the certificate. But the women brought trouble on themselves, revealing the secret when they had drunk too much brandy, and were imprisoned before trial. The ballad may be complete fiction but contains enough circumstantial detail to reveal something of street life in the riverside parishes.

Expanding trade offered London's seafarers new opportunities. Merchant sailors were quite well paid and promotion to officer status opened a route to higher social rank that was simply unavailable to rural labourers. Ship masters might retire with enough money to set up a shop or small business, especially if they married well. Or they might become shipowners like Bowrey. But sailors without means needed patrons and luck to become ship masters; Edward Barlow, who left a journal about his long career at sea from 1659, worked hard for promotion but only made it to chief mate. Ordinary seamen who left the sea often found jobs as riggers, ship watchmen, or porters on London's quays.

The state could build up the navy because it had introduced permanent taxes and could borrow on the strength of secure revenues. This fiscal innovation would survive the collapse of the Commonwealth after Cromwell's death in 1658. The feeling that it was England's destiny to be a great sea power also endured: its navy would protect trade, make the nation wealthy, and secure the precious liberties of the people. This was the message expressed in art, literature and even the Lord Mayor's Show, when City livery companies took care to represent overseas trade as the natural and essential activity of an island nation.[47] By the end of Cromwell's rule, England was recognized, and feared, as a great naval power, and London seemed positioned to take advantage of trading opportunities all around the world.

11

COFFEE-HOUSE CULTURE
NEWSPAPERS AND GOSSIP

During the troubled years of the Interregnum, key questions surfaced about contemporary society that seemed central to the country's future. One political commentator made a list of them. He included dysfunctional government, London's rapid expansion, and the relationship between individual liberties, Church and State. To guard against prosecution, perhaps, he put frivolous questions among contentious topics. He suggested, for example, that the learned College of Physicians should examine newfangled drinks like coffee, chocolate and tea to determine whether they agreed with English constitutions. He concluded by reflecting on the mess that England had got itself into: 'Whether it be not strange news that the *English men* have almost all lost their way in their own Country? and whether the several guides they chose to direct them, have not brought them into a wood that they have now work enough to enquire one of another how to find the way out.'[1] Beneath his merriment lay a serious message: in a bewildering and divisive age, citizens had to work together to sort the mess out themselves; there was no point in relying on tarnished political leaders. Although he only mentioned coffee as a new fad, oddly London's burgeoning coffee-house culture turned out to be crucial in the search for a way forward.

London's first coffee house opened in 1652. Merchants and their close associates trading with Turkey were among the first to be seized with the coffee-drinking habit in England. The merchant Daniel Edwards returned mid-century from Smyrna (Izmir) bringing a Greek servant called Pasqua Rosee to prepare the drink for himself and his family. Some say Edwards tired of giving out free coffee at his premises each day, when acquaintances turned up just as it was being brewed. He certainly saw a business opportunity and set Rosee up in a shop where he could sell the drink. This first establishment was little more than a shed, but centrally located in the churchyard of St Michael Cornhill, at the heart of London's financial district. Rosee proved an energetic entrepreneur and soon produced a handbill, *The Vertue of the Coffee Drink*, promoting coffee for alleged medicinal effects. He claimed it was good for digestion and headaches, that it prevented miscarriages in pregnant women, cured gout, dropsy, scurvy, and (more credibly) that it quickened the spirits.

Alehouse keepers in the City saw competition and complained that Rosee, no freeman of London, was not qualified to trade. Rosee was forced to go into partnership with Christopher Bowman, a servant of Edwards's father-in-law and free of the city. Their business thrived and in 1656 moved to a nearby site now known as 3 St Michael's Alley, although afterwards the two men went their separate ways, Rosee being forced to leave London after some unexplained offence. Other coffee houses were quick to open. By the end of the decade, Thomas Rugg, a Covent Garden barber who used them as a 'market place for news', wrote that practically every street had one, and a survey by City Magistrates in May 1663 recorded eighty-two in the City alone.[2] For the price of 1d., customers of any rank could take a dish of scalding hot coffee and read the papers (though a pipe of tobacco and fireside seat cost 2d. extra). All were welcome, so long as they could pay; someone at the door would take note of those who left without settling their bill.

Coffee needed complex roasting and grinding, so it was difficult to prepare at home and initially struggled to gain popularity. Suspicious onlookers variously compared the boiled concoction served in coffee houses to muddy water and syrup of soot before the addictive properties of caffeine won converts, especially among the business and intellectual elite.

Before the advent of hot, non-alcoholic drinks, most Londoners were daily inebriated to a greater or lesser extent. Untreated water from wells and conduits was, quite rightly, judged dangerous to drink, so people of all ages drank beer (children were served weaker, 'small beer'). John Evelyn, fresh from his continental travels, described the effect of alcohol on the English character with evident distaste. The English were boorish, lacked conversation, and were absurdly rude to foreigners. A heavy drinking culture permeated all social levels. Even ladies of quality were happy to be treated in a tavern to Spanish wines and other liquors:

'they drink their *crowned Cups* roundly, strain healths through their *Smocks*, daunce after the Fiddle, kiss freely, and tearm it an honourable *Treat*'.[3] Business deals were routinely concluded over a pot of ale. Still, the advantages of drinking coffee and keeping a clear head soon became apparent: 'For whereas formerly Apprentices and Clerks with others, used to take their mornings draught in Ale, Beer, or Wine, which by the dizziness they cause in the Brain, make many unfit for businesse, they use now to play the Good-fellows in this wakefull and civill drink.'[4] Puritans especially valued coffee houses as non-alcoholic places of debate and decent talk compared to other public spaces such as theatres, which were renowned for lecherous conversation.

Coffee soon transformed the social habits of the middling sort. Tea and chocolate were still quite expensive, although chocolate (prepared with milk, sugar and egg yolks) was acknowledged to be a hearty and nourishing drink; Samuel Pepys once drank his morning draught in chocolate as a hangover cure. Why did coffee catch on so quickly? By chance, coffee houses satisfied a growing range of urban needs. For one thing, most Londoners lived in rented accommodation, often without facilities for easy entertaining. But now businessmen need not be embarrassed about a shabby address. They simply gave clients the name of their coffee house, where they could be found at regular hours or where letters could be left for them. This early form of 'hot-desking' supplanted any comparable use of alehouses and taverns, not least because coffee was cheaper at a time of rising beer prices. As one convert enthused, 'A Tavern reckoning soon breeds a Purse-consumption; in an Ale-house you must gorge yourself with Pot after Pot, sit dully alone or be drawn in to Club for others' reckonings' (have to split the bill); but in a coffee house, 'for a Penny or two you may spend two or three Hours, have the Shelter of a House, the Warmth of a Fire, the Diversion of Company and Conveniency if you please of taking a Pipe of Tobacco, and all this without any Grumbling or Repining'.[5] Many coffee houses issued metal or leather tokens to compensate for the lack of small change, which helped to secure regular customers even before the Crown issued copper farthings in 1672.

Another advantage of coffee houses was that they freed users from the social constraints that normally governed polite conversation. Customers could make acquaintances without formal introduction, an openness that was especially welcome in a city with a high immigrant population. The historian and gossip, John Aubrey, whose pen-portraits of contemporary figures are a form of early biography, appreciated this. Before coffee houses, he wrote, 'men knew not how to be acquainted, but with their owne Relations, or Societies'.[6] And to drink coffee, an exotic import, was a mark of status. In a coffee house, customers felt themselves to be men of standing, at liberty to take centre stage whenever they had news or opinions to impart. The coffee-man flattered this sense of individual importance, striking an affected pose as he poured the liquid into each dish. Respected coffee houses not only signified a new openness to foreign influences, they also offered users an enticing identity as the kind of person who was up to date with current affairs, had need of a professional address, and might well be a member of a regular coterie that offered companionship and status.

Coffee houses were heavily clustered in the City near the Royal Exchange, where a network of alleys protected by overhanging buildings offered a good location for doing business, a use that increased after the Fire of London destroyed the Exchange in 1666. Coffee houses were also plentiful in St James's, near Westminster and the court, and on either side of Fleet Street and the Strand linking Westminster to the City; by now the Strand was mostly lined with three- or four-storey houses, many with shops.[7] Outside central London, alehouses outstripped coffee houses by far, but Wapping and the other suburbs did have coffee houses. Their clientele included not only merchants, scholars, wits and politicians, but also workmen and the less well-off, who acquired the habit of starting their day by reading the latest news. Some coffee houses sold more than coffee, offering tea, chocolate, and whey (favoured by those, like the natural philosopher Robert Hooke, who suffered from poor digestion). After the restoration of Charles II in 1660, others offered spirits but there remained establishments that prided themselves on exclusively offering non-alcoholic beverages. By the end of the century, the Marine coffee house in Birchin Lane was selling water-gruel before noon, while Shipton's, near Fleet Ditch, was selling jelly-broth to workmen from four o'clock in the morning.

Coffee houses were sometimes large but often modest affairs, occupying a first-floor room or part of a basement. They were simply furnished because clouds of tobacco smoke, combined with the smoke from coal fires, ruined fine decoration, just as it seeped into scented periwigs and troubled people with hacking coughs. Some premises were lit by oil lamps as well as candles, but a roaring fire, heating coffee in a great copper pot in the chimney, always gave a welcoming light. Walls might have a painting or two, but were mostly peppered with notices of all kinds, including for quack medicines. Dr Butler's Ale was still a popular purge available at Ned's Coffee House in Old Jewry, and various potions and restoratives were kept under the counter for sale, not least pills for rotting ulcers, running sores and venereal disease, usually promising desperate customers a safe cure without sweating or fluxing.

Early coffee rooms were furnished with large, communal tables that encouraged group conversation. Coffee-house keepers provided the newspapers *gratis* – both printed and manuscript, since the two kinds of newspaper coexisted. The *London Gazette*, printed from 1665, was the official organ of the state, but many thought manuscript newsletters, produced by a known compiler, more trustworthy. Coffee houses also displayed the myriad pamphlets that tumbled off the press and some even kept small libraries. Cards and chess might be offered. Polite forms of social behaviour were encouraged by default: coffee houses had open rooms, so customers had to learn to moderate their conversation lest it interfere with that of other groups; ideally people listened to a range of opinions and spoke in turn. Many coffee houses had bar women, usually selected for their looks in order to attract customers. The women lent a degree of ceremony to proceedings but were an easy target for male banter, being forced to endure unwelcome raillery since they could not leave their post.

Different coffee houses soon became associated with certain businesses and professions, although never exclusively. Will's in Covent Garden was favoured by the Wits: the poet and dramatist John Dryden had his own chair there, placed by the fire in winter and near the balcony in summer. From this comfortable seat he held forth to awestruck admirers. Will's, close to the King's Theatre in Drury Lane, was used by actors, including Thomas Killigrew, the actor-manager who in 1665 notably miscast Nell Gwyn in Dryden's *The Indian Emperour*, making her the emperor's virtuous daughter. In contrast, Garraway's in Exchange Alley, Cornhill, was linked to banking but also favoured by scholars like Hooke. The Young Man's coffee house near Charing Cross was the haunt of military types and notorious for gambling. The Grecian, first set up at Wapping

Old Stairs around 1665, moved to Devereux Court, Temple Bar, where it was favoured by lawyers and scholars. Famously, the coffee shop opened by Edward Lloyd, first in Tower Street then at the corner of Abchurch Lane, Lombard Street, became popular with merchants and shipowners, who used it to gather shipping intelligence, auction cargoes and report disasters. It grew into a maritime insurance brokerage, and Lloyd's flourishes in the City to this day.

London's growing commerce boosted the demand for coffee houses after the Restoration. But despite their usefulness as places for auctions, lotteries, stock sales and the exchange of news, they could not easily shake off their early association with republican and Puritan values – few could forget that the Nonconformist church leader, John Owen, had argued defiantly in 1659 that it was as lawful to kill a tyrant as it was to drink coffee.[8] This link, and the opposition of alehouse keepers to coffee-drinking, may account for some of the scare tactics used to get men to revert to taverns once Charles II became king. Coffee, it was said, made men effeminate and impotent: 'In this Age Men tattle more than Women, and particularly at the Coffee-house,' wrote one critic. Another author, supposedly female, accused men of losing all interest in sex, living instead for the coffee house where, dish in hand and a pipe at the nose, they puffed out offensive smoke, 'like a Brewers Stoke-hole'.[9]

Later criticisms of coffee-drinking, including *The Women's Petition* in 1674, repeated complaints that the drying effects of coffee and tobacco left men little better than eunuchs. But these ribald objections had a political basis and may not have been written by women at all. In an age of growing party politics, coffee houses became dangerously associated with rival political factions. Some were linked to those who supported parliamentary sovereignty; others to those who upheld divine-right monarchy. In 1679–81, when there was an attempt to exclude the Catholic James Duke of York from the succession, these groups were called Whigs and Tories respectively. Coffee houses around the Exchange were mostly aligned with Whig trading interests, but Jonathan's, in Exchange Alley, was accused of hosting a 'loyall, Tory-Rory, Drunken, Damming Meeting' where papists were present.[10] Garraway's was associated with Catholic plots. Partisan newspapers continually name-dropped coffee houses where the different parties met, so that these establishments became part of political life in the capital.

One undeniably feminist work, *An Essay In Defence of the Female Sex* (1696), criticized a certain type of 'coffee-house politician', who lodged at home but lived at the coffee house, addicted to political dispute.[11] Given the high price of coal and the severity of seventeenth-century winters, the source of female angst might have been that an absent husband meant less justification for a glowing fire in the domestic hearth. Women were not totally barred from coffee houses: Pepys took his wife to one in Covent Garden in 1668. Women are likely to have gone to auctions in coffee houses, especially to sales of books, textiles and lace. Some premises were run by women, usually widows continuing the family business. But the evidence for women visiting them is sparse and it is likely that respectable women patronized only the better establishments, and then merely at certain times of day when accompanied by their menfolk. Coffee houses were not necessarily safe spaces for women. Mary Watts, who met up with two men at the Bull's Head tavern in St Martin's Lane, testified in court that they robbed her after taking her to nearby Jones's coffee house. 'One of them stopp'd her mouth with his Coat-sleeve, and the other rifled her', taking a knife, fork and two shillings.[12] The men escaped punishment.

Despite criticisms, coffee houses were rapidly absorbed into London's commercial system: coffee was subject to excise tax from 1660, a move discussed as early as 1654. Merchants noted with approval that coffee-drinking stimulated the sale of other consumer goods, including tobacco, sugar and earthenware dishes. Marvels and monsters were displayed in some coffee houses: La Belle Sauvage on Ludgate Hill, formerly a coaching tavern, made a tidy sum from exhibiting a rhinoceros in the 1680s. Annual county feasts and society meetings were held in coffee houses, eventually leading to London's club culture. Some clubs formed in the seventeenth century. A club for duellists, for example, admitted none who had not 'fought his man'; it was a short-lived affair, most of its members succumbing to their fencing passion. The first notable club was the Rota Club, which met from 1659 at Miles's coffee house at the sign of the Turk's Head at New Palace Yard, Westminster. It had a large, purpose-built, oval table, with a square recess so that Miles could reach over to serve all members their coffee. At the Rota, the republican James Harrington propounded his ideal constitution, arguing that MPs should be replaced on a rotational basis by ballot to avoid the tyranny of permanent parliaments, and the club used a ballot box whenever members voted. Pepys was a member and recorded attending several lively debates. But when it became clear that Charles II would be restored, the Rota Club broke up: 'all these aierie modells vanished. Then 'twas not fitt, nay Treason, to have donne such.'[13] Members saw republicanism was doomed.

THE DARK SIDE OF COFFEE HOUSES

The popular conception of coffee houses today is that they were uniformly places of polite conversation, intellectual debate and sober business. But the streets of Stuart London were frenetic and filthy; many coffee houses were a continuation of this experience. The satirist Ned Ward described them as offering an assault on the senses, 'where a parcel of muddling muckworms were as busy as so many rats in an old cheese-loft; some going, some coming, some scribbling, some talking, some drinking, others jangling, and the whole room stinking of tobacco like a Dutch scoot, or a boatswain's cabin'.[14] He complained of being half-choked by stinking breaths. Standards of personal hygiene placed clean linen above bathing. Some – like Hooke – occasionally washed their feet for medicinal reasons and some – like Pepys – because their wives required it, but one advantage of tobacco smoke was that its pungent smell overpowered body odours.

In a city as varied as seventeenth-century London, it is not surprising that many coffee houses offered illicit opportunities. Ned Ward, who published *The London Spy* detailing 'the vanities and vices of the town' in monthly parts between November 1698 and May 1700, described one late-night visit to 'the Widow's Coffee-house' near St Paul's:

> We blundered through the long dark entry of an ancient fabric, groping our way like subterranean labourers in the caverns of a coal-pit, till we found the stairs, which were raised as perpendicular as a tiler's ladder, so that had I not had the use of a rope which was nailed along the wall, as a clue to guide me, I could have climbed a country maypole, or have crawled up the buttock-shrouds of one of Her Majesty's first-rate men-of-war, with less danger and difficulty.[15]

As the sexual innuendo implies, Ward's fictional characters had hit upon a brothel. Pasted on one wall was an abstract of the Acts of Parliament against drinking, swearing and profaneness. On another was an advertisement detailing 'the excellence of Doctor John Case's pills for the speedy cure of a violent gonorrhoea without loss of time, or hindrance of business'.[16]

For those in the know, coffee-house signs were coded: 'Where the Sign is Painted with a *Woman's Hand in't*, 'tis a Bawdy-House. Where a *Man's*, it has another Qualification; but where it has a *star* in the sign, 'tis Calculated for every Leud purpose.'[17] Coffee houses doubling as brothels were mostly in the Covent Garden area. Pepys noted the many places of ill-repute near Long Acre and worried about allowing his wife to visit her family there, 'in so ill-looked a place, among all the bawdy-houses'.[18] The link between brothels and coffee houses was so well known that when it was suggested to the confidence trickster Mary Carleton that she set one up to earn a living, 'she was mighty angry at it and said it was a Flam given out to sully her Name and Reputation'.[19] Carleton had been caught masquerading as a German princess to find a rich husband; the idea that she should run a coffee house might not have been a bad one – as she ended up on the gallows.

It is also a mistake to think of coffee houses as uniformly sober places; many drinkers went there from taverns and alehouses to sober up. And establishments like the one Ned Ward describes sold brandy and cock-ale (beer flavoured with a parboiled, skinned and gutted cock, spices and fruit). London authorities tried to enforce morality by forbidding tippling, and in 1695 banned it after ten o'clock at night, but although watchmen were supposed to clear taverns, illegal drinking continued, as Ward's tale illustrates. Nor were coffee houses free from violence: energetic debate spilled over into argument, and since men wore swords, murders took place inside and duels were fought outside.

Because some coffee houses stayed open late into the night, together with the introduction of street lighting along arterial routes from 1684, they helped to turn London into a twenty-four-hour city, at least in the prosperous central areas. In Paris, paving and lighting schemes had been paid for by a new tax as early as 1638; now London was fast catching up.[20] The curfew that had once sent citizens to their beds after nightfall gradually eroded as the fashionable found entertainments in the theatre, pleasure gardens and coffee houses. Robert

Hooke recorded in his diary that he often tarried in a coffee house until after 10 p.m. But if the well-to-do could walk the main streets with impunity under the glimmer of oil lanterns, other nightwalkers prompted suspicion: apprentices, given to roistering when they should have been asleep under their masters' roofs; the poor, likely to be vagabonds; and, of course, women. Female nightwalkers were assumed to be strumpets.[21] John Dunton's periodical, *The Night-Walker*, published from 1696 and often stocked in coffee houses, promised to expose and reform lewd practices on London's streets. Of course, it was packed with titillating stories about prostitutes.

Even the supposedly egalitarian policies of coffee houses could be abused. All were welcome and people sat without regard to rank, but highwaymen – often impoverished Cavaliers in the 1660s – used coffee houses to gather intelligence about when the wealthy would be on the road. 'Pray, sir,' says Aimwell to highwayman Gibbet, in Farquhar's play, *The Beaux' Stratagem*, 'Ha'n't I seen your face at Will's Coffee-house?' 'Yes, Sir,' came the brazen reply, 'And at White's too.' With the increase in trade, more Londoners were carrying consumer goods – watches, snuffboxes, cheap jewellery, silk handkerchiefs – tempting to pickpockets. Criminal gangs, which attracted destitute former soldiers, were often run on military lines and organized under 'captains'. Gang members hid in plain sight in coffee houses and other public spaces, observing gang rules and identifying each other by signs known only to themselves.

Coffee-house walls were often pasted with lost-and-found notices. And people who had lost valuables, or been robbed, advertised in newspapers for information or the return of goods, 'no questions asked', giving the name of the coffee house where they could be contacted. It was an invitation to steal in the hope of scooping a reward. Some gangs stole to order, targeting items of purely personal value such as pocket books, account books and legal papers that victims would pay to recover. London had no police force; night watchmen and parish constables were mostly elderly and ill-equipped. Some were even corrupt, happy to take bribes and to fence stolen goods. Coffee houses were wholly implicated in London's criminal underworld of theft, receivership and prostitution, as much a part of the network of illegal activity as the cant or rogues' language that helped to disguise criminal dealings. Notorious coffee houses even gained a kind of cachet, visited by rakes for the frisson of dabbling in danger.

By 1700 there were around 400 coffee houses in London – a substantial number for a city of about half a million people. Essentially, they remained places for networking and obtaining information. Those seeking news of runaway sons, servants or strayed animals, as well as victims of robbery, gave their nearest coffee house as a point of contact. Merchants hoping for sightings of missing ships similarly pinned up notices asking for information. In coffee rooms the latest news sheets were passed from hand to hand or read aloud for discussion. By 1700 the metropolis had several newspapers besides the *London Gazette*, including the *Post Boy*, *Post Man* and *Flying Post*, published three times a week and distributed to coffee houses.[22]

The natural philosopher Robert Hooke went almost daily to coffee houses, sometimes visiting three or more. His favourites were Garraway's and Jonathan's in Exchange Alley – both grand premises. These visits were an extension of his scientific enquiries. In 1662 he had been appointed Curator of Experiments at the Royal Society, a learned society founded in 1660 that promptly gained royal approval, and he carried out demonstrations and experiments at coffee houses, as well as giving lectures there. Hooke used Garraway's for meeting Fellows and officers of the Society, but he also found coffee houses useful places to meet with the artisans who constructed his bespoke scientific instruments. This face-to-face contact with skilled craftsmen reflects the social aspect of Hooke's scientific enquiries. It also helped to validate the methodology for his next experiment: if his approach could withstand the test of a wider audience, it was likely to have merit.

In coffee houses Hooke also shared information about his latest discoveries with men of learning and contributed to larger projects. For example, he suggested cartographic symbols for a new map of London to the map-maker John Ogilby, 'the way of Letters for marking his map and also the way of shadowing'.[23] A resourceful man, Ogilby had recovered from a series of personal disasters by translating the classics and setting up a publishing business that also produced magnificent atlases. The unspoken rule in such conversations seems to have been that a theory shared deserved another hypothesis or discovery in return; the exchange ceased if they observed strangers eavesdropping. Hooke got information from a range of coffee-house customers. He learnt about the metal-works near Leipzig from a sea captain who had seen how alloys were hammered into thin sheets, 'many plates beat under the Hammer at once like leaf gold or tinfoyle, the great difficulty is how to turne it under the hammer quick enough'.[24] Hooke also valued medical tips from coffee-house acquaintances; he was lean, and short because he had grown crooked, and he suffered from chronic ill health.

Learned conversations could lead to trouble. In 1698 a chance meeting of two men in Pall Mall led to a good coffee-house exchange about mathematics. But one of them was intent on a money-making scheme: he showed the other an 'excellent Liquor' that would remove about 18d. worth of gold from a guinea without obviously defacing it so that it might still pass for legal tender.[25] His new friend denounced him. He was arrested and found guilty of treason for tampering with the king's coinage.

The notion that the coffee house was a key factor in the development of polite, rational discourse, a celebration of English liberty of speech, is largely a construct, popularized by the early eighteenth-century essayists Joseph Addison and Richard Steele. Both politicians, they claimed that they wanted to bring philosophy 'out of Closets and Libraries, Schools and Colleges to dwell in Clubs and Assemblies, at Tea-Tables and in Coffee–Houses'.[26] Their reforming ambition may have owed something to the fact that coffee houses were notori-ously liable to spread fake news, while the quality of coffee-house debate could lapse into windy declamation. The best coffee houses aspired to be polite, sociable spaces, but some were linked to sedition as well as criminal activity and were targeted by government spies.

Still, the establishment of coffee houses under Cromwell shows that his regime fostered a degree of religious toleration and free speech. He even allowed the philosopher Thomas Hobbes to return to London and live in Fetter Lane, though Hobbes had tutored the exiled Prince Charles in Paris, was accused of atheism, and his book, *Leviathan*, about the structure of society and legitimate government, was highly controversial. In London, Hobbes conversed freely about his ideas – John Evelyn, for example, was one of his visitors. Readers of *Leviathan* were genuinely confused since, as Cromwell doubtless realized, Hobbes's belief that individuals were bound to submit to the power that offered the best protec-tion could be used to support the monarchy or the Commonwealth. Hobbes wrote that to avoid an ugly state of nature, in which life was perpetual warfare, individuals must put themselves under the power of an absolute ruler in exchange for the protection of their remaining key rights. He thought the best kind of government was an absolute monarchy, but his crucial point was that a ruler must wield absolute power, and that could reside in a Cromwell. London, which had experienced both royal and republican government, was a questioning, dynamic city, and *Leviathan* was a text made for coffee-house discussion. It helped to sharpen people's ideas about society and the nature of government. Yet Hobbes also believed that the Church should be subordinate to the power of the state; some accused him of being an atheist. Growing criticism of *Leviathan* meant that it became a tool with which to damage the reputation of coffee houses.

Because coffee houses were unable to shake off completely their association with republican views, royalist authors attacked them, especially later in the century during political crises. Satirists mocked the health benefits of coffee-drinking, claiming that it damaged the trade of brewers and vintners, and encouraged the lower ranks to meddle in topics beyond their intelligence:

A coffee-House is a *lay-conventicle*, good-fellowship turned *Puritan*, ill-husbandry in *Masquerade*; whither people come, after *Toping* all day, to purchase, at the expense of their last peny, the repute of *sober companions*: a *Rota-Room*, that (like Noah's ark) receives animals of every sort . . . He that comes often saves *two pence* a week in *Gazettes*, and has his News and his Coffee for the same charge, as at a *three peny Ordinary* they give in Broth to your Chop of Mutton; 'Tis an *Exchange* where Haberdashers of *Political small ware* meet, and mutually abuse each other, and the Publique, with bottomless stories, and headless notions; the Rendevous of *idle Pamphlets*, and persons more idly imployed to read them; a *High Court of Justice*, where every little *Fellow* in a *camlet-cloke* takes upon him to transpose Affairs both in Church and State, to shew reasons against *Acts* of Parliament, and condemn the Decrees of *General Councils*.[27]

Defenders of coffee houses claimed that debate neutralized extreme ideas and that anyway people argued about trifles. A coffee house might stoke diverse opinion 'yet is free from effects of Sedition or War. For there are no bloody

Challenges here made, much less Duels fought, or Blows given'.[28] But as we know, trifling arguments over a cup of coffee led to fatal stabbings. Pepys had left off visiting coffee houses by the late 1660s, partly because he had risen too high in public office to fraternize with their mixed clientele, doubtless also because some were again dangerously associated with republicanism. Given his rising status, he might also have avoided coffee houses because they were associated with lechery – for he was a known womanizer.

Royalists promoted ale-drinking as more patriotic than sipping coffee and less likely to lead to sedition, but there was no simple division of opinion about coffee houses along party-political lines. Coffee houses had strong defenders among both royalists and members of the opposition party. This was apparent in 1675 when Charles II was persuaded to crack down on coffee houses. On 29 December he issued a proclamation announcing their closure within twelve days. The proclamation stated that they were 'the great resort of Idle and disaffected persons', they encouraged tradesmen to waste time better spent at their business, and spread sedition: 'False, Malitious and Scandalous Reports are devised and spread abroad, to the Defamation of his Majesties Government, and to the Disturbance of the Peace and Quiet of the Realm.'[29] The royal proclamation triggered an immediate outcry. After all, coffee houses provided a variety of services. They offered spaces for business and pleasure under one roof; they had become essential to daily life.

Coffee houses were now caught up in a debate about power. Many thought the king's proclamation smacked of illegal tyranny and that alcohol, not coffee, was linked with discord and faction:

> It is wine and strong drinks make tumults increase;
> Choc'late, tea, and coffee are liquors of peace:
> No quarrels nor oaths amongst those that drink 'em;
> 'Tis Bacchus and brewers swear, damn 'em, and sink 'em!
> Then, Charles, thy edicts against coffee recall;
> There's ten times more treason in brandy and ale.[30]

What's more, in Londoners' minds, open debate in coffee houses was tied to the ancient liberties of the City. Opponents of closure repeated the view that a coffee house was no echo chamber tending to confirm like-minded people in prejudicial views but a forum for debate, which moderated extreme opinions. Thomas Garraway, whose coffee house had brought him wealth and influence, led the commercial opposition, cannily proposing that coffee-men should apply tighter regulations, keep good order on their premises, and report any sedition. Within ten days the king was forced to back down, although to save face he extended the period in which coffee houses might trade, without lifting the threat to ban them completely.

In the early years of coffee houses, they may have brought people together and helped to heal the wounds of civil war, but some later fanned the flames of faction. Certain coffee houses fostered opposition to the government; others, like Will's, were wholly loyal. Changes to coffee-house interiors reflected a tendency to cater for separate cliques: convivial, large tables were replaced with smaller ones, or boxes for semi-private conversation. Far from producing a polite consensus, coffee houses might prompt unsettling fears about morality and masculinity. Some became noted for heavy gambling rather than news and business. If rational, urbane conversation was the ideal customers aspired to, in the closing decades of the seventeenth century when information became more readily available, there was greater scope for mendacity. People were caught writing seditious letters to be circulated in coffee houses.

The Penny Post was introduced in 1680. It was a huge advance, both cheap and effective, and larger coffee houses were nominated as places where the postmen could collect or leave letters. But a pro-government author claimed that the service was immediately open to misuse:

> Well! Certainly this Penny-Post was the most happy Invention of this fortunate Age: there was never anything so favourable to the carrying on and managing Intrigues . . . one may Write, Print, Publish and Disperse ingenious Libels, either against particular Persons of the Tory Party, or the Government itself, and no Body the wiser or the better for it.[31]

Coffee houses did help to promote a growing awareness of the impact of collective private opinion, especially when that opinion was informed by political discussion. Of course, collective opinion had earlier been a force in daily life, often shaped by the Church through the pulpit. And many of the business activities that took place in coffee houses had taken place before in sociable alehouses and taverns where the comings and goings of carriers from across the country provided a flow of news. The difference was that in coffee houses, opinions were partly formed by consulting the news in written form, in newspapers and pamphlets, with less reliance on oral report. It was a development that built on the explosion of print and political discussion during the Civil Wars and it changed the nature of debate. The context of that debate was also new, shaped by scientific discoveries, commercial advances, and political developments that tied religion strongly to questions of civil government. And coffee kept wits sharp and propelled the discussion forward.

By the end of the century, the concept of 'The Publick' had acquired new force. Admittedly, it was overwhelmingly composed of men, often with no say in the formal political process, and contemporaries understood that opinion was fickle: 'The *Publick* is the Nicest and most Severe *Critick* in the World; yet a Dull Execrable *Ballad*, is enough to *Amuse* it for a whole Year. It is both Constant and Inconstant.'[32] But if this collective opinion comprised innumerable points of view, not all of them educated or urbane, it would henceforth be given more status, and be something to consider in political struggles. The coffee-house phenomenon helped to create this new development.

Londoners had long been a barometer of political opinion. Their ambivalent reaction to the death of Cromwell in September 1658 signalled imminent change. Cromwell's embalmed body lay in state for three weeks at Somerset House, beneath a lifelike effigy placed on a sumptuous hearse, as if he were a king. The corpse was buried privately in Westminster Abbey, as the family wished, while the effigy took centre stage in an elaborate and costly state funeral. John Evelyn – admittedly a hostile witness – remarked, 'It was the joyfullest funerall that ever I saw, for there was none that Cried, but dogs, which the souldiers hooted away with a barbarous noise; drinking, & taking *Tabacco* in the streetes as they went.'[33] Cromwell's nominated successor was his son Richard. Competent enough, he lacked his father's charisma and failed to quell competing factions. When it became clear that the monarchy was likely to be restored, collective opinion was strongly manipulated in Prince Charles's favour. Pamphlets were industriously circulated praising his magnanimity, his loyalty to the Anglican religion, and his repugnance for all forms of debauchery (though it was well known he had an illegitimate child). The explosion of debate during the Civil Wars would be further shaped in the reign to come and, channelled by the coffee-house experience, would leave a permanent legacy.

12

RESTORATION AND A LICENTIOUS COURT

On 29 May 1660, Thomas Rugg the barber, a committed royalist, jostled for a place in the Strand with thousands of others to see King Charles II make his triumphant entry from Southwark into London. The event, carefully aligned with Charles's thirtieth birthday since he had landed at Dover three days earlier, proved to be a spectacular assault on the senses. The crowd's outward enthusiasm for the return of the monarchy was something Rugg struggled to capture in his diary. 'Such shouting as the oldest man alive never heard the like,' he wrote.[1] The drawn swords and pikes of guards in the procession glinted in the spring sunshine, as did the gold and silver lace of their velvet costumes. Trumpeters and drummers lifted the crowd's excitement, and young women cast flowers along the route. Windows, rich carpets flung over their sills, were crammed with cheering people. Later there were bonfires at almost every door. The City had paid for wine to flow from its water fountains, and celebrations became rowdier as dusk fell; there were scenes of utter drunkenness. At a huge bonfire in Westminster, effigies of Cromwell and his wife were burnt, together with the arms of the Commonwealth. The following night, John Adler, a fervent royalist merchant who had managed to lie low during the Interregnum, organized fireworks outside his home in St Martin's Lane. He provided claret, which people took in their hats, cups or glasses. And he threw souvenir medals from an upper storey for people to catch, each stamped with the king's portrait.

This use of the king's image illustrates the crucial role of iconography in re-establishing the monarchy. Ireland, Scotland and Wales all played their part in the Restoration, but it was in London that the most politically important ceremonies took place and it was Londoners who performed key rituals that helped Charles bridge the chasm between his father's execution and his own accession, as if the Commonwealth had never occurred. Ceremonials and the reinstatement of royal arms took place across the kingdom, but London had the historic venues that gave proceedings enhanced legitimacy. After important events marking the Restoration in the capital, prints and other commemorative items were disseminated across the realm.

People welcomed the return of the monarchy because after Cromwell's death the government had descended into military rule and chaos. The lawyer, Bulstrode Whitelocke, found himself sitting up all night to protect his family from rowdy soldiers. Apprentices saw that their trades were suffering and petitioned against the power of the army in London, calling the hated soldiers in their red coats 'lobsters'. All this time, General George Monck, who had put aside royalist sympathies and become Cromwell's able governor in Scotland, watched cautiously from afar. When he judged he was likely to succeed, he marched into London, restored the Presbyterian members who had been purged from parliament in 1648, and counselled ministers to invite Charles to return. As he nudged events in the direction he favoured, he used iconography to help him judge the temper of the times. After Charles I's execution, the king's statue in the Royal Exchange had been removed and the pedestal defaced with the words 'Exit Tyrannus'. In March 1660, Monck arranged for a painter to mount a ladder with a pot and brush and erase this inscription. Far from causing an outcry, people gathered near the Exchange and made a joyful bonfire to celebrate. Thames watermen even started to wear their old royal badges again.

In a significant move before Charles II returned, parliament had proclaimed that the royal arms should replace those of the Commonwealth throughout the land. London livery companies were quick to comply and decked out their halls with celebratory flags. The House of Lords took steps to reassemble the magnificent art collection of Charles I, knowing that its potent symbolism would help to assert the power of the monarchy. Amazingly, some 80 per cent of the collection was recovered. Many works had been stored in a fruit warehouse in Thames Street for the use of Cromwell's wife. Some individuals were coerced into handing over the items they held; others proudly handed over great works of art, claiming only to have safeguarded them for the day when Charles II would return.

The king's accession was ceremoniously proclaimed in the traditional manner: first in Palace Yard, Westminster, then in the City after the lord mayor had formally granted the courtiers permission to enter at Temple Bar. This was an important nicety, the gate marking the boundary between two centres of power: Crown and City. As Charles was proclaimed king, cannon were fired from the Tower and church bells rang out, although Rugg reported that even Bow Bells were deafened by cheers. People were suddenly free to drink the king's health publicly in the streets. Anticipation of Charles's return grew to fever pitch. Huge bonfires were erected from pitch barrels, ready for lighting, the one in Southwark rising higher than a house. Pubs were renamed the King's Head or the Duke's Head, although John Evelyn complained about the quality of royal portraits on pub signs, the work of 'vile, and wretched Bunglers'.[2]

The restoration of the monarchy meant different things to different people. Charles signed the Declaration of Breda on 4 April 1660, offering reconciliation and a new beginning. He extended a general pardon to those who had committed crimes during the Civil Wars and Interregnum (excepting the regicides), provided they recognized his sovereignty, and he promised religious toleration. For some, who believed that the nation had learned at great cost that monarchy was its most perfect government, the Restoration meant peace, a return to parliaments and the rule of law. For others, freedom to worship according to one's conscience was most important. Royalist families trusted that their loyalty would be rewarded. Merchants wanted a king who would exert his power on the international stage to obtain better conditions for trade. Could Charles heal social division and meet all expectations? He genuinely wanted tolerance, but the Anglican clergy soon gained ascendancy in his reign and thwarted that. Still, in 1660 his Restoration was achieved without bloodshed; iconography and ritual helped to accomplish this smooth transition.

Any lingering discontent was muffled by the treatment of former Puritan rebels. An effigy of Cromwell was hung from a window in a courtyard of Whitehall Palace with a rope around its neck. An abusive crowd spared it no insult before the king ordered its removal. The trials of ten regicides went ahead at the Old Bailey. Found guilty, they were dragged on hurdles to Charing Cross or Tyburn for execution. Major-General Thomas Harrison was hanged, drawn and quartered at Charing Cross on 13 October. Samuel Pepys, never one to miss an entertainment, went to look, reporting that on the scaffold Harrison looked 'as cheerfully as any man could do in that condition'.[3] Yet Pepys may have been more disturbed than he let on. He went home and picked a quarrel with his wife, kicking and breaking a fine basket that he had bought her as a present, regretting it afterwards. Prudently, the king curtailed such bloody executions before the public mood turned to revulsion.

Westminster Abbey, which Cromwell had used to enhance his regime, was cleansed of that taint. The remains of the General at Sea, Robert Blake, were removed and thrown into a pit outside with other corpses. On 26 January 1661 the bodies of Cromwell, Henry Ireton, John Bradshaw and Thomas Pride were exhumed. Cromwell's vault excited great interest; people paid sixpence for a good view. They spread the word that his coffin was a very rich thing, 'full of guilded hinges and nayles'.[4] Pride's corpse was too decomposed for the next part of the ritual. The other bodies were taken to the Red Lion Inn in Holborn and the next day dragged on hurdles to Tyburn, the crowds cursing as the procession passed by. At Tyburn they were hanged until sunset, decapitated, and buried under the gallows. Their heads were skewered on poles at Westminster Hall by the common hangman. Commemorative items were produced, including tobacco boxes with Charles I on the lid, Charles II on the inside lid and, at the bottom, Cromwell with a halter round his neck and the Devil next to him, open-mouthed, to show how despicable the Protector had become.

Charles, who must have felt some trepidation on returning to a city where his father had been executed, set great store by traditional ceremony. Straight after his return, he and his brothers James and Henry dined at great expense in Guildhall at the invitation of the lord mayor, although bad weather in July curtailed the lavish procession into the City that had been planned. Charles was ardently committed to the Order of the Garter, his one badge of kingship in exile. Now he installed new Knights with the greatest pomp and magnificence at Windsor Castle. And under his influence the Knights' ceremonial costume was redesigned to be deliberately archaic, with trunk hose and round breeches reflecting an earlier Stuart court. Continuity with the past underlined his right to rule. Charles also instituted elaborate new ceremonies for creating Knights of the Bath, inviting influential Londoners and foreign dignitaries to watch.

Charles planned his coronation for St George's Day, 23 April 1661 (St George being the patron saint of the Order of the Garter and a focus of national pride). He made no dangerous claim to rule by divine right, but this choice of date allowed him to merge his identity with that of St George. The coronation was the occasion of yet another royal procession through London from the Tower to Whitehall; the City, having collected the usual financial contributions from livery companies, spared no expense. The route had been gravelled to conceal the unsavoury filth of the streets and was guarded by the Trained Bands. The procession passed under four ceremonial arches decorated with streamers, where crowds were entertained with speeches and pageantry. Music was played from balconies and again the conduits flowed with wine. London's maypole had been re-erected in the Strand, almost opposite Somerset House, in preparation for May Day. It stood an impressive 134 feet (41 metres) high, and morris dancers stepped around it for the coronation; sadly they proved out of practice, 'the worse that ever were'.[5]

The crown jewels had been melted down for gold coinage during the Interregnum and Charles had been obliged to order new regalia for the coronation ceremony in Westminster Abbey. He prudently opted for silver gilt but was careful to order a faithful copy of the originals, and he followed the traditional ceremony in every detail. His robes echoed those of Tudor and Stuart predecessors, again affirming his right to rule while tactfully eliminating traces of his father's coronation dress. His official coronation portrait, copied, printed and widely circulated, shows that the total effect was one of unassailable power.

The king's marriage had been under discussion even before his coronation; it seemed best to get him respectably married, given his mistresses. Charles and his advisors chose the bride who brought the largest dowry, since the Crown needed money. A Portuguese match with Catherine of Braganza was announced less than two weeks after Charles's coronation. She came with the Portuguese possessions of Tangier, Bombay (Mumbai) and a promised £300,000, although when it came to settlement Portugal could not find so much cash and sent sugar and spices as a stop-gap. The princess was Catholic, but London's royalist press focused on the potential benefits of the match in terms of trade and status; Charles had set up a Council for Trade to improve commerce and to show that he was listening to his subjects, and the port of Tangier seemed to promise rewards.

After much positive propaganda, Catherine eventually arrived at Portsmouth in May 1662. The couple were married there, perhaps because Charles and his advisors were apprehensive about how unruly Londoners would receive a Catholic queen. In August she made her state entry into London by water, as Henrietta Maria had done, but the couple stayed well upstream, travelling only from Hampton Court to the Palace of Whitehall. Even so, the procession was magnificent: thousands of barges rowed to the sound of trumpets and other music; pageants were performed on boats anchored in the middle of the river. It was enough to secure favourable publicity.

Charles keenly understood that his crown depended on popular support. Unlike his father, he kept himself in the public eye, taking a daily walk in St James's Park, dining regularly in public in the Banqueting House. His father had rarely attended the royal service on Maundy Thursday, but Charles did so from the start of his reign: in 1661 he washed the feet of thirty-one poor men in the Banqueting House, giving them food, clothes and money. These ceremonies were formal court occasions attended by visiting ambassadors. He also revived the practice of touching for the King's Evil, which his father had neglected; in the course of his reign Charles II physically touched an estimated 92,107 of his subjects.[6] These rituals, too, were heavily publicized across the land in prints and broadsides.

The increasing market for consumer goods meant that the Restoration and royal marriage were commemorated in a range of products from rings, thimbles and fork handles to earthenware flasks, jugs and wallpaper. The very first coronation mug was produced in this reign. Charles's distinctive appearance, especially his abundant curly hair, lent itself to reproduction in items ranging from pipe-stoppers to playing cards. His escape from the Roundheads after the Battle of Worcester in September 1651, when he hid in an oak tree, was romanticized and reproduced on fire-backs, dishes and in prints. Some items, notably the heart-shaped silver medals marking Charles's coronation, could be sympathetically paired with the relics that had been made to venerate the martyrdom of his father. Novelties bearing the new king's image were produced at prices to suit every purse. His portrait even appeared on tokens admitting people to the theatre and on hornbooks for teaching children to read.

Despite these efforts, not all Charles's subjects were won over. In London's eastern suburbs particularly, where many worshipped in independent churches, there was pointed criticism of the new king. As early as January 1661, Jane Blunstone of Whitechapel was accused of vilifying Henrietta Maria and her sons: 'the Queene is the Great Whore of Babilon and the King is the son of a whore and the Duke of Yorke is a rogue'.[7] Parliament soon passed laws that discriminated against Protestant Nonconformists: the 1662 Act of Uniformity stated that all ministers had to swear an Oath of Allegiance to Charles and preach according to a standard Book of Common Prayer. And the royal couple's water pageant had been deliberately scheduled to take place the day before the contentious deadline for ministers to swear the oath. Charles used his marriage as an opportunity to release some Quakers, imprisoned because their faith barred them from swearing oaths, but disturbances still took place in London. Presbyterians who refused to accept the Anglican service hauled Anglican ministers from their pulpits, tore their robes, and trashed the Book of Common Prayer.

FASHION

The Restoration brought a great revival of interest in fashion, both at court and among those who could afford to imitate court dress. Clothes not only indicated status, but sometimes political allegiances and religious beliefs as well. During the civil war period they proclaimed whose side you were on, since Cavaliers and Roundheads dressed differently. Broadly, the Interregnum had been a time of austerity and now people coveted luxury, but clothes continued to have political meaning and the cloth they were made from reflected national, commercial interests.

Charles consciously fashioned his image with his tailors, understanding the value of clothes in affirming the status of monarchy. When he arrived in England after the Restoration, he was dressed in the height of French fashion. Although this vogue was widely admired, it had its critics too: why ape Paris fashions when France's Catholicism and system of absolute monarchy were loathed and feared? Numerous London trades were making money from royalty by turning out commemorative items; cloth dealers also sought to profit from royalty, urging the king to wear textiles made in England. In October 1665, Charles duly announced that he and the queen would wear only English cloth, except linen and calicoes, and encouraged the court to do the same.

The royal couple soon saw that it would be expedient to claim to break with French fashion and create an 'English' style. Samuel Pepys recorded how, in October 1666, Charles ostentatiously began to wear a vest, or long waistcoat. It may well have been influenced by examples of Turkish dress worn on stage; John Evelyn credited the new fashion with being of Persian origin:

> Thence to Court, it being the first time of his *Majesties* putting himselfe solemnly into the *Eastern fashion* of Vest, changing doublet, stiff Collar, [bands] & Cloake &c: into a comely Vest, after the *Persian* mode with girdle or shash . . . resolving never to alter it, & to leave the French mode.[8]

Suits were now usually of sombre-coloured velvets, although vests were in brighter, contrasting colours; male dress gradually settled on coat, vest and breeches, foreshadowing the modern suit. Charles I had mostly worn flashy satin, but Charles II preferred woven cloth: camlets, made of wool and silk, or velvet. Although he wore English cloth, he augmented it with luxury fabrics from France and Italy. So in 1668 parliament petitioned the king and his brother James to set an example by wearing only English manufactures. The king's personal taste was for casual, quite plain clothes for everyday wear, but fashionable court dress ran to extremes. For women, dresses became more structured, with a tight, low-waisted bodice that was very low-cut; full, high-waisted gowns went quite out of fashion.

Among elite men, extravagant, long, curling wigs became the norm, because when Charles began to go grey towards the end of 1663, he started to wear them. Possibly he was already trapped by his royal image. Pepys cut his hair short and put on a periwig for the first time on 3 September 1665; he was rather nervous in case he was teased. Many others followed court fashions and bought royalist accessories for tactical reasons, as a demonstration of loyalty. Such behaviour prompted cynicism: turncoats, for example, who with regime change had switched political and perhaps religious allegiances, found it politic to sport snuffboxes bearing the king's portrait.[9]

The Restoration brought prosperity to some and encouraged demonstrations of wealth and status after the levelling effects of the Interregnum. Social climbers eagerly purchased items of dress and domestic goods that would convey prestige as well as patriotism. Consequently, in December 1662, Pepys recorded how ashamed he was that his wife was still wearing her taffeta dress when all fashionable women had purchased warmer mohair gowns. The number of Londoners who could afford luxury fabrics remained small, so novelty was at a premium among this elite. Nobody wanted to be wearing the same patterned fabric as everyone else.

Fashion trends posed challenges for cloth importers. Alderman Sir William Turner, a textiles merchant based in St Paul's Churchyard who mostly imported fabrics from Genoa and Paris, found that he had to satisfy new trends quickly and not overstock. At the beginning of September 1664, for example, he wrote to his chief foreign supplier, Boquelin and Sons of Paris, to explain 'there will be newer fashions for winter and therefore I will not order any tabys [silks] yet till the fashions are settled for winter'. He later added, 'As for the Brocades which you would fain persuade mee to keep I have already said enouf to make you understand the nature of flowred silks the fashion Changing so often that they are worth nothing when something newer comes.'[10] Turner certainly profited from the extravagance of others: already in 1660 his estimated annual income was £2,000.[11] But he was a Puritan and devoted much of his earnings to charitable works, winning a knighthood for public service in 1662.

In Restoration times, as now, fashion was big business. In 1671 a hot news item was that French drapers had come to London and bought up all English light-coloured broadcloth to the value of many thousand pounds. It would be the only material worn in the French court that winter.[12] This was welcome news, unless Londoners were determined to follow the French style. All the while, fashion trends were becoming more complex with the expansion of trade routes. Sir Joseph Williamson, royalist MP and master of the Clothworkers' Company, noted at a committee for trade in 1676 that 'Fashions of ribbons, stuffs, &c. run round the world'.[13] Outdated fashions from France were brought to England as new, and then passed to Ireland and the West Indies. When the manufacture of one sort of goods was established in England, the French would set up another fashion, and when that too was adopted in England, they would change it for a third. Canny merchants bought English cloth direct from weavers, then sold it as French at a higher price. Williamson warned that England imported so much linen, silk, wine and brandy from across the Channel, the balance of trade favoured France. To encourage English manufactures and limit French imports at a time of depressed trade, ministers again proposed that the king should wear only English textiles, and that ladies of the court should only wear English silks or silk mixtures. Because the king's mistresses were Catholics (excepting only Nell Gwyn), their fondness for French fashions rankled. Prudently, Charles did now adopt English medley cloth, which was made of multicoloured fibres woven together.

London's parks were places where people could display their fine dress. Charles made improvements to parks so that they offered even more attractive walks, although John Wilmot, the libertine Earl of Rochester, remarked that after dusk they were used mostly for sex. In October 1660 the king ordered a river to be cut in St James's Park and a new alley for the game pall mall, an early form of croquet, to run along the south side of the park wall. These alterations, together with the improvements to Whitehall Palace, employed some 300 men. Unfortunately, on the other side of the park wall lay the highway between Charing Cross and St James's Palace; carriages created so much dust that players often found they could not continue with their game. At some expense Charles was forced to move the highway further north, creating today's Pall Mall.

Nonconformists, Quakers especially, still wore sober costumes that set them apart, although they dropped the uncompromising Puritan habit of the earlier period. They might not wear black, which was associated with mourning, but still favoured muted colours. They rejected ornament and despised fashion trends. The poor struggled to appear respectable enough to go to church, often pawning Sunday clothes to tide them over for the rest of the week. Because clothing was expensive, London had a thriving second-hand clothes market, with many dealers to the east of Tower Hill, the place of execution for high-profile traitors. Because garments could so easily be turned into ready cash, street robbers targeted victims for their clothes as well as their valuables. In 1661 a gang of nine labourers assaulted the elderly Sir John Scudamore in

St Giles-in-the-Fields, taking not only his money and jewels but also his hat, cloak, breeches, doublet, shirt and gloves. The estimated value of his clothes alone was £17 2s. All the robbers were arrested and sentenced to death.[14]

The sumptuous costumes of the aristocracy, soon associated with the sensual pleasures of the Restoration court, elicited disapproval tinged with envy. The outrageous behaviour of some aristocratic rakes hardened criticism. Lord Rochester killed a waterman merely for commenting to another that Rochester was a handsome man. Hearing this as he passed by, Rochester turned back, swore, and asked the waterman who made him a judge of beauty. He gave the man a box on the ear and when the waterman seemed about to retaliate, drew his sword and ran him through.[15] Gentlemen routinely wore swords – usually rapiers – as a mark of their honour and status, almost as a decorative element of dress, so minor disputes easily escalated. They set a poor example; London's homicide rate, although decreasing, was higher than it is today.[16] The violence was disturbing; one resident of St Martin-in-the-Fields was prosecuted for wishing 'all the gentry in the land would kill one another, so that the comminalty might live the better'.[17]

The fascination that the court inspired slowly came to be mixed with repugnance at its immorality; people understood that silks and fine wigs often concealed the ravages of syphilis. Contemporary advertisements promising discreet cures pulled no punches in the description of sexually transmitted diseases. One medicine promised to:

> . . . Cure a Gonorrhaea, Running of the Rein or Clap, Pain, Heat, Scalding in making Water, &c. in a few Days: And very speedily take away all Aches or Pains in the Head, Back, Shoulders, Arms, Legs, or Night-Pains; Sores or Ulcers in the Mouth or Throat; All Sorn and stubborn Scabs, or breaking out in any part of the Body; preserve the Palate and Bridge of the Nose; purifie the Blood; perfectly free the Body of the Remains of any Pox or Clap formerly ill Cured.[18]

Prince Rupert, the king's cousin, reputed to be suffering from chronic syphilis, finally submitted to operations on his skull to release corrupted matter. Pepys saw him at Whitehall Palace less than two months afterwards, 'pretty well as he used to be, and looks well; only, something appears to be under his periwig on the crown of his head'.[19] The prince may simply have undergone treatment for an old injury, since he was once shot in the head, but this was not Pepys's understanding. Many writers who brooded on appearance and reality developed a corrosive cynicism; it was a theme that permeated through to popular literature and coloured the spirit of the age. The ballad 'News from Hide Park' describes a country gentleman's encounter with a prostitute, who seemed an 'armful of Sattin' but divested of her wig and fine clothes became 'Like a Lancashire witch of fourscore and ten'.[20]

RESTORATION THEATRE

Charles II, punctilious in observing traditional ceremonies at court, also forged stronger links between the court and everyday entertainments in London. This contributed to his image as a king who was accessible to his people. Cromwell had never quite managed to suppress the acting of plays in London. With Charles's accession, theatres reopened with a flourish and Londoners could once again enjoy an exuberant cultural life. As early as November 1660 the barber Thomas Rugg noted, 'Playes much in request and great resort to them'.[21] The king's obvious love of the theatre made plays even more popular.

In 1660, Charles licensed two theatrical companies to act full-length, five-act dramas (as opposed to song-and-dance shows that might be performed in minor playhouses). The King's Company flourished under the actor-manager Thomas Killigrew, and the Duke's Company under Sir William Davenant. By licensing loyal courtiers to run the two major theatres, Charles hoped to control what was presented on the stage. The Licensing Act for published works, renewed in 1662, controlled the printed word.

The two acting companies set up theatres in the best spaces available: former tennis courts. Killigrew opened in Vere Street, east of Drury Lane, and then Davenant opened in Portugal Street, Lincoln's Inn Fields. Both men chose to work within the conventions of the private court and continental theatres, rather than revive the Elizabethan public stage. They each built playhouses with a proscenium arch and as much scenic machinery as their premises could hold.[22] In 1663, Killigrew was able to move the King's Company to a more spacious and lavishly decorated theatre between Drury Lane and Bridges Street (now Catherine Street), where the current Theatre Royal still has its main entrance.

For a while, Londoners enjoyed a third company of professional actors: at the end of 1660, Charles granted the actor-manager, George Jolly, a licence to perform 'such plays as are free from all profanity or obscenity'.[23] Jolly, whose splenetic disposition was quite at variance with his name, took over any playhouse that was vacant. He used the Cockpit, near Drury Lane, the open-air Red Bull in St John's Street, and the Salisbury Court Theatre in Whitefriars, where clandestine performances had been staged during the Interregnum. But by 1667, Jolly was forced out by his two more powerful rivals; afterwards his troupe focused exclusively on the provinces.

The two patent theatres became magnificent. In 1671, the Duke's Company moved to lavish premises in Dorset Garden, further south from Salisbury Court on the Thames. The new theatre, said to have been designed by Sir Christopher Wren, had steps down to the river for those arriving by boat. It also had coach parking for patrons who chose to arrive ostentatiously in their own vehicle. The king was said to like the new playhouse so much that he gave £1,000 towards the cost of its construction.[24] And when fire destroyed Killigrew's theatre, he opened a more resplendent one in 1674, calling it the Theatre Royal Drury Lane.

The audience for the theatre was smaller than before the Civil Wars, averaging between 400 and 500 at each performance. In the patent theatres it was also socially narrower, dominated by noblemen and their ladies, town rakes and gallants, all mostly loyal to the Crown.[25] One reason for this was that going to the theatre cost more than in Shakespeare's time. The cheapest tickets in the upper and middle galleries cost 1s. and 1s. 6d. respectively. The pit, favoured by the elite, cost 2s. 6d., while boxes, reserved for royalty when present, cost 4s. Even so, the location of the two main theatres was calculated to be within distance of both court and city. Well-off tradesmen and their apprentices might take up the less expensive seats, especially on holidays. Further from the stage, these seats happened to be less well lit by the wax candles on stage and in wall brackets, so the presence of ordinary citizens was less evident.

Just as audiences were mixed, so men and women sat indiscriminately. Parties of aristocratic ladies often dispensed with a male escort at the theatre, although women of lower rank took female servants to preserve their reputation. When a husband and wife went to a play together it was a statement of domestic harmony. The intimate atmosphere of small playhouses fostered a seductive familiarity not permitted elsewhere in London, where social distinctions were usually carefully maintained. This licence could be exhilarating, although Pepys, for one, disliked any visible intrusion of apprentices and meaner citizens into the more prominent seats; having climbed up the social ladder himself, he preferred to keep the auditorium exclusive.

Most of the plays staged in the 1660s were adaptations of the work of earlier playwrights such as Shakespeare and Jonson. Gradually new material emerged; audiences were offered heroic tragedy and city comedy. The heroic tragedies, featuring conquests, tyranny and tragic romance, were sharply divorced from everyday London life of the 1660s and 1670s. Yet they served as a means of airing some of the issues facing Londoners in an age of mounting global trade and imperial expansion. Critics were tempted to mock the inflated poetry of the tragedies, but it was well understood that a nation of any standing should be able to support heroic drama. In contrast, most of the comedies focused on London society. They referenced known London attractions such as Hyde Park and Mulberry Garden, helped by moveable scenery, and linked theatre-going more closely with London life. Thomas Shadwell's plays, set in the provinces and spa towns, also enacted for a London audience the social tensions dividing the nation at large.[26]

One of the big changes to the theatre was that women now routinely performed, often in breeches parts that showed off their legs. Female actors became the pin-ups of the day, commodified and literally possessed by male admirers who made them their mistresses and sometimes their wives. The common assumption was that women on the stage were high-class courtesans. Nell Gwyn, a leading actor in the King's Company with a talent for comic parts, famously became Charles's mistress in 1669. Her friend Aphra Behn, the first woman to earn her living by the pen and foremost among a group of writers known as 'the Female Wits', recognized the scale of Gwyn's achievement. Behn dedicated her comedy *The Feign'd Curtizans* to Gwyn in 1679; as far as Behn was concerned, Gwyn owed her success to her intelligence *and* her beauty. Yet the notoriety of female actors contributed to a general perception that the Restoration had encouraged immorality. A London newsletter casually reported in 1668, 'Miss Davies the player at the Dukes house is with child by somebody. She hath left the stage, and keeps her Coach and footmen, and hath lodgings very richly furnished in Suffolk Street.'[27]

Cultured citizens were expected to have an opinion about the latest play and the quality of the acting. Samuel Pepys went to 118 performances in the 1667–8 theatrical season alone. The theatre was also a place to be seen and it encouraged displays of high fashion. In 1663, Pepys wrote:

> The play being done, we home by water, having been a little shamed that my wife and woman were in such a pickle, all the ladies being finer and better dressed in the pit than they use I think to be.[28]

Dramatists made a point of addressing the audience directly in prologues and epilogues, drawing spectators into the performance. One of the attractions of the theatre for different social types in the audience was that they might be singled out for comment, however impudent. Inevitably, such dramatic techniques fostered a sense of social importance: spectators felt themselves to be part of a privileged elite.

During the Interregnum impoverished Cavaliers had become adept at asserting their status through their behaviour, seeming confidently at ease and perfectly urbane, if poor. It was a kind of performance, moulded by an awareness of its effect on others, and it lent itself to imitation on the stage. The king's own affability, emulated at court, further dispersed in coffee houses, theatres and other public spaces, also influenced English manners. With some confidence, city comedies soon represented London's social round as the very standard of civility. The life of a lady of quality in the capital was depicted as the epitome of pleasure and liberty compared to life in the countryside. Heroic tragedies that censured life under Catholic or oriental powers, and particularly the tyrannical treatment of women, also indirectly celebrated 'liberty' in England. The London stage became a notable means of celebrating national characteristics and forging national identity. And the most popular songs were printed so that they could be performed outside the theatre.

The entire theatre district between Covent Garden and the Strand, and further south to the river, became a cultural hub. Yet, in the imagination of some, it helped to create an image of London as a place of licentious excess where youth was easily corrupted. The disturbances caused by crowds of play-goers after a performance encouraged this view. In 1684, for instance, the adventurer George Porter took offence when he was jostled outside the Duke's Theatre. He drew his rapier and stabbed Sir James Halkett clean through the thigh. The unlucky Halkett, a major in Dumbarton's Regiment just returned from garrison duty in Tangier, died a fortnight later. The killing was not premeditated so Porter obtained a pardon.[29] The theatre district was close to the fashionable Covent Garden and St Martin's Lane but set apart from the exclusive West End, where elegant squares were being developed: St James's Square from 1662, then Golden Square and King (later Soho) Square. Residents near both patent theatres found the traffic congestion on play nights intolerable. And the district was crowded with other places of entertainment, some of them suspect if not actually unsafe. It attracted the demi-monde and its reputation declined. By 1700, Salisbury House, built by Sir Robert Cecil south of the Strand, where Elizabeth I had been entertained, was home to 'whores, coiners, highwaymen, pickpockets, and housebreakers'.[30]

Charles's easy mingling with his subjects in the context of the public theatre was unprecedented and discontinued after his reign. Sometimes he also commissioned plays at Whitehall Palace, but then admitted non-courtiers and even charged to help cover costs, which John Evelyn thought 'very Scandalous, & never so before at court Diversions'.[31] Perhaps Charles calculated that accessibility would keep key individuals close to him and win public support. After 1677, as play texts engaged more closely with politics, the Crown raised an increasing number of objections to their content. Political pressures afforded Charles less time for playgoing. But ordinary citizens had picked up on the links between a licentious court and the theatre. In 1681 a woman who ran a chandler's shop in Long Acre accused a customer of being 'a whore and a bawd', saying she could get proof that the woman 'gets her living by shewing her Cunt. She lyes with all Nell Gwynne's footmen.'[32] The debauchery of the Restoration court may be understood as a reaction to the restraints of Puritanism, and at least Charles was no hypocrite as regards his personal life. But no king had been so open about his mistresses and bastard children as he was, or had ennobled so many at the expense of the public purse.

The poor, excluded from the world of the fashionable theatre, had ready access to the tradition of the spoken word at fairs and in taverns, where artists, like performance poets today, found ways to express their anger and sense of unfairness. Ballads offered commentaries on topical events. *The New Courtier*, for example, exposed court gallants who gambled, swaggered, lied and did not pay their bills.[33] Charles could ensure that those who published treason received the full, gory punishment, but he found it harder to control rumour and street entertainment, outlets that could be manipulated to influence popular opinion. After the Licensing Act temporarily lapsed in 1679, criticism of the court was unbounded. The royalist ballad 'The Licentiousness of the Times' complained that 'It is now grown an Epidemical disease,/For people to talk and to write as they please.'[34] Charles had returned to London in 1660 on a wave of enthusiasm, but natural disasters and his own lax behaviour would sour public opinion.

13

PLAGUE, FIRE AND WAR

In the mid-1660s terrified Londoners were forced to develop a new spatial sense of the town they knew and loved. The City had been brimful of historic buildings that held personal as well as national meaning. Certain suburbs had a reputation for being unhealthier than others. Now catastrophic events swept away the old certainties. First came the plague, which struck parishes with varying degrees of intensity and left survivors with a vivid mental map of the areas vulnerable to disease. Then came the Great Fire, which destroyed landmark buildings in a blaze lasting four days, almost erasing the City's street plan. And citizens were also being forced to reassess their relationship to the Continent. During the years of the Second Anglo-Dutch War, 1665–7, anxious Londoners could hear cannon fire from opposing fleets at sea, an urgent reminder that their prosperity and trade depended on English sea power and control of the oceans. The Dutch invaded the Thames and Medway rivers in 1667, capturing the very warship that had brought Charles back from exile to England. It was a humiliating episode that undermined Londoners' remaining sense of security. These terrible events took an emotional toll; people became even more susceptible to rumour and more critical of the monarchy. Perhaps the lax behaviour of the court had tempted fate?

The year 1665 seemed cursed from the start. Thomas Rugg, the Covent Garden barber, recorded a blazing comet on 17 December 1664, which some thought a sign of war or pestilence. When another comet appeared on 5 April, bigger than the last and only a month after war had begun against the Dutch, pessimists foretold impending doom. In London isolated cases of plague had appeared but normal life continued. Rugg noted that the playhouses were 'thronged with people of all sorts and sizes', while plague was 'in and about

London but 5 or 6 houses in all'.[1] Plague was endemic in the capital: few years passed without some cases, but major epidemics were expected only about every twenty years. Doomsayers worried that another was overdue. In 1659, Justices of the Peace in London's suburbs tightened up procedures for compiling parish Bills of Mortality: Churchwardens were reminded to hire searchers to view corpses and report on cause of death, as in the City, so that the Bills would be a more effective tool for measuring plague.

London was still a medieval city, built mostly of wood. Impressive in size, even the patriotic John Evelyn had to admit that it was cramped: 'a congestion of Houses; some of the principall streets so narrow, as there is nothing more deformed.'[2] Poor areas, webs of lanes and alleys lined with mouldering buildings, were even more ill-lit, airless and foul. Londoners knew that disease was linked to dirt and overcrowding. They feared 'uncleanly & unholesome keepeing of dwelling, where many are pestered together', but most physicians thought plague came from infected air.[3] Preventative concoctions routinely featured in domestic herbals, and housewives shared recipes that carried some kind of endorsement, such as 'Dr Burgeses watter against ye Plague'.[4] They were all useless: the pestilence was carried by fleas and lice; in 1665 a more virulent form may even have passed through the air.

There were suspicious deaths in St Giles-in-the-Fields at the end of 1664, and in other parishes too, but winter temperatures checked the plague's advance. Authorities may have suspected that it had reached England from Amsterdam, where it was raging. To avoid panic, it seems they concealed its presence: deaths were attributed to 'spotted fever'. Families themselves may have bribed searchers not to record plague deaths for fear of being quarantined. Early symptoms could be inconclusive but painful buboes, tumours in the armpits, groin and behind the ears, usually meant plague. The dreaded 'tokens', discoloured spots spreading over the skin, invariably signalled death. By April 1665, London's weekly death rate was rising fast; on the 26th the Privy Council finally introduced household quarantine. Where plague was confirmed, whole families were locked inside their homes. Samuel Pepys was shocked to see some houses shut up in Drury Lane on 30 April. A red cross was painted a foot high on the door, and 'Lord have mercy upon us' above. Watchers were appointed to ensure the quarantine was kept for forty days and to supply families with food. Nurses were hired to visit the sick. If the family was poor, costs were covered by parish funds. But incarceration was a death sentence for the healthy confined with the sick; when the first houses were locked up in St Giles-in-the-Fields, a mob smashed the locks to set inmates free. Rioters were imprisoned, but it was too late: they had released the contagion into the streets.

London had two pesthouses dating from the last significant outbreak of the plague in 1647; here victims could be isolated. One pesthouse stood at the far end of St Margaret's, Westminster; the other at St Giles Cripplegate, north of the city wall. The Privy Council quietly ordered infected parishes in the west to build two more, keeping victims well away from Whitehall. St Giles-in-the-Fields built its pesthouse in the village of Marylebone. St Martin-in-the-Fields joined with Covent Garden to build one in Soho Garden; it was the largest in London, with room for ninety people, but it soon filled up. Another was built in Stepney for the eastern parishes. Plague victims were often carried to pesthouses in sedan chairs fitted with straps; the chairs were supposed to be aired for several days before being used by healthy people.

As summer approached, the death toll increased. There had been no rain for weeks, so the streets and sewers – just open ditches – were filthier than usual. By 2 May there was a death in Bearbinder Lane, off Lombard Street: the plague had reached the City. The lord mayor issued a series of orders: laystalls (stinking rubbish heaps) were to be moved further from the city walls. Householders must sweep outside their door every day, the sweepings to be carried away by a 'raker' who would give notice of his coming by blowing a horn. No nightman was to empty a cesspit into any garden or space close to the City. No unwholesome, rotting food was to be sold. Dogs, cats and tame pigeons were to be killed, and dog killers were appointed. The number of alehouses in each parish was to be reduced, partly to discourage people from meeting, partly because authorities feared civil disorder; 'fanatics' – the general term for Nonconformists – were always under suspicion. Soldiers were quartered in rowdy areas. More regulation followed as plague deaths soared: surgeons were to carry white wands four foot in length so that people could avoid them in the streets; now householders were to wash the street outside with water, and scour the drain, two or three times a day – a futile instruction when so few had piped water. Street hawkers were banned, as were public funerals; beggars were removed from the streets; all openings into infected houses had to be stopped up so that no one could creep into cellars or take shelter there.

In June tens of thousands of Londoners left the City; every dusty exit route was thronged with carriages and carts piled high with possessions. Only the rich could afford to retreat into the country, although Dryden, who had married well, decamped to his father-in-law's estate and a friend of Milton hired him a cottage in Chalfont St Giles. Middling tradesmen mostly stayed in London, although some sent their wives and children away. Watermen above London Bridge rowed their families further upriver, where they remained until the plague ceased, putting up tents made from sails on the riverbank and retiring to their boats at night. At this stage, servants who had emigrated to London were still able to return to the provinces if they had a certificate signed by two Justices of the Peace, confirming that they were free of the plague.

Many physicians and clergymen fled with the elite, claiming that they were tending their flock. As the plague worsened, fleeing Londoners were met on the road by angry villagers, armed with pitchforks and cudgels, who forced them back to stop them spreading the disease. The court had left London for Salisbury in the first few days of July, and later moved to Oxford. Samuel Pepys sent his wife to Woolwich on 6 July, and in August, John Evelyn sent his wife and most of his household to his brother-in-law's house in Wootten. The king entrusted London to George Monck, now Duke of Albemarle, who stayed at the Cockpit in St James's Park. Monck was supported by William, Earl of Craven, an old soldier and Privy Councillor who fearlessly kept to his house in Drury Lane. London's lord mayor, Sir John Lawrence, also stayed at his post, helping to maintain law and order. Citizens continued to make charitable donations; important centres like Taunton and Bristol also collected money to relieve the capital.[5] These funds helped London officials to carry on, but much civic activity lapsed. From July, for instance, the Middlesex quarter sessions were either hastily adjourned or not held at all due to poor attendance.

Ballads of the time offer a low opinion of the merchants, priests and physicians who fled and left the poor to their fate: 'What shall the Poor do that behind do stay?/Death makes them rich, by taking them away.'[6] To counteract these powerful, subversive messages, ballads were circulated to justify the exodus and praise the king's care of his people. One urged, 'Rejoyce O London in thy King,/Who to thy City does such comfort bring.'[7] Charles did order one of his surgeons back to London, but otherwise did little more than issue the time-worn regulations for dealing with plague, almost all of them ineffectual.

Some physicians and apothecaries stayed to help the sick. William Boghurst, an apothecary in St Giles-in-the-Fields, made his name by treating as many as sixty patients a day, by his own account. Another apothecary, Nathaniel Hodges, was paid £100 'for his care & pains in looking after the Poore visited with the Plague'.[8] Both men must have had some immunity to the disease, although Hodges attributed his preservation to burning herbs over hot coals on entering sick rooms, taking nutmeg, and copious drafts of sack or fortified wine. Other doctors died in great numbers, to judge by the sums that the City paid afterwards to their widows and dependants.

Terrified citizens fell prey to a host of quack doctors advertising pastes, powders and potions. Pomanders, 'made according to advise from the Colledge of Physicians for preventing of the Plague', could be had in St Paul's Churchyard for 12d. each.[9] Some quacks even claimed their medicines had royal approval. Pepys, who stayed in London, put his trust in his hare's foot and he chewed tobacco. Boghurst was adamant that tobacco, pomanders and stopping up the nose with rue and wormwood were all futile measures; Hodges ridiculed those who trusted to dried toads and amulets of wax and arsenic. The plague was relentless: it 'crept downe Holborne and the Strand, and then into the City, and at last to the East end of the Suburbs', reaching Stepney in July, falling on many parishes at once 'like raine'.[10] Thieves looted empty houses, spreading contagion still further.

The king ordered public fasts in July and August; many viewed the plague as God's punishment for sin. Church services continued, although sports were banned, public places closed, and even Bartholomew Fair in Smithfield was cancelled. There was a ban on dealing in second-hand clothes, but all business declined and London's trade with the provinces was badly affected. Thousands of common people had no work and no wages. The merchant Edward Wood wrote from the countryside to his London agent, John Pack, telling him to discharge workmen, 'Lock upp the Dores, & shun the danger what you can & to goe abroad as little as may be.'[11] The streets fell strangely silent and in some places grass began to grow where once there had been heavy road traffic. There were no cries of street hawkers or sounds of manufacture. River traffic declined as overseas trade took a hit. The textiles merchant, Sir William Turner, left in the general exodus but returned to the city in August to look after his affairs. He explained to his chief client in Paris that because his debtors had fled to the country, he could get no money to pay him, 'the sicknesse Encreaseth and the Towne is empty'.[12] In November, Turner was still placating his French supplier, 'The merchants doe not yet come to Towne so that I have not received one penny of our money But you may bee confident I watch all oportunityes.'[13] Four mercers in Paternoster Row went bankrupt.

People lived knowing that they might die at any minute. It was clear that filthy alleys were more dangerous than wider streets, that wealthy central parishes suffered less than poorer suburbs. Pepys travelled by water whenever he could, although he took fright in early September when one of his watermen got the plague and died next day. In desperation the lord mayor ordered bonfires to be kept burning in most streets, day and night. A blanket of smoke nearly suffocated people in their houses for almost three days before torrential rain put the fires out. The experiment was not repeated. Boghurst and Hodges railed against the inhumane practice of shutting up the healthy in plague-ridden homes, but London had too few pesthouses for the sick. Those who refused house quarantine faced prison; fears rose so high that charitable people who took in children from infected houses were prosecuted. Yet people with raging fevers and plague sores were walking the streets and often died there. Witnessing a corpse, Pepys mused, 'Lord to see what custom is, that I am come almost to think nothing of it.'

Not all were numbed by familiarity with horror. Parishes had been forced to hire drivers with carts who collected bodies for night burial, crying 'Bring out your dead.'[14] Rugg recorded that some were so uncouth they spread fear by cursing people and swearing at their horses. A driver called Buckingham finally prompted outrage:

> . . . a foul and wicked fellow that in the night time with the pest cart having his load of dead would cry when hee had any children in his cart would cry ffaggotts ffaggots five for six pence and take a child up by the leg . . . would lay yong women to open view and such unseemly actions that I am ashamed to express heare his cryme.[15]

Lord Craven had Buckingham dismissed, whipped in front of the pesthouse, and put in Newgate.

Churchyards were so stuffed with corpses that, in many places, the ground was disturbingly higher than before. Nor were graves so well covered with lime or bodies buried as deep as they should have been. Since local burial grounds were overflowing, plague pits were dug beyond the city walls. Rugg recorded a 'Great Hole' near the pesthouse for Covent Garden and St Martin-in-the-Fields for up to forty bodies.[16] There were plague pits in Moorfields, Finsbury Fields, and in the open spaces of Tothill Fields and Southwark. But excavations have shown that corpses were mostly coffined, and that coffins were stacked in neat rows up to four deep. People clung on to ritual, even in mass burials.

Samuel Pepys, and others, suspected that numerous plague deaths went unrecorded: searchers of the dead were usually old women, possibly threatened with loss of parish relief unless they undertook the dangerous work and hardly competent judges of cause of death. They were poorly paid, commonly receiving just 4d. to view a body, and easily bribed to say it was no plague victim. Nurses, also badly paid, were suspected of killing patients in order to rob them. Several looters were prosecuted, and others caught the infection from stolen goods: death helped to enforce law and order.

By October the poor were desperate and unwilling any longer to endure plague regulations, now viewed as forms of tyranny. There was no Lord Mayor's Show; the new mayor was sworn in at a comb-maker's shop at Tower Gate, decorated for the purpose, and returned quickly to his house. But at last plague deaths began to decrease with colder weather. By December many judged it safe to return to London, although the court did not appear until the following February; plague cases continued to be reported for the rest of the year. The official number of plague deaths in 1665 was 68,596; probably it was closer to 90,000, almost a quarter of all Londoners.

'THE WHOLE HEAVEN ON FIRE'[17]

The New Year did not bring much lightening of mood. Astrologers had long issued warnings about 1666 because the Book of Revelation gives 666 as the number of the Beast of the Apocalypse. London's poor still simmered with resentment that the rich had deserted the city during the plague, dodging their obligation to provide charitable relief; at the two social extremes there was no common experience of the crisis, no sense of unity in misfortune. In the winter of 1665–6 the poor suffered badly: fuel was dear, and employment hard to find. Middling tradesmen had financial losses, too, because the court had long been absent, and returning courtiers were slow to pay their debts.

During the plague, Justices of Middlesex had denounced unhealthy over-crowding in the suburbs caused by:

Receaving harbouring and placeing of inmates and undersitters in houses and cellars, and by erecting of new buildings, and by divideing and parcel-ling out the said buildings and other houses into severall petty tenements and habitacions, and pestering and filling the same with inmates and poore indigent and idle and loose persons.[18]

When the Middlesex quarter sessions resumed in February 1666, the Justices meant to evict lodgers and restore subdivided houses to their former state. They encountered a wave of protest: the poor could not afford whole houses; if they did not live in tenements, how would London employers recruit local labour? For the moment nothing much was done, although crowded dwellings were a known fire risk.

On Sunday 2 September, between 1 a.m. and 2 a.m., the baker Thomas Farriner woke to find his house in Pudding Lane thick with smoke. The oven in his bakehouse had not been raked out properly the night before, and now his lower storey was on fire. The family's only escape route was over the roof, but their maid was too afraid to climb out; she perished in the flames. Neighbours had gone to bed later than usual, Saturday being the end of the working week, and they were in their first, dead sleep. As the flames spread to nearby houses and workshops, people woke too late to do more than save themselves. It had been another dry summer; London's wooden buildings were like tinder. Worse, a stiff, easterly wind was blowing, fanning flames and causing them to jump over houses. Watchmen alerted the lord mayor, Thomas Bludworth. The lanes around Farriner's bakehouse were too narrow to admit fire engines, so fire-fighters advised Bludworth to have buildings pulled down to make a firebreak.

He hesitated – most of the houses were occupied by tenants; did he need the owners' permission before tearing down property? Fires in London were commonplace; he decided this one wasn't serious. Allegedly remarking that a woman could piss it out, he went back to bed. It was the biggest mistake of his life.

From Pudding Lane the flames spread northwards to Gracechurch Street and the Royal Exchange, south towards London Bridge, and west towards the warehouses in Thames Street. Here the fire fixed on quantities of combustible materials: oils, hay, spices, rope and timber. People carrying buckets of water began to panic; tall buildings and narrow streets made it impossible to judge where the fire was heading. Soon it was completely out of control. In the centre of this chaos the heat was intense, the noise of the devastation terrifying: timbers cracked, houses crashed to the ground, and above the roar and desperate shouting, sudden screams rang out. Overhead, the wind blew tongues of fire to reach distant buildings; drifts of falling sparks made faces smart and singed hair; the acrid smoke reached deep inside people's lungs, sending them away coughing and spluttering. Already rumours were spreading that the Dutch and French had fired the city.

By Sunday night around a thousand shops and houses had been destroyed. The king, knowing that his throne probably depended on saving London, put his brother James in charge of fighting the flames, overriding the lord mayor. First thing on Monday, the Duke of York organized teams of men to pull down houses. The fire had already consumed Thames Street and part of Cannon Street; John Evelyn, watching from the Southwark shore, estimated that 10,000 houses were ablaze. There were reports that the inferno could be seen forty miles away. By now, most Londoners had stopped trying to put it out and were intent on saving themselves and as many possessions as they could take with them. The City's narrow roads became choked with people and wagons: some moving south to get their goods into boats, others heading for the open fields to the north. With so many on the move, the price of carts rocketed. Usually costing 10s. or 12s. to hire, the price rose to £10; some drivers were said to be asking £30 and more.

London was still ablaze on Tuesday. The king joined his brother, riding through the streets to encourage the firefighters, and he ordered the use of gunpowder to create wider firebreaks. Despite all efforts, the flames reached Cheapside; merchants were facing huge losses. Most booksellers, printers, and some drapers shifted their wares into St Paul's, then under restoration, thinking the cathedral's stone walls would offer protection, but flames soon lapped at the scaffolding around it. The fire was burning at intense temperatures, reaching 1,700°C since it melted pottery; the lead in the cathedral roof began to melt and ooze to the ground.[19] Stained-glass windows sagged and shattered; stone walls splintered and exploded outwards. The merchants lost everything. Charred paper blew westwards as far as Eton. Pepys, watching the apocalyptic scenes from his garden in Seething Lane, feared he would soon lose his house; he buried his wine and precious Parmesan cheese in the garden.

Moorfields, where thousands of citizens had fled, became a refugee camp. Stupefied and disconsolate families sat with their children, guarding their few possessions, 'Some under tents, some under miserab(l)e Hutts and Hovells, without a rag'.[20] Hundreds had escaped with only the clothes on their backs. The king, who had gained a great deal of support by fighting the fire in person, ordered supplies of ships' biscuit to be distributed so that people did not starve, and later issued a proclamation to provide food for the destitute. Schools, churches and other public places were made available to store the goods of the homeless. A loyalist ballad was printed, warning merchants not to charge inflationary prices, urging citizens to help each other, and praising the decisive action of the royal brothers.[21] Inevitably, there was profiteering.

By Wednesday evening the fire was under control and by Thursday it was out, although cellars continued to smoulder and, where flammable goods remained, small fires erupted for months afterwards. Around four-fifths of the walled city had been destroyed: some 13,500 houses, 87 of the 109 parish churches, 43 livery halls, and other important buildings like the Royal Exchange and the Custom House. Sir Edward Atkyns, a prominent judge, wrote that he could hardly tell where parishes had been:

> There is nothing but stones and rubbish, and all exposed to the open air. Soe y^t [that] you may see from one end of the Citty almost to ye other . . . . and you can compare London (were it not for ye rubbish) to nothing more than an open field.[22]

Officially, only six people died but the death toll was certainly higher. The Venetian ambassador in France claimed, 'The old, tender children and many sick and helpless persons were all burned in their beds and served as fuel for the flames.'[23] And William Taswell, a boy at Westminster School, found a dead woman who had taken refuge near the east walls of St Paul's. Years later he vividly remembered the body, 'every limb reduced to a coal'.[24] No one was counting dispossessed street dwellers, or the old and sick with no family. As over 65,000 people had been made homeless, some died from exposure in the fields around London.

Although the authorities knew that the fire had started in a baker's shop, Londoners looked for scapegoats: it was the work of Catholics, foreigners or plotters. Any Dutch or French person was suspect. Some were formally accused of throwing fireballs and prosecuted; others fell prey to vigilante groups. Suspicion remained even after one disturbed Frenchman, Robert Hubert, confessed to arson and was hanged. The judges knew he was innocent, but since he wanted to part with his life, they took it. Meanwhile, looters seized what they could. The burnt-out areas of the City became extremely dangerous: thieves waylaid travellers, dragged them into cellars, robbed and sometimes murdered them, hiding bodies underground.

Rival nations predicted that the Fire would be a death blow for the Stuart monarchy, but Charles swiftly planted the idea that London would recover and, phoenix-like, rise more beautiful than before. Within a week, on 13 September, he issued a proclamation stipulating that houses should be rebuilt with brick exteriors and that building regulations would follow. Robert Hooke was appointed chief City Surveyor for London's reconstruction. He came up with a street plan that incorporated wide boulevards and open spaces. Christopher Wren and John Evelyn also drew up proposals for a new city, more regular in design than before. The cartographer Richard Newcourt even suggested the kind of grid plan that would be adopted in America. None of these ideas came to fruition: the vital thing was to get London trading again to help pay for the cost of rebuilding; there was no time, money, or even administrative capacity for a redesign. Former property owners started to rebuild where their houses had stood, and London's medieval street plan was mostly retained. The only marked improvement was the creation of King Street and Queen Street for

1. This ink drawing shows the chariot carrying Queen Elizabeth's coffin, drawn by four horses and flanked by earls and barons carrying banners. It is taken from a seventeenth-century work presenting the first ever visual record of an English monarch's funeral procession.

2. London viewed from Southwark in 1616, taken from a four-piece panorama. This section shows London Bridge, Billingsgate to the right, and the City bristling with church spires. Barges and small boats on the River Thames take people and goods upstream.

3. James I of England aged fifty-five in 1621, when he had lost teeth and was already suffering chronic ill health. The tapestry behind him incorporates the Tudor rose and the motto BEATI PACIFICI: 'blessed are the peacemakers'.

4. Charles I aged thirty-one, painted at Greenwich in 1631. He had inherited his father's unshakeable belief in the 'Divine Right of Kings' and from 1629 to 1640 ruled England without a parliament. Portraits like this were sent to friends, servants and officials overseas.

5. Oliver Cromwell, Lord Protector of England, based on a 1656 portrait by the miniaturist Samuel Cooper. Cromwell famously demanded to be painted 'warts and all', but doubtless benefited from his standing as a plain man who disliked flattery.

6. A preparatory work for a larger painting of Charles II with the governors, masters and boys of Christ's Hospital, a London charity school. The king poses as benefactor and educator of his subjects, promoting mathematical studies to eager pupils. Charles died suddenly and the finished work depicts his successor, James II.

7. A digitally constructed birds-eye view of the Great Fire on 2 September 1666, the day that the inferno began. It shows the scale of London at the time, major roads leading into the City, and building developments along the route to Westminster.

8. A dramatic view of the Fire on the evening of 4 September 1666, when it had taken firm hold. The imagined viewpoint is from the safety of a boat near Tower Wharf. Sparks fly high over the city and terrified Londoners try to escape with their goods.

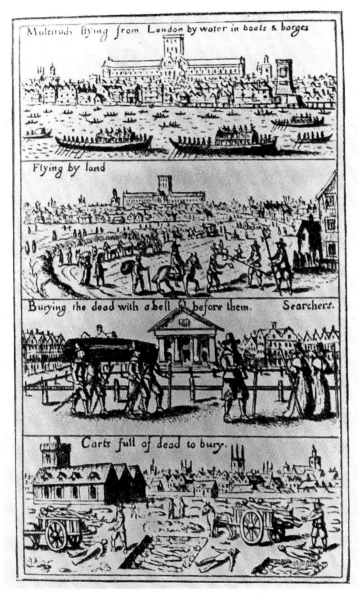

Multituds flying from London by water in boats & borges
Flying by land
Burying the dead with a bell before them.   Searchers.
Carts full of dead to bury.

9. A contemporary print of London scenes during the Plague of 1665. Some flee by water. Others go by road but are challenged by guards placed to stop the spread of infection. Funerals are minimal; a bell-ringer warns people to stay clear. Cartloads of naked bodies are placed in plague pits.

10. A rare drawing of the inside of a London coffee house. A woman in a white lace fontange sits behind the counter near a roaring fire. One servant pours coffee; another takes clay pipes from a chest. The walls are dotted with paintings and notices.

11. John Flamsteed and two assistants working in the Octagon Room at the Royal Observatory, Greenwich. The telescope and large quadrant could be moved from window to window. Tompion's clocks are in the centre; portraits of the Observatory's patrons, Charles II and James II, are above the door.

12. Samuel Pepys aged fifty-six in 1689. This was the year he resigned from his post as Secretary to the Admiralty after his patron, James II, was driven into exile. It shows a solemn, dignified Pepys embarking on a new stage of his life.

13. A Dutch engraving of the Duke of Monmouth's execution at Tower Hill after his failed rebellion in 1685. Of noble birth, Monmouth was spared hanging. Unhappily, as the caption records, it took several strokes to behead him.

Monmouth ongelukkiglyk met verscheidene Slagen Onthooft.

14. East Indiamen being built at Deptford in the 1680s; after 1649, the East India Company realised it was cheaper to charter ships than to build their own. Two other vessels in the river fly the striped Company flag. In the left foreground is the royal yacht, *Henrietta*.

15. This view from One Tree Hill in Greenwich Park artfully depicts London's prosperity under Charles II. To the left is the Royal Observatory and, in the centre, the Queen's House. The Monument to the Fire, completed in 1677, is in the middle distance.

better access to Guildhall from the river. But numerous streets were widened, and the stony rubbish of St Paul's was used to raise the low parts around Fleet Street and to reduce the steep gradient of routes west of the Tower leading to riverside quays.

City authorities also took swift action. The Court of Common Council met on 10 September and began to make provision for the homeless. It offered seven-year leases in designated open spaces to those who wished to make dwellings while they rebuilt former premises. Moorfields was the most important site. It was mostly open pasture and used as tenter grounds for stretching and drying cloth. According to Pepys, by 1667 its quaggy fields had been replaced with paved streets and houses two storeys high. London's Guildhall had been badly damaged, so the lord mayor and aldermen used Gresham College, which was unharmed. Merchants also used the college as an exchange, so overcrowding there acted as a spur to reconstruction.

Many livery companies, who had long sustained the City with their charity, as during the Plague, were now impoverished. The priority for the Apothecaries, Blacksmiths, Brewers, Merchant Taylors, Glaziers, Painterstainers, Skinners and others was to rebuild their halls and help their destitute members. In the Grocers' burnt-out hall, the Company's plate had melted. The parcels of metal were collected, amounting to nearly 200 pounds of silver, and sold. With little money to spare for wider charity, companies ceased to maintain their corn granaries, which were lost in the fire. A Lord Mayor's Show in 1666 was unthinkable – apart from lack of funds, the streets were in no condition to host a pageant.

In October the king and the mayor set up a commission that included Wren and Hooke to oversee rebuilding the following spring. In bitter winter temperatures Hooke and other surveyors carried out a basic survey of the burnt neighbourhoods to inform the commission's recommendations. These were encapsulated in the First Rebuilding Act, which became law in February 1667. The Act defined four categories of building and standardized the dimensions of each. Buildings were to be of brick or stone, overhanging gables were banned, major routes were to be widened. Any compensation for loss of land would be paid by a new tax levied on coal brought into London for the next ten years. A new court – the Fire Court – would be set up to deal with boundary disputes and compensation claims. The twenty-two Fire Judges worked tirelessly to encourage swift rebuilding, so much so that a grateful City had portraits painted of them to hang in its newly restored Guildhall. Some still hang in the Guildhall Art Gallery today, with a note explaining that eight of the carved, gilded frames were supplied by one Mary Ashfield at £12 each.

Hooke played the major role in supervising London's reconstruction. The regulations set out in the 1667 Rebuilding Act were mostly followed – not least because builders found that standardization saved money.[25] New premises, largely funded by private money, went up on old foundations; fire rubble was sifted for materials that could be reused. Trade slowly recovered. Sir William Turner was probably typical of merchants in that he lost his accounts in the Fire. He had to write to overseas clients and ask for duplicates. In 1668 he was elected lord mayor, winning praise for the efficiency with which he oversaw the restoration of the City. A new Exchange was completed in 1669, one of the first corporate buildings to be rebuilt; a new Custom House, a two-storey, classical design by Wren, was in use by 1671. The price of building materials was monitored, although importers of timber, bricks and tiles made a lot of money. London's timber trade was handled by a few powerful merchants who benefited in the longer term, too, since the Fire boosted trade with Scandinavia. The enormous growth in colonial trade also helped to pay for the rebuilding of London.

Many merchants who fled settled in the suburbs and did not return to the City and only about a third of the houses destroyed by fire were rebuilt, so the City was significantly depopulated; for a while playhouses had smaller audiences. But Londoners did pull together. In just six years the City was largely restored. The Monument to the Fire, designed by Hooke with Wren's input, was finished in 1677. Most city churches and St Paul's Cathedral took longer to rebuild. Wren, appointed King's Surveyor of Works in 1669, was responsible for over fifty new churches; his masterpiece, St Paul's, was only completed in 1711. Most people admired the new London but although it had fine modern buildings, the total effect was not as uniform as some had wished. The architect, Nicholas Hawksmoor, later dismissed the City as 'a Chaos of Dirty Rotten Sheds, allways Tumbling or takeing fire, with winding Crooked passages (Scarse practicable), Lakes of Mud and Rills of Stinking Mire Running through them'.[26]

The regulations of the Rebuilding Act applied only to the City; outside its walls, many wooden buildings continued to be constructed.

In one instance the City did drag its feet. Charles insisted that Temple Bar had to be replaced, although it was undamaged by fire. The gate was a visual marker of the City's independent power from Westminster, so Mayor Turner and his aldermen disliked the intervention. How much was Charles involved in designing the replacement? We do not know, but the new stone structure, built between 1669 and 1672, featured statues of himself, his father and grandfather, powerfully upholding the continuity of Stuart rule. It also asserted royal control over a city that had opposed monarchy during the Civil Wars.

Some royalists claimed the Fire was fit punishment on London, given its earlier rebellion; others said it was God's retribution on a sinful people. But not a few muttered that the house of Stuart met with nothing but misfortune.

WAR WITH THE DUTCH

Domestic tragedies made it harder for England to sustain its new war against the Dutch. Charles and his brother deliberately provoked the conflict, hoping for booty and greater royal authority. They circulated anti-Dutch propaganda to whip up trade rivalries, and Charles formally declared war on 4 March 1665. This Second Anglo-Dutch War was popular at first but there was no money to pay for it. Hopes rested on quick victories at sea but, after a heartening victory at the Battle of Lowestoft in Suffolk on 13 June, outright success eluded the English fleet. Meanwhile, the treatment of wounded seamen and prisoners of war grew scandalous. John Evelyn had been made one of the commissioners of the Sick and Hurt Board that provided medical services to the navy. With plague raging in London and no funding, he became increasingly desperate, complaining to the Navy Board that thousands of prisoners and wounded seamen at Woolwich and Gravesend were dying for want of food and shelter.

In October workers in the royal dockyards at Deptford and Woolwich mutinied. To prepare for war they had been asked to work twelve-hour days and longer, but they had not been paid. By early 1666, men were desperate. Two ropemakers and two ship's carpenters petitioned the Duke of Albemarle, still in London during the plague, for swift relief. Their pay was nine months in arrears, co-workers had died of want during the epidemic; families were all in debt and could no longer get credit.[27] But the demands of war took precedence. Naval shipwrights were in such short supply, many had to be 'pressed' into service from the better-paid merchants' yards. Inevitably, men were truculent; pilfering in the dockyards increased and naval management suffered.

Seamen also went unpaid. The Navy Board was forced to keep ships in commission for no military reason, incurring more expense, because it could not afford to pay off crews; meanwhile, seamen's families starved at home. In May 1665 the Board resorted to the system of paying seamen with tickets, not ready money. Unscrupulous dealers only bought them at a heavy discount; sailors might have to sell a ticket representing a month's wages for just one shilling. By October, Pepys was seeing seamen starving in the streets. Their wives and widows also petitioned for speedy payment of their husbands' wages, and the compensation promised them, many walking hundreds of miles to London to make their case in person. After the Four Days' Battle, 7–11 June 1666, wives whose husbands had been taken prisoner besieged the navy office, demanding the money owed them. Pepys confessed:

> Their cries were so sad for money, and laying down the condition of their families and their husbands, and what they have done and suffered for the King, and how ill they are used by us . . . that I do most heartily pity them.[28]

Naval officials became so worried for their own safety that in 1667 they applied for 'twelve well-fixed firelocks with supply of powder and bullet' to defend their office against angry mobs.[29]

The Navy Board had no money to pay contractors either. Merchants with deep purses or credit continued to supply materials, quietly inflating prices to cover the effort and so deepening the war debt. Smaller contractors grew needy. William Wood of Wapping, for example, begged the navy commissioners to pay his £500 bill for ships' masts, explaining that he had 'freely parted with his goods, and not demanded money till compelled by urgent occasions'.[30] Many went bankrupt, increasing the poverty of maritime communities.

Press gangs found obtaining crews increasingly difficult: men saw that naval supplies were short and that sailors could go hungry at sea. By 1666, labourers and householders usually exempt from impressment were being torn from their families; to Pepys it seemed 'a great tyranny'.[31] In May that year the ban on pressing Thames watermen was lifted, although afterwards press gangs were discovered taking bribes to release them. Sailors went into hiding, causing government to urge press gangs to search houses in maritime districts and deliver to the fleet any seamen found; discontent rose. And as impressment increased, London's industries suffered: in July brewers pleaded to be left with enough men to continue their businesses. Yet there were still isolated cases of girls disguising themselves as men in order to join the fleet.[32]

The Plague had confronted Londoners with scenes of horror, but now the lasting human cost of war made a deep impression. While beds were available, English sick and wounded were taken to the Savoy, a military hospital since the Civil Wars. John Evelyn visited it in August 1666 to see the 'miserably dismembred & wounded men dressed'.[33] Thomas Carter's petition to the king for a pension reveals the disfiguring injuries that men sustained; in the last battle, he wrote, a terrible wound broke his jawbone, 'so that he could only eat spoon meat since'.[34] The maimed and disfigured were daily reminders of the consequences of war.

In these years of crisis the monarchy tried hard to control the news. Potentially dangerous works, like Hobbes's *Leviathan*, were investigated for promoting atheism; Londoners were encouraged to celebrate every success in battle with bonfires and bell-ringing. In June 1666, after citizens had spent anxious days listening to cannon fire off the east Kent coast, the government newspaper, the *London Gazette*, described the Four Days' Battle as a 'victory' although it was not. Repeated catastrophes and setbacks took a mental toll on Londoners. In November 1666 the porter of Bethlem Hospital and his wife reported a great increase in lunatics, making their work dangerous – a coincidence, perhaps, but contemporaries were aware that insanity as a cause of death was under-reported.[35]

A Dutch invasion had long been feared. But when, in June 1667, the Dutch sailed up the Medway, attacking the English fleet, Londoners went mad with anger, humiliation and disappointment. Some feared a conspiracy was under way to reverse the Restoration and plunge them into deeper poverty; the king, it seemed, had been badly advised by his Privy Council. A mob attacked Clarendon House, the mansion that the king's Chief Minister, Edward Hyde, Earl of Clarendon, had just completed on Piccadilly. Rioters trampled his newly planted trees and broke expensive windows. The rumour on the streets was that Charles had been distracted by his pleasures even as the Dutch attacked; some even dared to say that things were better ordered under Cromwell.

Government overcame the naval funding crisis; Charles went on to nurture the navy and left it in a better state than he found it. But he had lost much of his people's trust: he had not won prestige for the country abroad, he presided over a degenerate court whose pleasures had an insidious effect on the nation, he was increasingly suspected of favouring Catholicism and absolute rule. The shared trauma of the Fire certainly brought Londoners together: moderate loyalists, defining themselves against perceived extremes of Nonconformist 'fanatics' on the one hand and papists on the other, became a powerful force. But a rebellious element still smouldered in London. It was plain to see in the Bawdy House Riots, which broke out on 23 March 1668. That Easter Monday demobbed sailors and rowdy apprentices pulled down brothels in Poplar. This unrest differed from the usual apprentice holiday riots: satires were published directed at the court; Dissenters fuelled the rioting, bitterly disappointed that Anglicans in parliament had thwarted the king's promise of religious tolerance. On 24 March large crowds headed for London's red-light districts in Moorfields, East Smithfield, St Andrew Holborn and St Leonard's Shoreditch parish. They targeted notorious brothel keepers, including Damaris Page, 'the Great Bawd of the Seamen', and Mother Creswell, who ran a network of high-class brothels.[36] The final assault came on Wednesday, when rioters, joined by reinforcements from Southwark, focused on brothels in Moorfields.

The violent disorder was a sign of widespread opposition to the Restoration monarchy. Courtiers even feared that apprentices and rioters were supported by former soldiers in Cromwell's army. Charles was especially irritated by *The Poor-Whores Petition*, a printed letter in the form of a satire aimed at the morals of his court. Allegedly written by brothel owners and prostitutes, it was addressed to Lady Castlemaine, court whore and Catholic, facetiously asking for her help to repair riot-damaged property. The ringleaders were convicted of treason, then brutally hanged, drawn and quartered.

In these terrible years the physical spaces of the City changed beyond recognition, and so too did citizens' mental grasp of their capital. But though disaster crushed some spirits, it put others on their mettle. Divisions surely remained but a common purpose, born of common experience, saw the rapid rebuilding of the City and the formation of a new outlook. Fortunately, London could call upon some of the finest brains of the century and many worked now as if doubly conscious that they had only limited time in which to make their mark; their advances in knowledge increasingly helped to inspire London's adventurous and resilient citizens.

14

THE SPIRIT OF DISCOVERY
CURIOSITY AND EXPERIMENT

On 23 November 1667, Arthur Coga, a crazed and impoverished former student of divinity, became the first person in England to undergo a blood transfusion. The procedure followed gory experiments in London to transfer the blood of one dog into another, and a blood transfusion into a human carried out some months earlier in Paris. Coga was given nine or ten ounces of sheep's blood, which seemed a good choice because the Bible describes Jesus as the Lamb of God, so it was hoped that the young sheep's blood would have healing powers. William Harvey, physician to Charles I, had discovered that blood circulates around the body, rather than being continually created and used up, so doctors reasoned now that it was worth trying to improve the quality of blood in the sick. Coga was paid 20s. for his compliance. Some weeks later the experiment was repeated but there was no improvement in Coga's mental state; he drank his fee at the nearest tavern. He was lucky to survive: the incompatibility of blood between different species had not been discovered; there was no understanding of blood types. After the death of a Frenchman in another transfusion, these operations were outlawed in France and abandoned in England until the nineteenth century.

The experiment on Coga was carried out by members of the Royal Society of London for Improving Natural Knowledge, to give this learned Society its full title. Founded on 28 November 1660, it is the oldest national scientific institution in the world. Members aimed to 'Improve the knowledge of Natural things and all usefull Arts, Manufactures, Mechanick practises, Engynes & inventions by Experiments', vowing not to meddle with touchy subjects like divinity, morals or politics.[1] They turned their backs on dogma and took as their motto 'Nullius in verba', which roughly translates as 'take nobody's word for it'. They meant to test ideas and phenomena by experiment before accepting them, although in practice they also relied on detailed, convincing description. The Society did not spring into the world with the Restoration; its approach owed much to Francis Bacon's insistence at the beginning of the century that the natural world should be documented by close observation.[2] It was indebted to the influential thinker Samuel Hartlib, who died in 1662, and to the programme of lectures at Gresham College. Its members were also broadly swayed by the challenge to authority in the civil war period; even during the turbulent 1640s and 1650s groups of scholars and amateur enthusiasts had continued to meet in London and Oxford, in coffee houses and taverns, to discuss mathematics and test theories by experimentation.

The divisions of the Civil Wars and Interregnum had constrained political and religious thinking, so scholars, experts and keen amateurs (wealthy, leisured men who pursued special interests and connoisseurship) relished free discussion about the natural world as a breath of fresh air. They corresponded with European scholars, exchanging findings even when their countries were at war. Patriotic Londoners believed that they stood to gain from such networks; that they were 'not so apt to invent' themselves but could improve on the inventions of others.[3] Gentlemen who had travelled on the Continent, like John Evelyn, kept up their foreign contacts. Evelyn had met Thomas Hobbes in France and took care to visit him in England. Learned groups also exchanged the latest instruments: in 1653, for example, Evelyn received a selenoscope for observing craters on the Moon.

Under Cromwell, learned groups, fired by the growing ambition for their country and the excitement of discovery, came to believe that London's ingenious citizens were on the cusp of greatness. Christopher Wren, appointed Professor of Astronomy at Gresham in 1657, claimed unscientifically, when giving his first lecture, that the planets themselves smiled on London. Mercury, he said, nourished its mechanical arts and trade, encouraged the liberal sciences, and fostered 'a general Relish of Mathematicks'.[4] In an evident crowd-pleaser he went on to link scientific discovery with navigation and sea power. In no other city, he explained, did the ocean come so far inland; he hoped that Londoners might be always called 'Masters of the Sea' and that London, like Alexandria before it, might become 'the establish'd Residence of Mathematical

Arts'.[5] Wren's buoyant enthusiasm was justified: after the Restoration, economic and social conditions were ripe for the new scientific spirit to extend to commerce and industry. London was poised to become the most important location in the world for scientific enquiry.

The Society, meeting in London to discuss experimental learning, obtained royal approval almost as soon as it was founded, just five months after Charles was restored to the throne. And in 1662 he granted its first charter. Evelyn is credited with suggesting the term 'Royal' to help secure the king's support, but Sir Robert Moray, an army officer with keen scientific interests, was central to the establishment of the new Royal Society. He was close to the king, had supported him in exile, and understood that Charles, with ambitions to extend his dominions and increase trade, had a specific problem: he was desperate to strengthen his navy through improved navigation and ship design, but lacked the funds for it. As far as Moray was concerned, the men best able to advance maritime knowledge were already loosely based at Gresham College. A free-mason, and therefore at ease with the convention that an organization might leave sectarian faith and politics at the door, he encouraged royalists and parlia-mentarians to unite in studying the natural world. These natural philosophers (today we would call them scientists) met weekly at Gresham. To defray expenses, they paid an initial fee of 10s. and then 1s. weekly, whether they attended meetings or not. Fellows were elected by secret ballot and anyone curious to find out more about the natural world might apply to join. In the early years almost half of them were noblemen: courtiers and politicians who enjoyed the kudos of belonging to an exclusive, fashionable circle. Their money helped to fund the Society's work. Evelyn was one of the founding Fellows, linking the earlier period of curiosity to the later concerns of these experimental philosophers. In the 1640s he had attended anatomy lectures in Padua and purchased rare tables of human veins, arteries and nerves, which in 1667 he donated to the Society.

As many early Fellows were physicians, discussions often focused on the circulation of blood, respiration and the effect of poisons. Other Fellows included university professors and men of letters, like Dryden. They could be asked to prepare experiments or papers for subsequent meetings. Consequently, in the Society's early months, Wren was asked to demonstrate the characteristics of a pendulum. Sir Robert Boyle's leisured experiments with air and gas led to the discovery of Boyle's Law, published in 1660, when he proved that the volume of gas varies inversely with pressure. His assistant, Robert Hooke, who developed the vacuum air-pump Boyle needed, was made the Society's Curator of Experiments in 1662. Hooke had a wonderfully inventive mind as well as great mechanical ingenuity, and for a while he produced new experiments or discoveries at almost every meeting. The Society's range of interest is indicated by the list of research topics Hooke made in the 1660s. It included theories of motion, light, gravity, magnetics, gunpowder, and of the heavens, and the improvement of shipping, watches, optics, and engines for trade and carriage. Other Fellows were interested in husbandry, mining and the chemical industries. In these early years the Society encouraged work on the histories of specific trades. This was something Francis Bacon had suggested, and scholars had begun the task in Cromwell's time, aiming to revolutionize industry, although it would take decades for such work to have practical effect. The physician William Petty, for example, investigated the production of wool cloth. As the son of a clothier, he may have had a personal interest; in 1664 he also wrote a treatise on techniques for dyeing cloth.

Founding Fellows were enormously excited, even liberated, by the latest forensic method of investigating the natural world and ordering knowledge. It seemed that if they proceeded by experimentation and mathematical reasoning, if they reported their findings in plain language so that each step was a building block, they would surely come to a genuine understanding of natural phenomena. Yet several of them still dabbled in alchemy; magical thinking coexisted with the new experimental philosophy. Hooke pursued dubious experiments involving spiders and what he took to be unicorn's horn. Isaac Newton, who in 1687 revolutionized scientific thought with the publication of his *Principia Mathematica*, setting out universal laws of motion and gravitation, was perhaps the greatest alchemist of all. He spent years looking for the secret of transforming base metal into gold.

The Society's live experiments featured horrific vivisections. In 1664, Hooke cut away the chest of a dog to investigate its breathing. He inserted a hollow cane down its throat into its windpipe and found that he could keep the dog alive for as long as he wished by pumping air into its lungs with bellows. Few living things survived the Fellows' avid curiosity. In 1663 fishes were gagged; in another experiment frogs were daubed in turn with pitch, mercury and vinegar. Mercury and vinegar proved harmless, 'but good store of pitch being put upon one killed it at last'.[6] In 1665, Pepys, who had been elected a Fellow for his naval contacts and administrative ability, witnessed a 'little kitling' put to death with tobacco oil.[7]

Other investigations seemed more immediately practical. The Commissioners of the Navy appealed for advice on woodland management because oak trees were urgently needed for shipbuilding. This resulted in Evelyn's *Sylva, or A Discourse of Forest-Trees and the Propagation of Timber*, published in 1664. Evelyn always referred to 'My *Sylva*' and had his portrait painted, book in hand, but although his own role had been central, the book was a collective project. Wren and Petty were also tasked with finding practical improvements to shipping. The king himself asked Petty, who had gone to sea in his youth, to turn his mind to naval matters. Petty came up with a fast, early version of the catamaran, but work on it stopped after a prototype was lost in the Irish Channel. Petty remained interested in ship design: from 1661 he investigated the sheathing of ship hulls in protective thin lead. Around 1670, metal workers invented a process known as milled lead, rolling lead bars between two drums to get an even thickness, making lead sheathing feasible. The king himself visited Deptford dockyard in 1673 to examine the hull of a ship that had been sheathed and sent to the Mediterranean. Encouraged, he decreed that only milled lead should be used to sheath his warships but over time dangerous corrosion appeared in their iron rudder bolts. No one understood this electrochemical process and the experiment became mired in controversy. Although a failure, lead sheathing is a prime example of how the Society's scientific enquiry became entwined with practical technology, manufacturing and military concerns.

There were also close ties between the Society's work and foreign trade. Fellows cooperated with the East India and Royal African Companies to collect tidal data. They experimented with dyestuffs from the New World. They eagerly amassed information about the skills of the Chinese, Japanese and native peoples in North America that might benefit English manufacturing, and they were keenly interested in the medicines used overseas. Thomas Sprat, a churchman and man of letters elected a Fellow of the Society in 1663, and soon afterwards asked to write its 'history', remarked on this international network. 'In short time,' he wrote, 'there will scarce a Ship come up the *Thames*, that does not make some return of *Experiments*, as well as of *Merchandize*.'[8] But if the Society was open to foreign influence and admired the skills of indigenous peoples, it mostly saw knowledge as a way to strengthen England's grip on distant lands and exploit others' natural resources. As a scientific institution based in London, it was at the heart of a growing imperial network.

After the Fire, Gresham College was used as a temporary Exchange until 1673 when a replacement was completed. In this period the Society met in Arundel House on the Strand, home of Henry Howard, Duke of Norfolk. Evelyn soon persuaded Howard, a Fellow of the Society but no book lover, to donate his valuable library to the Society for safekeeping. The Society also built up a 'Repository' of specimens, which helped Fellows to identify rare finds. Collecting natural rarities and other 'wonders' had long been an elite pastime. These curiosities testified to a person's wealth and status; the rooms where they were displayed provided an ideal setting for amiable conversation. Elite tourists to London, including ambassadors, were sure to take in the Society's Repository and John Tradescant's 'Ark', the museum he and his son assembled in Lambeth. And both venues helped to extend the culture of curiosity to women: Evelyn met an Irish bishop and his wife visiting the Repository, noting, 'She seemed to be a knowing Woman, beyond the ordinary talent of her sex.'[9] The social aspect of collecting was also demonstrated in Don Saltero's coffee house in Chelsea. Its owner, James Salter, had been a servant to Sir Hans Sloane, the physician and naturalist whose great collections helped found the British Museum. Sloane gave unwanted curiosities to Salter, turning his Chelsea coffee house into a visitor attraction. All these venues enhanced the reputation of London.

The Society was fashionable when founded. Curiosity about natural and artificial rarities was the mark of a gentleman, and during the winter season when the nobility and gentry were in London, attendance at its meetings rose. Its experiments and demonstrations became topics of conversation, so the experience offered had to be something all Fellows could understand and put into words. This circumstance sat well with the Society's ambition to cultivate 'a close, naked, natural way of speaking', favouring the language used by arti-sans and merchants over that of scholars.[10] The links that Fellows had with the art world – some donated portraits and prints to the Society – also appealed to the elite. And after 1666, when France set up its Académie Royale des Sciences in Paris, the frisson of international competition also helped to make support for the Society patriotic.

Scientific interests filtered down to the aspiring middling classes. Numerous men and women bought and tried to understand scientific books. Some purchased expensive microscopes and telescopes to see for themselves; Pepys was thrilled with his microscope, 'a most curious bauble'.[11] At first he and his wife had trouble seeing anything through the eye-piece, but once he had got the hang of the instrument he eagerly used it to impress dinner guests. He was also capti-vated by Hooke's book, *Micrographia*, with its magnified images of the flea and the louse; he gazed at its pages by candlelight until 2 a.m., rating it 'the most ingenious book that ever I read in my life'.[12] Later Pepys amassed a library of rare publications, creating a haven of his own where he could entertain his circle, and where a shared admiration for objects of curiosity strengthened friendships. His interest in mathematical instruments – a professional necessity – was long-lasting. When his coach was held up by highwaymen in 1693, he was robbed of a silver ruler, gold pencil, magnifying glass and five mathematical instruments. One of the robbers advised him to ask next day at the Runner Tavern in Charing Cross if he wanted his favourite instrument back. It was an error of judgement that would result in two of their number being caught and hanged.

Thanks to the premium the Society placed on talent, by the end of its first decade it had also ventured into the realm of the social sciences. It enthusiastically welcomed the work of a mere tradesman, John Graunt, a button maker and friend of Petty. In 1662, Graunt presented the Society with fifty copies of his *Natural and Political Observations* on London's Bills of Mortality. In this work, prompted partly by the Society's emphasis on useful knowledge and partly by Londoners' curiosity about matters related to their own lives, he analysed avail-able data on deaths in London and presented findings about the health of its population. The Bills had been published weekly since 1592 and recorded cause of death since 1629, probably to help manage epidemics. Bacon had argued that the state should collect and analyse just this kind of data in order to improve its administration, but until Graunt applied what he modestly called his 'shop-arithmetic' to the Bills, no one had demonstrated what could be done. Graunt found that deaths from plague and from syphilis were probably under-reported. Few in London died from starvation. More than a third of those born would die before the age of six, and just 7 per cent would live to die of old age. Autumn, it seemed, was the unhealthiest season.[13] Although Graunt acknowledged that he was working with imperfect data, he also offered a way to estimate the population of London. The Society promptly made him a Fellow. He had given London's cultural world a new perspective from which to reflect, and his analysis soon launched further studies in social statistics and demographics.

THE ROYAL OBSERVATORY

The king grew disappointed that the Society discovered no quick breakthrough to serve the navy or promote trade. Improvements to navigation were essential: ocean-going ships needed to know where they were and how to get to where they wanted to go but mariners still had no reliable method of calculating longitude, their north-south position. In 1674 there was revived interest in working this out by tracking the position of the Moon across the background of fixed stars. If the location of the Moon could be predicted a year or two ahead, and if tables giving this information were supplied to seamen, in theory they could work out their position at sea. There were rumours that the French had come up with a way to do this. Reassuringly, a young, self-taught astronomer, John Flamsteed, pointed out that no one had charted the positions of celestial bodies with anything like the accuracy needed. Hearing this, Charles at once said that the heavens would need to be mapped again for the benefit of his seamen. The race to find longitude was a matter of national defence; in 1675 he appointed Flamsteed his 'Astronomical Observator'.[14] Flamsteed was confident that he could succeed where other astronomers had failed because new pendulum clocks had made timekeeping more accurate, telescopic sights meant that star positions could be measured more exactly, and the latest instruments allowed angles to be measured with greater precision.

A Royal Observatory had to be built. Sites at Hyde Park and Chelsea were considered before Wren put the full force of his influence behind the choice of a steep hill in Greenwich Park, topped by a decayed, fortified tower dating back to the fifteenth century. A small party of Royal Society Fellows, including Hooke and the mathematician Sir Jonas Moore, visited the site in June 1675. All approved the location, which offered good viewing conditions, but, as ever in Charles's reign, money was short. Moore, Surveyor of the Board of Ordnance and responsible for its stores and fortifications, was a great supporter of Flamsteed. He raised funds by selling old gunpowder to the Dutch. The builders also used recycled materials: wood and metal from an old gatehouse at the Tower, and bricks from a disused fort at Tilbury. Wren is usually credited with being the Observatory's architect, but Hooke had the major role in its design and construction. He used the strong foundations of the old castle and completed the building in record time, exceeding his meagre £500 budget by less than 10 per cent. From such unpromising circumstances rose a display-piece, built 'for the Observator's habitation & a little for Pompe'.[15] In July 1676, Flamsteed took up residence to begin his systematic observations. It would be his home for the next forty years.

Sir Jonas Moore, 'a good Mathematician and a good fellowe', paid for some of the expensive instruments Flamsteed needed from his own pocket.[16] They included two pendulum clocks by Thomas Tompion, which only needed winding up once a year, so Flamsteed could make consistent, annual observations of the Moon and stars. Unfortunately, building constraints meant that none of the walls in the Observatory aligned with a north-south axis. Flamsteed absolutely needed this for his observations and so did most of his work in a small, unheated outhouse constructed on the meridian in his garden. He had suffered delicate health since childhood and the many cold nights he endured charting the stars were proof of his dogged determination. He was soon under pressure to publish his results. He resisted, partly because he feared premature findings might be misleading. Even today, scientists searching for Black Holes must calculate and compensate for the pull of gravity on radio telescopes; Flamsteed the perfectionist struggled with imprecise instruments, and his assistants had to do hours of manual calculation to correct each reading. Critics who wanted results just did not understand the immense labour involved: 'They may as well ask,' the perfectionist sighed, 'why St. Paul's is not finished.'[17]

Flamsteed's distance from the court and from London's coffee houses placed him at a disadvantage, as did the unsocial hours he was forced to keep. Misunderstandings arose when cooperation was needed. He would accuse Newton of failing to acknowledge in his *Principia* that the celestial observations he used to test his theories about gravitation and motion came from him. He also fell out with the astronomer Edmond Halley, even though Halley was a genial man, able to persuade the suspicious Newton to let the Society publish his *Principia*; Halley saw it through the press and even paid for its publication when the Society ran out of funds. Flamsteed never did solve the essential problem that the Observatory had been set up to address: how to help ships find their longitude at sea. And it was decades before his painstaking work was published in full. Yet the impressive Observatory, overlooking the Thames and visible to all shipping, was a constant reminder of the nation's maritime ambitions. Tsar Peter the Great, who visited London in 1698 to obtain the latest developments in shipping, visited the Observatory at least twice. His embassy was welcomed as a sign of London's growing prestige in maritime affairs; the Society and the Observatory, with their links to London instrument makers, played a role in this.

At the time the Observatory was being built, Hooke and Wren were also at work on the Monument to the Fire, near Pudding Lane where the blaze had begun. They chose a 200-foot (61-metre) hollow pillar, designed to hold an immense telescope to measure the exact position of stars directly overhead throughout the year. The idea failed. The Monument moved too much in the wind; the brickwork expanded and contracted with different temperatures, although Hooke could use it for other experiments. But the Monument shows how, in this period, scientific interest could affect the very fabric of London. It is also testimony to the irrepressible spirit of Londoners, that even when commemorating the disaster of the Great Fire, they also looked to the stars.

THE EFFECT OF NEW SCIENTIFIC THINKING ON LONDON

The Royal Society had a diffuse effect on London: its activities were a talking point among the urban elite, it stimulated the manufacture of instruments, it also impacted on art and literature. But the Society had its opponents. Hobbes never joined, still believing that rational deduction was superior to any sense-based experimentation. Universities were sometimes critical; they had vested interests in the classical approach to learning, as opposed to the Society's experimental methods. Other critics believed that the findings of natural philosophers were bound to be flawed because they used artificial aids such as magnification. Today we accept that microscopes reveal accurate detail but, in an age when lenses might be imperfect, many held that observation with the human eye was best. This was one of the objections that Margaret Cavendish, Duchess of Newcastle, had to the Society's work. She was one of the very few women of the time with opportunities to engage in scientific enquiry. She visited the Society in 1667, causing John Evelyn to dismiss her as 'a mighty pretender to Learning, *Poetrie* & *Philosophy*' and Samuel Pepys to scoff at her antiquated dress.[18] She was a controversial figure and perhaps they feared she would bring the Society into disrepute. But she could not dent its growing reputation; nor did she censure all aspects of its work.

Behind Cavendish's intermittent hostility to the Society lay her personal outrage that women were excluded from such learned bodies. They could only operate behind the scenes, as did Lady Ranelagh, Robert Boyle's elder sister, whose circle of friends included Wren and other founding Fellows of the Society. She introduced her brother to this circle and encouraged him in his studies. From 1668, Boyle lived with his sister at her house in Pall Mall, and the two of them nurtured the take-up of the Society's thinking by arranging social events at which Fellows were present. Women lower down the social scale, like Pepys's wife, Elizabeth, would be lucky to glimpse the latest discoveries through their husbands' interests (many men tried to keep up with the new experimental philosophy from a desire to appear fashionably up to date). Flamsteed's wife, Margaret, on the other hand, proved an able mathematician, willingly supporting him.

The most wounding criticism of the Society came in the form of satire. In 1676 the cantankerous Hooke went to the Dorset Garden Theatre to see Thomas Shadwell's *Virtuoso*, about a wealthy, leisured man who pursued special interests and connoisseurship, only to find that the play lampooned the Society mercilessly. Before long he was squirming in his seat, convinced that he was

Shadwell's principal target. The virtuoso in the play, Sir Nicholas Gimcrack, studies spiders and insects and is described as 'a sot, that has spent two thousand pounds in microscopes to find out the nature of eels in vinegar, mites in a cheese, and the blue of plums which he has subtly found out to be living creatures'.[19] These and virtually all the experiments ridiculed in the play had actually taken place. Once home, Hooke condensed his outrage and humiliation into a scribbled diary entry: 'Damned Doggs. *Vindica me Deus*. People almost pointed.'[20] It was a low point in the Society's history.

Public investment in Flamsteed's work at the Observatory did not immediately bear fruit. He did, though, publish accurate tide-tables for London Bridge between 1682 and 1684, and his appointment inspired other useful work. The young Edmond Halley sought to complement Flamsteed's observations by recording the star positions in the southern hemisphere. A Londoner, his father was a wealthy soap-boiler and freeman of the Salters' Company who could afford to indulge his son's love of astronomy. Soon Halley found powerful patrons in the capital willing to send him on a voyage to St Helena with his telescope. On return, he was elected a Fellow of the Society and frequented the same coffee houses as Hooke, especially Jonathan's in Exchange Alley. He continued his interest in navigation, sometimes going to sea to make observations, producing work of practical importance to mariners. Halley was also useful in international diplomacy: he instructed Tsar Peter in seamanship at Deptford and showed him experiments that could be carried out at sea. In the 1690s he captained two voyages in the north and south Atlantic to chart variations in the Earth's magnetic field, already known to affect compasses. Lively and energetic, his personality was vastly different to Flamsteed's. Professional and personal rivalries soon spiked their relationship: a jealous Flamsteed spread rumours that Halley's religious beliefs were unorthodox, and by the end of the century he complained openly that Halley drank brandy and swore like a sea captain – which he did.[21]

The value of encouraging scientific and mathematical expertise was readily appreciated. Pepys did not have the scientific training to understand all the Society's activities, but as a naval administrator he was an ardent supporter of mathematical education for boys who would become officers. Louis XIV, eager to make France a great maritime power, had opened schools on the coasts of

France in the 1660s giving boys free lessons in navigation. Alderman Sir Robert Clayton, a banker and later lord mayor, thought that London needed just such a school and he won the king's support. The Mathematical School of Christ's Hospital opened in 1673; Pepys would be immersed in its progress for the rest of his life. He wrote to individual Fellows of the Society for advice about the boys' curriculum. He also sent some of the boys to Flamsteed for extra lessons, helping to make sure that the Observatory influenced mathematical training in the capital.[22] Elected President of the Royal Society in 1684, Pepys worked hard to put the Society on a more stable footing, encouraging links between its programme and the navy.

The Society had a big advantage when promoting its work and fostering new experiments: from 1665 it began publishing its *Philosophical Transactions of the Royal Society*, still the world's longest-running scientific journal. Scholars had long maintained private networks of correspondence extending overseas, but the Society's second royal charter of 1663 gave it the right to license mathematical, technical and scientific publications. At first the Secretary of the Society published the *Transactions* as a personal venture to supplement his meagre salary. Yet it rapidly became an institutional production, coordinated with the Society's correspondence network, and highly respected. The journal was popular with readers who could not attend meetings. It provided intellectual stimulation for provincial scholars who otherwise worked in isolation and offered a means for individuals to register their rights as the author of a discovery. By 1682, Evelyn noted that it was 'much desired & called for by the Curious from abroad, & home'.[23] The Society always had an open international attitude, publishing research from overseas and electing foreign Fellows. Botanists and naturalists began to correspond with the Society, too, providing another link with the maritime world since exotic plants and animals were brought to Europe by ship. This openness and wide dissemination of knowledge was essential to the success of the Society, which placed London at the hub of an international web of scientific activity.

At home, the Society was able to benefit from an improving postal service. In 1660, Charles II had established a 'General Post Office' in the City. After the Fire its headquarters moved first to Gresham and then to a building in Lombard Street. Mails left London for all parts of the country three times a week along six great roads: to Holyhead, Bristol, Plymouth, Edinburgh, Yarmouth and Dover. But there was no post in London between one place and another until Robert Murray set up his Penny Post in 1680 and assigned it to William Dockwra. For one penny, payable in advance, letters and parcels up to one pound in weight were delivered within London and its suburbs. There were four deliveries a day to most parts of the city and six or eight to the business centres. Almost every street had a shop or coffee house where letters and parcels could be left for the postman. In 1683, just when Dockwra was making a profit, the Duke of York claimed that the London service infringed his monopoly on revenue from the Post Office. He won his case and the Penny Post was incorporated seamlessly into the General Post.

Meanwhile, the Society's reputation as a disinterested judge of scientific quality meant that its name was increasingly used as an endorsement. Henry Bond, teacher of navigation and mathematics in Ratcliff, implied that he had the Society's support when he said he could find longitude at sea by observing magnetic variation. He designed a dip circle to measure the angle between the horizon and the Earth's magnetic field; Henry Wynne, the instrument maker who built the dip circle, claimed that the Society had approved it. London opticians also used the Society's name freely in marketing material, allowing careless readers to think their lenses had the Society's endorsement. In 1695 the watchmaker Daniel Quare, advertising in the *London Gazette*, said the Society approved of his portable barometer. Fellows of the Society themselves cashed in on their status: Evelyn mentioned his Fellowship in the 1660s when advertising his books on printmaking and gardening.

The Society's prestige as a scientific institution slowly helped to drive a wedge between scientific knowledge and magic. The Society did not categorically denounce magical thinking – some of its members were ambivalent about magic in any case – but it avoided the topic, sensing potential embarrassment, and that was enough.[24] Its preference for plain, objective language, particularly in the *Transactions*, also helped gain a readership for its work and credibility for science as a discipline.

In 1664 the Society had set up a short-lived committee to improve the English language for scientific writing. Sprat, in his history of the Society, associated extravagant, metaphorical language with political instability, clearly remembering the manipulative rhetoric used to sway emotions during the Civil Wars. In contrast, he argued, intellectual, scientific debate could be conducted without the intemperance that marked disputes in politics or religion. This proved to be an aspiration, but in recommending plain speech the Society did help to develop a standard English, distinct from vernacular dialects, and grounded this effort firmly in the capital. Dryden, briefly involved in the committee, used plain sea terms alongside poetic devices in *Annus Mirabilis*, which he published in 1667 and dedicated to the City of London. In a moment of crisis for Stuart rule, when England was engaged in an expensive, indecisive war against the Dutch, this was an important poem that encouraged readers to see 1666 as a year of wonders, and to think of the Plague and the Fire not as disasters but as trials from which Charles emerged triumphant. Dryden prophesied that 'a city of more precious mould' would rise from the ashes of the Fire and that the Society's work would bring commercial and military success.[25] His stylistic preferences changed during his long career, but the Society's attitude to language had enduring impact. Towards the end of the century, the philosopher John Locke adopted an 'Historical plain Method' in his *An Essay Concerning Human Understanding*, a highly influential work largely because he described the powers of the human mind and the development of our intellectual faculties with rigorous empiricism.[26]

The fabric of London benefited directly from the experimental philosophers, who were not lone geniuses but mostly practical men: Wren and Hooke found great use for their talents in rebuilding London after the Fire. Hooke, as City Surveyor, also oversaw the production of a new map of London which the mayor and aldermen commissioned to improve their administration. John Ogilby published the map in 1677 but it represented years of work by a team of surveyors and Hooke maintained quality control. Newton improved coinage when put in charge of the Mint. The natural philosophers also fostered close links with the artisans on whom they depended for their equipment, so that London became the go-to place for optical and mathematical instruments. Hooke and others particularly advanced the development of timekeepers. Tompion gained such prestige from the clocks he supplied to the Royal Observatory that he was soon unable to fulfil all his orders from his own workshop (on the site of 67 Fleet Street). He bought in components for assembly, which led to batch production in the manufacture of watches. And scientific knowledge was closely linked to experiential craft skills and material culture. Hooke designed surveying, navigational and astronomical measuring instruments, while watches and clocks were prized as beautiful objects. The Society's history of trades programme proved short-lived with little immediate impact on industry, which continued to be crafts-based. But it did help to create in London a greater willingness to innovate than elsewhere in Europe. The evident expansion of London's commerce also helped to win support for the Society's emphasis on the benefits of useful knowledge. Petty's *Political Arithmetic*, written in the 1670s, reassured readers that England's trade and wealth was increasing; similar studies measuring the data then available to government helped to stimulate national ambition.

The Observatory and the Royal Society, with its useful Repository, had a big impact on the creation and dissemination of knowledge. Natural philosophers not only elevated enquiry over dogma but also altered people's sense of the civic and urban. Knowledge was linked to power relations; the Society's key founding Fellows believed that to promote useful arts and sciences was to contribute to successful government. By the 1680s the Society was caught up in the political and religious controversies of the times, and its reputation for disinterested enquiry was dulled by exploitation for political ends. Yet from the first it shone a light on the benefits of coordination and the value of building on the efforts of others, despite obvious class distinctions between natural philosophers and lesser craftsmen. Even Newton repeated the adage, perhaps with a whiff of mock humility, 'If I have seen further it is by standing on ye sholders of Giants.'[27] By the end of the century, to London's great benefit, the Royal Society had overcome internal dissensions and lack of money to become the leading scientific society in Europe.

15

DOMESTIC ANXIETIES
HOME IMPROVEMENTS

In 1676 or thereabouts Mary, the wife of John Evelyn, sat down to do her husband's bidding and produce some advice about household management for his young friend, Margaret Godolphin, recently married and nervous about exceeding her annual domestic budget of £500. Mary started with essential kitchen equipment because the young couple had moved into lodgings in Scotland Yard, Whitehall, already furnished with beds, hangings and chairs. She grouped the various kitchen pots, pans, shovels, pails and baskets in a way that would not occur to us now, by the material they were made from: plate, tin, iron, brass, pewter, wood and earthenware. It was an exercise that her daughter-in-law, Martha, would echo some twenty years later, when her husband took up a government post in Dublin. She could not buy the kitchen equipment she needed there and sent Mary a long list, asking her to pack key items from her London kitchen and send them to Ireland. Again, items were grouped by material, partly because different metals affected the price of goods. In 1676, Mary estimated that it would cost £313 1s. to set up a genteel household for eight people in London (linen included). By way of comparison, the utensils from a modest kitchen in Wapping in 1659, including a pewter chamber pot, were valued at just £2 16s. 9d. second-hand.[1]

The kitchen was understood to be the wife's province even if she dictated little else about the house. It had become a recognizable space, though other rooms might be put to flexible use: the inventory of a house in St Giles-in-the-Fields in 1661 listed beds in every room except the kitchen and parlour, 'three paire of stairs backward', furnished with tables and a bench.[2] (A parlour offered some privacy.) Building regulations after the Great Fire meant that, in the City at least, kitchens were usually sited in basements. This made sense if the house had piped water, since gravity made it easier to channel water through leaky elm pipes into the basement. But some London kitchens were still on the ground floor. Many men worked 'at home' and the wife of an artisan renting just one or two rooms might have to cook over the hearth in a space that doubled as his office or workshop.

Cooking was still done over an open fire, but in Evelyn's time the fuel was likely to be coal, more efficient than wood. Coal prices fell during the second half of the century so consumption in London almost doubled; the pall of smoky air over the metropolis was overwhelmingly due to domestic coal fires.[3] Yet, as Mary's household instructions show, wood might still be burnt in upper chambers, if furnished with rich textiles that coal smoke would damage. Coal fires meant a grate was needed, superseding fire dogs and the cast-iron fireback used for burning logs. The grate was inserted between two hobs – brick pillars – that made small shelves where food could be kept warm; Pepys modernized his 'hearth and range' in 1661.[4] Few houses had ovens, so pies were sent to be cooked at the nearest baker's. But wives and maidservants could toast, fry, grill and roast meats using jack-driven spits or a vertical jack to rotate a joint over a dripping pan. The jack was operated by clockwork, or a system of weights, or even – in larger premises – by a small dog, specially bred with a long body and short legs to run in a treadmill. There was also a smoke jack, with fan-like blades, turned by the hot gases from the fire below it. Coal grates did lead to some new equipment. The three-legged skillet was replaced by a flat-bottomed saucepan in the mid-1680s; sauce-making then became more popular and recipe books gestured towards the new French taste in cooking. Mary's daughter-in-law carefully specified that she wanted her flat saucepan and trivet in Ireland. Only the poorest cooks were restricted to boiling food in a cauldron.

A skilled housewife had to be able to judge the heat of different parts of a fire, and the cooking times of different joints of meat. Pepys's wife, Elizabeth, got this badly wrong on Christmas Day 1661, which led to a row about the maid's 'sluttery'.[5] Cooking had some parallels with contemporary experimental science; when Hannah Woolley, a writer on household management, introduced a new recipe book, she wrote, '*I hear some of you say,* I wish Mrs. *Wolley* would put forth some New Experiments.'[6] Cookery books rarely specified quantities and never gave cooking times because different fires produced different results. Much in a recipe remained intuitive, a matter of trial and error.

The mistress of the house needed to be proficient in more than cookery to earn respect. According to *The English House-Wife*, she had to be able to order great feasts, preserve wines, extract oils, make and dye cloth, and run a dairy; she had to understand distillation, perfumes and malting as well as brewing, baking, 'and all other things belonging to an Household'.[7] First published in 1615, this domestic manual went through nine editions and at least two other reprints by 1683, testimony to women's growing literacy. While some of the skills the manual describes might be suited to country living rather than city life, London women needed an exact knowledge of the plants to be found in a town house garden, not only for culinary purposes but also to freshen rooms and relieve common ailments.

Households often kept a book of recipes and cures, handed down through generations and compiled over time. Theories of disease were a matter for physicians, but women were expected to know plant-based home remedies, which might help to avoid unexpected medical bills that could wreck a household budget. *The English House-Wife* has remedies for disorders such as haemorrhoids, sciatica, pimples, 'pissing in bed' and rather alarmingly, 'the falling of the fundament'.[8] Where animal ingredients are called for, they signal fading traces of magical thought; London women were still being accused of witchcraft in the 1680s.[9] But extravagant ingredients might also signal desperate measures to be tried when all else failed. *The Queens Closet Opened* has a horrific cure for consumption that begins, 'Take a running cock, pull [pluck] him alive, then kill him.'[10] Published in 1655, the book was highly regarded, saw ten new editions before 1700, and was one of the volumes in Mary Evelyn's closet.

Syrups and herbs might soothe a cough or help to expel wind but of the thousands of remedies in common use, few were effective. When Charles II contracted his final illness in 1685, the doctors did not even know what it was. Kidney disease? A stroke? They inflicted on him every medical torture in their armoury and with their bleedings, purges and emetics certainly hastened his departure. The efforts of the royal medical team made such an impression on John Evelyn that he recorded their copious bloodletting in a letter to his wife – another 12 ounces was taken from the king on his last morning. Evelyn did not mention the king's deathbed conversion to Catholicism, which was not widely known.

Domestic skills apart, a good housewife was expected to be religious, modest and obedient. Men were brought up to think that their strength and allegedly superior reasoning powers justified male domination over women, supporting the biblical injunction that wives should obey their husbands. The duties of a housewife were even documented on the backs of playing cards.[11] Evelyn took pains to mould his wife, whom he married in 1647 when she was just thirteen years old. Couples could marry young: the minimum legal age was twelve years for women and fourteen for men; children could get engaged from the age of seven, with the right to break off the engagement when they reached the age of consent.[12] But Evelyn and his friend Pepys – who fell in love and married Elizabeth when she was not quite fifteen – were both unusual. On average, high-ranking men married women in their mid-twenties when they themselves were perhaps a decade older.[13] Even lower down the social scale women tended to wed later: female servants married in their early twenties.[14] Because Evelyn's new wife was so young, she continued to live with her parents in Paris, where her father, Richard Browne, was English Resident or ambassador to the court of France. In this period Evelyn presented her with a handwritten manual on her domestic duties.

The couple set up home at Sayes Court, Deptford, in 1652. Evelyn expected Mary to bend to his way of doing things and she conformed. But she had been brought up to value intellectual development: she spoke three languages, had read the classics in translation and learnt mathematics. As a young wife she retained her verve. In one letter she wittily marvelled that men could change the appearance of an entire landscape and expect praise for their husbandry yet mock women as vain creatures if they altered a little thing like their dress or the pattern of a gorget.[15] Evelyn for his part grew to rely on his wife, writing in 1652, 'You are my selfe, & I trust you wth all'.[16] In his early advice on household economy, Evelyn had included the maxim that 'A prudent Husband should by no means discover unto his wife the utmost secrets of his Estate.'[17] But during the Great Plague, when work kept Evelyn in London and he feared for his life, he sent Mary the key to his most private trunk which held money and important papers, asking her only to keep it locked. He trusted in her discretion, even sending her updates on his painful piles which prevented him taking a regular dose of rhubarb. If she responded with a salve from *The Queens Closet Opened*, it would have been made with 'a spoonful of white dogs turd' mixed with perfumes, honey and egg yolk.[18]

Not all couples lived harmoniously: Pepys's marriage was turbulent. And since there was no need for a church ceremony, marital irregularities were common. The poor might even dispense with a marriage contract altogether since a public declaration of intent made a lawful marriage. Those who wished for secrecy could always find an obliging parson to marry them in an empty church, tavern room or private house. When marriages failed, dependent wives might be thrown onto the parish for relief. Court cases in Middlesex include petitions from wives complaining that their husbands have deserted them and refuse to maintain their children, or that a husband 'pretends to be married' to someone else, or has lived with another woman 'for some time past'.[19] The legality of marriage in London's densely populated suburbs was hard to police.

Most wives found their pursuits were restricted by childbearing: Mary Evelyn gave birth to eight children, of which only four lived to adulthood and only one, Susanna, survived her; she also had at least three miscarriages. Elite women, who put their babies out to wet nurse, had more frequent pregnancies. Wet nurses were often drawn from the middling sort and the idea was to give babies a better start in life, perhaps in cleaner air outside London, though some fashionable women may simply have wished to avoid the bother of regular feeds.[20] Mary Evelyn was expected to supervise her household and sometimes share the employments of upper servants, but most poor women had to find work to contribute to the household budget, despite pregnancies. Some helped their husbands if they ran shops or taverns; many had wholly separate employments. Seamen's wives were often silk winders, since the Spitalfields weaving district was an easy walk from the eastern maritime parishes. Others found 'women's work' in kitchens, as washerwomen, or in casual trades like street-hawking, which could be fitted around the needs of their family. Given the nature of such temporary work, many experienced poverty. Working women had more freedom about the streets than those running households, sometimes ranging further than men.[21] Yet women were quick to call each other out for immoral behaviour; they had to maximize earning power and credit, so their street reputation was important to them.[22]

Astonishingly, the City parishes were about three times more crowded than even the most densely populated London boroughs today. Houses might be occupied by two or more households, but individual family units tended to be fairly small. Towards the end of the century a household in Cheapside averaged 6.6 people and in poorer Aldgate 4.5 people. Cheapside had more lodgers, servants and apprentices, which explains the difference in household size.[23] In both these districts, households had relatively few children – they either died or were nursed in the country, and soon made their way in the world as teenagers. Any vacant space in a house would be rented to lodgers – who might be wealthier than the host family, given the pressure on accommodation in the City.

It is rare to find London housekeeping records in this century, but the advice that Evelyn's wife prepared for Margaret Godolphin in the 1670s indicates the lifestyle of the modestly genteel. Mary Evelyn prepared sample menus for a week, catering for a family of eight people, including servants. Dinners were heavily meat-based (a joint, followed by a course of fowl and fish, then a dessert of fruit, sweets and cheese), although Evelyn's own book on 'sallets' (salads) – to which Mary contributed recipes – recommended eating more plants and herbs. The annual cost of running such a household, omitting extravagances and eating rabbit and cheaper fowls more often than partridge and pheasant, came to £480 4s. 0d.[24] Her instructions about linen reveal that sheets were washed fortnightly, although servants' bed linen was changed only once a month.

The papers of Evelyn's daughters show that conscientious parents taught girls to keep household accounts. And Mary warns Margaret not to hire a gossiping out-servant to help with her accounts but to find a trusty housemaid:

She should bee the first of servants stirring, & last in bed, & have some authority over the rest. . . . It is necessary also she shoud know to write & cast up small sums, & bring you her book every Saturday-night, which you may cause to be enter'd into another for yr Selfe, that you may from time to time judge of prices & things which are continualy altering . . . & such a

Servant (I tell you) is a Jewell not easily to be found, but such there be & such I wish you.[25]

Mary's own letters show how such upper servants might be identified, revealing too how women could help other women who made unfortunate marriages in an age when divorce was almost impossible. She wrote to Pepys, recommending a new housekeeper:

She is not in so prosperous a way as formerly, yet in no want; has no charge of children, one only daughter and that provided for, and from her; she has a husband, but he is absent by consent for many years; so that she is allmost a free woman; ever very neat, an excellent housewife, not ungentile. Sightly, and well behaved, yet of years to allow the necessary experience and prudence to direct in a family, and preserve respect.[26]

Her description shows what employers valued, though Pepys found the woman a bit of a shrew. Adult domestics were surprisingly independent as wage earners: there was a demand for their service and a premium on their behaviour, which reflected on a family's reputation.[27]

Poorer households had few servants or none, used wooden rather than pewter plates, and ate a much more restricted diet than that set out by Mary Evelyn. Staple foods were bread, cheese, onions and beer. Pottage was another basic, made by boiling grains over the fire, adding vegetables and sometimes meat. Those with limited cooking facilities, or just pushed for time, bought food from street vendors or victualling houses; in May 1668, Pepys made a good meal of half a breast of mutton off a spit in the Rose Tavern, Covent Garden, before the play started.

FURNISHING THE HOME AND THE MIND

How did the genteel and middling sort aspire to live? In 1696 the advertisement for a sale of goods in an upmarket house in Buckingham Street, off the Strand, lists hangings, looking-glasses, lined beds, chests of drawers, carpets of several sorts, a Japanned cabinet, and pewter and brass items from the kitchen.[28]

Hannah Woolley, who was something of a social climber, gives further clues in her books on domestic management. She had worked as a servant in an aristocratic household before marrying a schoolmaster and moving to Hackney. When her husband died, she married an eligible widower in Westminster. In *The Queen-Like Closet* she gives directions for embroidering chair covers, making wall hangings, framing pictures, and decorating wainscot by cutting out prints and gluing them to the wood. Her recipes for using up food scraps suggest that she imagined housewives would economize in some areas in order to emulate the latest home decorations. Pepys, also upwardly mobile, spent a great deal on home improvements once he moved into a house in Seething Lane, west of Tower Hill, a perk of his navy office job.

The growth in foreign trade meant that the moderately well off now enjoyed a greater range of foodstuffs and wine. The main meal was taken at midday. Table manners were improving; it was common to use smaller forks at meals so that people no longer needed to eat with their fingers. Life for the rich became more refined, if not more luxurious. Furniture became lighter; there was a shortage of oak from overuse and wartime shipbuilding, so chairs were often made of walnut and, from the 1670s, featured cane work which was cheaper than upholstery. Families might have lighter, folding tables since, in a major advance towards privacy and status, many no longer dined with servants and apprentices. The demand for oriental textiles soared, encouraged by the East India Company which now imported calicoes and chintzes from Bombay, a port that formed part of Catherine of Braganza's dowry. The Company also traded Indian goods with the Far East, bringing back tea and porcelain from China, and lacquer furniture from Japan. These luxury imports were much sought after and stimulated domestic production of pottery, glassware, silk and textiles.

Some things remained the same. In an age when laundry day brought turmoil and housewives battled with coal dust, clean linen remained a mark of status. But the use of new luxury items was an index of wealth and a means to compliment guests. When Susanna Evelyn got engaged to William Draper in 1693 and visited her future mother-in-law in Surrey Street, her parents were breathlessly gratified that 'she was received magnificently her Apartment Damask bed and hangings her dressing roome filled with a Japan styled Cabinet

China tea table Cups tea pot Chamber plate in the best manner'.[29] Fine 'Indian things' made popular wedding presents, and drinking chocolate, increasingly popular since the 1650s, was considered a refined gift: Evelyn's eldest daughter, Mary, had been 'not a little pleased' with a present of twelve boxes of chocolate and two fine cups trimmed with silver filigree.[30]

London was central to this genteel world of elegant consumption. People routinely visited London to order their winter and summer clothes. Branches of elite families renewed their acquaintance in town, and women journeyed there to give birth, unless they trusted a midwife in the country. As Mary Evelyn aged, she visited less often, complaining, 'The Ayre is so moist and thick with the seacoale smoake that one lives in a continuall mist', but she recognized that a young bride needed access to London life, since to put her in 'a mere Country Gentlemans hands is to bury her alive so litle contentment is there in a hawking drinking squire'.[31] London was a vital hub. Even if families stayed in the countryside, they kept up a stream of correspondence with friends and relations in the capital thanks to the postal service. Letters helped to create a 'polite society' and failure to observe the social niceties of correspondence was soon noticed. Susanna wrote dismissively to her mother about cousins who had not notified her of their arrival in the capital: 'I supose they dont understand yͭ to be a piece of good manners'.[32] From a young age, girls of middling ranks and above were schooled in the correct manner of address. Their first letters in the correct form, signalling the moment of entry into this polite world of patronage and influence, were often carefully preserved by family members.

In London, female literacy in Evelyn's time was close to 50 per cent and rising.[33] Woolley included sample letters for different situations in *The Queen-Like Closet*, understanding that some readers would wish to improve their writing skills. Sadly, many women wrote to commiserate about the deaths of children. They also shared remedies for common ailments; so many cures were circulated that authors of household manuals often collated recipes rather than inventing them. But elite women also used letter-writing to advance family interests. Mary Evelyn wrote to one of the queen's ladies-in-waiting, sending home-made cake as the queen had lately wished for cake, but asking to remain anonymous as it was such a lowly gift.[34] (It surely did her family no harm.) She also wrote to Pepys to secure employment for a sea captain, married to a relation, who had fallen on hard times. In turn, she received letters from friends whose husbands wanted to be presented at court.[35]

Letter-writing offered women a route into flourishing amateur literary networks and participation in other aspects of intellectual life. Females were not allowed to join the Royal Society but could at least read Thomas Sprat's history of the Society and hold opinions about the style he advocated for scientific writing. Mary Evelyn engaged in this discussion, writing about Sprat's book to Ralph Bohun, her son's tutor:

> I never liked anything more, not only because it is written in the defence of worthy and learned men, or of a cause which promises so many future advantages; but that his notions are conveyed in so just, easy, and polite expressions, in knewn and yet not vulgar english.[36]

Letter-writing also gave women opportunities to engage with politics and current affairs. When Captain Thomas Bowrey was at sea, his wife Mary was careful to send the latest news about English relations with the Barbary states on the north African coast, since Barbary corsairs regularly attacked merchant shipping.[37]

Yet there were conflicts. Mary Evelyn was torn between fulfilling her household duties and keeping up to date so that she could discuss intellectual matters with male acquaintances without fear of ridicule. Ralph Bohun praised her 'even style, & masculine notions', and said it was hard to believe a woman could write so well. Yet when she sent him her opinion of Dryden's latest play, *The Conquest of Granada*, she added pointedly that if she had not done the play justice, it was as much as could be expected 'from the leisure of one who has the care of a Nurcery'.[38] Her son Jack was a young man, but she had three daughters under the age of six at home. Later, when Bohun complained that she had not written in a while, she set out the nature of her dilemma. She might live 'under the roofe of the learned, and in the neighbourhood of science', but:

> Woemen were not borne to read Authors and censure the learned, to compare lives and Judge of virtues, to give rules of morality, and sacrifice to the Muses, wee are willing to acknowledge all time borrowed from family

duties is misspent, the care of Childrens education, observing a Husbands comands, assisting the sick releeving the poore, and being serviceable to our friends.[39]

She added with some bitterness that if a woman did rise above her station and do something extraordinary, she was rewarded with wonder, not esteem. Such comments may help to explain her uncharacteristic harshness towards the writer Margaret Cavendish, whom Mary Evelyn dismissed as vain, ambitious and affected, with a way of speaking as 'empty, whimsicall and rambling, as her Books, ayming at science difficulties and high thoughts, terminating commonly in nonsence, Oathes and folly'.[40] She may have correctly judged Cavendish's character, if not her books; but she may also have envied the opportunities that Cavendish had to study without distraction.

Conduct books aimed at genteel women might insist on female submissiveness, but not all women of Mary Evelyn's rank were happy to be compliant in male-run households or eager to practise their writing skills for polite correspondence. This much is evident from her own daughters. Mary, the eldest, made notes on sermons, sang opera songs in French and Italian, played the harpsichord, and was the delight of her parents (who were devastated when she died of smallpox aged nineteen); Elizabeth, their middle daughter, eloped with a dockyard official, tragically succumbing to smallpox soon afterwards. Their youngest, Susanna, never took to learning – her letters as a teenager are a mess of blots, and as the sole surviving daughter she struggled to live up to expectation.

Fortunate women did manage to pursue their own interests at home. Well-educated families placed value on women's artistic skills and Susanna mercifully found that she had a talent for art and japanning. It accorded well with her father's artistic interests (he had got his own recipe for the Japanese varnish on his travels but failed to patent it). Susanna's mother-in-law also proved supportive; she herself found time to paint as well as carry household and social responsibilities. Susanna would also have liaised with the network of female amateur artists in London, and at least known of Mary Beale, who made a living in her own home as a portrait painter. Beale had an egalitarian view of marriage. In her 'Discourse on Friendship' (1666) she stated that God made Eve as 'a wife and Friend but not a slave'.[41] She was the family breadwinner and her husband acted as her studio manager. From their rented house in Pall Mall, they used the familiar situation of a well-to-do woman entertaining friends and acquaintances with music and refreshments to make sitters relaxed about having their portrait painted by a professional female artist.

The first public concerts in London began only in the 1670s, in Whitefriars, so there was a long tradition of making music in the home. And the increased number of printed music books during the closing decades of the century gave women more options. In some households, music-making was an extension of the family's political and religious position – the Bowreys, for example, had a collection of anti-popish songs; the domestic world was rarely isolated from the public.

HOUSEHOLD PERILS AND VALUES

Wives were expected to make homes congenial but could never make them perfectly safe. Hearths posed a great peril, although coal fires in enclosed grates were safer than open wood fires. The physician, builder and businessman, Nicholas Barbon, responsible for much housebuilding after the Fire, opened the first office for household insurance behind the Royal Exchange in 1680. It was still up to families to take the greatest care. Other dangers were more insidious. Home remedies for invalids might do more harm than good, as indicated by the letter Mary Evelyn received from her granddaughter, Betty:

> I find the snaile watter agree so well with me that I desir you will send me another botel of it all other things that I take makes me very sick I would be glad to have the receipt of it to make some if you plese to give it to me.[42]

If Mary Evelyn had turned to *The Queens Closet Opened* for the 'admirable and most famous Snail water' for invalids, it would have contained garden snails, washed in beer and popped in the oven, 'till they have done making a noise', then pounded with earth worms, herbs and flowers.[43] The tonics that Betty rejected must have been nauseous indeed.

Home-made cosmetics presented another hazard. While people preferred to sprinkle their bodies with fragrant powders rather than immerse themselves in water, they did want their exposed flesh to be blemish-free. A clear complexion was a sign of health and good character. Many household manuals dealt with the removal of pimples and itchy pustules or 'tetters', promising a whiter skin. Unfortunately, their concoctions contained harmful ingredients. Hannah Woolley, for example, offered a potion for removing smallpox scars that contained caustic lime. Salves with dangerous ingredients were recommended for sunburn, breast reduction and stretch marks after pregnancy, indicating the kinds of conditions that might tempt women to use them. Only at the end of the century did George Hartman warn in his *Family Physitian* against all cosmetics containing mercury, white lead or lime. Mercury gave the user convulsions or paralytic fits, discoloured the teeth and made them loose, he explained; lead eventually turned skin black, while corrosive lime roughened the skin instead of smoothing it.[44] He recommended his own face powder made from oyster shells instead.

Parts of Europe were in the grip of what has come to be known as the 'Little Ice Age' in the second half of the seventeenth century and the snow lay longer on the ground than it does today. This had consequences in the home. Waste removal from seventeenth-century households was an unpleasant business at the best of times. During harsh winters when the Thames froze over, as in 1676 and 1683–4, it was difficult even to get water to keep homes clean. Extreme cold sapped people's strength. In rooms where there was no fire, water froze as surely as it did outside. Mary Evelyn wrote half-jokingly to a relative in 1669: 'The Crackling of the Ice, and whistling winds are our Musick, which if continued long in the same quarter may possibly freese our witts as well as our penns.'[45] The poor always suffered most. The bad harvests of the 1690s led to more burglary and housebreaking, even though during the last decades of the century levels of prosecuted crime stayed low. Around 1700, Thomas Bowrey's sister, Anne, complained to him that her house had been broken into for the second time in three weeks. She had lost pewter, brass, the clock he had given her and linen.[46] House thieves often stole clothes, which they could easily pawn for cash, and targeted silver items which they could melt down.

The household unit was valued as essential for social stability, just as marriage seemed fundamental to the structure of society and accepted gender hierarchy. Mary Evelyn's housekeeping budget for Margaret Godolphin set aside £40 to be given to the poor each year; her daughter Mary's teenage accounts recorded her charity to poor women as well as the modest sums she lost at cards. And just as a woman's role as mistress of the house was defined, so too was the man's, especially when his husbandry involved land management. The possibility of taming nature through careful husbandry was related to contemporary ideas for solving social and economic problems. Husbandry was a word used in many contexts. The king was expected to lower court spending and use husbandry, or the skilful management of resources, in his costly foreign wars.[47] In the context of colonial expansion, the concept of husbandry could be used to support new English colonies in the Americas and West Indies, where ostensibly virgin territory would be farmed and made productive. But husbandry could also be used to defend domestic trades, like beekeeping, at risk from increasing amounts of imported sugar. And if formal gardens in the French taste were fashionable status symbols, gardening often had subtle links to foreign and colonial policy as more exotic plants were brought from overseas.

At Deptford, John Evelyn kept a personal notebook on husbandry. Among other things, he made a note of the weekly and quarterly jobs that needed doing in his grounds, when to sow kitchen foods, how to graft different plants, how to kill pests, and how to preserve fish in frosty ponds by breaking surface ice. It is unlikely that he did this work himself, but he equipped himself to oversee it. He planned and costed a family still-house for pressing and distilling oils, and a brew house, noting that tuns could be bought second-hand from vinegar-men in St Olave's Street by London Bridge.[48] He had a hive at Sayes Court carefully designed so that he could take honey without destroying the bees. He also made notes on elegant stable design, listed horse medicines, and recorded how best to train hunting dogs. Even Bowrey in Wapping owned books of husbandry. They included *The Compleat Distiller*, *A New Art of Brewing Beer*, *England's Interest: Or the Gentleman and Farmers Friend*, and *Mechanick Exercises*, a book which covered blacksmithing, joinery, carpentry, turning wood, bricklaying and plastering.[49]

Whatever the social and international contexts influencing the way people thought about their households, they were places full of personal meanings – chambers where children had been born and died, closets where confidences were whispered or letters placed in the secret compartments of writing desks, parlours associated with the sound of tuning strings, and kitchens full of familiar pots and pans. In Cromwell's time the long handles of skillets had carried mottos such as 'the Wages of Sin are Death' or 'Pity the Poor'.[50] But everyday objects often had meanings and associations that brought comfort. It was in the home that many created a sense of self.

Some women feared that a housewife's skills were undervalued. The author of *An Essay In Defence of the Female Sex* was angered by men's dismissal of women's conversation about household affairs: 'the *Regulation* of the *Family*, and *Government of Children* and *Servants*, the provident management of a *Kitchen*', the planning of meals, and matching of furniture; male contempt seemed unfair given that women's intellects were forcibly confined to domestic matters and given that homes would be 'meer *Bedlams*' without female effort.[51]

Female education became a topic of increasingly heated debate. Hannah Woolley was provoked into claiming that 'Most in this depraved later Age think a Woman learned and wise enough if she can distinguish her Husbands Bed from anothers.'[52] She argued that women were born as intelligent as men and only deprived of learning in case they rivalled their husbands. In similar vein the author of *Advice to the Women & Maidens of London* assured her readers that the 'masculine Art' of book-keeping was no more difficult than lacemaking, and women had better master it in case they had to run the family business as widows.[53] But even when women received education and couples ran their home as a partnership, women's ultimate subservience to men was understood to be the norm, and at all social levels firmly embedded in the country's religious and legal frameworks.

It is impossible to tell how women began to view the larger world from their homes but Evelyn's clever daughter, Mary, wrote a satirical poem that he published after her death, which yields rare insights. In it she describes the contents of a lady's dressing room (as women's supporters and detractors often did), offering a mock defence of the fashions and ornaments that women of taste thought essential. She added a 'Fop-Dictionary' to explain the latest terms for cosmetics, hairstyles and clothing. Evelyn may have published his daughter's satire as evidence of her own good sense and virtuosity. Yet her poem reveals a detailed knowledge of the latest accessories and furnishings, and the trendy French names for them, just when French immigration and the growing demand for luxury goods was causing concern. Worse, her satire promptly elicited a poetical response, apparently by a woman, criticizing men of fashion as effeminate fops.[54] It warned that fops were liable to ruin themselves and end up in seamy Alsatia – the Whitefriars district of London, outside the City's jurisdiction, where debtors claimed sanctuary. Just a few streets away from mainstream London, Alsatia had its own customs and thieves' cant. This second satire contains references to homosexual activities and semi-criminal lifestyles, lightly masked in cant terms and in the affected French that fops used. Taken together these two satires suggest that few women exposed to London society could maintain a cloistered mindset. The complex urban perspective they brought to household duties was likely to fuel conflict and frustration.

16

IMMIGRANTS, OR 'STRANGERS'

August 1675 was extremely hot; many in London's crowded weaving districts in and about Spitalfields left their upper windows open while they slept. On the night of 9 August protestors intent on destroying new-fangled 'engine looms' entered weavers' houses through these windows, climbing to the roof or upper storeys when they could not break through a front door. Wreckers knew which of their neighbours had these looms and chose their targets carefully. Soon the streets echoed with shouts, oaths, and the screams of women and children. Gangs numbering from 30 to 200 forcibly removed the great looms and burnt them in open ground. They met with fierce resistance; many were injured, and some killed. Rumours also circulated that English hatters were ready to join them, prepared to cut the throats of French rivals who had introduced new styles and worked for less. Would dissident political groups arm the rioting weavers and trigger outright revolt? The king sent companies of horse and foot to help the militia quell the disturbances, which raged for several nights.[1]

Engine looms had multiple shuttles so that weavers of ribbons, tapes and narrow trimmings could make up to twenty-four pieces at the same time. Such looms were not power-driven, despite the name, but their skilled operators, mostly French immigrants, massively outperformed single-loom weavers who soon despaired of their livelihoods. An engine loom cost between £12 and £16, and the riots revealed that clusters of five to ten looms might be housed in one place, owned by a loom-master who hired journeymen to work for him. Punishment for the rioters was swift but tempered by sympathy for poor weavers and their families; those caught were mostly just pilloried and fined, although imprisoned until they paid up. The Weavers' Company continued to lobby hard to get the looms banned, but the demand for ribbons was huge after the Restoration and the government concluded that engine looms would reduce imports. The French and Dutch were using the looms already and could easily undersell English weavers who did not modernize. Authorities reasoned that if the technology was not developed in England, ingenious minds would be deterred from making similar advances in sawmills, printing presses and cranes.[2] The weaving districts of Whitechapel, Stepney and Shoreditch remained unruly and tense.

Protestants fleeing religious persecution in France and the Low Countries had long sought refuge in England, giving us the word 'refugee'. They were granted the use of the priory church in Austin Friars as early as 1550. Within months the French-speakers established a church in nearby Threadneedle Street; its worshippers numbered 1,400 by the 1630s. This French Church in London was Calvinist and grew in political might: it supported parliament against the king when Archbishop Laud tried to impose Anglican Church government on its congregation. French Protestant refugees were called Huguenots. Those in the weaving industry lived in or near the City but as London developed westwards, Huguenot artists and silver workers followed customers closer to the court in Westminster, where an established community of French wool traders was already recognized by a street named Petty France. Another Huguenot community lived in Greenwich, notably the eminent Lanier family of court musicians, based in Croom's Hill.

Protestants in France faced renewed persecution from 1661, prompting a steady trickle of refugees to London. That year Charles II sanctioned a second place of worship for Huguenots: a chapel in the palace of the Savoy (south of the Strand, not the modern Savoy Chapel). Services there were held in French but had to conform to the Church of England, even though the Threadneedle church maintained its independence. Not all Huguenots were happy with this but saw advantages in having another church close to the court.

If the elite valued French craftsmanship, ordinary citizens regarded immigrants with suspicion. Londoners blamed them for starting the Great Fire, and for numerous other blazes afterwards, claiming that foreigners threw fireballs into houses, or rented basements intending to stuff them with combustibles and set whole buildings alight. Some feared that papist spies hid within the French community.[3] In 1668 a London newsletter reported, 'The people here and in the adjacent maritime counties are much frighted at the great numbers of French that have lately come into England and have sheltered themselves in this towne.'[4] Fear was yoked to resentment. London shipowners and mariners complained to parliament that French vessels had taken over much of the export trade with France, while in 1670 the weavers of Spitalfields protested that they were impoverished 'by forraigne nations' trading within England, 'espetially by the French'.[5] An Italian traveller noted, 'The common people of London, giving way to their natural inclination, are proud, arrogant, and uncivil to foreigners, against whom, and especially the French, they entertain a great prejudice, and cherish a profound hatred, treating such as come among them with contempt and insult.'[6]

Yet Londoners sympathized enormously with the sufferings of fellow Protestants in France whose plight worsened from 1679. Louis XIV had determined that France would be an entirely Catholic nation. In 1681 he began a policy of billeting soldiers on Protestant households with licence to do all they could to convert them, short of murder. Forced billeting, or *dragonnades*, would give us the term 'to dragoon'; billeted soldiers put Protestant families to insupportable expense and daily intimidation. Protestants caught fleeing suffered terrible punishment: women were imprisoned, men sent to the galleys. Those who made it to England had to dodge guard ships at sea and often arrived with only the clothes on their backs. Londoners watched them come up the Thames, often crowded into small fishing boats, mostly women and children, sent to safety first by their husbands. In 1685, Louis XIV revoked the Edict of Nantes, withdrawing all recognition of Protestantism in France. In the next two decades some 25,000 Huguenots came to London, a dramatic influx given that in 1680 its population was around 500,000.[7]

In the language of the time an alien immigrant from overseas was a 'stranger', denied the full privileges of a subject of the realm. A 'foreigner' was someone who had merely emigrated to London from an outside parish. Cosmopolitan London was home to strangers from many nations. Its black population was increasing due to commercial activity in the East Indies and England's growing involvement in the slave trade. Yet the status of black Londoners was becoming uncertain: black seamen might have full liberty but black servants, acquired by ship captains and sold or presented to wealthy families, might not. By the end of the century footboys included 'East India Blacks' as well as Africans who, to judge from notices placed in newspapers, led disempowered, unhappy lives. At the turn of the century a Mrs Thwaites of Stepney offered a reward for news of 'a slender middle sized India Black, in a dark grey Livery with Brass Buttons', thought to have run away to sea; another reward was offered for the return of Peter James, 'An East India Black, middle sized, pitted with the Small-pox, about 20 years old', who had also fled.[8]

London also housed Jews from Spain and Portugal, who lived openly, growing in number, since Cromwell had adopted a more tolerant policy towards them in 1656. Denied the freedom of the City and so forbidden to open shops, Jews focused on wholesale commerce. Many became established merchants: the export of salt fish and import of currants were largely in Jewish hands. Jews also became respected brokers in the Royal Exchange, acting as agents for the sale and purchase of commodities. By 1699 the Jewish community of some 185 households had outgrown its small synagogue in Creechurch Lane and acquired a nearby site for Bevis Marks, now the oldest working synagogue in Europe.[9]

The Huguenots differed from other strangers in that as refugees they began to arrive in great numbers from 1679. Their sufferings in France were well reported; Londoners could read about the savagery of French soldiers and how Protestants were turned out of their trades and professions unless they converted.[10] This Protestant exodus inflamed English distrust of absolute monarchy as practised by Louis XIV just at the time when England and Scotland were gripped by the Popish Plot. This was the claim, first made in 1678, that Jesuits were plotting the assassination of Charles II. It was utterly fictitious, but anti-Catholic hysteria raged until the 'plot' was exposed as nonsense some three years later. Meanwhile, the Puritan (Whig) faction at court exploited the situation to try to remove Catholic peers from parliament and to inflame fears about a Catholic monarchy in England. Their aim was to get bills passed to exclude Charles's Catholic brother James from the throne, a struggle known as the Exclusion Crisis. When the Protestant magistrate Sir Edmund Berry Godfrey was found murdered near Primrose Hill in October 1678, there was rising panic. Catholics who were neither tradesmen nor property owners were ordered to stay at least ten miles from London and Westminster, unless they attended Protestant church services. Suspected Catholics were rounded up and only released if they could prove that they had recently taken the Anglican sacrament. Trained Bands patrolled London's streets day and night. In this anti-Catholic furore, Londoners were predisposed to welcome Protestant refugees.

Charles II had shown real generosity in welcoming Huguenots to England from as early as 1666. When the dragonnades increased their terror, he offered Protestant refugees free letters of denization in 1681, guaranteeing them privileges as residents and the right to pursue their trades and handicrafts. He also ordered a public collection to relieve their needs. Some £14,000 was collected and distributed to refugees through the French churches. Yet Charles was also being astute. Huguenots were known to be hard-working Calvinists. They brought valuable skills and types of manufacture that England sorely needed. The king had already called a halt to French imports in 1678 because England's trade deficit with France was causing alarm: imports of French silk, wine, brandies and other luxury goods exceeded English exports to France by at least £1 million.[11] He also saw that refugees would swell the English population, which experts feared was in decline just at a period when a nation's wealth was judged to depend on the number of its people. Finally, current anti-Catholic feeling incriminated Charles as well as his brother. Rumours circulated that he had succumbed to Catholicism as a young exile in France and would introduce it someday into England.[12] By actively welcoming distressed Protestant refugees, Charles was disassociating himself from Louis XIV.

Charles meant to naturalize the Huguenots, giving them rights equal to those of his native subjects. In 1682 he wrote to the East India Company, requesting that Huguenots be allowed to buy stock as if already naturalized.[13] But naturalization required an Act of Parliament and time and again the House of Commons refused to pass one. Equal rights would deprive livery companies of the hefty fees they charged aliens to trade in London, and prejudice against foreigners was strong. Most companies made life difficult for immigrants: the Goldsmiths complained that French craftsmen were given equal rights though they lacked proper qualifications; Gunmakers zealously searched Huguenot premises for evidence of illegal trading and issued fines. Lord Dartmouth, Master of the Ordnance, had to insist that one talented immigrant, Andrew Dolep, be admitted to their Company.[14] Dolep, originally from Germany, was one of the first to make rifled guns and went on to make pistols with revolving chambers. The Gunmakers had to comply since their members relied on contracts for military arms from the Board of Ordnance. The king himself wrote to the Pewterers' Company about their unfair treatment of James Taudin, a pewterer in St Martin's Lane.[15] Charles also asked the Weavers' Company to be lenient when members complained that strangers were working as master weavers although they were not members of their livery. The Company still ruled in 1676 that it would be 'very sparing' of admitting Huguenots 'unless upon some weighty grounds or reasons'.[16] It had grounds for caution; when the Company agreed with Huguenot weavers that they should employ as many English journeymen as French, the rule was evaded before long.

This friction with the livery companies was one aspect in a growing conflict between the king and the City of London. In 1683 it reached a climax when Charles used the law to impose his will on the City, a prime source of revenue in his realm. The City was forced to surrender its charter and submit to the rule of a royal commission. Afterwards livery companies were made to surrender their individual charters and apply to the king for new ones. The new charters stated that a Company's governing body was subject to royal approval, so if the king disapproved of any member, he could replace him at will. A key reason for replacement would be so that Charles could influence the election of the City's four MPs. This development was a great blow for the citizens of London, who muttered darkly that if the City lost its charter, it would not be long before the king lost his head.[17] Meanwhile, continuing harassment from the livery companies encouraged Huguenots to migrate westwards where they could avoid the companies' regulation and fees. Huguenots occupied hundreds of properties standing empty in Soho, thanks to the building boom after the Great Fire, and they also settled in Lambeth, Battersea and Wandsworth (where they specialized in hat-making).

Huguenot textile workers mostly stayed in Spitalfields, in the eastern suburbs; a Huguenot community had lodged in Spital Square since the mid-century and, south of the square, the area just outside the City saw rapid development. By 1675 this district had more than 1,336 houses, crowded into narrow streets about White's Row and Fashion Street, both laid out before 1660. These new dwellings were mostly two-storey tenement houses with frontages from 10 to 16 feet wide (3 to 4.8 metres), intended for humble occupants. The standard of building was shoddy, and no remnants of them survive today. In the 1680s the developer Nicholas Barbon acquired the old Artillery Ground; since the Restoration it had only been used for proofing guns because the Trained Bands moved to a new Artillery Ground in Bunhill Fields. Barbon and his associates laid out streets of cheap, modest houses with good sanitation, on slightly wider plots of up to 20 feet (6 metres). These attracted more French weavers.[18] By the early 1680s, Spitalfields was populous enough to have its own market, built by the mid-1680s, although fields to the south were still reserved as tenter land, where fabric was stretched to dry on tenterhook frames to keep its shape. Spitalfields had pockets of wealth. Prosperous silk families continued to favour Spital Square, although the silk-masters' houses in Princelet, Wilkes and Fournier Streets, with their distinctive weavers' garrets, were not built until the eighteenth century. Poorer immigrants made the best of cramped housing, growing plants where possible and cherishing caged song-birds. The very poor and disreputable found cheaper housing further out, along Cock Lane, now Bethnal Green Road.

When King Charles died suddenly in the spring of 1685, James, his heir, had no choice but to continue the policy of state support and public collections for Huguenots. He did so reluctantly, because he thought strict Protestants would oppose the kind of monarchy he meant to have. John Evelyn noticed that the official newspaper, the *London Gazette*, had stopped carrying stories of Huguenot suffering in France even though, with the Revocation of 1685, suffering had reached new heights. James also censured books about the perse-cution. He ordered that the work of a banished pastor, Jean Claude, which seemed to blame the French king for the torment of Protestants, be publicly burnt by the common hangman at the Royal Exchange. James II's behaviour increased fears that he meant to bring in popery and overturn the liberties of his subjects just as easily as Louis XIV had abolished the Edict of Nantes.[19] But the immigrant situation was complex: in 1685 alone 13,500 arrived in the City and suburbs, threatening to overwhelm all generosity; support for refugees from the Bishop of London, Henry Compton, led some to accuse the Church of England of encouraging Nonconformism. Refugee numbers temporarily fell off.

IMMIGRANT OCCUPATIONS

In Spitalfields successful Huguenot silk-masters created jobs for waves of new immigrants coming from textile centres in France. They brought skills that English weavers simply did not have; their exquisite taffeta, with its deep sheen, entranced Londoners. Huguenots also brought the dyeing and finishing skills needed to produce beautiful colours and lustrous blacks. Since the cut of clothes changed slowly, fashion centred on new patterns and textures. Voluminous dresses and long waistcoats provided ample canvases for pleasing designs, while silk was luminous, soft to the touch, and produced a rustle that announced wealth even before a dress came into plain view.

James II's coronation ceremony in 1685 boosted the fashion for luxurious silks. Due to the bitter political divisions caused by opposition to a Catholic king and the removal of London's charter, there was no traditional procession through the City the day before. The public focus was on his coronation day when James and his entourage walked from Westminster Hall to the Abbey. The route was entirely covered with blue broadcloth, and six women, two to a basket, strewed the route ahead with flowers and sweet herbs. Spectators, crowding into windows, balconies and nearby streets, were treated to an experience in which the colour and luxury of courtiers' dress were paramount. James wore silks, satins and velvets in expensive shades; he had a cloak of crimson velvet as he walked to the Abbey, and of purple velvet as he returned. He walked under a canopy of iridescent cloth of gold, held up by Barons of the Cinque Ports, of whom Pepys was one. The queen was superbly dressed in purple velvet, and the aristocracy also wore velvets fringed with gold and silver. Even the soldiers guarding the route were dressed in bright green, yellow and crimson.

Spitalfields weavers tended to specialize in one type of fabric – sumptuous damasks and other figured or flowered silks, crisp taffetas, glossy satins, striped silks, or brocades woven with costly silver and gold thread. Some of the designs were so complicated that a weaver might only produce half a yard a day. Master weavers often subcontracted the work out to home weavers, supplying the patterns and silk, and paying men weekly. And many others depended on the silk-weaving trade, including dyers, throwers who twisted the silk filaments onto spindles, and drawboys who worked on the loom alongside the weaver, raising groups of warp threads for complex patterns.

In contrast, Soho attracted Huguenots with a range of artistic and intellectual skills, including makers of lace, shoes, gloves and periwigs; bookbinders and stationers; jewellers and perfumiers; and instructors who set up as teachers of dancing, music or languages. Many language teachers were former churchmen, as was John Cairon, who kept a school in Orange Street where he taught boarders and day pupils French, Latin, Greek, Hebrew, geography, writing, arithmetic and merchants' accounts. The ability to speak French was a mark of social status and gentility in London, but many immigrants struggled to find pupils. Monsieur Switterda, who lived in Arundel Street, taught Latin and French to his boarders but also gave lessons in taverns during the daytime and two evenings a week. He advertised that he would teach pupils anywhere if it proved worth his while.[20]

French dancers became part of the cultural life of the capital, performing, teaching and influencing the London stage as well as gracing elite gatherings. The upper ranks of society had to be able to dance well. Some families hired French dancing masters (although there were fears that they might be introducing papist spies into their homes); others sent their children to boarding schools. The French school near Charles Street, now King Charles Street, Westminster, boasted a dancing room 27 feet (8.2 metres) long. Spacious dancing schools also provided accommodation for public concerts of instrumental music and singing. These attracted only the well-to-do since, in west London, tickets were typically 2s. 6d.[21] Entertainments like this encouraged the publication of sheet dance music, advertised as being the music of the court, the theatre and public balls. Engraved and printed on good paper so that the ink would not seep through, even the production of sheet music benefited from French skills. White paper was made in England, but the best quality was mostly imported until Huguenots brought their paper-making skills to England.

French perfumiers had skills that were much sought after, considering that perfumes were needed for body powder, wash balls, oils, pomatums, rose water, scented gloves and fans, and perfumed snuff. High-end French hairdressers and wigmakers were in demand for complicated and expensive coiffeurs. From about 1685 the fashion for women was the imposing 'fontange', a French head-dress that sat forward from the crown of the head. Stacked curls, usually of false hair supported on a wire frame, were topped with a cap trimmed in front with ribbon and rising pleats of expensive muslin or fine linen. The pleats were held rigid with wires and edged with gold or silver lace. This frothy tower became so high it could make getting into sedan chairs difficult. As Mary Evelyn's 'Fop-Dictionary' explains, the individual curls had French names, as did the components of the bonnet. A headdress might be decorated with pearls and flowers until it cost as much as £1,000 or £2,000.[22] In 1691 it was reduced to two pleats and this more practical version was termed the 'commode'.

English goldsmiths put up strong opposition to immigrant rivals, but there was no curbing the growing market for smaller, domestic gold and silver articles that Huguenots tapped into. Much heavy Restoration plate was melted down to supply such items, and French designs, featuring the florid Rococo work popular at the French court, were highly sought after. Coffee and chocolate pots, teapots, tea caddies, tobacco boxes, snuffboxes, flat-handled spoons and forks, were all introduced before 1700. Under the French influence, decoration was usually based on scenes from mythology or the sea. The technical skill of French craftsmen was remarkable; they adorned even small items with dolphins, mermaids, sea-gods, shells and foam-work. One characteristic French piece is the helmet-shaped ewer, introduced towards the end of the century – but hardly anything sold without a French name.[23] Even the stick for stirring and crushing hot chocolate, otherwise quite gritty, was known as a 'molionet' (it slipped into the aperture of a chocolate pot). French gunmakers responded to a demand for lavishly decorated weapons that few English makers could produce, and French immigrants also brought valued clock-making skills. The fashionable new shopping area for many of these goods was Charing Cross, near wealthy customers from Westminster and Whitehall. Here 'toyshops' sprang up selling engraved watches, ivory and tortoiseshell trinkets, and gold and silver goods, providing a new shopping experience for Londoners.

Meanwhile, French furniture-makers introduced eye-catching styles into domestic settings. Cornelius Gole, the son of a leading cabinetmaker in Paris, reached England by 1689, living in Stepney and then Soho. He made expensive furniture and richly carved mirror frames for the royal palaces and noble houses, specializing in floral and metal marquetry, gilding and inlay work. He also publicized his designs, holding at least one sale in 1694, which took place in a dancing school in Bow Street, Covent Garden. Later he published a set of engravings to show that his baroque designs could also be used to decorate watches.

Ralph, first Duke of Montagu, who twice served as Charles II's ambassador to France, decorated his London home in the French style in the 1690s.[24] It stood in Bloomsbury where the British Museum now stands, and Montagu spared no expense in making it the finest house in London. He enticed a team of French artists over the Channel to complete ceiling and wall paintings. The famous Huguenot designer, Daniel Marot, who had taken refuge in Amsterdam, advised him on interior decoration, and Montagu employed a range of other Huguenot craftsmen and gardeners. This project, a showcase for French fashion, had a great impact on interior design in London. Montagu's clock cases, upholstery for chairs and beds, marquetry tables, mirror and picture frames, and household pewter, all exhibited the best French craftsmanship that others greatly envied. Montagu was an unscrupulous politician but cherished his reputation as patron of the arts. He certainly worked to change the look of London; the trends in domestic design that he helped to introduce found imitators among the wealthy, who now had access to an increasingly wide range of textiles.

Some talented Huguenots became members of the Royal Society. Denis Papin, for example, demonstrated an early version of the pressure cooker in 1675, called a 'New Digester of Bones'. John Evelyn was so delighted with its jelly that he sent some home in a glass to his wife. Papin had trained as a physician, but Protestant surgeons and apothecaries were effectively banned from working in French towns after 1669, when new rules barred them from joining professional guilds and crafts. They emigrated and Londoners benefited instead. Paul Rotier, for example, set up a practice in Beaufort Buildings, off the Strand, where he specialized in making ingenious trusses to alleviate ruptures, common among seamen and other labourers.

In 1679, France banned Protestants from running military academies. Solomon Foubert promptly moved his renowned academy from Paris to London, luckily escaping with his money, tapestries and books. Foubert's supporters, including Evelyn, helped him to build a new clientele, explaining that English gentlemen and noblemen could now avoid the expense of sending their sons to Paris for tuition. Foubert rented premises near Piccadilly at the corner of Brewer Street and Sherwood Street; his wealthy pupils practised their military drills in adjoining fields. His son, Henry, who served as a major in the English army, took over the academy on his father's death in 1696 and relocated to what is now Foubert's Place off Regent Street. Here aspiring army officers learned swordsmanship, dancing, modern languages and drawing. Montagu gladly sent his eldest son to Major Foubert's Academy.

Fortunately for the refugees, public demand for French goods and services remained high. Self-proclaimed arbiters of taste, so-called 'Wits', were easily satirized for talking up French fashions. In Thomas Otway's play, *The Atheist* (1684), one character complains:

> We are overrun with a race of vermin they call wits, a generation of insects that are always making a noise, and buzzing about your ears, concerning poets, plays, lampoons, libels, songs, tunes, soft scenes, love, ladies, perukes, and cravat-strings, French conquests, duels, religion, snuff-boxes, points, garnitures, milled stockings, Foubert's academy, politics, parliament-speeches, and everything else which they do not understand, or who would have the world think they did.[25]

But even adverse publicity helped to make French styles popular.

From the 1650s, in the City and its suburbs, Huguenots contributed to a marked growth in different types of occupation. This was especially the case in London's most populous parish, St Giles Cripplegate, now absorbed by the Barbican, where many Huguenot families settled. An estimated 260 new trades took root in Cripplegate in the second half of the century.[26] An example of one new manufacture, 'draped milled stockings', was patented in 1682 by Francis Ammonett and two associates, advancing the production of close-fitted stockings. Between 1685 and 1695 about a hundred joint-stock companies were founded in England, offering a range of new investment opportunities.[27] These included companies making glass, white paper, linen, and a luxury fabric called lustrings. The technical expertise of Huguenot refugees was crucial to this development; hitherto England had been slow to build manufactures and industries that demanded great technical skill. London's growing prosperity and enterprise owed much to a buoyant economy, increasing colonial trade, and wartime spending, but Huguenot immigration was a prime factor.

Huguenots also contributed to London's intellectual life. Westminster's French Protestant community favoured Old Slaughter's coffee house in St Martin's Lane, where artists and intellectuals from different nations met. French bookshops, close to St Martin-in-the-Fields near Charing Cross, served a growing clientele. And Pierre Motteux, who worked from the Black Boy coffee house in Ave Maria Lane off Ludgate Hill, founded the *Gentleman's Journal*. It ran from 1692 to 1694, an important forerunner of the monthly magazines of the next century.

Understandably, then, Londoners grew annoyed when French agents, worried about the loss of skills in French towns, tried to lure Huguenots back. In 1698 it was reported that papers, written in French, had been nailed to the doors of French churches in Westminster, urging refugees who had a mind to abjure their heresy and return to France to apply to the French ambassador. This was treated by the English as an 'impudence' and an affront to their cherished anti-Catholic laws.[28]

THE IMMIGRANT EXPERIENCE

In London's suburbs, pockets of rich and poor often lived side by side. Wealthy Huguenots and those with skills that were highly sought after lived well, while journeymen weavers toiled six days a week in cramped tenements for low pay.[29] Needy immigrants clustered around their churches. At first, they flocked to the established church in Threadneedle Street and the reformed church in the Savoy, but by 1700 there were twenty-eight French churches in London. The Threadneedle Street church gave much practical help: food, clothes, schooling for children, care for the sick, and help to find work. Anxious to avoid criticism, the churches were selective in their charity; immigrants of higher status tended to receive more money. Those inclined to spend their allowance on tobacco and brandy received vouchers which they could exchange for food.

French leaders understood that in a city that was already crowded, Londoners would fear refugees bringing more dirt and disease. Their charity was a means of social control; they aimed to remove from the streets anyone who might bring discredit on their community. In 1681 the lord mayor and Bishop Compton persuaded the City to make over to the refugees a former isolation hospital in Bunhill Fields, used during the Plague. Known as the Pest House, it housed the sick and infirm free of charge, attracting donations. In 1689 the Maison de Charité was set up in Spitalfields. Known as 'La Soupe', it fed poor families according to need up to six times a week. Each meal consisted of 'a Pan of good Broth, mix'd with Six Ounces of Bread, half a Pound of Meat, and the same Weight of good Bread'.[30] Westminster soon had a similar institution. The Huguenots' efficient charities won respect. They also introduced friendly societies into England, rivalling the kind of care that livery companies might offer members.

Silk-weavers enjoyed growing demand for their fabrics but faced competition from imported Indian silks. The East India Company insisted, disingenuously, that it never imported wrought silks mixed with gold and silver, since that would harm domestic trade. Yet the Company licensed others to do so, claiming that wrought silks could only be smuggled into London, as French silks were, despite the Act banning them. The Company also claimed that any disadvantage caused by its imports of plain Indian silks were outweighed by its import of essential raw silk.[31] As well as competition, London weavers had to cope with slack periods and interruptions in the supply of raw materials. In such cases journeymen weavers and lesser workers always suffered most: master weavers just halted production, leaving their dependants without work. Even in good times, conditions of employment could be harsh: it could take days to set up a loom for complicated patterns, during which time a weaver might not be paid.

Partly owing to fluctuations in the market for silk cloth, poor weaving districts became increasingly associated with crime. Yet in the early years of Huguenot immigration most prosecutions involving French offenders also had French victims so did not greatly aggravate their host community: poor workers stole from masters; violent crimes were largely domestic. It was the same with cases that made the headlines. There were suicides, runaway apprentices, and a lunatic Frenchman who killed his weaver father-in-law; he was sent to Bedlam.[32] All the same such cases throw light on the dislocation and trauma that refugees suffered.

Resentment and prejudice were part of the immigrant experience. One Englishman complained sullenly that consumers seemed 'bewitched with an affectation of *French* Commodities':

> We must have all *French* about us; their Behaviour, their Fashions, their Garb in wearing them … *French* Musick, *French* Dancing-Masters, *French* Air

in our very Countenances, *French* Legs, *French* Hats, *French* Compliments, *French* Grimaces; only we have not so frequent the *French* shrug of the shoulder because we are not so low – and itchy.[33]

Even when English workmanship was superior, he claimed that retailers had to swear, and even lie, that goods were French-made before they would sell. Some hostility was understandable.

Outstanding Huguenot goldsmiths were soon admitted to the Goldsmiths' Company, and they did train English apprentices, leading to new styles of work.[34] London goldsmiths still worried about competition and accused the strangers of undercutting prices, but the Company took no action because these exceptional French craftsmen had the patronage of the court. Essentially, the welcome given to Huguenots was class-based: masters welcomed skilled craftsmen who could help them fulfil lucrative contracts; workers resented immigrants with superior skills who seemed likely to undercut their wages. An Italian traveller remarked of Londoners that the lower orders neglected work, however urgent, daily spending time in taverns yet still expecting rewards: 'Hence it is, that the French make fortunes in London, for being more attentive to their business, they sell their manufactures at a lower price than the English, who would fain derive the same profit as other artizans, however little they work.'[35] So French refugees were objects of sympathy but their welcome was mired by contradiction: Samuel Pepys donated money to the fund for Huguenots but confided to his diary, 'we do naturally all . . . hate the French'.[36]

English prejudice fed on easy stereotypes: the mincing, perfumed and curled French dandy; the wooden-shoed, frog-eating French beggar. The diet of poor Huguenots included much that could be gathered for free: snails, mushrooms, roots, onions and garlic. They also introduced oxtail soup, making a nourishing meal from a part of the animal that the English discarded. Such thrift often met with scorn. When the Reverend Richard Welton, a High-Church Tory, was appointed to the parish of Whitechapel, he took issue with the extreme level of Nonconformity there and spurned Huguenot immigrants as a threat to religion, declaring, 'This set of rabble are the very offal of the earth.'[37] The streets in London's Huguenot heartlands even sounded different; those working for French masters had little incentive to learn English. But most understood that it was in their interest to assimilate. Many anglicized their names, and succeeding generations spoke English well. Their willingness to work hard and help each other into employment made integration easier, so the new French churches fell into disuse in the next century. Only a modest percentage of Huguenots chose to pay for denizen status or full naturalization; the livery companies failed to extend their regulatory framework into the sprawling suburbs, so refugees found that they could mostly get by without having full rights.[38] An Act to naturalize foreign Protestants was finally passed in 1709.

What is striking is the sheer range of crafts and skills that the refugees brought to London, and the vacuum in Londoners' skill set which they filled. Almost every sector of the economy enjoyed a boost from Huguenot expertise. They also improved England's international trade: many still had contacts in France and could tap into a network of fellow Huguenots who had emigrated to the Netherlands, Ireland and the New World. Those in the silk-weaving industry, for example, did business with agents in Maryland. French vintners profited, as can be seen for an advertisement for red and white wine from a cellar near the French Church in Soho; one gallon in twelve was given free of charge to those who bought in quantity.[39] At a domestic level, probate records show that Huguenots, devoted to a different cuisine, were early adopters of the flat saucepan.[40]

England's negative trade balance with France would be reversed in the first part of the eighteenth century, and the Huguenots had a large part in this. By 1700 about 5 per cent of London's population, then around 500,000, was French. All foreigners in London, not just the Huguenots, broadened people's horizons and made the capital more dynamic. Immigration was a positive factor in creating a city that was set to play a larger role on the world stage. None of this was evident at the time. What Londoners did notice was society's growing consumption and the change to lifestyles brought about by overseas trade. John Evelyn, preparing his daughter's satire for the press, lamented the introduction of 'foreign manners' and the general increase in luxury. Time was, he wrote, when 'the sturdy Oaken Bedstead, and Furniture of the House, lasted a whole Century', when 'Things of Use were Natural, Plain, and Wholesome'.[41] But London society, and language itself, had quite changed.

17

INSURRECTION
JAMES II LOSES HIS WAY

In 1685 most Londoners seemed to welcome James to the throne. He was an inflexible Catholic, but the common view was that his religion would be a temporary problem. At fifty-one he was considered elderly, all his children with Mary of Modena had died young, and next in line were his Protestant daughters by his first marriage, Mary and Anne. Anti-Catholic protests had reached fever pitch from 1678 with the Popish Plot and the Exclusion Crisis but, since the early 1680s, the Crown had brutally suppressed Whig opposition. During those crisis years there had been 'Papers, Speeches, Libels, publiquely cried in the streetes' against Catholic James.[1] But Charles II had managed to fill public offices with loyal, Tory supporters equally able to sway crowds; his firm hold on London increased royal authority over the rest of the kingdom.[2] James was in a strong position when, against all odds, he came peaceably to the throne.

In a deliberate display of continuity, James was proclaimed king at Whitehall, Charing Cross and Temple Bar in the same ritual form as when his grandfather succeeded Elizabeth I. Observers hoped that the new king would clean up the lax court and enforce much-needed economies in the royal household. James was stubborn and lacked his brother's quick wit, but he was less dissembling. When, in October 1685, John Evelyn discovered that Charles had converted to Catholicism on his deathbed, he declared that he much preferred James's openness about religion, that James was an honest man who could be trusted to keep his word.[3] If James had been content to worship in private, all would have been well, but he was determined to advance Catholicism in his kingdom.

James cherished ambitions to create a new state-building bureaucracy, curbing the press, building up his army, and making new Catholic institutions prominent in government. He did seek religious toleration, but many assumed his chief aim was to remove discrimination against Catholics. The model James pursued was Louis XIV's France, Catholic and absolutist, firmly under the control of its king, not the Pope. But if James thought that London was stable enough to permit far-reaching reform, he was mistaken. The Londoners that Charles had promoted to office were complaisant, but the removal of the City's treasured charter had caused deep ill feeling; Evelyn doubted whether it was even legal.[4] People valued their civil liberties, and anti-Catholicism was endemic in the metropolis. London's Court of Common Council had even insisted on a change to the inscription on the Monument; in 1681 a phrase was added to the north panel blaming the Fire on 'popish frenzy'. When James became king, he had the additional words removed; but it was not so easy to change opinion. A hard core of Londoners had also grown used to mass petitions and street protests in the Protestant cause. It was this undercurrent of popular protest, extending to wealthier members of society, that James would ignore at his peril.

For the first few months of his reign James had a smooth ride; then the Duke of Monmouth, Charles II's eldest bastard son, launched a rebellion against him. Monmouth was dashing but easily swayed. His move in 1685 was impetuous, yet he had long courted the common people and ballads glorified him. Some believed that he had as good a claim to the throne as James. After all, Henrietta Maria, James's mother, had often been denounced as a whore, and some thought Monmouth could have been legitimate, though Charles II had repeatedly denied ever marrying Monmouth's mother. Others just called for Monmouth to be legitimized. He was the obvious figurehead for a Whig plot. On 1 June, Monmouth arrived in the West Country from Holland, expecting to ignite a mass uprising in the Protestant cause. But powerful men did not answer his call; local dissenters, farmers and artisans mostly flocked to his standard. This ragbag army was easily defeated on 6 July at the Battle of Sedgemoor in Somerset. In the retribution that followed, George Jeffreys, Lord Chief Justice, sentenced some 250 to death in the 'Bloody Assizes' – an excruciating attack of kidney stones sharpened his cruelty. Hundreds more rebels were transported as cheap labour to the West Indian colonies.

The government feared an insurgence in London that summer; Monmouth had the backing of many Nonconformist ministers and was popular in the capital.[5] In March, John Hathaway of Stepney had been fined and whipped from East Smithfield, through Wapping to Ratcliff Cross, for swearing that he was ready to fight for Monmouth; Deborah Hawkins of Holborn was fined and pilloried for disparaging the king and declaring, 'if there were wars as I believe there will be, I will put on breeches myself to fight for the Duke of Monmouth'.[6] The rebellion in June was followed by a crackdown on sympathizers in London; ninety-two were arrested.[7] The horrific executions of those convicted of treason deepened the climate of fear created by reports of the hundreds hanged in the West Country. William Disney, condemned for printing Monmouth's declaration of intent, was hanged, drawn and quartered on Kennington Common on 29 June, his limbs afterwards fixed to the City's gates. In October, Elizabeth Gaunt was burnt at the stake in Smithfield for helping traitors, although she claimed she had only given charity to a rebel's wife and children 'ready to perrish for want of bread and cloathing'.[8] She was not allowed to be strangled first, as many such cases were. Supporters tried to make her into a Protestant martyr; a version of her last speech proclaiming her innocence was issued in Dutch and English.

Monmouth's execution on 15 July was also harrowing. He had begged James for his life but was now too great a liability for his uncle to pardon him. On Tower Hill, Monmouth gave the executioner Jack Ketch six guineas, promising he would get more if he made a clean job of it. Then, feeling the axe he said, 'I fear it is not sharp enough.' Ketch growled, 'It is sharp enough, and heavy enough.'[9] But whether irritation or nerves put Ketch off his stroke, he botched the execution horribly. After the first blow, Monmouth raised his head in anguish. After the second and third strikes, he was seen to mutter some words. Ketch gave two more desperate clouts with his axe before pulling out a long knife and hacking through the remaining sinews. The crowd watched in horror and rising anger, groaning and screaming at the spectacle; when Ketch held up the head, they rushed forward to dip their handkerchiefs in the blood. The official account of the execution was bland, but a Dutch propaganda print depicted Monmouth on the block, his head twisted sideways, his face contorted as Ketch sawed with his knife.[10] To counteract popular sympathy for Monmouth, loyal songs mocking his ambitions were rapidly licensed and distributed, typically calling him a 'sham' prince.[11]

London would play a major part in opposing James as he pursued autocratic rule and the advance of Catholicism. First, he failed to disband the extra soldiers recruited to quash Monmouth's rebellion. It was a worrying sign; Charles had kept a standing army but always reduced its size in peacetime, partly because he could never afford a large army. Thanks to England's growing overseas trade, James got higher revenues from the taxes that parliament granted him and increased his army from about 8,500 to just under 20,000 men.[12] The increase was a source of fear and discontent because people understood that a strong army allowed a king to impose his will on the people. Evelyn was disgusted by the creation of a 'mighty Land Army . . . doubtlesse kept & increased in order to bring in & Countenance Popery'.[13] And although penal laws and the Test Acts made it illegal for Catholics to hold office or serve as military officers, James manipulated these laws to appoint the Catholic army officers he trusted.

A large army brought daily annoyances. England had no barracks, so soldiers were quartered in taverns; many refused to pay for food, drink or lodging. In London, soldiers were traditionally stationed on the outskirts, in the Tower, Southwark and the Savoy, ready to support the Trained Bands in emergencies. But in early 1686, James requisitioned Dissenters' meeting houses in Old Gravel Lane, today's Wapping Lane, converting the houses into barracks. He also moved soldiers from the Savoy and Charing Cross to Fleet Street, a clear sign that he meant to extend his authority into the City itself. Every summer he held a training camp for the army on Hounslow Heath. At first, this was unpopular: critics complained that the camp was a hotbed of immorality, that soldiers were poxed and that their tents attracted 'Multitudes of Women', if not whores.[14] Later, annual military exercises became a visitor attraction; Londoners also flocked to Blackheath to watch impressive artillery displays, 'the Granadoes whirling like a flight of Partridges thro: ye Aire and alighting halfe a mile distant'.[15] If James wished to awe Londoners, such spectacles produced mixed reactions.

Londoners were not easily reconciled to the military presence in their city. As early as June 1686, leaflets were circulated justifying resistance whenever civil rights and liberties were threatened; hand-outs urged soldiers and seamen to rebel against their Catholic officers.[16] In the streets, scuffles took place between regiments and London's constables and watch. Soldiers were implicated in murders and robberies; they abused women.[17] Regiments were also used in cases of heavy-handed peacekeeping. For instance, one Sunday in July 1687, a cowkeeper called Griffiths, a testy character, found some apprentice boys washing in his ponds in Lambs Conduit Fields. He seized their clothes and set his mastiff on them; several boys were mauled. An avenging rabble formed to damage the cowkeeper's house and goods. Griffiths called for soldiers, who fired live ammunition into the crowd, killing one and wounding others. Reinforcements of horse and foot guards quelled the disturbance, and the militia stood guard afterwards. Some apprentices were sent to prison, provoking more riots days later when supporters demanded their release.[18] The king sent George Jeffreys, now made Lord Chancellor, to complain to the mayor about rioting in the City, but many felt the cowkeeper should get the blame.

The ease with which James came to the throne, and his firm belief in the divine right of kings, encouraged him to edge towards absolute rule. In fact, his security depended on the loyal Tory Anglicans whom Charles had put in public offices, and James only undermined his position by promoting Catholicism. Put simply, there were three religious groups he had to consider: Dissenters, Anglicans and Catholics. People's political and religious beliefs were never completely aligned but Dissenters were predominantly Whigs, whereas Anglicans were predominantly loyal Tories. In order to advance the Tory-Anglican interest, Charles had inflicted terrible hardship on Dissenters. London's Trained Bands had interrupted them at prayer and broken up their meeting houses, smashing pulpits, galleries and seats.[19] Ministers had been thrown out of their livings, fined and imprisoned. Many Dissenters were still uneasy in their own city, shuddering with fear as they passed law courts and other government buildings. The third group, Catholics, accounted for only about 1.2 per cent of the population; like Dissenters they were banned by the Test Acts from holding office or sitting in parliament.[20] Naturally, Anglicans had expectations that James would protect their Church from other faiths in return for their loyal support. In London particularly, Anglican clergymen railed against popery and stirred up anti-Catholic feeling from the pulpit, although many Catholics were tolerant of other faiths. James was outraged.

In September 1686, James suspended Henry Compton, Bishop of London, for failing to clamp down on anti-Catholic preaching. The move was 'universally resented', all the more so because signs of popery were becoming daily more visible on London's streets, thanks to royal policy.[21] For the first time since Henry VIII's break with Rome, the Pope's nuncio, Fernando D'Adda, had been welcomed to the capital. The papal representative began to appear publicly that September, taking precedence over other ambassadors. Catholic chapels and religious orders proliferated, popish pamphlets and pictures were openly sold. Papists seemed favoured with the best posts because James used his powers of dispensation to get around the Test Acts and anti-Catholic penal laws. Citizens soon feared that the rule of law was under threat as well as their Protestant religion. John Evelyn recorded bitterly that after the City lost its charter, the Lord Mayor's Show in October 1686 was a hollow affair, evidence of civil rights lost. James had advanced his reforming agenda rapidly and broken the Anglican stranglehold on office, but were his actions legal?

Around this time, John Dryden, now Poet Laureate and a convert to Catholicism, composed *The Hind and the Panther*, a poem in which he urged Catholics and Anglicans to unite against Dissenters. The different faiths were represented by different animals who improbably discussed the nature of the true Church. The poem was greeted with satire and ridicule when published in 1687. Nor could Dryden keep up with James's changing policy. The king had grudgingly realized that Anglicans would never support the repeal of the Test Acts. Already, at the outset of 1687, he had changed tack and began to court Dissenters who, like Catholics, stood to benefit from toleration. This alarmed Anglican groups in London; they circulated 'libels' against removing the Acts.[22] But on 4 April, James published his Declaration of Indulgence, entirely suspending the Test Acts since he could not obtain parliamentary approval to repeal them. People were now free to worship according to their conscience. Anglicans like Evelyn were dismissed from office, and the Church of England seemed as beleaguered as in the time of Cromwell.[23] James was fast losing vital Anglican support. Army barracks around Old Gravel Lane were removed and the meeting houses restored, but even Dissenters were unhappy with toleration on this basis: they worried that if James so readily used his authority to overrule Acts of Parliament, he could easily trample on laws that upheld the liberties of his subjects. But at least his Declaration encouraged more Huguenot refugees to head for England.

James next turned his attention to the City livery companies. A legal loop-hole put the companies outside the Test Acts, so office-holders did not have to be members of the Church of England. Companies had allowed Dissenting congregations to worship in their halls; some even harboured radicals. Charles II had regarded the companies as hotbeds of opposition and purged them of Dissenters. But his overhaul of company charters brought inefficiency and delay as judges began legal proceedings against no fewer than fifty companies. It also led to incompetence; expertise counted for more than faith when over-seeing London's complex trading networks, and there were simply not enough Anglicans with the skills and experience to fill vacant positions. Routine business was neglected. In February 1687, James had to remind the Court of Aldermen to prosecute all people keeping shops, selling by retail, or following any trade in City and surrounding Liberties who were not freemen.[24] And James was about to make matters worse.

By the time that he issued his Declaration removing the ban on Dissenters holding public office, London's companies were governed by new charters which insisted their officials had to be Anglican. Confusion reigned. In the autumn of 1687, James purged the companies of Anglican officials who objected to his Declaration. Then he weeded out as many as 1,795 opponents among the lesser liverymen; more dismissals followed in February 1688.[25] Citizens were shocked that the king should take it into his head to meddle with their aldermen, and they noticed that many Anglican officials had been replaced by 'Fanaticks', because inevitably radicals crept into office alongside sober administrators.[26]

There was another problem: from the autumn of 1687, Dissenters were free to resume their City offices, but many were reluctant to serve, irritated by the disruption to trade and wary of the king's arbitrary tendency to ride roughshod over rules. The livery companies drifted towards paralysis and James found that the new men he put in office were hardly more willing to do his bidding than the old. His stubborn determination to alter the religious balance in his kingdom had alienated powerful businessmen and aggravated London's poor. For years, companies had been plagued by debt; now the charity they normally dispensed dried up. It mattered, because London's reaction to James's policies was crucial to the success of his reign.

With James's Declaration of Indulgence, one newsletter reported, 'Popery was upon ye gallop'.[27] The queen's new chapel opened at Whitehall provoking outrage since Catholic priests always sought converts. Jesuits set up a school in the old Savoy hospital, a Benedictine monastery was founded in Clerkenwell, and the Carmelites established a church in Bucklersbury, right in the heart of the City. The Franciscans and Dominicans opened chapels in Lincoln's Inn Fields and Somerset House, and monks openly walked the streets in their habits. The king's Jesuit advisor, Father Edward Petre, was admitted to the Privy Council in November 1687, although fastidious peers were reluctant to sit with him. The new Dissenting aldermen even invited the papal nuncio to dine with the king and queen at Guildhall.[28] In this climate, James summoned key individuals to meet him face to face and demanded to know whether they would support him in repealing the Test Acts. This 'closeting campaign' put enormous pressure on Anglicans and was clearly aimed at packing parliament so that James would get his way.[29] Following London's lead, Catholic chapels began to spring up in other English cities as James urged city corporations across the land to appoint men who would support him. All knew he could rely on his army to crush protest. Many drew parallels with Louis XIV's treatment of Protestants in France and dreaded the life they would lead if James remained on the throne. Fear of popery and absolutism outweighed the benefits of freedom of worship for all.

SEVEN BISHOPS AND A BIRTH

On a tour of the West Midlands in 1687, James travelled to Holywell to pray for a male heir at St Winefride's shrine. The queen opted for more physical measures and took the waters at Bath. Whether it was a miracle or the medicinal waters, when the couple met again in September the queen soon got pregnant. Given her history of miscarriages, she waited until November before announcing the pregnancy. After a proclamation of the news in December, the king appointed 15 January 1688 as a day of thanksgiving in London. Henry Hyde, Earl of Clarendon, attended the service at St James's, Christopher Wren's new fashionable church in Piccadilly. He saw that few had bothered to bring the official form of prayer with them and was worried by people's behaviour: 'It is strange to see, how the Queen's great belly is every where ridiculed, as if scarce any body believed it to be true. Good God help us.'[30] Libels about the pregnancy were pasted to walls or scattered about the streets at night. One pinned to the pillar of a church called on people to give thanks to God for the queen being great with a cushion.

Jubilant Catholics seemed so confident that there would be a male heir, it was rumoured that whether the outcome proved a stillbirth or a daughter, Catholics at court would find a way to ensure that a healthy boy was declared Prince of Wales. Even Princess Anne gave an ear to such rumours and communicated them to her sister, Mary, living in Holland with her husband, William of Orange. Anne had just suffered yet another miscarriage; she found it galling that her father's young wife was enjoying a healthy pregnancy. A male heir would place Mary, Anne, and any children they might have, further from the throne. Many scurrilous libels about the pregnancy were printed in Holland; James had the booksellers who distributed them arrested but he could not quash gossip. Against this background, Londoners found signs of advancing Catholicism and the street clashes with soldiers doubly aggravating. Prominent among many annoyances were the £5,000 that James gave the Franciscan friars in Lincoln's Inn Fields to enlarge their chapel, already too small, and his plans to fit out a royal armoury in the Tower, able to equip 30,000 horse and foot, and an artillery train.

James reissued his Declaration of Indulgence on 27 April 1688. Few Anglican clergy had welcomed it when the Declaration was first issued on 4 April 1687. Now bishops were told to instruct their clergy to read it from the pulpit on two successive Sundays in May. Clearly, obedience would signal approval of the king's suspension of the penal laws and Tests. It was a trap. And if James thought that the bishops would comply, he was mistaken. They understood that if the king could operate outside the law, no one was protected from his arbitrary power. Archbishop Sancroft of Canterbury and six others decided to petition the king to be excused on the grounds that parliament had already affirmed such a declaration to be illegal. They presented their petition with respect at Whitehall on 18 May, but James was outraged; he believed that his dispensing power came from God. Soon 'the Bishops affair' was on everyone's lips.[31] Few London clergy chose to obey the king; in the whole of the metropolis, the Indulgence was read in just seven churches.

This was something James could not ignore. He summoned the seven bishops to an audience on 8 June. They refused to explain further because legally they could not be forced to incriminate themselves. James demanded that they give bail to appear at the Court of the King's Bench; again, the bishops refused because, as peers of the realm, bail was not required of them. Instead, they offered their personal promise to appear. James now lost all patience and ordered them to the Tower. As they were taken under guard to the river, citizens fell spontaneously to their knees and asked for their blessing. Even blaspheming watermen cried out, 'God bless the *Bishops!*'[32] The river workers were mostly Dissenters and cared little for prelates, but now that they saw these men suffering in defence of religion, liberty and property, they took a different view. London was already on edge because an aguish fever raged through the town, attributed to unseasonably cold northeasterly winds, with few families escaping it. During the bishops' imprisonment, vast numbers flocked to the Tower. John Evelyn visited the bishops, as did Clarendon, who hoped to be able to mediate.

Two days after the bishops were locked up, Clarendon was in church on 10 June when a great whisper rippled through the congregation. He could not learn what the matter was, but on the way home his servant told him that the queen had given birth to a son. The lord mayor at once sent dutiful congratulations. He ordered great bonfires to be set ablaze at Guildhall gate, the Royal Exchange, and outside his own house, and provided wine so that people could drink to the health of the royal family. About the City and the court end of town there were other bonfires, fanfares and window illuminations. In the rest of the capital the news was received with little zeal or loyalty; in some places it even met with fear and denial. The very next day there were rumours that the prince had died, and another baby substituted. The baby's health was followed in detail, not least because he was often very sick. The doctors had decided that milk would be bad for him, so he was fed gruel and pap. Only in August, as he faded fast, did they cease to advise he should be brought up 'by hand' and seek a wet nurse.[33]

The royal birth was overshadowed by the case of the bishops, summoned to appear at Westminster Hall on 15 June. Lord Chancellor Jeffreys, for one, regretted that the king did not seize on the birth of a son as an excuse to drop the trial. The atmosphere in London grew more uneasy. Catholics were targeted covertly; an official at one Catholic chapel was murdered near the Haymarket.[34] On 15 June the streets were full of angry people and Westminster Palace Yard was thronged. Waiting crowds made way for the bishops as they passed and pressed for their blessing but cursed and intimated the lawyers. In court, the bishops were charged with publishing a seditious libel against the king. They pleaded not guilty and this time were released on bail. Outside, the crowd mistook their release for a complete discharge; that evening London was illuminated with bonfires celebrating the bishops' delivery, many more than had been lit for the birth of the prince.

The appointed Thanksgiving Day for the birth was 17 June. Again, the City made a great show of loyalty, paying the musicians £6s. 8d. each for their performances, finding ten guineas for the messenger who brought the news of the birth to the lord mayor, and setting aside another sixty guineas to be distributed among the nurses whenever the king gave permission for aldermen to attend the young prince.[35] It was merely an interlude; all minds were focused on the bishops' trial on 29 June. Samuel Pepys was called to give evidence but said nothing to favour either party. The king reviewed two or three battalions in Hyde Park while the trial took place; he meant to have soldiers armed and ready in case of civil unrest. And crowds were gathering in Westminster for news of the verdict.

The jury took a long time over their decision. They were shut up all night in a private room at the Bell Tavern in King Street. Next morning, they returned to Westminster Hall and declared the bishops not guilty. Great shouts erupted in the hall from onlookers. Afterwards church bells were rung and bonfires lit, although they were forbidden, and in a striking departure from recent practice, the crowds burnt effigies of the Pope. The authorities had lost control of public ritual; it was a decisive sign that James had lost his cause. That night, watches were doubled in the City, but a watchman was shot with a brace of bullets as he tried to quell demonstrators in the Strand; his attacker was never identified. Around midnight the butchers of Clare Market, armed with cleavers and chopping knives, rampaged through the streets, breaking the windows of great houses, notably that of the Catholic Earl of Castlemaine, crying 'No Declaration No Toleration'.[36] The watch dared not oppose them.

Seven eminent men, including Henry Compton, Bishop of London, had already written secretly to William of Orange, a dedicated Calvinist, inviting him to invade England and defend the Protestant religion.

THE LONDON MOB AND REVOLUTION

London's backing would be crucial to William in the events that followed. The word 'mob' dates from these years, and William benefited from mob action as well as from men in power. During the Exclusion Crisis of the early 1680s, London's underclass had been primed to take part in elaborate and impassioned Pope-burning processions. The Whigs, hostile to the court, organized these rituals at their Green Ribbon Club, named after the colour of the radical Leveller movement of the 1640s. Club members met at the King's Head Tavern, at the corner of Fleet Street and Chancery Lane, where they organized an annual procession on 17 November, the birthday of Protestant Queen Elizabeth I.[37] At dusk, marchers wound past the Royal Exchange, along Cheapside, then up Ludgate Hill to Temple Bar, the gateway marking the boundary between City and Court. Thanks to the renovation in stone that Charles II had insisted on after the Fire, it now included a female statue assumed to be Elizabeth I. A procession of many thousand was choreographed in 1681 by the playwright Elkanah Settle, who would later write pageants for the Lord Mayor's Show. Men, dressed as cardinals, carried aloft an effigy of the Pope, stuffed with live cats, who shrieked horribly at the event's climax when the effigy was burned on a giant bonfire at Temple Bar. These were rituals of enormous excitement and passion which helped to focus popular opinion and turn it into a political weapon.

James had managed to control London during his remodelling of civic institutions, but his policies had not been given a smooth ride. In the spring of 1686, when Catholic chapels were being built, the mob attacked construction workers and broke furniture. Afterwards, crowds gathered at chapel doors, hurling anti-Catholic insults, and even throwing stones and oranges at the altars inside. In September 1686 the unrest reached a climax when London apprentices attacked the house of the Spanish ambassador, located near today's Wild Street. He was celebrating that year's great Christian victory over the

Turks at Buda, the ancient capital of Hungary, but the mob broke his windows from top to bottom, threw firebrands inside, and shouted that they would rather see Buda in the hands of the Devil than occupied by Catholics.[38] Scenes of violent disorder erupted on 5 November, even though at the start of his reign James had banned anniversary celebrations of the Gunpowder Plot and had mostly quelled all bonfires the previous year. Now there were bonfires and illuminations near the Monument and elsewhere in the City and suburbs. Representations of the Pope were burnt in some places and carried in effigy in others. Catholic rituals were mocked, and in one place 'a piece of flesh burnt which was a great reflection upon the Sacrament, and a great reproach to Christianity'.[39]

The king issued a stern warning to the lord mayor, aldermen and Justices of the Peace not to allow such demonstrations in future. Accordingly, they tried to stamp out protest: in 1687 soldiers opened fire on demonstrators objecting to any repeal of the penal laws and Test Acts; but libels against James continued to circulate, despite arrests of printers and booksellers. The unrest was partly due to anti-Catholic feeling but also a response to the king's policies, which had increased the power of the Crown. There were rumours in various parts of the country, eagerly repeated in London during 1688, that Monmouth was still alive. Such rumours had started soon after his execution but now they spiced London's heady mix of libel and speculation. In some accounts, James was accused of poisoning Monmouth.

The king's opponents had long been in communication with William of Orange. They spread favourable propaganda about the Dutch court that contrasted with affairs at Whitehall, such as news that William had decided to dismiss all his Catholic servants unless they embraced Protestantism. In 1688, James was unwilling to believe that William, his own nephew and son-in-law, would invade England, but he did take precautions. Warships were provisioned from March, ready to be ordered to the Downs, an anchorage off the Kent coast, to guard the Channel during the summer. After a Dutch fleet put to sea in April – allegedly to protect trade – rumours circulated that the Dutch were building more ships, so a hundred extra shipwrights were hired at Deptford to speed the fitting-out of English warships. By the autumn it was common knowledge that William had adopted the role of deliverer and meant to invade.

Londoners did not trust James and were weary of his regime; many were disappointed with the entire Restoration monarchy. Rich English merchants even helped to fund William's invasion force.

The prevailing cynicism made it easy to cast doubt over the legitimacy of the young Prince of Wales. Prints showed the queen beside the baby in its crib, a Jesuit priest behind her, his hand suggestively clasping her neck.[40] The message was both that the royal family was in thrall to Rome and that the queen may have been having illicit sex with her confessor, Father Petre. Gossips said that, when she recovered, she meant to take the waters at Bath again, opening the prospect of still more Catholic princes. Many believed that the prince was not royal at all, that the queen had feigned pregnancy and a baby had been smuggled into the birth chamber. Because she had delayed making her condition public, it appeared that she had mysteriously been brought to bed two months early even by her own calculation. Some insisted that the baby had been sneaked into the royal bed in a warming pan. This was absurd, given that by tradition English queens suffered the indignity of giving birth in a room full of courtiers who acted as witnesses. But Anne, a potential key witness, had made sure that she was too distant to be summoned when the queen went into labour; Anne had headed for Bath to treat her own gynaecological problems, although her usual resort was Tunbridge Wells, not so distant. Now she cast aspersions on the prince's legitimacy – she had never seen the queen's great belly, never been asked to feel the child kicking (not that this had happened in the queen's earlier pregnancies), and she nursed these seeds of doubt in letters to her sister Mary. Clarendon was horrified in October 1688 to find the princess and her women openly making jokes about the birth.

The previous summer, a faction within the army that had ill-defined links to the circle around Anne began to plot against James. Bawdy rumours about the royal birth even circulated among the troops. One of the horse guards was committed to the Marshalsea prison for suggesting that the prince was spurious, 'wee have had too many shamms already'.[41] Even the corpulent Bishop of Chester, Thomas Cartwright, who had sided with the king against the Seven Bishops, was not convinced that the baby was legitimate; he suggested that since the child was often sick, it might be better if he died.[42] Some would believe the child was genuine only if he did die. On 22 October the king organized a meeting of the Privy Council at which statements were taken on oath testifying that the prince was his true son. It did no good: despite the evidence, Protestants did not want to believe in a Catholic heir.

By September, James himself accepted that William meant to invade. Events now took on a curious two-speed momentum. There were frenetic preparations in the capital: more ships were fitted out, seamen were pressed, horses were requisitioned and, as in the Civil Wars, female households made desperate pleas to keep their carriage horses so that they could escape if threatened. On Lord Mayor's Day, 29 October, press gangs were out in such force, 'there were hardly any watermen seen on board of the Barges of the lord mayor and the different companies, even not on that of the King, as they dare not show themselves'.[43] All the while, William's fleet made its stately progress westward down the Channel, as the wind dictated. Occasional sightings of his fleet off the south coast were relayed to London. The same wind that propelled William's force westwards kept the English fleet pent up in the Thames estuary. Yet there was a suspicion that not all naval officers wanted to give chase. Just like the army, the navy harboured a faction opposed to James. When two warships returned to the Thames for provisions, many sailors deserted. Ordered to return to the fleet, the warship captains complained that they were undermanned. The Admiral of the Fleet, Lord Dartmouth, offered to send men from other ships, but the two warships still lingered in the Thames until truly trapped there by adverse winds, a sign to all that the king's forces were divided.

In September, James began to make hasty concessions. He pledged to restore the Bishop of London, to remove Catholics from office, and to call a parliament rather than freely using his dispensing power. On 2 October he restored the City of London's charter. The following day, when his bishops demanded that he restore all things to the state they were when he came to the throne and that he cease proceedings against the corporations, James began to comply, reversing his reforms. It was too late: the patience of London's populace snapped. On 30 September a Jesuit priest slighted the King James Bible during a service in the Lime Street chapel. A crowd quickly formed, tore him from the pulpit, smashed the altar, and broke the chapel windows before the Trained Bands arrived. The following week, crowds again attacked Catholic chapels. Two weeks later, on Lord Mayor's Day, apprentices stirred up trouble. They gathered along

Cheapside up to the entrance of Cornhill and threw dirt at passing coachmen. Then a mob attacked the chapel in Bucklersbury. Crowds pulled down the altar and dragged pictures, doors and windows into the open street, setting fire to the lot. The Sheriff managed to protect the chapel in Lime Street, but rioting continued all night.

The guards in the City were doubled; two companies of Trained Bands stood on duty at night and files of musketeers were sent to each city gate to support the constable and watch. Citizens were fearful because the king had quartered some 2,500 Irish troops, foot and horse, in and about the town. The Irish had not been in London long, but several had already been confined to Newgate for murder and other crimes. The mayor found he needed a large force to keep the peace: by 5 November there were ten companies of Trained Bands under arms, in addition to the constables.

For days now, a northeasterly wind had blown hard. Londoners were sure that William's fleet would have landed somewhere; they expected news hourly but saw their fate would be decided by others. That 5 November, William had indeed made landfall in Torbay – the significance of the date was not lost on commentators. A messenger galloped to London with the news, covering more than 160 miles in less than 20 hours. He arrived 'so disordered' that people feared he would hardly recover, while from the west came other reports of terrible apparitions in the air, 'flashes of fire like the fighting of two Armies'.[44]

18

TAKING SIDES
THE DUTCH INVASION, 1688

With a large army and thirty years' military experience, King James should have had powerful options when Prince William invaded, but he found himself cornered. His need to defend and control London meant that he could not apply all his energy to confronting William in the west. In any case poor roads made it nearly impossible to move his troops swiftly in winter. Nor did he have the supply network to feed them on the march. He could fix on no steady plan: every option seemed plagued by drawbacks. Worn out by weeks of frenetic preparation, he succumbed to heavy nosebleeds and slept only with the help of opiates.[1] He grew emaciated and dwelt morbidly on the fate of his father and Richard II, kings killed by their subjects. Precise details of William's movements were hard to come by, but rumours of influential men defecting to William's camp soon turned out to be true. James no longer trusted that his forces would stay loyal in battle, yet he feared to open negotiations with William from a position of weakness. His confidence seeped away.

Londoners were left to wait in suspense during this uncertain time. At the end of October, William had sent a *Declaration* over from Holland explaining clearly why he had decided to invade England. His sole intent was to uphold the English constitution and preserve liberty. This manifesto was widely circulated and, by the time of his invasion, had won many hearts and minds. His invasion fleet carried not just troops and weapons, but a printing press, paper, and thousands of leaflets printed in English to rally people to his side. But skilful propaganda alone could not ensure people's loyalty to either cause. Radical groups had been galvanized and soon there were street disturbances. In taverns the singing of subversive songs about the City's lost charter and other grievances fostered popular resistance. Rioters had often targeted Catholic chapels, and on

11 November troops finally fired live ammunition into the crowd. That night Trained Bands were guarding the chapel in Lincoln's Inn Fields, when 'the loose Youth of the town' broke through and smashed its windows.[2] Then they swarmed towards the monastery in Clerkenwell where, according to rumour, long knives, gridirons and cauldrons had been stockpiled to wound and torture Protestants. Its monks climbed onto the roof and threw bricks and tiles into the angry crowd surrounding the building. Rioters managed to smash down the door and would have destroyed the chapel had not horse and foot guards fired on them, killing several individuals.

James promptly ordered all chapels in London to close, except those belonging to foreign ambassadors and the palace. But next day, as dusk fell, when the Clerkenwell monks tried to remove their goods to safety, the rabble overtook their carts in Holborn and set fire to the contents. Then, with flaming torches, they marched through the streets and returned to the monastery, intent on destruction. They found the building guarded, and in another ugly fight soldiers again fired, wounding and killing many, 'a Blacamore' among them.[3] To keep the peace, several hundred members of the Trained Bands were ordered to patrol the streets and watches were doubled in the City and suburbs. In Blackfriars, a close guard was placed on the king's official printer, Henry Hills, whose premises had been attacked three times, most recently by crowds over a thousand strong, because he had issued propaganda opposing William's *Declaration*. In another move to quell discontent, Lord Chancellor Jeffreys ordered London's mayor and aldermen to lay in a stock of corn for the poor during the winter months, a practice that had long since lapsed.[4] Even so, the trickle of defections to William's camp became a torrent and there were riots in other major cities.

At the end of November, James learned that his daughter, Anne, had fled London to join the rebels. Whom could he trust? By 2 December, John Evelyn, whose son had also joined Prince William, perhaps with his blessing, was writing, 'it lookes like a Revolution', although by that term he may have meant a reversal of government rather than a popular, violent uprising.[5] The more practical Pepys, who also saw which way the wind was blowing, made certain he had James's signature on a document certifying that he was owed money for services since 1679. The atmosphere in London grew fearful; citizens were especially intimidated because the Tower was garrisoned by newly recruited troops under Catholic officers and a Catholic governor. The Dutch envoy, Aernout Van Citters, underlining the sentence to show his emotion, complained in his November dispatches that Catholic threats had confined him to his house for a month:

> And what hurts my family most, is that I must remain to live under the execration and threats of a heap of ignorant priests who would every hour or every moment if they had it in their power break my neck, plunder my House, or set fire to it by night.[6]

In this emergency, James finally agreed to demands for a free parliament, saying he would call one in the New Year. He sent the moderate Marquis of Halifax and other peers to talk terms with the prince but had secretly decided that his only option was flight. He had already hurried his queen and baby son to France; on the night of 10 December he followed.

In London, news of the king's 'withdrawing' broke next day. Terrible violence erupted that same evening. Chapels, embassies, and the houses of wealthy Catholics, mostly protected before, were attacked with unbounded fury. The mob, thousands strong, tore down the chapel in St James's; they made a bonfire of the vestments and ornaments of the mass-house in Lincoln's Inn Fields. Catholics who tried to flee the city with their goods were stopped by guards and robbed. Cartloads of royal propaganda and Catholic works from the printer Henry Hills were burned near Fleet Bridge. The streets from Whitechapel to Westminster were full of angry people, but Londoners had no cause to fear massacre or even wholesale damage to property because mob and militia were on the same, Protestant, side. In contrast, the tumultuous violence against Catholic centres was terrifying and uncontrollable fires were feared as the mob attacked chapels, burnt furniture, pulled down structural timber, and even carried away bricks in baskets so that little remained. The Spanish ambassador's residence, Weld House, was ransacked and torched. The rabble stole valuables worth £20,000, destroyed a library worth £8,000, and plundered goods that Catholics had taken there for safety. In contrast, the mob left the French ambassador's house untouched; he was popular because he paid his bills promptly, whereas tradesmen loathed the Spanish ambassador, who contracted great debts and paid no one. If James had looked back as he journeyed to the coast, he would have seen the sky above London flaming red.

Rioting continued the following night. Women took part as well as men, and the crowds included disbanded soldiers, outright thieves and looters who plundered as much as they could. At Charing Cross the mob killed a captain of a Trained Band sent to keep order, then swept through Southwark and Peckham, attacking more Catholic houses. In Marshalsea prison, inmates rioted and many escaped. Real terror began to take hold, as reports circulated that Irish soldiers were marching on London, killing and burning everything in their path. Although several thousand Trained Bands were on patrol, citizens stayed up all night, their houses lit from top to bottom so that an eerie light flickered in the streets. The hated Lord Chancellor, Jeffreys, was found hiding in Wapping. The lord mayor ordered him to the Tower under armed guard to prevent an angry crowd from tearing him to pieces; he ended his days there. The Bishop of Chester was caught, disguised as a Swiss mercenary 'with artificiall Mustaches', but allowed to escape.[7] At the height of the crisis, John Evelyn wrote from Deptford, 'we are here as yet (I thank God) unmolested; but this shaking menaces every Corner'.[8] Catholics were the prime target but the extreme violence rattled law-abiding moderates. They condemned what they saw as an attack on liberty and property 'to the great Scandall of the City', not least because it damaged London's economy.[9]

Among the motives spurring the mob were social, economic and political grievances. Radical groups in London, persisting long after the Civil Wars, railed against James's policies; he had threatened civil liberties and his remodelling of the livery companies had disrupted their charitable payments to the poor. It is striking that the French ambassador was spared because he was known to fulfil his responsibilities to those lower down the social scale. Among merchants there was a European context to the dissatisfaction with James's programme. The king was allied with Catholic Louis XIV of France, but the City wanted to curb France's ambition to be the leading power in Europe. Instead, they wanted war with France to preserve the balance of power. An anti-French policy, merchants thought, would offer better opportunities for English trade. The Florentine agent in London, Francesco Terriesi, whose home and chapel in the Haymarket had been attacked, was certain that 'great men' had manipulated the lower orders and contrived the political agitation.[10]

City authorities now took stock of the destruction of property and the damage to trade from civil disorder, fast spreading to other major cities. Firm action was needed because a serious setback to trade would jeopardize the nation's prosperity. In the political vacuum caused by James's departure several peers met at Guildhall to discuss the way forward. Given the severity of public disorder and fears that armed papists roamed London ready to set fire to buildings or attempt a sudden massacre, they agreed to summon Prince William to control the situation. London's mayor and aldermen formally invited the prince into the City to demonstrate that he did not take it by force, and their letters were printed and distributed in a show of transparency. Leading peers then ordered the king's Irish soldiers to surrender their arms and told the navy not to clash with William's fleet, thereby giving the prince complete military supremacy. Rioting in London had helped tip the scales in William's favour.

Meanwhile, James had reached Faversham, where brigands were on the lookout for Catholics fleeing the country with valuables. They stopped the king without recognizing him, even pulling down his breeches in a strip search before someone realized who he was. James was escorted back to London on 16 December, a broken man. The mayor and aldermen decided against laying on the usual civic welcome – after all they had just invited William to take charge of the capital. Even so, crowds loudly cheered the king as he rode, escorted, through the City to Whitehall. Either citizens were fickle, or they chose to distinguish between James's hated policies and his actual person, or they assumed he would restore order and so greeted him with relief. For the moment no one was sure which way the tide of popular opinion would turn, towards the king or towards Prince William. For his part, James was convinced that it was only a matter of time before he was killed. Despite the encouraging welcome, he was still intent on flight. This was just as well because William, camped to the west of London, now had serious designs on the throne, whatever his earlier motives had been. He was appalled that James had returned and sent Halifax and other lords to the king requiring him to retire to Ham House. James asked to go to Rochester instead; William agreed and conveniently left him unguarded there so that he could escape to France.

On the afternoon of 18 December, Prince William entered London. He rode from the west straight to St James's Palace, sending only his troops into the City. They were a disciplined force: English and Scots regiments from Holland, Swedes and Germans, Swiss mercenaries, Dutch guards, Huguenot volunteers, and some 200 Blacks from the Netherlands' plantations in America. Anxious onlookers, mindful of the great store Londoners set on a procession, regretted that William had dispatched only second-rate baggage horses with the men. But the citizens had prepared for a magnificent entry and welcomed the soldiers with joyful enthusiasm and bellringing as if it were a second Restoration. Some waved oranges on sticks and, at Ludgate, a female orange seller distributed several baskets of oranges to the prince's officers and men. As further evidence of women's interest in politics, when the soldiers turned into Fleet Street, several women took them by the hand crying, 'Welcome God blesse you, you came to redeeme our Religion, Lawes, Liberties and Lives God reward you.'[11] Roger Morrice, a Puritan Whig clergyman, reflected on the momentous transfer of power he had just witnessed and noted the role of the London mob. 'It is true the King had legall Authority,' he mused, 'but the Prince they had invited had power &c And there was another power tho*ugh* it were very unwarrantable that the Mobile [mob] had.'[12] William now occupied London but strong divisions remained.

THE SUCCESSION

The wealth of London was enormous, and its financial support was crucial to the success of the revolution. So was its political support needed to inspire confidence in the new regime. William acted promptly to smother unrest in the capital: within two weeks he was in control of the military and civil government. He made sure that the Tower was in loyal hands and he took James's disbanded soldiers into the army, allegedly for London's defence but mostly to prevent mischief. Already, on 20 December, one of William's guards had been found in Long Acre with his throat cut.[13] The soldier had been quartered with papists, who were quickly arrested. Two days later all papists who were not householders or tradesmen were sent out of London. William tried not to quarter soldiers in private houses and expected to pay for those quartered in taverns. For this he needed money. The City raised over £150,000 in six days to help pay the expenses of government, certain that the prince alone could guarantee peace.[14] To help win loyalty and to smother discontent in the middle of a bitterly cold winter, William sent money to the poor, to workhouses and to prisons. The gesture helped to create an image of royal paternalism which was especially powerful given that England was not his own country. London's mayor and aldermen paid tribute, inviting him to a great dinner. The Royal African Company, switching its allegiance, was quick to thank him for the 'Hazard and Expense' he had demonstrated in saving the nation from popery; it chose him for their governor and gave him 'a considerable Present'.[15] But what could be William's next move?

The prince had claimed to be invading England to save the kingdom from popery and slavery; his *Declaration* had said nothing about replacing the king. And the complaints against James itemized in the *Declaration* had already been addressed by James himself who, in his panic, had even agreed to call a free parliament. So not everybody accepted that a change was needed to the succession. All William could do was summon a Convention Parliament in the New Year and wait. Because the king had left the country, the licensing laws were not enforced, and a flood of publications poured from London's presses setting out different options. Should the king be recalled? (But then, if returned to power, would he pardon rebel Protestants and respect the laws in future?) Should there be a regency? Should William's wife, Mary, be declared queen? Should William and Mary rule together? Or, more radical, should the monarchy be replaced by a commonwealth?

When the Convention Parliament met in January, members spent much time debating whether James had abdicated at all. Opinion divided along political but also religious lines, since discussion was still grounded in a deeply religious world view. Most Anglican Tories favoured restoring James or settling the throne on Princess Mary alone, since she was first in the order of succession. Whigs, on the other hand, especially Whig merchants who wanted better trading conditions and a boost for manufacturing, favoured giving William power. Many Whigs were Nonconformists. One positive outcome of this intense debate was an increase in people's understanding of the nature of government and the relationship between ruler and ruled.

Parliament eventually concluded that James had abdicated, freeing the path for a new monarch. At this juncture MPs saw an opportunity to make sure that the Crown could never again abuse its power. They drew up a list of conditions, known as the Declaration of Rights, to preserve civil liberties from arbitrary government. Chief among these was that there should be no standing army in peacetime and that no monarch could raise taxes without the consent of parliament. Other clauses in the Declaration insisted that there should be freedom of speech, free election of MPs to parliament, and that parliaments should be called frequently.

The version of this 1688 revolution commonly transmitted to later generations explained that an oppressed population, firmly rejecting popery and tyranny, had come together in a spirit of moderation to restore the people's ancient rights and liberties. The revolution was called 'Glorious' because, it was said, people had neither been dragooned against their will nor put through violent religious conflict of the kind then raging on the Continent. But the truth is more contested and muddled; the emerging political solution in 1689 was a compromise that left ambiguous several crucial points that people found too difficult to sort out. And when, with government encouragement, William imposed his rule in Ireland and Scotland by force of arms, his victory brought slaughter.

The Marquis of Halifax was made Speaker of the House of Lords. A self-declared 'Trimmer' who cut his way between extremes, Halifax was the chief architect of the political settlement, but ordinary Londoners played a crucial role. William's supporters organized petitions, signed by thousands of citizens, urgently pressing for the Prince and Princess of Orange to be crowned. And during parliamentary debates noisy Whig demonstrations took place around Westminster, when the crowd especially intimidated MPs thought to be hostile to William. In this complex and shifting situation, many of the tactics used had parallels in the civil war period but there were also differences. The commercial context came into sharp focus because merchants and tradesmen, mostly Whigs, saw France as the great threat to free trade and prosperity, and they wanted its power curbed. The public had become accustomed to coffee-house debate fuelled by printed news. And the fall-out from James's policies had fostered a greater willingness of Dissenters and some 'low' Anglican churchmen to work together.

The rush of pamphlets from London presses explaining the different options for rule fostered debate across the kingdom, and the prevailing judgement in

London influenced the rest of the country. A Scottish minister, Robert Kirk, wrote:

> Tis a great advantage in England that whatever by the changes continually occurring in Church or State there be so many learned men who immediately publish their advice *pro* and *con* that each may see and quickly choose what is safest and best to do without much study.[16]

According to Kirk, clearly not a man of deep-seated opinion, 'If any get example from the citizens or clergy of London (the centre of wisdom) the whole nation is influenced by it', although he did also see that religious arguments were used for political ends.[17] The experience of civil war meant that people were determined to avoid bloodshed – which, in England at least, they largely managed to do. William was praised for his skilful intervention, but English subjects were tactfully given credit for their refusal to submit to slavish rule. Religious and political factions in London grew sufficiently aligned to support a compromise solution that ensured most people largely got what they wanted.

By mid-January the talk of the town was that William and Mary were to be crowned king and queen, the prince to be king during his lifetime in case his wife died without children. The deciding move came from William himself, who told Halifax and other Lords that he had not invaded England to be tied to his wife's apron strings and would depart for Holland if Mary were given the crown alone. For her part, Mary let it be known that she had sworn to obey her husband when she married and would not take the crown for herself. On 12 February parliament agreed to offer them the crown jointly, the executive power to be invested in William. By this time Mary had reached London, having been held up because the ports were frozen. On 13 February the couple accepted the throne jointly in the Banqueting House, symbolically holding hands. At the ceremony Halifax read aloud the Declaration of Rights. It was not a condition of William and Mary taking the throne, but it was certainly a firm statement of their subjects' legal rights which, as rulers, they should uphold. William spoke for both when he replied that he had no intention but to preserve the country's religion, laws and liberties; Mary gave a little curtsy. In December the Bill of Rights was made law.

London-based rituals were used to help establish the new regime. On 13 February the new king and queen were proclaimed in Whitehall and the City of London according to tradition. As usual, when the procession reached Temple Bar, the herald knocked for admission to the City. On the other side an officer for the mayor and aldermen asked who was there. 'We are come to proclaim the Prince and Princess of Orange King and Queen of England' was the reply. 'Where is James II?' asked the officer. 'He is dead, he is dead, he is dead', came the reply.[18] Others added that he had abdicated, and the gate was duly opened. The new king and queen were proclaimed at Temple Bar, and afterwards at the Royal Exchange. That evening there were bonfires in most streets; three enormous pyramid structures were set alight in St James's Square and others in Leicester Fields. William and Mary were crowned on 11 April, when the ceremony echoed James's coronation: the procession walked from Whitehall to Westminster Hall, on blue cloth, then proceeded to the Abbey. Such details were important because so much of the coronation was unique: there were two monarchs, and the oath itself had to be specially adapted. As Speaker, Halifax formally offered the two crowns; he had also drafted the speech of acceptance. In another familiar detail, after the ceremony the royal couple changed their crimson velvet costumes for purple velvet before returning to Westminster Hall.

Visual propaganda was used to the full. Before the coronation new uniforms were ordered for the Yeomen of the Guard, the monarch's bodyguard, and for the yeomen warders of the Tower of London. The uniforms were of fine red cloth, lined with blue, with the letters W. M. RR. in silver and gilt spangles emblazoned on the breast and back. A celebratory print of the coronation procession was issued, and portraits of the crowned couple holding their sceptres were printed and advertised for purchase in the *London Gazette*. Medals were struck to celebrate William and Mary's accession and legitimize their rule. One silver medal shows William bringing peace and crushing the serpent of Discord; in the background, James and Father Petre are taking flight with the baby prince, James Stuart.[19] As in much contemporary satire surrounding the birth, the prince holds a toy windmill. Millers were traditionally associated with fraud and many claimed the baby was a miller's son.

Another print shows William brutally trampling underfoot several Catholic priests, one of them vomiting. The caption explains that William has reclaimed the kingdom from 'these vermine'.[20] It was printed by Grace Beckett, at a time when only about 4 per cent of London's booksellers and printers were women. As she had earlier produced an attractive print of the baby prince, she may have been eager to signal her loyalty to the new king.[21] It was also possible to buy packs of playing cards illustrating key episodes in the narrative of the revolution: James's tyranny, his flight, and William and Mary's accession. Such items helped to normalize the extraordinary event that had taken place. The Mint soon produced gold and silver coinage stamped with the heads of the new king and queen, alongside traditional symbols: Britannia or a lion rampant. There was a shortage of small currency, but the couple's portraits featured on alloy penny tokens since it was crucial that all levels of society accepted the succession. Images of the new monarchs also decorated earthenware pottery, pewter spoons and jewellery so that people could display their allegiance in different ways according to their spending power.

Early in the new reign, parliament passed a Toleration Act giving Protestant Dissenters the right to hold their own religious services without fear of prosecution. Catholics were explicitly excluded from the terms of the Act: 'no popery' remained a convenient slogan with which to gain support for policies at home and abroad. The Test Acts that excluded Dissenters and Catholics from holding office remained law, although Dissenters in London organized protests and petitions to try to get them repealed. And not all Londoners were content with the change in regime. There were numerous prosecutions for sedition; someone even boldly defaced William's portrait in the Guildhall 'by cutting out the crown and scepter'.[22] Even those who were broadly in favour of William and Mary mistrusted the secrecy surrounding court politics. According to the minister Kirk, anything controversial was kept 'under a veil and undiscovered', to dissuade opponents from forming conspiracies.[23]

William grew nervous about the activities of radical Whig leaders in the City, partly owing to the prevalence of sedition. In 1689 the Lord Mayor's Show was used to proclaim the Whig understanding of the revolution as a triumph of the people's will over tyranny. Whigs also tried to revolutionize the City's government to make it more democratic. James had restored the City's charter, but it was one of his last acts as king, of dubious legality, and had to be ratified by a new bill. Whig leaders drafted a radical new charter for discussion in parliament. They claimed to be restoring ancient procedures, but their new charter would make it harder for the City's elite to ignore the wishes of ordinary citizens. Its supporters included the same wealthy Whig merchants who, when James fled, had pushed hard for a republic rather than the monarchy of William and Mary. A hint of the continuing political debate and discontent is evident in a print of William III, identical in every respect to an earlier print of Cromwell except for the head, where the copper plate had been reworked to portray William not Cromwell.[24] The printer may have adapted an old plate for speed or economy. Or the motive may have been to suggest that Londoners had lost a lawful king and gained an unlawful 'protector', another cunning Cromwell.

Soon William began to align himself with the Tories, and in parliament there was a reaction against the City's radical Whig leaders. When the bill about the City's charter came to parliament in 1690, it was rejected as hasty work that would turn London's corporation into a commonwealth. London's old charter was restored without revision. Whig leaders saw that they would have to temper their politics if they wanted power, and Tories also found they would have to adapt to the domestic and foreign policies of the day. Radicalism in London might remain a constant presence, but the two main opposing parties now evolved different identities from those proclaimed earlier in the century.

PROVIDENCE AND THE NEW REGIME

When John Evelyn first encountered William, he thought him 'very stately, serious, & reserved'.[25] It was up to Mary to provide a welcoming, friendly presence at court. Her role was a complex one. She accepted contemporary gender roles, deferring to her husband, but as a monarch she could not help but influence views about women. It may be no coincidence that in 1688 Halifax finally acknowledged authorship of an advice book he had written for his daughter, publishing what had circulated in manuscript for some years. In it he urged her just as a matter of prudence to accept the view that women are inferior to men. In marriage particularly, women as 'the weaker Sex' must submit to 'Masculine Dominion' rather than threaten an institution so essential to the social order: 'You are therefore to make your best of what is *settled* by *Law* and *Custom*, and not vainly imagine, that it will be *changed* for your sake.'[26] Mary clearly needed no second bidding, but other women should not be seduced by her status to get ideas above their station.

Since Mary was the legitimate heir, her image was fashioned to help reconcile opponents to the revolution. William's new subjects found him cold and distant. It did not help that William was asthmatic, gaunt, and some 4 inches shorter than his attractive wife who stood 5 feet 11 inches tall. (The height discrepancy was never represented in joint portraits.) Because, in accepting the throne, Mary could be accused of breaking the fifth commandment to honour one's father and mother, her allies circulated reports of her many virtues in advance of her return to England. She was described as 'the best Natur'd Princess in the World', religious, studious, humble and charitable.[27] Like most women, she had received a superficial education. It was understood that she had made up for its deficiencies, completing a broad programme of religious and philosophical reading. And she was genuinely pious: at one point, James had tried to convert her to Catholicism, but she was able to reply with a long, intelligent letter, presenting cogent arguments for her Protestant faith.

Even so, on her return to Whitehall in 1689, she made a bad impression. William had told her not to look unhappy when entering her father's palace in case detractors accused her of a guilty conscience or began to doubt that there were sound reasons for his invasion. She overplayed her part, breezing through rooms, examining beds and turning down coverlets as if she were at an inn. Shocked onlookers felt that some show of regret at having to assume her father's crown would have been in order. She soon registered her mistake and afterwards became acutely aware of the impact of her behaviour on others. She was closely observed and did much to fashion her own image. Rarely idle, in a courtly way she played the part of a good housewife, embroidering hangings and cushions with her ladies whenever she had time, because sewing was a potent symbol of the woman's role in a family.

Since William's claim to be rescuing the nation from popery and tyranny had been undermined by James's late concessions, supporters of the revolution restructured the event as a providential deliverance. According to this view, William was doing God's work in protecting Protestantism and would restore the nation to piety and virtue. As early as January 1689, when William was still waiting for the Crown, a solemn day of thanksgiving was declared for the nation's deliverance. Church services were followed by bellringing, the firing of great guns from the Tower, and bonfires. The couple's own personal dispositions meant that they easily presided over a regular, reformed court. Mary increased the number of divine services held at court and altered arrangements at Hampton Court so that she could be seen worshipping in the chapel's royal gallery. She authorized the publication of sermons given in her presence, averaging no fewer than seventeen publications a year in her short reign. They sold well and helped to create the impression of godly rule. Both William and Mary favoured low churchmen who were more likely to work with Dissenters and help to heal religious divisions. From this foundation it was possible to address the moral reform of the kingdom.

The first Societies for the Reformation of Manners were set up in London from 1690, building on Anglican religious societies for young men that had become established during the previous decade. Societies for the Reformation of Manners often used informers to identify individuals engaged in prostitution, sodomy, gaming, cursing and drunkenness; offenders were then punished in the courts. Both William and Mary supported the societies, but Mary was more active, ensuring that Justices of the Peace elected in London and Westminster were already members. Possibly she was attracted to the cause of reformation because she bore the heavy burden of her father's curse, which he delivered to her around the time of her coronation. Certainly, she was behind proclamations enforcing laws against adultery, blasphemy and Sunday trading. The fight against supposed immorality disproportionately hit the poor, although the middling sort also suffered when trading was banned on Sundays. The kingdom was soon at war with France, and reform societies promoted ideals of manly virtue, arguing that lewd vices could lead to military defeat. From the late 1690s, officials especially targeted homosexuality, raiding the molly houses where gay men or 'mollies' met. In London there was a thriving queer subculture that some now thought too overt; the king, never popular, was rumoured to have homosexual leanings. Anyway, it was convenient to associate Englishness with the Protestant, heterosexual males that the military wanted, and just as normal to slur foreign enemies as effeminate, luxurious and Catholic.

In her lifetime Mary was explicitly compared to Elizabeth I, both in her defence of the Protestant faith and for her stout bravery when the country was threatened by invasion. For, despite earlier worries about entrusting the throne to a woman, Mary exceeded expectations when she had to shoulder the burden of rule. Each year, during the campaign season from the beginning of May to late October, William fought with his troops in Ireland or on the Continent. He toyed with the idea of having the Privy Council rule in his absence but in the end trusted his loyal wife, though he did provide her with a council of advisors. As regent, she referred the important decisions to him anyway. She took care to avoid differences of opinion between husband and wife, and happily restored power to him as soon as he returned. She was a model of how a devoted wife ought to behave while her husband was at war. But occasionally there were crises that demanded urgent action. At these times her firm response inspired confidence and respect. She also had a personal touch that stood her in good stead. When James threatened to invade with a French force to regain his throne in 1692, Mary delivered inspiring words to the navy. Her address deliberately recalled Elizabeth I's speech to the troops at Tilbury in August 1588, when England was threatened by an invasion from Spain; it likewise spurred the fleet to victory.

As a paragon of piety and wifely devotion, Mary was a central figure in the propaganda that cemented the new regime. She helped create the mythology that the revolution was a providential delivery from tyranny. Her image was that of a just and pious ruler sent by God to reform the nation. But James still had his supporters in London. Printing houses had to be inspected regularly for seditious material that could be distributed across the kingdom through the mails. Women were prominent among those who conspired to spark unrest among disadvantaged groups such as weavers; several women were arrested on suspicion of plotting treason. Mary's opponents circulated libels in manuscript and print form, some cruelly mocking her weight gain. But Mary's pious image survived the onslaught and, alongside the work of the reforming societies, helped to reconcile some of James's followers to the revolution. Commentators said that the societies had 'done much Good, and put some considerable stop to Vice, that was running on in a high and desperate Degree in the Nation'.[28] But the joint reign of William and Mary would do more than influence the outlook and behaviour of metropolitan society. It would have an impact on London's institutions, its style and even its built environment.

19

A NEW REGIME
WILLIAM AND MARY'S TOWN

When Mary returned from Holland in 1689, after an absence of eleven years, she would have noticed the many changes that new building had made to the fabric of London. When she had left with William in 1677, she was a tearful bride of fifteen, unhappy to leave the city she loved. The queen tried to comfort her, saying that she, too, had left her homeland to marry young, and without first meeting the king. Naively, Mary replied, 'But, madam, you came into England; but I am going out of England.'[1] Yet to her surprise, Mary grew to love Holland, its cleanliness, propriety, and the informality of Dutch palaces compared to the ritual of the English court. She returned to take her father's throne with deeply mixed emotions, able now to make a fair appraisal of life in the capital. Both she and William knew that they would never enjoy the same freedom again.

London was still a place of narrow, twisting streets. One in ten English people lived in the metropolis and population density in its business centre was among the highest recorded for any city. More than three-quarters of its citizens now lived outside the City walls.[2] It was a place where most people still travelled on foot. For longer journeys there were around 500 hackney carriages for hire, but water transport was cheaper and often faster. At the court end of town, there was elegant new building, but in the suburbs low-density, sprawling housing was the norm, intermingled with wretched shanty towns for the poor. Even in the City, uneven streets made travel dangerous. Dorothy, wife of the merchant Thomas Wood, complained that she had been 'sadly frited' the previous night when her coach turned over coming down St Dunstan's Hill to their town house in Thames Street. She would be glad to leave such a troublesome location but would have to extend her stay; the bodice man had still not got her garment right after three fittings. She even doubted that her coach would make it back to their country home in Littleton, 'for it tis verey rotten'.[3] The importance of London as a shopping centre must have outweighed many inconveniences.

Mary II, who was childless, spent large sums on clothes once crowned. She found that even when shopping she had to guard her reputation. One day she dined with Mrs Graden, a seller of fine ribbons and headdresses; William accused her of entering a brothel and desired, pointedly, that next time she went, he might be of the party.[4] Alarmed, she replied that she had done nothing more than the late queen, Mary Beatrice, had done. 'And do you mean to make her your example?' he replied.[5] Mrs Graden was well known in Westminster Hall, which at that time was lined with booths – some no more than 8 feet (2.4 metres) wide – selling books and small items of clothing such as gloves and ribbons. What Mary might not have known was that top knots of ribbons had acquired lascivious connotations. Ballads circulated which hinted that women who sported these lavish, expensive adornments prized luxury more than virtue.[6] William's sharpness may also have owed something to a personal dislike of tall headdresses, which added inches to the height of his tall wife.

When Mary went shopping to the New Exchange in the Strand, she would have seen that most of the great noblemen's houses that once extended from the Strand to the Thames had disappeared. Northumberland House, south of Charing Cross, still stood, as did Somerset House, refurbished by Wren in 1685 for Catherine of Braganza and now her London home. But several impoverished peers had been forced to sell their great houses to developers. George Villiers, second Duke of Buckingham, had sold York House in 1672. A condition of the sale was that the streets replacing it would commemorate his name. This led to ridicule since every part of his title was used, producing Of Alley. Further east, Arundel House and its gardens had gone, and Arundel Street put in. Essex Hall had been replaced with Essex Street. And James, fourth Earl of Salisbury, had decided to pull down Salisbury House, already in disrepair, and put up shops and houses. Legal permission to do so was delayed; the house was finally pulled down in 1695 and Cecil Street created. The Savoy, just west of Somerset House, had become partly militarized since being used as a hospital in the Civil Wars; one building had been converted to barracks for foot guards in 1679, and although the Huguenots were using its chapel, the nobility had left the houses in its grounds and tradesmen had moved in.

Further north, a syndicate of bankers and merchants bought the Duke of Albemarle's Piccadilly mansion, Clarendon House, in 1684. It was the grandest private London residence of its era, with 101 hearths. Twenty years earlier, Samuel Pepys had written, 'it is the finest pile I ever did see in my life, and will be a glorious house'.[7] John Evelyn had proudly advised on the garden and interior decoration, but thanks to the spendthrift duke it had fallen into neglect. Clarendon House was in a prime location: it faced St James's Street but backed onto open fields at a time when the aristocratic residential district of Mayfair was being built. The house was soon demolished, and Dover, Albemarle, Bond and Strafford Streets were created on the site. People certainly registered these changes. The traveller and diarist, Celia Fiennes, wrote at the end of the century, 'There was formerly in the Citty several houses of the noblemens with large gardens and out houses . . . but of late are pulled down and built into streetes and squares and called by the names of the noblemen.'[8] The newly built Montagu House in Bloomsbury stood out as a jewel in this context.

London was becoming famous for its elegant squares. West of the City, Lincoln's Inn Fields had been enclosed on three sides by streets as early as the civil war period, and the square crossed by diagonal paths. In the 1660s the Earl of Southampton copied the Italian concept of the piazza and created a large open place to the south of his house on Great Russell Street. Southampton, later called Bloomsbury, Square was shown to foreign dignitaries as one of London's embellishments. St James's Square, with its large houses and gardens behind, was completed about 1676. And when Mary returned from Holland she would have found other squares in Westminster. Soho Square was begun in 1677 and tenants moved into houses there from 1681. The square was earlier called Frith, and then King's, Square, in honour of Charles II, and it was fashionable with the gentry who paid ten shillings a year towards 'the keeping in repaire the Rayles, Payles, Fountaine and Garden in the middle of the square'.[9] This secure, communal garden was an innovation and the same model of charging householders for the upkeep of the enclosed square was adopted at nearby Golden Square, begun in 1675 although not completed until the early 1700s. These fashionable squares were given piped water, sewerage and paved footpaths in front of houses; London's continued westward expansion meant that in 1696 William granted patents to Marchants Waterworks to lay pipes and raise Thames water to service more houses.

Smaller squares also appeared in the City. Crosby Square, off Bishopsgate, was built from about 1671. Then Nicholas Barbon, the energetic physician, economist and speculative builder, bought nearby lands from the Earl of Devonshire and, from 1678, he developed Devonshire Square. Around 1680, Heydon's Yard, later Square, was constructed just east of the Minories. It was followed by New Square in Lincoln's Inn and Bridgewater Square just north of the Barbican, both neatly paved, which date from 1682. The northern and eastern suburbs were not totally left behind. To the north, Hoxton Square was laid out in 1683, forming a fashionable development for Nonconformists. To the east, the indefatigable Barbon and his partner, Felix Calvert, built Marine or Wellclose Square off Ratcliff Highway from 1683. It would be popular with wealthy sea captains, but completion was slow; it was harder to sell large houses in maritime east London.

Squares sometimes helped to reconcile Londoners to the loss of open land. In 1684, when Barbon began to lay streets over Red Lion Fields in Holborn, the lawyers of nearby Gray's Inn Fields rebelled at the loss of recreation space and came to blows with Barbon's workmen. Justices of the Peace in Middlesex complained to the Privy Council that the project had blocked highways that had been free 'time out of mind'; that 'the air of Gray's Inn would be choked up'; and that Barbon had made 'severall laystalls there of garbage and offalls from severall marketts, sufficient to endanger the bringing of a plague into the neighbourhood'.[10] Barbon was forced to adjust his dense housing plans and leave a central square crossed by diagonal paths.

More houses meant more pollution. The smoke from London's coal fires aggravated William's asthma; he found it impossible to live for long periods in Whitehall Palace and retreated to Hampton Court. There Mary, who preferred a private life and loathed the restrictions and back-biting at the court, tried to recreate the tranquillity that both had enjoyed in their Dutch palaces. Sir Christopher Wren was employed to remodel Hampton Court. It proved impractical to demolish and start afresh; instead Wren created the baroque Fountain Court, with state apartments for both William and Mary, featuring newly invented, highly fashionable sash windows. Although Hampton Court was only two hours from London by water, it was still too distant from parliament for the couple to live there permanently. They purchased Kensington House for £20,000 from the Earl of Nottingham and ordered Wren to enlarge it quickly, moving in by Christmas 1689. Mary extended her suite by adding a gallery and, after a fire in 1691, the king's staircase was rebuilt in marble and a guard chamber added, so that the house grew more palatial. To make the route to Kensington safer, William had a new broad avenue built from Hyde Park Corner along the south side of the park with 150 oil lanterns each side. Later known as Rotten Row, it was the first highway in Britain to be artificially lit.

Whitehall Palace was badly damaged by fire in 1691, when the queen had a narrow escape. Another blaze completed its ruin in 1697, although the Banqueting House survived. William did not rebuild; he had never liked the rambling complex. Afterwards, St James's Palace became the chief royal residence in London, although the couple rarely lived there. John Evelyn had hoped that the library at St James's would be developed as a national resource because so many great libraries had been lost or neglected during the Civil Wars, but the project did not survive the death of the queen, its patron.

William and Mary were responsible for other building projects. Mary initiated the creation of Greenwich Hospital for retired and disabled naval seamen on the Thames. A baroque masterpiece, designed by Wren and Nicholas Hawksmoor from 1692, it was a visual reminder of her charity as well as of the value the nation placed on control of the seas, though the money for it came from various sources. In 1692, Chelsea Hospital for retired soldiers, founded by Charles II a decade earlier, finally opened its doors; Mary was determined to do the same for seamen, extending and adapting a royal building that Charles had left unfinished on the site of the old Tudor palace at Greenwich. Public buildings of the stature of Greenwich and Chelsea Hospitals added prestige to the growing capital, as was already evident from the reception given to the new Bedlam Hospital for the insane in Moorfields. Designed by Robert Hooke, it had opened in 1676 and its stately facade had many admirers.

The largest new development in 1690s London came after William granted Thomas Neale, a politician and entrepreneur, the freehold of land west of Covent Garden named Cock and Pye Fields, after a public house there. Covent Garden was already getting a bad reputation; Lincoln's Inn Fields, ten minutes' walk away, was troubled by beggars. William may have hoped that building on Cock and Pye Fields would improve the area but chiefly he wanted to raise money to fund his war against France. Neale had to pay ground rents on the land and needed to maximize his return. His solution was ingenious: he rejected fashionable squares and built in a star pattern of six radiating streets (seven in the final plan). The scheme, laid out in 1693, dramatically multiplied the number of houses that could fit on the site and increased his rental income. He hired Edward Pierce, a leading sculptor and stonemason, to make a sundial pillar at the centre of this set-piece, giving Seven Dials its name. Neale himself is still commemorated in Neal's Yard and Neal Street. He intended the houses for gentlemen and prosperous tradesmen but after 1695, when he sold his interest in the site to builders, houses were subdivided into shops and lodgings and Seven Dials became a bustling commercial district. It attracted Huguenots, who were flocking to London now that Protestant William and Mary reigned, and the Toleration Act of 1689 had granted freedom of worship to Nonconformists. Skilled Huguenot engravers helped to publicize the latest building achievements, producing topographical prints of St Paul's, now nearing completion, and of other landmarks, including Greenwich Hospital.

INTERIOR AND GARDEN DESIGN

One factor that helped to smooth the path of William's invasion was that, at the top of the social scale, Dutch tastes were already shaping domestic interiors and garden design in England. Dutch fashions were themselves filtered through powerful French influences, not least because William and Mary favoured French design and employed the Huguenot architect and designer, Daniel Marot, to help furnish their palaces in Holland. Once in England, William and Mary used interior and garden design to help cement their rule. At Hampton Court the decoration of the new Fountain Court was themed around the divine hero Hercules, glorifying William III as a great martial ruler. William's state coach, either created by Marot or influenced by his designs, shows the king being presented with the Magna Carta and the Bill of Rights, flanked by figures representing Liberty, Fame and Justice. It is still used by the Speaker today.

By 1690, Huguenots represented about 8 to 10 per cent of London's population, so there was a ready supply of accomplished craftsmen, able to produce technically complex pieces of metalwork, carving, gilding and painting in the French style. William had dined with the Earl at Montagu House and admired his decorative schemes. Later, the royal couple employed in their palaces many of the French artists and craftsmen that Montagu had used to rebuild his mansion in Bloomsbury. The royal accounts show that Queen Mary commissioned expensive furniture, sometimes decorated with the latest metal inlay. Cornelius Gole, a Huguenot cabinetmaker, was paid £100 in 1690 for 'a table dolphin fashion inlaid graved and richly carved and gilt the frame richly carved and gilt suitable with several figures festoons etc' and also 'a pair of stands and a table finely adorned with brass graved and gilt the frames finely carved and gilt' to be used at Whitehall and Kensington'.[11] Mary also commissioned Gole to produce ornately carved mirror frames.

The mansions of the elite attracted curious visitors, so fashions permeated down to lower levels of society, and French design was further popularized by importing and reprinting French pattern books. The Nonconformist minister Robert Kirk visited Montagu House and marvelled at the large sash windows and parquetry floors: 'Tis preferable to Whitehall banqueting house or any other I saw yet in England,' he declared.[12] Pictures and porcelain were increasingly used as part of the decoration of great houses. The inventory of Anne, Lady Belasyse, who died at her house in Queen Street, St Giles, in 1694, shows that French and Dutch tastes had been firmly adopted. She was the wife of John, first Baron Belasyse, a resilient Catholic royalist who had steered a precarious career as a soldier and member of parliament. He had endured a long imprisonment during the years of the Popish Plot, and her inventory shows how families might use fashionable objects to display loyalty to a new regime. In her various residences Anne owned 'dutch chairs' as well as cane chairs and 'jappan chairs'; in one home she decorated her ground-floor rooms with twenty-nine pictures, 'great and small'; she had a great deal of china and her gardens were furnished with 'leaden potts' and orange trees.[13]

Mary was a passionate collector of oriental porcelain and blue and white Delftware (tin-glazed earthenware). Such ceramics were already the height of fashion in England, but she brought her collection over from Holland and elevated the craze for decorating rooms with fine china to new heights. The writer Daniel Defoe claimed that she introduced the custom of 'furnishing houses with china-ware, which increased to a strange degree afterwards, piling their china upon the tops of cabinets, scrutores, and every chymney-piece, to the tops of the ceilings, and even setting up shelves for their china-ware, where they wanted such places'.[14] In this the queen was again influenced by Marot, whose designs for massed, symmetrical displays of fine porcelain, enhanced by lavish use of mirror glass, were a striking departure from earlier arrangements limited to mantlepieces and cabinets. An inventory of Kensington Palace, taken in 1697, records no fewer than 787 pieces of porcelain arranged throughout her suite of nine rooms there.

The secret of making porcelain had not yet been discovered in Europe, so examples from China and Japan were both precious and exotic, especially when combined to good effect with lacquer furniture, screens and rich textiles. These beautiful, lustrous objects, used to create a novel atmosphere, may have provided a form of escape for a queen under almost constant surveillance, but they also raised the status of the royal court. In 1693, Evelyn wrote, 'I saw the Queenes rare Cabinets & China Collection, which was wonderfull rich & plentifull, but especialy a huge Cabinet, looking Glasse frame & stands all of Amber, much of it white, with historical Basrelie(vos) & statues with Medals carved in them, esteemed worth 4000 pounds.'[15]

Porcelain urns, vases and jars from China and Japan were highly coveted; brightly coloured pieces from Japan were especially fine. When an East Indiaman came into port, its precious cargo was advertised in newspapers and later people could buy from auctions held in the warehouses of the East India Company or in coffee houses, no longer viewed as places of sedition since the revolution. The process of buying choice items of porcelain was therefore enhanced by anticipation and competition. Londoners' growing passion for tea boosted the demand for fine china, to the extent that thieves targeted cargoes of expensive porcelain when ships anchored in the Thames. Francis Purchase, master of the *Bonaventure* which docked at Ratcliff on 22 December 1698, testified that his ship was robbed in the early hours of the morning by four thieves who brought a wherry alongside. Under cover of darkness, they took 'divers Pieces of china stuffs' (porcelain) and garments, then divided the haul and concealed it in hideouts.[16]

Delftware was decorated in the spirit of oriental, blue and white porcelain, although the later pieces that Mary bought for her English palaces had western designs. She displayed the bulk of her collection at Hampton Court in her Water Gallery, a pavilion remodelled from a set of Tudor buildings overlooking the Thames. Defoe later described it as 'the pleasantest little thing within doors that could possibly be made'.[17] French tastes also meant that Delftware factories now manufactured items of tableware that had usually been of metal: spice boxes, butter dishes and salt cellars. This development altered people's experience of dining and entertaining. At mealtimes a display of china on a sideboard became a sign of wealth and sophistication.

Queen Mary commissioned several innovative Delftware pieces for displaying plants and blossoms: large jardinières in which to grow plants, and elaborate flower vases that could ornament an empty fireplace during the summer months. One ingenious tulip vase she once owned has nine tiers, each with six spouts to hold individual tulips. Behind each spout there is an enclosed space for water. This kind of 'portable garden' became popular and was often displayed in rooms with access to a garden, introducing a clever interplay between 'art' and 'nature'. By acquiring these striking vases for the display of expensive, rare plants, William and Mary were deliberately rivalling the splendour of the court of Louis XIV. The trends they set were copied in comparatively modest town houses: in rooms with a corner fireplace, a tier of pyramidal shelves might be built above the mantelpiece for the display of china. Often such rooms offered a view into a garden, however small, and so displays of flowers in vases were especially pleasing. The gentry and wealthy merchants eagerly emulated new court fashions in London and at their country estates. When Thomas Wood decided to pave the hallway of his country house at Littleton with black and white squares, he employed the same stonecutter who had worked at Hampton Court. The whole job cost him £50, which included the cost of the mason taking up the old tiles, providing mortar, and transporting black marble and white Purbeck stone from his house in Hampstead.[18]

William and Mary's interest in remodelling and furnishing their palaces was closely linked to their shared interest in gardens. When William invaded in 1688, he had even turned aside from his march on London to visit the famous gardens at Wilton House, near Salisbury. The fashion for formal gardens in the

French taste, with walks, symmetrical planting, and flat parterres and fountains, had revived in Charles II's time. London boasted fine examples of established gardens: the Apothecaries' Garden at Chelsea (Chelsea Physic Garden), with its underfloor-heated conservatories; secluded gardens at the Inns of Court; and the garden at Fulham Palace where Henry Compton, Bishop of London, had introduced numerous foreign trees, especially from North America. Already the aristocratic interest in gardening was fuelled by a complex web of associations and desires: the prestige of having fine grounds and exotic plants; the approval to be won by seeming to control nature for human benefit; the advancement of knowledge, given that the Royal Society took a keen interest in progressive horticulture; and the obvious link between the cultivation of newly discovered plants from distant countries and imperial expansion.

The royal couple spent lavish amounts on improving the grounds at Kensington House, which covered 26 acres. Their taste was heavily influenced by formal baroque gardens associated with Italy and France, of which Louis XIV's garden at Versailles is the most magnificent example. But they also introduced elements considered typically 'Dutch': evergreens, ornamental 'canals', orange trees in tubs, topiary, and copious use of box. The shrub was useful for hedging sections of formal garden and showing off colourful plants enclosed in patterns, which were often modelled on textile designs. Royal gardens were sometimes used for musical entertainments in the summer months, which helped to make the monarchy seem accessible and allowed the gardens to be admired. But they were also havens for contemplation, of a piece with the rulers' desire to preside over a godly court.

William and Mary ordered and supervised substantial remodelling of the gardens at Hampton Court. The Great Fountain Garden, probably designed by Marot, with thirteen fountains and two avenues of yew trees, was intended to complement Wren's new baroque building. The Privy Garden was largely reworked towards the end of the reign, but, early on, in 1690 they commissioned the French master ironworker, Jean Tijou, to make gates and railings for the end of the garden. Tijou's magnificent 'screen' enhances distant views across the Thames; his published book of designs would inspire English blacksmiths to emulate his work. The royal couple brought specialists from Holland to build glass cases and greenhouses for the cultivation of rare, precious plants. The greenhouses were over

50 feet (15 metres) long, heated by stoves and flues. Mary had an extremely large collection of more than two thousand different species of unfamiliar plants, some from India. She continued to collect, sending gardeners to Virginia, the Canary Islands and Mauritius in search of new species. She also brought over from Holland her collection of rare varieties of flower bulbs. George London and Henry Wise, who ran a nursery at Brompton Park where the Kensington Museums now stand, were appointed royal gardeners. William had his own team headed by his friend, Hans Willem Bentinck, but London and Wise knew what plants would thrive in an English climate. Naturally, their nursery profited from the vast expenditure on the creation and maintenance of royal gardens.

If elements of William and Mary's taste in gardening were fashionable in England before their reign, their example did much to encourage horticulture and the sourcing of novel plants. Dutch topographical paintings and prints helped to publicize garden designs and soon gardening was increasingly talked up as a genteel pursuit for merchants and the middling sort, as well as for the gentry. In a modest way gardening fashions were probably copied in the housing plots that Barbon and other builders were creating in London. It was a sign of the times when one gentleman advertised 'I want a Man to be a Groom that understands a Gun and a Garden'.[19] Newspapers carried notices from gardeners able to supply seeds, fruit trees, plants for greenhouses, hardy evergreens, and imported bay and lemon trees. Gentlemen and merchants increasingly wanted plants and seeds from abroad to furnish their gardens; where space was limited, the mark of status changed from grand garden designs to the display of rare plants from across the globe. London Traders advertised 'Flower-Pots of hardned Metal for Gardens', and 'all sorts of iron Rolls for Garden-Walks, ready fitted'.[20] Advertisements for the sale of London houses talked up fine gardens as an asset; nor were they solely aimed at the well-to-do. One notice describes 'a good Brick House with a Garden a long Shed and a large Piece of Ground by it, fit for a Carpenter, Silver-Spinner, or Twister [of metallic thread]' at £16 a year.[21]

John Houghton's periodical, *A Collection for Improvement of Husbandry and Trade*, offered tried and tested advice. It was reissued from 1691 with the support of Fellows from the Royal Society, following a similar periodical published in the early 1680s. One correspondent noted his success after watering his flowers with a mixture of saltpetre, lime and pigeon dung. Another commented on the good effects of soap suds: 'A very good Friend of mine that liv'd at *Islington*, used to wash his Hands and Face with Water and Soap daily in his Garden and upon some of the near Plants he sprinkled his *Suds*, which made them visibly thrive much more than their Neighbours.'[22] The effect was put down to the potash in the soap. Gardeners also had ready access to manuals, among them Leonard Meager's *The English Gardener*, published in 1670 and reprinted in 1683 and 1688, which had sections on fruit trees (good for garden walls), kitchen gardens and gardens of pleasure. There was also Meager's *New Art of Gardening* (1683), which went through four editions before 1700, and Roger Sharrock's *An Improvement to the Art of Gardening: Or, an Exact History of Plants* (1694), which advertised his credentials as a Fellow of the Royal Society on the title page. Even lowly homeowners could respond to this latest version of husbandry.

By 1722, Thomas Fairchild, a gardener in Hoxton for over thirty years, would be advocating that 'the pleasures of gardening' were as much the right of merchants and traders as 'Persons of Quality'; though their gardens were modest, industry would make the best of them, just as industry would bring them money with which to enlarge and improve their gardens.[23] He aimed his book at people 'who have little Gardens in *London*', who either did not know which plants would withstand the smoke of sea coal, or did not know how to manage their plants when they have got them, adding 'And yet I find, that almost every Body, whose Business requires them to be constantly in Town, will have something of a Garden at any rate'.[24] He observed that citizens furnished their rooms or chambers 'with Basons of Flowers and Bough-pots, rather than not have something of a Garden before them' and recommended decorating chimney pieces with living plants in summer, which he thought would look pretty on a pyramid of shelves.[25] He suggested that plants stand in Delftware pots, on dishes so that water would not run onto the floor.

This growing interest in town gardens prompted a desire to improve the quality of London's squares – after all they were more visible than private gardens. Most were featureless in the seventeenth century, possibly gravelled, often neglected and subject to fly-tipping, the haunt of gamblers and street entertainers. Crosby Square, used to provision horses, was encumbered with stabling, haylofts and dung heaps. Writing in 1694, the lexicographer, Guy Miège reported that 'no foreign City' could show 'so many Piazzas or fine

Squares' but commented that much remained to be done in the way of planting.[26] By the turn of the century there were calls for the central space in London's squares to be turned into gardens; Lincoln's Inn Fields were planted by 1700. As English tastes turned from formal gardens to a more natural effect, squares were planted with a variety of trees and shrubs to amuse the eye.

QUEEN MARY'S POPULARITY AND DEATH

On Sunday 2 February 1690 the Reverend Kirk watched William and Mary at their regular public dinner in Whitehall Palace. They sat on a dais, under a red velvet canopy woven with black, where they were served two courses on gold and silver dishes. The first was pig, turkey, duck, roast beef, venison. The second, fricassee, goose, capon, pigeon and tarts, followed by conserves and sweetmeats. The queen ate much better than king: 'He is phlegmatic, and did spit much at dinner. Queen Mary fat and of a lively colour'; Kirk also noted approvingly that there was 'nothing frolic or vain' about her dress.[27] These public spectacles increased Mary's popularity.

The queen often walked six or seven miles a day, supervising the works at Hampton Court or Kensington, but was the type to put on weight if stressed. She worried about weight gain but seems not to have tried eating less, perhaps finding that abstinence sent out unhelpful signals. When William was on campaign in Ireland, she complained, 'I must laugh and talk, tho' never so much against my will ... All my motions are so watch'd, and all I do so observed, that if I eat less, or speak less, or look more grave, all is lost in the opinion of the world.'[28] Her increasing girth was ammunition for Jacobite satirists, writing for supporters of James II. She 'grew in bulk and chin' as her wheezy husband grew leaner, prompting concealed smirks as they toured their gardens, William seeming to lean on her arm.[29]

But Mary's piety and kindness won many admirers; she became a focus for national loyalty, especially as the movement for the reformation of manners gained ground, when Catholics were blamed as corrupting influences in society. For instance, French Jesuits were suspected of supporting bawdy playhouses in order to corrupt youth.[30] As Mary proved an able ruler in her husband's absence, the sense that she had usurped her father's throne faded. From 1690 her image, fostered in medals, loyal addresses and poetry, became less conflicted. Court propaganda was especially important because the size of William and Mary's rather upright court was shrinking. There was less scope to influence significant individuals face to face, and anyway the political power of the court lessened as the importance of parliament grew.

Smallpox was rife in London during the winter of 1694; hundreds were dying every week. On the morning of 24 December, having felt unwell for some days, Mary woke in her bedchamber at Kensington to find a rash on her arm. She recognized that she had been given a death sentence. Doctors confirmed that she had caught the most virulent smallpox and that there was nothing they could do. She died on 28 December in the early hours of the morning. William, much to the surprise of courtiers, was utterly distraught. He had lost the woman he loved but, as he must have recognized, he had also lost a vital force that gave legitimacy to his rule. Jacobites lost no time in spreading the word that her early death was God's punishment for her disobedience to her father. Loyalists counterclaimed that her death was divine punishment on an entire nation that had been at fault; they encouraged an outpouring of grief. In uncertain times the best next step was to give the queen a magnificent funeral.

The court and London itself were plunged into deepest mourning. The Abbey, Houses of Parliament, Whitehall and Kensington were draped in black. The queen, embalmed, lay in state on a bed of purple at the Banqueting House for two weeks while a gilded and painted mausoleum was prepared for her to Wren's design. Thomas Wood's son, in London to seek an introduction that would help him make his way in the world, reported anxiously to his parents that he might need expensive mourning clothes:

> Here is a generall Mourning both in City & Suburbs & tis ye opinion of some wh[o]m I have consulted, yt I shall be ranked amongst ye Jacobites, if I do not, wch at this juncture of time will not be approved of very well, but I shall wait for yr advice, before I cloth myself.[31]

By 20 January, when John Evelyn went to see the queen lying in state, the frost and continual snow had lasted five weeks; the Thames was frozen over. Veiled Ladies of Honour kept vigil by candlelight at each corner of her resting place, relieved every thirty minutes. Despite the bitter cold, queues formed early each day to see Mary's body, although the public was admitted only between noon and 5 p.m. Her funeral did not take place until 5 March, when it rivalled that of Elizabeth I to whom she had been so often compared.

As with Elizabeth's funeral, the procession took place in daylight so that crowds could get the full benefit. In driving snow, peers, MPs, mayor, aldermen and 400 poor women in mourning gowns and hoods accompanied the hearse bearing Mary's coffin, crown, orb and sceptre from the Banqueting House to Westminster Abbey, while the entire route was hung with expensive black cloth. Henry Purcell wrote some of his most moving music for the service, while outside, the great guns in the Tower fired every minute. It was the largest funeral ever held for an English monarch and cost £50,000; conveniently, the queen's note expressing her wish for a modest burial was only discovered later.

William became less popular after Mary's death. He was disliked as a foreigner and there was a sense that the English were paying for an expensive war against France that primarily served the Dutch. When the king was due to ride through the City in November 1697, the mayor had to issue an order to make sure that local officials visited each house along the route to give notice to the inhabitants that they must decorate their balconies and windows and pave, mend and clean the streets.[32] The Dutch became a byword for dullness and lack of wit. To counteract William's unpopularity, Mary's memory was used in loyalist propaganda. Prints were made of her sombre lying in state, her funeral and her mausoleum. She was commemorated in poems, medals and some forty funeral sermons that insisted on her personal virtues, piety and charity. Her benign influence was heralded as a divinely ordered step towards national renewal. Her association with gardens ('royal huswifry'), fine china and cultured domesticity acted as a counterweight to William's militarism.[33] The important thing about her leisure interests was that they could be reflected in people's homes. Much popular Delftware pottery of the 1690s therefore showed the king in heroic poses on bowls, plates and tiles.[34] Patriotic display was absorbed into the routines of daily life, no longer reserved for special occasions, and London's rich cultural life camouflaged division. As increasing numbers accepted the revolution, grew to expect imported luxuries, and got on with business, national confidence blossomed.

20

NO TIME FOR CYNICS
TOWARDS A NEW CENTURY

London in the 1690s was gripped by lottery fever. Cash prizes allowed people to dream of riches and offered hope to the desperate. The lotteries were advertised in newspapers and on handbills posted in coffee houses and pubs. News also spread by word of mouth: lotteries were the talk of the town. Tickets were sold at the Royal Exchange and locally, from booths in major taverns and other venues. Women, with few opportunities in the world of finance, were enthusiastic subscribers. Chancers without much money clubbed together to raise the price of a ticket, so lotteries reached most social levels; John Evelyn's coachman won £40 in a lottery that Thomas Neale set up in 1693. Neale had hired Daniel Defoe as one of his managers – Defoe, then a bankrupt hosier, was keen to grasp any opportunity to make money. Neale's venture was such a success that the following year he set up the first state-run lottery, promising to raise a million pounds for the war against France. This Million Adventure lottery captured people's imagination; in some circles it even spurred discussion about the new mathematical concept of probability, still barely understood. A thousand shares were sold for £10 each and a prize fund of £40,000 set aside to be distributed in the form of annuities of varying amounts. The Million Adventure pandered to the contemporary addiction for gambling but also had patriotic appeal and sold out in no time; speculators afterwards pushed a separate trade in undrawn tickets.

Lotteries allowed citizens with just a little capital to dabble in London's growing financial markets. The early 1690s saw a stock-market boom which peaked in the years 1691–3. There were many companies in which to invest, thanks to a developing economy, earlier growth of foreign trade, and an increase in manufactures spurred by Huguenot craftsmen. Investors could now buy shares not just in the established East India, Hudson's Bay and Royal African Companies, but in new ventures like the Company of Copper-Miners, the Company for making imitation Russia-leather, or the Hollow Sword Blades' Company. And because the war hindered foreign trade, investors looked to put their money into domestic projects. Most share investments remained in the hands of aristocratic stakeholders and rich city merchants, but depositors from middling backgrounds were attracted to the expanding market. Evidence can be found in the apothecary John Houghton's weekly publication, *A Collection for Improvement of Husbandry and Trade*. Written with the support of like-minded members of the Royal Society for a general audience, it now included articles explaining in basic terms just how the stock market worked.

For many this giddy financial activity offered a completely new experience. Speculators could follow the price of shares in newspapers and discuss exciting money-making schemes in smoky coffee houses. Investment proposals included the recovery of sunken treasure ships, which explains the publicity given in 1693 to an intrepid Thames diver who allegedly managed to walk half a mile underwater from Vauxhall to York Buildings.[1] Would-be investors had to make fine judgements about risk and the quality of commercial information. The process had parallels with the careful assessments of the Royal Society, weighing up information received about the natural world. Increasingly, London was a conduit for intelligence from all over the world. At the Exchange, which now grew in importance, hundreds of merchants of many nationalities gathered daily; there was an incessant buzz of conversation, a kind of loud whisper that contemporaries compared to the sound of a hive or the drone of a bagpipe.[2] It was a place where reputations could be made or ruined. After stock-jobbers were found to be speculating on the value of guineas in 1695, all jobbers and brokers were forced to leave the Exchange; their frenetic behaviour was in any case thought too vulgar. They decamped to nearby Exchange Alley where their haunts were Jonathan's or Garraway's coffee houses.

Investors in shares were essentially betting on the fate of individual companies in wartime, in a period of high taxation. The line between gambling and investment was already blurred: merchants lay bets on the outcome of a battle or siege to hedge against the risks of overseas trade, although London's mayor banned such distasteful wagers at the end of 1692. Inevitably, stock-jobbers tried to manipulate share prices by circulating good or bad news from abroad; there were reports that corrupt brokers, in league with the French, were bribed to discourage investment in London's financial market.[3] Stock-jobbers were even blamed for the depression later in the 1690s when many new companies failed. Doubtless the core market in stocks continued to operate in an orderly way, supported by bonds of trust between respected merchants, but a new breed of stockbrokers devised financial instruments that allowed them to cash in on a range of speculative opportunities. Critics worried that the antics of upstart brokers and stock-jobbers, buying and selling for quick profit, were not just disruptive but a threat to the nation's economic stability. Defoe raged that they dabbled in 'a Trade founded in Fraud, born of Deceit, and nourished by Trick, cheat, Wheedle Forgeries, Falshoods and all sorts of Delusions, Coining false News . . . whispering imaginary Terrors'.[4] These sharpers not only profited from naive investors but also brought down honest tradesmen. They could ruin men silently, through impenetrable financial schemes that operated like poison at a distance. Perhaps drawing on his own experience, Defoe claimed that unsuspecting tradesmen were plundered without knowing who had hurt them.

By 1694, five years into war with France, William was running out of money despite generous loans from the City. Annual public spending had reached alarming levels, rising from under £2 million in 1688 to between £5 and £6 million from 1689.[5] Taxation, already heavy, could never be increased to cover this level of wartime expenditure, although from 1695 the Crown even taxed the registration of births, deaths and marriages. This was why William turned to schemes like Neale's Million Adventure. Lotteries were a sure way to raise money quickly and defer payment, and governments would raise revenue through state-run lotteries until 1826. In the long term, the Million Adventure brought little benefit to the exchequer, which struggled to maintain annual payments to winners. But it did mark the beginning of a revolution in the world of finance, ignited because William desperately needed still more projects to increase the flow of credit.

In July 1694 the Bank of England was founded by royal charter, chiefly to fund the war effort although it was touted as a public benefit that would improve general trade. The bank was a private venture, owned by stockholders, and London's internationally minded Whig financiers contributed £120,000 at

4 per cent interest. This alignment of Westminster government and monied interest in London greatly boosted the power of the state. Wealthy Huguenots, loyal to William III, contributed about 10 per cent of the bank's capital, making a massive contribution to the stability of their adopted country. Seven of the Bank's original twenty-four directors were of Walloon or Huguenot extraction. While the bank could be described as a patriotic venture, it offered investment opportunities that were more secure than the general run of trade. It opened an office in the Mercers' hall, Cheapside, but by October its governor, Sir John Houblon, had moved the bank to his own company, the Grocers, in nearby Poultry. After the death of Houblon's widow in 1732, the couple's house and gardens in Threadneedle Street would become the site of the present Bank of England.

The bank allowed for the creation of a national debt. Instead of risky short-term borrowing by the Crown there was a shift to long-term public borrowing under the auspices of parliament, with taxation providing a backstop against default. The state could now finance extensive wars. The bank also started a conventional banking business, accepting deposits from the public. Subscribers included the landed elite, but most came from London's canny merchant and professional classes. The bank issued hand-written 'bank notes', often for the exact amount deposited, which customers at first treated like loan bonds: Captain Thomas Bowrey in Well Close Square scrupulously kept copies of the Acts of Parliament relating to public funds in his document box, along with lottery tickets and share certificates in the East India Company because, to his mind, the Acts set out the contractual terms of his bank deposits and lottery purchases. But because the bank's notes were payable on demand and vastly more convenient than carrying coin, by 1697 they were circulating like money, despite attempted frauds and counterfeits. For a while the bank worked smoothly, loaning £2 million to the Crown in 1695, then it over-extended, opening a branch in Antwerp which lost money. But the real body blow that caused its credit to slump was England's coinage crisis.

Two groups of coin were in circulation: old, hammered money and new, milled coin which Charles II had introduced. The process of hammering money with a die left a fringe beyond the imprint of the image which could be clipped and melted down. The old money was also easy to counterfeit. The new money, mass-produced in the Royal Mint by horse-powered presses, was harder to forge and impossible to clip but it had a high silver content. Coins were worth more than their face value when melted down into bullion. To make matters worse, guineas made of fine African gold, nominally worth twenty shillings, traded for as much as thirty shillings according to fluctuations in the price of gold. Whenever the value of guineas fell, they were exported to Holland where they fetched more. No wonder that in the mid-1690s there was an extreme shortage of any sort of good coin.

By the 1690s most old, hammered coins had lost about a third of their original size. Clipping and counterfeiting were endemic, although both were capital offences (men were hanged while women were burnt at the stake). Between 1688 and 1698 there were over four hundred prosecutions for coining offences at the Old Bailey alone, with notable peaks occurring in 1693 and 1695. Clipping was not an activity confined to the poor in garrets and basements. It involved criminal networks, from the blacksmith who made clipping shears to the goldsmith who sold 'broad coin' at a premium rate, knowing it would be clipped. In 1696, Elizabeth and Thomas Driver, a husband and wife team, were caught red-handed with boxes of clippings. They implicated George Bilbee, a wealthy goldsmith in St Martin-in-the-Fields. He gave them four shillings a week to hide clippings in their cellar, and from time to time they took him some clippings and helped him melt them into ingots.[6] Outwardly respectable tradesmen grew rich on the back of this racket. When John Moor, a Westminster tripeman, was found guilty of clipping and coining in 1695, he had no trouble offering £6,000 for a pardon.[7] He was hanged at Tyburn, leaving a house worth £1,000 that was snapped up by a Scottish nobleman.

By 1695, London workers were complaining that they were paid in clipped coin that would no longer pass. Shipwrights in the naval dockyards protested that their wages were given in half-crowns that were mostly counterfeit. Something had to be done. That year the House of Lords set up a committee to discuss how to suppress clippers and coiners. It decided on wholesale recoinage: the old, clipped money would be recalled and melted down into new, milled money. One of the advisors on the committee was Isaac Newton, then mathematics professor at Cambridge. In 1696 he was offered the post of Warden of the Royal Mint, which was still housed in the Tower, moated and well-guarded.

The ever-present Thomas Neale was Master of the Mint, but he had many other calls on his time and his health was failing, so the bulk of the work fell to Newton, his deputy. Newton approached the task with the same intensity and attention to procedural detail that he had brought to his scientific and mathematical discoveries. Within a short space of time he had increased the production of coins to a record £100,000 a week and, as he was paid in proportion to the volume of coins struck, he was becoming very rich indeed. He moved out of temporary accommodation in the Tower to a house in Jermyn Street, Westminster. His duties as Warden included pursuing notorious counterfeiters and, after some reluctance, he threw himself into this activity as well, forging links with London's criminal underworld, infiltrating networks of semi-professional informers, taking evidence in taverns and prison cells, and successfully prosecuting twenty-eight offenders.

In the short term, the great recoinage project exacerbated the acute shortage of coin. John Evelyn thought it a great mistake to recall the corrupt old currency before new supplies were ready. In London no one had enough cash to do business; everything was done on trust and credit. Households had no coin with which to buy basic provisions in markets, and riots were daily feared. As usual, the poor suffered because there were no low-value copper coins to be had; local tradesmen issued tokens of dubious worth and used them as currency instead. Meanwhile, unscrupulous bankers and goldsmiths hoarded good coin in the expectation that its value would increase. To make matters worse, a new window tax was levied to help underwrite the recoinage.

In these years of economic crisis London's crime rate soared. As people walked the streets in the evening, especially in winter, they would be robbed of their hats, periwigs, cloaks and swords. In 1690 the residents of Red Lion Square complained that 'many of them have been very frequently robbd both by day and by night, through ye neglect if not connivance of ye Watchmen'. They asked to be allowed to appoint their own private watchmen instead of paying local taxes for them.[8] Major routes in and out of London were infested with highwaymen and footpads; merchants travelling to their country houses at the weekend routinely exchanged shots with highwaymen on the way. Some gangs were very large. A band of twenty footpads met regularly at a tavern in Southwark before dividing into smaller teams to go out and rob, and when the celebrated highwayman James Whitney was taken in Whitefriars at the end of 1692, he offered to bring eighty gang members into the king's service in return for a pardon. He was hanged in Smithfield the following February. Several members of his gang, taken later, clearly led double lives. One kept a livery stable in Moorfields; others were tradesmen, including a milliner and a gold-smith with shops in the Strand. In 1693 the Chief Justice had a list of eighty highwaymen to arrest, including several women.[9]

MARITIME LONDON

While much of London suffered wartime shortages and maimed soldiers and seamen became a familiar sight on the streets, war weighed most heavily on London's maritime parishes. Soldiers and cavalry horses boarding transports for the Continent were a regular disruption. Naval press gangs patrolled the streets, sometimes day and night. In 1693 the Privy Council even ruled that watermen were no longer exempt from pressing; new warships lacked crews and men were needed to row landing craft. Despite protests, the names of watermen were put on an official list. The number of seamen in the navy more than doubled in this conflict, rising from about 22,000 at the start to a peak of 48,500 in 1695.[10] Many died at sea of wounds or epidemics, or were made prisoners of war, or returned maimed and unable to work. While men were absent, families got into debt and became a burden on the parish. In 1691, Elizabeth Haley, arrested for owing £20, pleaded for a reduction in her fine; she had three small children and her husband earned just 23s. a month in the navy.[11] Partly to unite communi-ties, monthly fast days had been imposed since 1691 to seek God's blessing on the war effort, but the yawning gap between rich and poor was bound to cause tensions. On one day in August 1693 the diarist Narcissus Luttrell could record that Queen Mary's terrace at Whitehall, 'curiously adorn'd with greens', had been completed at a cost of some £10,000, while impoverished seamen's wives had marched on the palace to demand the arrears of their husband's wages.[12]

London's vibrant maritime parishes still retained a kind of scandalous allure. The Scottish minister Robert Kirk, visiting London in 1689–90, noted that Wapping was 'the most whorish place about London', and that seamen's wives, whose husbands were long abroad, were 'very impudent and lascivious', having children by other men who were then raised at their husband's charge.[13] The maritime parishes were bastions of Dissent: Wapping had no church, only two Dissenting meeting houses. Unsurprisingly then, the Society for the Reformation of Manners began its work in the Tower Hamlets area. From 1691 clergy, Justices of the Peace, and the well-to-do worked to bring its brothel keepers and Sabbath-breakers to court claiming, 'Here 'tis that Impudent Harlots by their Antick Dresses, Painted Faces, and Whorish Insinuations, allure and tempt our Sons and Servants to Debauchery, and consequently to embezel and steal from us, to maintain their Strumpets.'[14] Many men accused of keeping brothels escaped punishment by joining the navy. At the same time London's maritime communities were increasingly viewed as nationally important; seamen themselves became a resource to be conserved; religious and mathematical handbooks were targeted at them to improve their morals and their skills.

Thames shipbuilding flourished in these war years. London had always built strong, armed vessels, allowing builders to profit from the expansion of the East and West Indian trades. Now huge sums were spent on warships. The king visited Deptford to hasten the work and, on Christmas Eve 1692, sent orders that the royal dockyards were to work day and night with no breaks for Sundays and holy days.[15] Ship launches on the high-water spring tides became a common sight; in December 1693, at Deptford's naval dockyard, two ships were launched in two days, while another two ships were ready on the stocks. Large private shipyards were contracted to build warships, too, because naval yards could not meet the demand. War encouraged the growth of London's industrial satellites, like Rotherhithe and Deptford, soon linked in a continuous ribbon of Thameside development. Hundreds of extra men were employed in the naval dockyards: numbers fluctuated but by 1697 the workforce at Deptford had risen to a peak of 700.[16] A cash-strapped government might pay wages far in arrears, but dockyard expansion boosted local trades and services and Deptford grew rapidly. In 1703, John Evelyn recorded that in his lifetime the town had become nearly as populous as Bristol, which was one of England's three largest cities together with Norwich and London.

Contractors to the navy also prospered. The government spent vast sums on ordnance, shipbuilding materials and food supplies, including hogs and oxen to be slaughtered and salted in barrels for seamen. The quality of food supplied at the outbreak of hostilities had been bad: 'gutts and garbage' were found at the bottom of beer casks; 'galls and copperis' (bile and iron sulphate) in the salted meat, but the long war led to an improvement in logistics.[17] The iron-monger Ambrose Crowley is one example of someone who profited from the expansion of London's maritime infrastructure. At the end of the century he advertised that he was joining his trade at Ratcliff Cross to his trade in Upper Thames Street, where he was 'better sorted than ever', and well placed to benefit from the growing export of manufactures to the American colonies.[18] In these years the merchant John Cass extended his business empire by leasing proper-ties in Wapping. A Tory suspected of Jacobite sympathies, he found it hard to win high office but did become a member of parliament and, having profited from the slave trade, died a philanthropist.

In the short term, war with France severely damaged London's foreign trade. French privateers operating out of Dunkirk and St Malo attacked English cargo ships in the North Sea and the Channel; some even dared to enter the mouth of the Thames. In 1693 merchants petitioned Queen Mary to protect the Channel; she did assign two warships to patrol it, but losses continued. As the war dragged on, merchants protested that the Admiralty was failing to provide convoy escorts; shipowners resorted to hiring Dutch privateers to protect their vessels. It was safer to sail in convoy, but convoys meant merchant ships arrived in the river at the same time. In April 1691, in one day, 128 homebound ships regis-tered at the custom house, a higher number than ever before.[19] This was not necessarily a good sign: copious goods glutted the market and lowered profits.

From 1694 the French began sending out squadrons of up to a dozen ships, sometimes composed of a mixture of warships and privateers, able to overcome paltry convoy escorts. London merchants suffered heavier losses: between 1689 and 1697 the French captured about four thousand English ships.[20] Nor could the English navy make up for these losses by capturing enemy ships in large-scale sea battles, as in the Dutch Wars. The French preferred commerce raiding and privateering to fleet actions. Evelyn commented:

> Here's a sad town . . . the gentlewomen . . . without a yard of muslin in their
> shops to sell, while the ladies (they tell me) walk pensively by, without a
> shilling (I mean a good one) in their pockets to buy.[21]

Thousands of London grocers, drapers, milliners and other traders went bankrupt.

Merchants also suffered losses when ships were forcibly hired for the navy; in December 1692 forty were co-opted for naval use. But the overriding problem was a shortage of seamen; despite fierce pressing up and down the Thames, the navy could not get enough men. Various measures were tried: men were promised a month or six weeks' pay in advance if they volunteered.[22] Large warships were kept in pay at reduced rates over winters from 1691 to 1694, which seamen resented because voyaging was seasonal and they were used to being with their families during winter. A seaman's monthly wage shot up to as much as 55s., although in peacetime the navy usually paid 24s. to 25s., before deductions.[23] The Admiralty even tried to limit the number of seamen working on merchant ships, so cargo vessels left London under complement and more vulnerable to attack. Sometimes war almost paralyzed trade in London.

At this difficult juncture, pirate exploits suddenly grabbed the headlines. Odd as it may seem, there were often covert links between pirate and merchant activity. With the connivance of Whig interests in London, piracy flourished out of ports in the American colonies and found easy pickings in the Indian Ocean. But in 1695 the pirate Henry Avery pulled off one of the most notorious piracies of all time: he seized the *Gunj-i-Suwaee*, a ship belonging to the 'Great Mughal' Aurangzeb, emperor of India. It was full of treasure but also pilgrims on their way to Mecca, whom the pirates raped and killed. The Mughal reacted swiftly, imprisoning East India Company officials; England's valuable trade with India faltered, leaving the government desperate to bring the pirates to justice. But when several of Avery's crew were caught and tried at the Old Bailey, popular admiration for pirates and sympathy for poor seafarers meant the jury returned a verdict of 'not guilty'. A retrial was hastily arranged, and a fresh jury lectured on its patriotic duty. This time the pirates were found guilty. But in 1698 pirates again damaged relations with the Great Mughal when Captain Kidd, pirate hunter turned pirate, captured an Indian ship. He was arrested on his return to New York and brought to London for trial and execution amid huge publicity. Kidd's venture had wealthy Whig backers. Now that it had gone wrong, questions were asked in the Commons about the Whig lords who had planned to share the spoils. They escaped punishment but the episode weakened Whig political power.

Merchant shipowners still supported William because they saw this war as a means to extend England's colonial empire; they looked forward to making up their losses in peacetime. William signalled that this would be the case. In 1696 his parliament strengthened the Navigation Acts which protected English shipping from foreign competition, insisting that goods could only be imported, exported and traded between colonies in English ships. Vessels in the colonial trades would have to be registered, which gave England its first Register of Shipping – if incomplete – because many ships were not in colonial trades. And when the war ended, other commercial measures offered the prospect of free trade.

The Whig merchants who had supported the Revolution were also determined to break the monopolies of the chartered companies. In 1698 the Ten Per Cent Act broke the control that the Royal African Company had on trade with Africa. Private traders would be admitted, so long as they paid a 10 per cent duty to the Company on goods shipped to and from Africa, with silver, gold and enslaved Africans exempted. The tax would be used to help maintain the Company's forts on the coast. More merchants now entered the slave trade, which increased the number of Africans being transported in terrible conditions to the American colonies. London at this time still dominated England's slave trade, and the Act signalled an acceptance by all sides of political opinion that the trade was essential to England's economy. At mid-century it had been cheaper to ship indentured servants across the Atlantic to work in plantations rather than buy enslaved Africans (up to £8 as opposed to around £35).[24] But now slave plantations were the norm and London had a growing elite of wealthy planters.

Whig merchants succeeded in breaking the East India Company's monopoly. In the spring of 1698 parliament legislated for a new East India Company, giving the old Tory East India Company three years in which to dissolve itself. The backers of the new Company guaranteed a £2 million loan to the government, still short of revenue. The East India trade was financed with bullion, which merchants obtained from the profits of other trades, so London was at the centre of an increasingly complex trading system in which the Thames, and improving transport links to London, were vital.

In 1698, Peter the Great visited the Netherlands and afterwards Deptford dockyard to see shipbuilding for himself, planning to establish the industry in Russia. He stayed at the king's expense in John Evelyn's house, Sayes Court, close to the dockyard. Evelyn's bailiff soon warned his master that the house was 'full of people, and right nasty'.[25] The Tsar and his entourage did a shocking amount of damage: not just carpets but the floorboards beneath had to be replaced; in the garden they pushed wheelbarrows through Evelyn's carefully planted holly bushes. But the Tsar was feted for diplomatic reasons, touring the Royal Observatory and viewing the great presses at the Royal Mint. Aside from Evelyn's disappointments, his visit was reckoned a great success.

Meanwhile the slump in trade was clear to discerning observers. One wrote:

> It is a certain Truth, and Merchants know it full well (whatever the unthinking Vulgar may imagine to the contrary) that Ships are now but of little Value, notwithstanding the number of Merchants Ships are much less than they were before the War.[26]

Even so, England's overseas trade remained on an upwards trajectory, although growth was nothing like the expansion seen mid-century. And even in the darkest days of the war, with shipping harassed and the country prey to Jacobite plots and invasion fears, far-sighted Londoners nursed visions of commercial success.

This is seen in the building of the Howland Great Wet Dock. In 1695 the Duke of Bedford's grandson had married Elizabeth Howland, a granddaughter of Sir Josiah Child, former governor of the East India Company. It was a remarkable match, uniting prominent Whig and Tory families with financial stakes in the East India trade; the groom and bride were just fourteen and thirteen. Elizabeth's enormous dowry included a shipyard and lands in marshy Rotherhithe, which the Bedford family soon developed, wagering that luxury consumption would drive up commerce. They commissioned a second dry dock for the yard, where East Indiamen were built for Company use. Between 1695 and 1699 they also laid out the timber-lined Howland Dock; it covered an area of some 12 acres, boasting a depth of 17 feet (5 metres) during the spring tides. It was intended for the sheltered repair of shipping between voyages, mostly East Indiamen, and could hold 120 vessels. It was probably the largest dock in Europe, proof that basins on this scale could be built and operated. In 1699 a great fire in Rotherhithe destroyed ships and nearly 300 houses, but the new dock offered hope for the future.

AN END AND A BEGINNING

Poor harvests and bankruptcy drove the warring nations to the negotiating table in the autumn of 1697. With the peace, William returned from the Continent, making his triumphant entry into London on 15 November. The magnificent spectacle echoed former royal entries into the City and reinforced the message that William, as God's instrument, had brought military success to England. A day of national thanksgiving was kept on 2 December, when St Paul's was finally consecrated (Christopher Wren having been on half-pay since March to encourage him to finish it to the point where it could be used). Its soaring dome seemed to signify a resurgence of national power.

By the turn of the century England was the greatest trading nation in Europe. London, as both capital city and chief port, was dominant with a population of half a million and rising. It had survived revolutions and disasters. It handled 80 per cent of England's imports, some 65 per cent of its exports, and had long been a centre of conspicuous consumption. Increasing numbers of the gentry now made their home in London or stayed for 'the season', providing work for tailors, hairdressers, perfumiers and other service trades. Immigration had made the capital more cosmopolitan, if no less xenophobic. With the growth of London's commerce and manufacturing base, more residents were climbing the social ladder; middling ranks now accounted for up to 30 per cent of its population.[27] Literacy steadily increased and Londoners were much better informed, having access to trade and shipping lists for business and, from 1695, several tri-weekly newspapers, even if these papers contained more foreign than domestic news.

There had been dramatic changes in outlook in the course of this remarkable century: Newton's world was not the same as Shakespeare's. Defoe detected a new, energetic public spirit, a social transformation, which he traced back to 1680 and called the 'Projecting Age'.[28] People daily came up with new inventions and projects to make money or benefit humankind. They included machines to bore guns, contraptions to pull ships against wind and tide, and useful schemes like the Penny Post. Defoe himself suggested innovations including a registry of seamen and, since relations between the sexes were increasingly a matter of debate, better education for women. He promoted polite conversation, complying with the latest desire for the improvement of manners, and slated the English habit of larding sentences with pointless swearing. Not all such efforts bore fruit but taken together they suggest the drive and progressive outlook with which people approached the new century.

Much of London was new built: in the centre, where the Fire had destroyed the medieval city; to the west, where exclusive squares and town houses were built after the Restoration; to the north, where streets and terraces were laid out in Spitalfields; and in the east where maritime parishes saw rapid growth. Change was visible to all. About 45 per cent of houses now had piped water for at least part of the week, improving sanitation and transforming the lives of London's many female servants. And if developers and opportunists were influencing the way London expanded, so the new urban fabric was helping to shape attitudes. Once there were squares, for instance, Londoners beautified them with trees and plants, which in turn helped to make domestic gardening more popular. The expanding city with its government offices, coffee houses and luxury shops fostered new professional identities for men, and some women. Unsurprisingly, different districts offered a different experience of daily life, not least because there was no overarching governing authority. In the expanding suburbs, beyond the jurisdiction of the City authorities, people were governed by different benches of magistrates and by officers elected in each parish. Governance in the dispersed maritime districts was distinctly haphazard, although independent sailors' wives were quick to seek legal redress if their neighbours' language or behaviour caused offence.[29] Because parish loyalties were deep-rooted, some Londoners may have been slow to build a strong metropolitan identity.

Much remained unchanged. London's attractions were, as ever, counterbalanced by crime, disease and pollution. If anything, these problems seemed to be growing worse. The number of crimes prosecuted rose in the decade after 1688; women offenders increased to unprecedented levels, driven in part by the recruitment of men into the armed forces, leaving women to support families alone.[30] William and Mary cracked down on lawbreaking and immorality, supporting the Society for the Reformation of Manners which linked prostitution and crime. This cause briefly united all faiths, but because the Society used informers, it threatened to aggravate community tensions in the short term. And as London grew more populous it became unhealthier. Medicine was still largely ineffective; from mid-century, migrant workers had been essential merely to compensate for London's high mortality rates. No wonder that, despite the growing influence of the Royal Society, superstition and supernatural beliefs persisted.

The affluent were becoming accustomed to luxuries like sugar and chocolate, but the capital still had appalling levels of inequality. In the small wealthy parishes of the inner City, and in the West End, rents were nearly twice as much as in northern parishes and almost three times as much as in eastern parishes.[31] Poor families clustered in the suburbs, particularly in the eastern districts, where the air was especially polluted due to the processing of raw materials. But even the western suburbs were mixed, with fine houses for the elite, lesser developments for the middling sort and tradesmen who wanted retail space on main streets, and basic dwellings for the poor, packed into yards, alleys and side-streets.[32] Poverty was rising. In 1695 the churchwardens of St Margaret's parish, Westminster, sought permission to raise the poor rate by 50 per cent because the poor had 'abundantly increased within severall years last past'.[33] Relief almost always went to children, widows and the aged or infirm. The unemployed were expected to find work, so aggressive street begging was a plague in wealthy areas.

After war with France ended, there were schemes in London and other large cities to put the poor to work. A workhouse was set up in Bishopsgate Street which, by 1700, had room for 300 children. They were taught to read and write and to spin wool. Its governors also arranged for poor women to spin wool in their own homes, but the scheme had only local impact. Local taxation, always a bugbear, was a heavy burden for those living at subsistence level. In 1690, Edward Bayly asked to be exempted from paying the nine shillings poor relief in Shoreditch, claiming that he was a poor man himself 'carrying a Barrow about ye streets to sell apples & other fruit pease & the like in their seasons &

his wife keeping a small Chandlers shop (wth goods upon Credit) for the live-lihood of his family having 3 small children to maintain'.[34] The vegetarian hatter, Thomas Tryon, somewhat obsessed by cleanliness, worried about the poor, who 'fare very hard, having ragged Cloaths, and Shoes without sole, being all Dirty, going about the streets Cold and Hungry'.[35] At least, by the end of the century, the metropolis had a comprehensive system of parish-based poor relief, but the sums doled out in different parishes varied according to population, social make-up and local power structures – the seventeenth-century equivalent of a postcode lottery.

London remained a city where paradox and ambiguity were a feature of daily experience. Merchants who dined off fine china might have profited from networks created by the pirates hanged at Execution Dock; many had links with the slave trade. East India merchants prospered but weavers in Spitalfields starved, unable to compete with imports of rich finished silk. Government preached moral reform, but its recoinage crisis and the lack of small coin only encouraged theft. And prostitution thrived; the Nonconformist minister Robert Kirk, who back in Scotland indulged his parishioners' belief in fairies, thought that unless a man in London deeply remembered his God, his soul and death, it was 'hardly possible for him to escape the temptations of drinking and whoredom'.[36] A growing culture of politeness improved society, but the same concept would soon be used as a political justification for the colonization of 'barbarous' lands. The Royal Exchange was an icon of London's commercial identity, its magnificent architecture greatly admired but the easternmost column on the south side was used as 'a common pissing place'; authorities complained about 'the noisome smell'.[37] And there remained a strong under-current of sedition; despite the benefits of the 1688 Revolution, some still pledged loyal toasts to James II. On the Prince of Wales's birthday in 1695 at the Dog Tavern, a Catholic drinking hole in Drury Lane, there was street fighting when soldiers built a bonfire outside and drank to the prince's health. A mob gathered, threatening to pull the pub down.[38]

Religious divisions festered despite the relief given to Dissenters by the 1689 Toleration Act. As many as one in five Londoners was a Dissenter.[39] The Act acknowledged that Anglicans and Puritans could no longer be members of the same Church, as in Elizabeth's time, but offered Dissenters less than the 1650

Toleration Act, which had allowed them to worship freely. Under William and Mary, they had to register their meeting houses, which were closely controlled, and they were still banned from holding office. In 1699 parliament passed new laws against Catholics who refused to take the oaths of loyalty to William; once again, those considered dangerous were banished from London.

Criticism of the link between money and power grew more vocal. Some claimed that dearth and slow trade were God's punishment on the sins of the nation, but others were adamant that high taxes, coin clippers, bankers and close-fisted merchants were to blame.[40] The two explanations could sit side by side as belief in divine intervention remained strong. In the early 1690s there had been strong support for a revolutionary Whig regime which held that the country's future wealth depended on international trade not on any land-based economy. But as successive Whig ministries cosied up to monied interest in the City, the Whigs became identified as a party of power and privilege, unhealthily aligned with Dissent. It did not help that livery companies had become bastions of the wealthy; they still funded charity but seemed less connected to ordinary people. By the late 1690s the Tories had assumed the role of champions of London's less affluent, especially small tradesmen, ground down by wartime taxes. Tories lambasted the new class of financiers, stock-dealers and government contractors, whom they presented as social climbers lacking social responsibility, whose power came from new money not generations of wealth, from opportunism not good husbandry, and who collectively posed a threat to landed society. Tories easily tapped into disgruntled Anglicanism, xenophobia and latent support for the Jacobite cause in some quarters. Debates about the economic future of the country, and therefore about imperial policy, became more vocal and better understood, but in the City, common council elections were increasingly riven by party faction, and religion would continue to be embedded in party politics until well into the next century.[41]

Yet conflict with Catholic France had given the English a greater sense of identity and purpose as a commercial, Protestant power. People saw that as the French were pushed back in the West Indies, so England's colonial trade advanced, including that of the Hudson's Bay Company.[42] The astronomical cost of the war impelled some commentators to talk up the vital role of trade and the importance of naval protection. London had long been a great port;

travellers to London marvelled at the sight of Thames shipping. The minister Robert Kirk wrote, 'The ships of the river of Thames are like one entire wood or forest from below the Bridge of London to Gravesend, a distance of 20 miles', while Celia Fiennes, standing on Shooters Hill and viewing the Thames from Blackwall to Deptford and beyond, observed 'On this part of the River I have seen 100 saile of shipps pass by in a morning which is one of the finest sights that is.'[43] Increasingly London became, and felt itself to be, a modern commercial centre, too. The establishment of the Bank of England, a vital link between government and capital, made London the linchpin of national financial activity. In 1697 an Act was passed to regulate stockbrokers and stamp out corruption. The City licensed one hundred reliable brokers, and any found trading without a permit were pilloried for an hour on three successive days.

But despite the hardships of war under William, and Princess Anne's repeated failure to produce a Protestant heir, the Revolution continued to offer hope. One of Mary Evelyn's female relations affirmed her belief that it had been right to overthrow James II, 'if we woud not be Dragoon'd out of all that was dear to us', adding presciently, 'we are beholding to this revolution for many good laws of which future generations may find the benefit'.[44] Celia Fiennes was equally certain that England's reformed monarchy and constitution 'is by all the world esteemed the best'; the plot to assassinate William, discovered in 1696, had brought the country close to ruin: 'were it not for Gods providentiall care and miraculous works we should at this day been a people left to utter dispaire, haveing only the agraveteing thoughts of our once happy Constitution to lament its losse the more'.[45] Williamite propaganda suggesting that Protestant England was a chosen nation, favoured by God, had taken root; it would feed the energy and resilience of Londoners into the next century.[46]

Seasonal smogs fell on London towards the end of 1699. People lost their way in the streets because candles and torches failed to penetrate the gloom; drums were beaten to guide Thames watermen to the shore. For most Londoners the future seemed equally smudged. During a turbulent century London had shaped national events and been shaped by them. England now had a viable parliamentary system of government; it had developed the fiscal and administrative infrastructure needed to keep fleets supplied and armies in the field for a long war; it was poised to emerge as a world power. But nothing was easily deciphered from the multi-tonal buzz of this great hive. No wonder Londoners liked to survey their city from great heights: from the top of St Paul's, which offered amazing views 'Of this Unbounded, and still growing Town',[47] or from Greenwich Park where the sight of shipping in the river below confirmed London's dominant trade and manufacturing power. From such heights the city seemed to symbolize national aspirations and to hold out the promise of a glorious future.

NOTES

ABBREVIATIONS

BL	British Library
BM	British Museum
Bodleian	Bodleian Library, Oxford University
Chamberlain, *Letters*	John Chamberlain, *The Chamberlain Letters: A Selection of the Letters of John Chamberlain Concerning Life in England from 1597 to 1626*, ed. Elizabeth McClure Thomson (London: John Murray, 1966)
CSPD	*Calendar of State Papers Domestic* (London: originally HMSO, 1858–1937), 90 vols covering 1625–1702
CSPV	*Calendar of State Papers Relating to English Affairs Existing in the Archives and Collections of Venice and in Other Libraries of Northern Italy* (London: originally HMSO, 1900–47), 39 vols covering 1603–75
EBBA	English Broadside Ballad Archive, ed. Patricia Fumerton, http://ebba.english.ucsb.edu
Jeaffreson	John Cordy Jeaffreson, ed., *Middlesex County Records*, 4 vols (London: Middlesex County Records Society, 1887–1902; reissued 1974)
JE diary	John Evelyn, *The Diary of John Evelyn*, ed. E. S. De Beer, 6 vols (Oxford: Clarendon Press, 1955)
LMA	London Metropolitan Archives
LPL	Lambeth Palace Library
NPG	National Portrait Gallery, London
OBP	Old Bailey Proceedings Online, www.oldbaileyonline.org
RCPL	Royal College of Physicians, London
Rushworth	John Rushworth, *Historical Collections of Private Passages of State*, 8 vols (London: D. Brown et al., 1721–2)
SP diary	Samuel Pepys, *The Diary of Samuel Pepys*, eds Robert Latham and William Matthews, 11 vols (London: G. Bell and Hyman, 1970–83)
TNA	The National Archives, Kew, London

1 'OH WHAT AN EARTH-QUAKE IS THE ALTERATION OF A STATE!'

1. Penry Williams, *The Later Tudors: England 1547–1603* (Oxford: Oxford University Press, 1995), 386.
2. A. L. Beier and Roger Finlay, eds, *London 1500–1700: The Making of the Metropolis* (London and New York: Longman, 1986), 23.

3. Jeremy Boulton, *Neighbourhood and Society: A London Suburb in the Seventeenth Century* (Cambridge: Cambridge University Press, 1987), 231.

4. Thomas Dekker, *The Wonderful Year* (1603), quoted in *Elizabeth I and Her Age*, eds Donald Stump and Susan M. Felch (New York and London: W. W. Norton, 2009), 529.

5. Jennifer Woodward, *The Theatre of Death: Ritual Management of Royal Funerals in Renaissance England, 1570–1625* (Woodbridge: Boydell Press, 1997), 102.

6. John Stow, *Annales, Or, A Generall Chronicle of England*, continued by Edmund Howes (London: Richard Meighten, 1631), 815.

7. Southwark, created as the twenty-sixth ward, had no representation on City councils.

8. Ben Jonson, *Bartholomew Fair*, Induction l. 185, in *The Selected Plays of Ben Jonson*, 2 vols, ed. Martin Butler (Cambridge: Cambridge University Press, 1989), II, 161.

9. William Trumbull, *The Trumbull Papers: The Property of the Most Honourable the Marquess of Downshire*, auction catalogue (London: Sotheby's, 1989), 10.

10. Jonathan Swift, 'A Description of a City Shower', l. 61, *The Complete Poems*, ed. Pat Rogers (New Haven and London: Yale University Press, 1983), 114.

11. E.g. John Schofield, Lyn Blackmore and Jacqui Pearce, with Tony Dyson, *London's Waterfront 1100–1666: Excavations in Thames Street, London, 1974–84* (Oxford: Archaeopress Publishing Ltd., 2018), xx, 397–8.

12. SP diary, I, 269 (20 October 1660).

13. Stephen Porter, *Shakespeare's London: Everyday Life in London 1580–1616* (Chalford: Amberley, 2009), 22.

14. John Donne, *Selected Letters*, ed. P. M. Oliver (Manchester: Carcanet, 2002), 22.

15. Anne Clifford, *The Diaries of Lady Anne Clifford*, ed. D. J. H. Clifford (Stroud: Alan Sutton, 1990), 33.

16. Beier and Finlay, *London 1500–1700*, 22.

17. Porter, *Shakespeare's London*, 70.

18. Stephen Greenberg, 'Plague, the Printing Press, and Public Health in Seventeenth-Century London', *The Huntington Library Quarterly* 67, no. 4 (2004), 508–27 (p. 508).

19. CSPV X, 33 (22 May 1603).

20. Stow, *Annales*, 840.

21. CSPV X, 8 (20 April 1603).

2 'THE MOST HORRIBLE TREASON'

1. TNA SP 14/216/2.

2. John Gerard, *The Condition of the Catholics Under James I: Father Gerard's Narrative of the Gunpowder Plot*, ed. John Morris (London: Longmans, Green and Co, 1871), 34.

3. M. A. Tierney, *Dodd's Church History of England*, 5 vols (Farnborough: Gregg International Publishers, 1971), IV, 39n.

4. Tim Harris, *Rebellion: Britain's First Stuart Kings, 1567–1642* (Oxford: Oxford University Press, 2014), 34.

5. Matthew Sutcliffe, *A Briefe Examination of a Certaine Peremptorie Menacing and Disleal Petition Presented, as is Pretended, to the King's most excellent Majestie* (London: R. Bradock for William Cotton, 1606), 58.

6. Thomas Birch, ed., *The Court and Times of James the First: Illustrated by Authentic and Confidential Letters, from Various Public and Private Collections*, 2 vols (London: Henry Colburn, 1849), 37.

7. James F. Larkin and Paul L. Hughes, eds, *Stuart Royal Proclamations*, 2 vols (Oxford: Clarendon Press, 1973–83), I, 123.

8. Samuel R. Gardiner, *History of England from the Accession of James I to the Outbreak of the Civil War, 1603–1642*, 10 vols (London: Longmans, Green and Co., 1883), I, 266.

9. Larkin and Hughes, *Stuart Royal Proclamations*, I, 124.

10. [William Barlow], *The Sermon Preached at Paules Crosse, the tenth day of November, being the next Sunday after the Discoverie of this late Horrible Treason* (London: Mathew Lawe, 1606), 18, 36.

11. CSPV X, 293 (21 November 1605).

12. BM 1886,0410.1.

13. William Shakespeare, *Macbeth*, eds Sandra Clark and Pamela Mason (London: Bloomsbury Arden Shakespeare, 2015), 185–6 (II. 3. 8–12).

14. Thomas Dekker, *The Seven Deadly Sinnes of London* (1606), ed. Edward Arber (London: [E. Arber], 1879), 21.

15. Ibid., 31.

16. Owen Davies, *Cunning-Folk: Popular Magic in English History* (London: Hambledon, 2003), 17.

17. Keith Thomas, *Religion and the Decline of Magic: Studies in Popular Beliefs in Sixteenth- and Seventeenth-Century England*, rev. edn. (London: Weidenfeld and Nicolson, 1973), 9.

18. John Aubrey, *Miscellanies Upon Various Subjects* (London: Reeves and Turner, 1890; 1st edn 1696), 140–1.

19. The Museum of London has examples, e.g. B177, A17210.

20. Thomas Cooper, *A Brand taken out of the Fire, Or The Romish Spider, with his Webbe of Treason* (London: G. Eld for John Hodgets, 1606), 16; T. W., *The Araignment and Execution of the Late Traytors* (London: Jeffrey Chorlton, 1606), 1.

21. T. W., *The Araignment and Execution of the Late Traytors*, 21–2.

22. See Marion Gibson, *Early Modern Witches: Witchcraft Cases in Contemporary Writing* (London and New York: Routledge, 2000), 299–315.

23. William Rowley, Thomas Dekker and John Ford, *The Witch of Edmonton*, eds Peter Corbin and Douglas Sedge (Manchester and New York: Manchester University Press, 1999), 50 (II. i. 1–10).

24. Tai Liu, *Puritan London: A Study of Religion and Society in the City* (Newark: University of Delaware Press; London: Associated University Presses, 1986), 23.

25. LPL, Talbot Papers, MSS/3202 f. 257.

26. James I, *Letters of James VI and I*, ed. G. P. V. Akrigg (Berkeley, Los Angeles and London: University of California Press, 1984), 221.

27. Dekker, *The Seven Deadly Sinnes of London*, 13.

28. Anne Clifford, *The Diaries of Lady Anne Clifford*, ed. D. J. H. Clifford (Stroud: Alan Sutton, 1990), 22.

29. CSPV X, 70 (30 July 1603).

30. Chamberlain, *Letters*, 34–5.

31. James Howell, *Londinopolis: An Historicall Discourse or Perlustration of the City of London, the Imperial Chamber, and chief Emporium of Great Britain* (London: J. Streater for Henry Twiford et al., 1657), 346.

32. Chamberlain, *Letters*, 35.

3 FORGING CIVIC IDENTITY

1. Tim Leunig, Chris Minns and Patrick Wallis, 'Networks in the Premodern Economy: The Market for London Apprenticeships, 1600–1749', *The Journal of Economic History* 71, no. 2 (2011), 413–43 (p. 417).

2. Chris Minns and Patrick Wallis, 'Rules and Reality: Quantifying the Practice of Apprenticeship in Early Modern England', *The Economic History Review* 65, no. 2 (2012), 556–79 (pp. 559–60); Patrick Wallis, 'Apprenticeship and Training in Premodern England', *The Journal of Economic History* 68, no. 3 (2008), 832–61 (p. 836).

3. Chamberlain, *Letters*, 140.

4. CSPV XV, 60–1 (29 November 1617)

5. LMA CLA/048/PS/01/052 (7 April 1628).

6. SP diary, II, 186 (29 September 1661).

7. TNA STAC 8/177/23.

8. LMA MJ/SP/1695/12/002.

9. LMA MJ/SP/1691/05/006.

10. LMA MJ/SP/1690/01/003.

11. LMA MJ/SP/1691/02/020. He died in 1693: TNA PROB 11/416/205.

12. Patrick Wallis, 'Labor, Law, and Training in Early Modern London: Apprenticeship and the City's Institutions', *Journal of British Studies* 51, no. 4 (2012), 791–819 (p. 804).

13. LMA MJ/SP/1691/02/011.

14. LMA MJ/SP/1691/02/012.

15. LMA MJ/SP/1695/04/002.

16. Ian W. Archer, 'The Charity of Early Modern Londoners', *Transactions of the Royal Historical Society*, 12 (2002), 223–44.

17. Nigel Sleigh-Johnson, 'The Merchant Taylors Company of London 1580–1645' (PhD thesis, University College London, 1989), 162, 195.

18. LMA COL/CHD/AP/05/018/019.

19. Ian W. Archer, 'The Government of London, 1500–1650', *The London Journal* 26, no. 1 (2001), 19–29 (p. 20).

20. Sir Walter Sherburne Prideaux, *Memorials of the Goldsmiths' Company, Being Gleanings from their Records Between the Years 1335 and 1815*, 2 vols (London: Eyre and Spottiswoode, [1896–7]), I, 138.

21. Baron Heath, *Some Account of the Worshipful Company of Grocers of the City of London*, 3rd edn (London: [n.p.], 1869), 90, 92.

22. CSPV XV, 59 (29 November 1617).

23. R. T., *The Art of Good Husbandry, or The Improvement of Time* (1675), reproduced in J. Thirsk and J. P. Cooper, eds, *Seventeenth-Century Economic Documents* (Oxford: Clarendon Press, 1972), 98.

24. Ross W. Duffin, 'To Entertain a King: Music for James and Henry at the Merchant Taylors Feast of 1607', *Music & Letters* 83, no. 4 (2002), 525–41 (p. 536).

25. J. Caitlin Finlayson, 'Jacobean Foreign Policy, London's Civic Polity, and John Squire's Lord Mayor's Show, "The Tryumphs of Peace" (1620)', *Studies in Philology* 110, no. 3 (2013), 584–610 (p. 592).

26. Prideaux, *Memorials of the Goldsmiths' Company*, I, 116.

27. CSPV XV, 59 (29 November 1617).

28. R. T. D. Sayle, *Lord Mayors' Pageants of the Merchant Taylors' Company in the 15th, 16th & 17th Centuries* (Reading: Eastern Press, 1931), 74.

29. Thomas Platter and Horatio Busino, *The Journals of Two Travellers in Elizabethan and Early Stuart England* (London: Caliban Books, 1995), 115.

30. SP diary, I, 277 (29 October 1660).

31. Ian Anders Gadd and Patrick Wallis, eds, *Guilds, Society & Economy in London 1450–1800* (Loughborough: Centre for Metropolitan History, Institute of Historical Research in Association with the Guildhall Library, Corporation of London, 2002), 5.

32. John Nicoll, *Some Account of the Worshipful Company of Ironmongers* (London: John Bowyer Nichols and Son, 1851), 184.

33. Francis Bacon, *The Works of Francis Bacon, Lord Chancellor of England. A new edition*, ed. Basil Montagu, 16 vols (London: William Pickering, 1825–34), XII, 73, Letter to King James, New Year, 1609.

34. Walter Harris, *Hibernica: Or, Some Antient Pieces Relating to Ireland* (Dublin: W. Williamson, 1757), 130.

35. T. W. Moody, *The Londonderry Plantation 1609–41: The City of London and the Plantation in Ulster* (Belfast: William Mullan and Son, 1939), 70.

36. James Stevens Curl, 'Reluctant Colonisers: The City of London and the plantation of Coleraine', *History Ireland* 17, no. 6 (2009), 28–31 (p. 30).

37. Tim Harris, *Rebellion: Britain's First Stuart Kings, 1567–1642* (Oxford: Oxford University Press, 2014), 157.

4 'FORRAIGN TRADE ... THE MEANS OF OUR TREASURE'

1. Thomas Mun, *England's Treasure by Forraigne Trade. Or, the Ballance of our Forraign Trade is The Rule of our Treasure* (London: J. G. for Thomas Clarke, 1664), 219–20. Written *c.* 1630.
2. TNA HCA 13/70 f. 30; 13/70 f. 29.
3. George F. Steckley, 'Collisions, Prohibitions, and the Admiralty Court in Seventeenth-Century London', *Law and History Review* 21, no. 1 (2003), 41–67 (pp. 41–2).
4. Raymond Smith, *Sea-Coal for London: History of the Coal Factors in the London Market* (London: Longmans, 1961), 25.
5. Architell Grey, *Debates of the House of Commons, From the Year 1667 to the Year 1694*, 10 vols (London: D. Henry, R. Cave and J. Emonson, 1769), I, 442. Colonel Birch (13 April 1671).
6. CSPV X, 739 (30 May 1607).
7. Stephen Hipkin, 'The Coastal Metropolitan Corn Trade in Later Seventeenth-Century England', *The Economic History Review* 65, no. 1 (2012), 220–55 (p. 220).
8. Thomas Roe, *Sir Thomas Roe. His Speech in Parliament. Wherein he sheweth the cause of the decay of Coyne and Trade in this Land, especially of Merchants Trade* (London: printed for John Aston, 1641), 7.
9. *Journal of the House of Commons: Volume 1, 1547–1629* (London: HMSO, 1802), 215.
10. Ralph Davis, *The Rise of the English Shipping Industry in the Seventeenth and Eighteenth Centuries* (Newton Abbot: David and Charles, 1962), 4.
11. Thomas Cogswell, *James I: The Phoenix King* (London: Allen Lane, 2017), 84.
12. Antony Farrington, *Trading Places: The East India Company and Asia 1600–1834* (London: The British Library, 2002), 22.
13. LMA CLC/B/227/MS29393, letters 1632/3–6.
14. F. J. Fisher, 'London's Export Trade in the Early Seventeenth Century', *The Economic History Review*, n.s., 3, no. 2 (1950), 151–61 (p. 152).
15. M. J. Power, 'East London Housing in the Seventeenth Century', *Crisis and Order in English Towns 1500–1700: Essays in Urban History*, eds Peter Clark and Paul Slack (London: Routledge and Kegan Paul, 1972), 237; CSPV XXIII, 460 (13 April 1635).
16. M. J. Power, 'Urban Development in East London, 1500–1700' (PhD Thesis, University of London, 1971), 182; Derek Morris and Ken Cozens, *Wapping 1600–1800: A Social History of an Early Modern London Maritime Suburb* (London: East London History Society, 2009), 2–3.
17. Power, 'Urban Development in East London', 39, 75, 177–8.
18. Davis, *The Rise of the English Shipping Industry*, 390.
19. LMA MJ/SP/1699/05/004; MJ/SP/1667/02/001.
20. LMA MJ/SP/1667.
21. Brian Lavery, *The Colonial Merchantman Susan Constant 1605* (London: Conway Maritime Press, 1988), 10.
22. CSPV XXIII, 460 (13 April 1635).
23. CSPV X, 739 (30 May 1607).
24. Sir Henry Mainwaring, *The Life and Works of Sir Henry Mainwaring*, eds G. E. Manwaring and W. G. Perrin, 2 vols (London: Naval Records Society, 1920–2), II, 25.
25. Ibid., II, 153.
26. K. N. Chaudhuri, *The English East India Company: The Study of an Early Joint-Stock Company* (London: Frank Cass and Co. Ltd., 1965), 21.
27. CSPV XXIII, 460 (13 April 1635).
28. Lavery, *Susan Constant*, 10.
29. Erin Griffey, ed., *Sartorial Politics in Early Modern Europe: Fashioning Women* (Amsterdam: Amsterdam University Press, 2019), 16.
30. Robert Brenner, *Merchants and Revolution: Commercial Change, Political Conflict, and London's Overseas Traders, 1550–1653* (Cambridge: Cambridge University Press, 1993), 25.

31. BL Add MS 69877 ff. 10–11; Add MS 69880 f. 49; Add MS 69878 f. 93.
32. Linda Levy Peck, *Consuming Splendour: Society and Culture in Seventeenth-Century England* (Cambridge: Cambridge University Press, 2005), 57.
33. BL Add Ms 69880 f. 82.
34. Peck, *Consuming Splendour*, 10.

5 A CITY OF EXTREMES

1. Richard Cust, *Charles I: A Political Life* (New York: Longman, 2005), 29, 148.
2. Malcolm Gaskill, 'Witchcraft, Politics, and Memory in Seventeenth-Century England', *The Historical Journal* 50, no. 2 (2007), 289–308 (p. 295).
3. [Sir Balthazar Gerbier], *The None-Such Charles His Character: Extracted, Out of Divers Originall Transactions, Dispatches and the Notes of Severall Publick Ministers, and Councellours of State as wel at home as abroad* (London: R. I., 1651 [1650]), 85.
4. James F. Larkin and Paul L. Hughes, eds, *Stuart Royal Proclamations*, vol. 1 (Oxford: Oxford University Press, 1973), no. 152 (16 July 1615).
5. Felicity Heal, 'Art and Iconoclasm', in Anthony Milton, ed., *The Oxford History of Anglicanism, Vol. I: Reformation and Identity, c. 1552–1662* (Oxford: Oxford University Press, 2017), 199.
6. F. H. W. Sheppard, ed., *Survey of London, Vol. XXXVI, The Parish of St Paul, Covent Garden* (London: The Athlone Press for the Greater London Council, 1970), 28.
7. William Prynne, *Hidden Workes of Darkenes Brought to Publike Light* (London: Thomas Brudenell for Michael Sparke Senior, 1645), 196.
8. [Gerbier], *The None-Such Charles*, 116.
9. T. C. Dale, *The Inhabitants of London in 1638*, vol. I (London: Society of Genealogists, 1931), iv.
10. Derek Keene, 'Growth, Modernisation and Control: The Transformation of London's Landscape, *c.* 1500–*c.* 1700', in P. Clark and R. Gillespie, eds, *Two Capitals: London and Dublin 1500–1840*, Proceedings of the British Academy, vol. 107 (Oxford: Oxford University Press, 2001), 7–39 (p. 13).
11. Lena Cowen Orlin, 'Boundary Disputes in Early Modern London', in *Material London, ca. 1600*, ed. Lena Cowen Orlin (Philadelphia: University of Pennsylvania Press, 2000), 344–77.
12. Jeremy Boulton, *Neighbourhood and Society: A London Suburb in the Seventeenth Century* (Cambridge: Cambridge University Press, 1987), 189, 267.
13. Donald Lupton, *London and the Countrey Carbonadoed and Quartered into Severall Characters* (London: Nicholas Okes, 1632), xxx.
14. Lena Cowen Orlin, 'Temporary Lives in London Lodgings', *The Huntington Library Quarterly* 71, no. 1 (2008), 219–43 (p. 231).
15. Ibid., 242.
16. William Petty, *A Treatise of Taxes and Contributions* (London: N. Brooke, 1662), 23.
17. A. G. H. Bachrach and R. G. Collner, eds and trans, *Lodewijck Huygens: The English Journal 1651–1652* (Leiden: E. J. Brill/Leiden University Press, 1982), 134.
18. Peter Brimblecombe, *The Big Smoke: A History of Air Pollution in London since Medieval Times* (London: Routledge, 1987), 34; John Evelyn, *Fumifugium: Or, The Inconvenience of the Aer, and Smoak of London Dissipated* (London: W. Godbid for Gabriel Bedel and Thomas Collins, 1661), 16.
19. Evelyn, *Fumifugium*, To the Reader.
20. Ibid., 10.
21. Ibid., 14.
22. Thomas Mun, *England's Treasure by Forraigne Trade. Or, the Ballance of our Forraign Trade is The Rule of our Treasure* (London: J. G. for Thomas Clarke, 1664), 179–80. Written *c.* 1630.
23. Chamberlain, *Letters*, 70.
24. Ibid., 190.

25. Emily Cockayne, *Hubbub: Filth, Noise and Stench in England 1600–1770* (New Haven and London: Yale University Press, 2007), 30, 61.

26. Thomas Tryon, *A Treatise of Cleanness in Meats and Drinks* (London: [n.p.], 1682), 5–8.

27. BL Add MS 69878 f. 151.

28. Chamberlain, *Letters*, 127.

29. Margaret Pelling and Frances White, 'WINCHE, Thomas', in *Physicians and Irregular Medical Practitioners in London 1550–1640 Database* (London, 2004), *British History Online*, http://www.british-history.ac.uk/no-series/london-physicians/1550-1640/winche-thomas (accessed 27 April 2020).

30. Pelling and White, 'BEVEN, Humfrye', in *Physicians and Irregular Medical Practitioners*, http://www.british-history.ac.uk/no-series/london-physicians/1550-1640/beven-humfrye (accessed 27 April 2020).

31. RCPL, MS-MANUS/447.

32. LPL, Talbot Papers, MSS/3203 f. 296.

33. Cust, *Charles I*, 170.

34. Chamberlain, *Letters*, 218.

6 THE PATH TO CIVIL WAR

1. *Journal of the House of Lords: Volume IV, 1629–42* (London: HMSO, 1767–1830), 43.

2. Tim Harris, *Rebellion: Britain's First Stuart Kings, 1567–1642* (Oxford: Oxford University Press, 2014), 279.

3. Nehemiah Wallington, *Historical Notices Occurring Chiefly in the Reign of Charles I*, [ed. R. Webb], 2 vols (London: Richard Bentley, 1869), I, 220.

4. Ibid., II, 320.

5. Kevin Sharpe, *The Personal Rule of Charles I* (New Haven and London: Yale University Press, 1992), 593–4.

6. http://www.bruzelius.info/Nautica/Ships/War/GB/Sovereign_of_the_Seas(1637).html (accessed 14 April 2020).

7. Sir Simonds D'Ewes, *The Journal of Sir Simonds D'Ewes*, ed. Wallace Notestein (New Haven: Yale University Press, 1923), 37.

8. BL Egerton MS 2646 f. 30.

9. BL Egerton MS 2645 f. 347, f. 327; 2646 f. 17.

10. Nehemiah Wallington, *The Notebooks of Nehemiah Wallington, 1618–1654: A Selection*, ed. David Booy (Aldershot: Ashgate, 2007), 53.

11. Ibid., 59.

12. LMA CLC/521/MS00204 f. 340.

13. LMA P92/SAV/0409; Wallington, *Notebooks*, 103.

14. LMA MJ/SR/0913/8.

15. LMA MJ/SR/0913/13.

16. CSPD 1637–8, 550 (1 July 1638).

17. LMA ACC/1360/528.

18. Michelle Anne White, *Henrietta Maria and the English Civil Wars* (Aldershot: Ashgate, 2006), 35–6.

19. Bodleian, MSS. Bankes 18/31.

20. BL Egerton MS 2651 f. 95.

21. Wallington, *Historical Notices*, I, 224.

22. BL Egerton MS 3383 f. 18 b.

23. Wallington, *Historical Notices*, I, 245.

24. John Walter, *Covenanting Citizens: The Protestation Oath and Popular Political Culture in the English Revolution* (Oxford: Oxford University Press, 2017), 51.

25. Philip Lee Ralph, *Sir Humphrey Mildmay: Royalist Gentleman* (New Brunswick: Rutgers University Press, 1947), 156.

26. BL Egerton MS 3383 f. 51.
27. *The Trve Speech of Thomas Wentworth, Late Earle of Strafford upon the Scaffold, the twelfth of May, 1641* (London: [n.p.], 1641), 5.
28. Wallington, *Notebooks*, 131.
29. BL Egerton MS 2646 f. 161.

7 'I SEE ALL THE BIRDS ARE FLOWN'

1. TNA SP 16/488/25.
2. Rushworth, IV, 479.
3. Nehemiah Wallington, *The Notebooks of Nehemiah Wallington, 1618–1654: A Selection*, ed. David Booy (Aldershot: Ashgate, 2007), 156.
4. Thomas Warmstry, *Pax Vobis or a Charme for tumultuous Spirits* (London: George Thompson, 1641), 20.
5. Dorothy Gardiner, *The Oxinden and Peyton Letters 1607–1642* (London: Constable and Co, 1933), 272.
6. Wallington, *Notebooks*, 253.
7. James Howell, *Epistolae Ho-'Elianae. Familiar Letters, Domestick and Foreign*, 7th edn (London: printed for T.G., 1705), 514.
8. Thomas Hobbes, *Behemoth or the Long Parliament*, ed. Paul Seward (Oxford: Clarendon Press, 2010), 108.
9. Sir Walter Sherburne Prideaux, *Memorials of the Goldsmiths' Company, Being Gleanings from their Records Between the Years 1335 and 1815*, 2 vols (London: Eyre and Spottiswoode, [1896–7]), I, 202, 206, 208.
10. CSPV XXVI, 90 (4 July 1642).
11. Rushworth, IV, 754.
12. LMA MJ/SR/0906/3; MJ/SR/0913/154.
13. CSPV XXVI, 192 (7 November 1642).
14. TNA SP 116/528/18.
15. *The Diary of Bulstrode Whitelocke 1605–1675*, ed. Ruth Spalding (Oxford: Oxford University Press for the British Academy, 1990), 139.
16. CSPV XXVI, 257 (27 March 1643).
17. David Flintham, *The English Civil War Defences of London* (Bristol: Stuart Press, 2014), 21.
18. Wallington, *Notebooks*, 254 cf. 74.
19. Ben Coates, *The Impact of the English Civil War on the Economy of London 1642–50* (Aldershot: Ashgate, 2004), 144.
20. CSPV XXVI, 269 (8 May 1643).
21. Wallington, *Notebooks*, 214.
22. BL Egerton MS 2646 f. 207, Martin Bayldon to Sir Thomas Barrington, 1643.
23. Coates, *The Impact of the English Civil War*, 90, 92.
24. CSPV XXVII, 11 (28 August 1643).
25. Philip Lee Ralph, *Sir Humphrey Mildmay: Royalist Gentleman* (New Brunswick: Rutgers University Press, 1947), 168–9.
26. Wallington, *Notebooks*, 253–4. Cf. Paul S. Seaver, *Wallington's World: A Puritan Artisan in Seventeenth-Century London* (Stanford: Stanford University Press, 1985), 171.

8 'THE MEMORY OF THE WICKED SHALL ROT'

1. John Taylor, *A Swarme of Sectaries, and Schismatiques* (London: [n.p.], 1641) title page; *A Cluster of Coxcombes; or, Cinquepace of five sorts of Knaves and Fooles* (London: Richard Webb, 1642), 4–5.
2. Taylor, *A Cluster of Coxcombes*, 5.

3. [J. Birkenhead], *Mercurius Aulicus, Communicating the Intelligence and affaires of the Court, to the rest of the Kingdome* (Oxford: [n.p.], 1643–8), 34th week (20–26 August 1643), 466.

4. Ibid., 468.

5. Ibid., 39th week (25–30 September 1643), 32.

6. *The Character of an Oxford-Incendiary* (London: Robert White, 1645), 5, 6.

7. Philip Lee Ralph, *Sir Humphrey Mildmay: Royalist Gentleman* (New Brunswick: Rutgers University Press, 1947), 162.

8. *Mercurius Aulicus*, 36th week (3–9 September 1643), 499–500.

9. John Milton, *Complete Prose Works of John Milton*, eds Don M. Wolfe et al., 8 vols (New Haven: Yale University Press; London: Oxford University Press, 1953–82), II, 560.

10. Ibid., II, 515, 564.

11. Ibid., II, 553–4.

12. Philip Baker, 'Londons Liberty in Chains Discovered: The Levellers, the Civic Past, and Popular Protest in Civil War London', *The Huntington Library Quarterly* 76, no. 4 (2013), 559–87.

13. *The Clarke Papers: Selections from the Papers of William Clarke*, ed. C. H. Firth, 4 vols (London: Camden Society, 1891–1901), I, 301.

14. *The Diary of Bulstrode Whitelocke 1605–1675*, ed. Ruth Spalding (Oxford: Oxford University Press for the British Academy, 1990), 212.

15. Jeaffreson, III, 103.

16. Ibid., 93 (20 May 1644).

17. J. G. Muddiman, *Trial of King Charles the First* (Edinburgh and London: William Hodge and Co. Ltd., 1928), 77.

18. Ibid., 74.

19. Ibid., 82.

20. Ibid., 93.

21. Ibid., 94.

22. Ibid., 106.

23. Ibid., 101.

24. Ibid., 154.

25. Barbara K. Lewalski, *The Life of John Milton: A Critical Biography* (London: Blackwell, 2000), 260.

26. Sir Walter Sherburne Prideaux, *Memorials of the Goldsmiths' Company, Being Gleanings from their Records Between the Years 1335 and 1815*, 2 vols (London: Eyre and Spottiswoode, [1896–7]), I, 268.

9 CROMWELL: A KILLJOY REGIME?

1. From a 1640s ballad, *The World Turned Upside Down*, protesting against the banning of Christmas celebrations during the Interregnum.

2. Quoted in A. L. Morton, *A People's History of England* (London: Lawrence and Wishart, 1992), 218.

3. CSPV XXIX, 77 (27 May 1653).

4. *The Diary of Bulstrode Whitelocke 1605–1675*, ed. Ruth Spalding (Oxford: Oxford University Press for the British Academy, 1990), 281.

5. James Howell, *Londinopolis: An Historicall Discourse or Perlustration of the City of London, the Imperial Chamber, and chief Emporium of Great Britain* (London: J. Streater for Henry Twiford et al., 1657), 387.

6. Ibid., 46.

7. Edward Holberton, *Poetry and the Cromwellian Protectorate: Culture, Politics, and Institutions* (Oxford: Oxford University Press, 2008), 47.

8. Lucy Hutchinson, *Memoirs of the Life of Colonel Hutchinson with the fragment of an autobiography of Mrs. Hutchinson*, ed. James Sutherland (London: Oxford University Press, 1973), 209.

9. Barry Coward, *Oliver Cromwell* (London: Routledge, 2013; first published 1991), 100, 169.

10. CSPV XXXI, 82 (13 July 1657).
11. J. F. Merritt, *Westminster 1640–60: A Royal City in a Time of Revolution* (Manchester and New York: Manchester University Press, 2013), 117.
12. Hutchinson, *Memoirs*, 209.
13. Jeaffreson, III, 246–7.
14. *Unto every individual Member of Parliament: The humble Representation of divers afflicted Women-Petitioners to the Parliament, on the behalf of Mr. John Lilburn* (London: [n.p.], 1653), 1.
15. William Cobbett, *Cobbett's Parliamentary History of England*, vol. 3 (London: R. Bagshaw, 1808), 1,347.
16. JE diary, III, 97 (11 May 1654).
17. CSPV XXX, 184 (3 March 1656).
18. BL Add MS 38100 f. vi.
19. Edward Maunde Thompson, ed., *Correspondence of the Family of Hatton*, 2 vols (London: Nichols and Sons, 1878), I, 14.
20. JE diary, III, 214 (31 May 1658).
21. Ibid., 97 (8 May 1654).
22. Ibid., 77 (5 November 1652).
23. Jerry Brotton, *The Sale of the Late King's Goods: Charles I and his Art Collection* (London: Macmillan, 2006), 320.
24. Ibid., 197 (15 September 1657).
25. Nehemiah Wallington, *The Notebooks of Nehemiah Wallington, 1618–1654: A Selection*, ed. David Booy (Aldershot: Ashgate, 2007), 296–7.
26. Howell, *Londinopolis*, 350.
27. [John Evelyn], *A Character of England, As it was lately presented, in a Letter, to a Noble Man of France* (London: J. Crooke, 1659), 13.
28. CSPV XXX, 308 (1656).
29. JE diary, III, 166 (11 February 1656).
30. CSPV XXX, 124 (22 October 1655).

10 THE UNCERTAINTIES OF WAR AND COMMERCE

1. JE diary, III, 195 (3 July 1657).
2. N. A. M. Rodger, *The Command of the Ocean: A Naval History of Britain 1649–1815* (London: Allen Lane, 2004), 38.
3. CSPV XXVIII, 187 (21 June 1651).
4. Derek Morris and Ken Cozens, *Wapping 1600–1800: A Social History of an Early Modern London Maritime Suburb* (London: East London History Society, 2009), 135.
5. Linda Levy Peck, 'Luxury and War: Reconsidering Luxury Consumption in Seventeenth-Century England', *Albion* 34 no. 1 (2002), 1–23 (p. 5).
6. CSPV XXIX, 264–5 (4 October 1654).
7. G. F. Steckley, ed., *The Letters of John Paige, London Merchant, 1648–58* (London: London Record Society, 1984), 14.
8. CSPV XXX, 308 (miscellaneous, 1656).
9. LMA CLC/526/MS30045/004 f. 64.
10. Ralph Davis, *The Rise of the English Shipping Industry in the Seventeenth and Eighteenth Centuries* (Newton Abbot: David and Charles, 1962), 23.
11. Ibid., 138.
12. Jeaffreson, III, 239.
13. John Cordy Jeaffreson, ed., *A Young Squire of the Seventeenth Century*, 2 vols (London: Hurst and Blackett, 1878), II, 4.
14. Jeaffreson, III, 248.

15. Steckley, ed., *The Letters of John Paige*, 77.
16. Imtiaz Habib, *Black Lives in the English Archives, 1500–1677: Imprints of the Invisible* (Aldershot: Ashgate, 2008), 243–5.
17. LMA ACC/1302/1H.
18. JE diary, III, 194–5 (16 July 1657).
19. Ibid., 577 (25 May 1671).
20. LMA CLC/526/MS30045/004 f. 89.
21. CSPD 1652–3, 497 (14 December 1652).
22. CSPV XXIX, 16 (1 February 1653).
23. CSPV XXIX, 25 (15 February 1653), 29 (23 February 1653), 38 (15 March 1653); CSPD 1652–3, 527 (3 February 1653).
24. Edward Maunde Thompson, ed., *Correspondence of the Family of Hatton*, 2 vols (London: Nichols and Sons, 1878), I, 9.
25. CSPV XXIX, 145 (13 November 1653).
26. Peter Elmer, *Witchcraft, Witch-Hunting, and Politics in Early Modern England* (Oxford: Oxford University Press, 2016), 155.
27. Jeaffreson, III, 277.
28. LMA P93/DUN/327 f. 115.
29. Jeaffreson, III, 223, 259, 270.
30. Ibid., 229, 260.
31. Randolph Roth, 'Homicide in Early Modern England 1549–1800: The Need for a Quantitative Synthesis', in *Crime, History & Societies* 5, no. 2 (2001), 33–67; W. Tomlinson, *Seven Particulars* (London: Giles Calvert, 1657), 11–19.
32. Philip Banbury, *Shipbuilders of the Thames and Medway* (Newton Abbot: David and Charles, 1971), 35.
33. CSPD 1651–2, 542 (15 January 1652); 1652–3, 496 (10 December 1652).
34. CSPD 1664–5, Pt 1, 181 (28 January 1665); 1656–7, 392 (4 July 1656).
35. CSPD 1664–5, Pt 1, 168 (11 January 1665).
36. JE diary, IV, 203 (13 May 1680); LMA P78/NIC/044 f. 73.
37. TNA ADM 42/485 (24 June 1660).
38. CSPD 1660–1, 550 (28 March 1661).
39. Rodger, *Command of the Ocean*, 46; D. C. Coleman, 'Naval Dockyards under the Later Stuarts', *The Economic History Review* 6 (1953), 134–55, p. 139; C. W. Chalkin, *Seventeenth-Century Kent* (London: Longmans, Green and Co., 1965), 31.
40. LMA CLC/526/MS30045/004 f. 107.
41. JE diary, III, 60 (15 February 1652).
42. Ibid., 149–50 (9 April 1655).
43. 'The First Anniversary of the Government', l. 357, Andrew Marvell, *The Complete English Poems*, ed. Elizabeth Story Dunno (Harmondsworth: Penguin, 1972), 135.
44. Edward Ward, *The Wooden World Dissected, in the Character of 1. A Ship of War*, 2nd edn (London: H. Moore, 1708), 1.
45. LMA CLA/036/02/1686/05/001.
46. *A Mad Marriage; or, the Female Fancy of Debtford* (London: I. Deacon, [1671–1704]).
47. Thomas Jordan, *London's Glory, Or, the Lord Mayor's Show* (London: John and Henry Playford, 1680), 11.

11 COFFEE-HOUSE CULTURE: NEWSPAPERS AND GOSSIP

1. *Endlesse Queries: Or, An End to Queries . . . for the Peoples Information* (London: [n.p.], 1659), 8.
2. *The Diurnall of Thomas Rugg, 1659–1661*, ed. William L. Sachse, Camden 3rd series, vol. 91 (London: Offices of the Royal Historical Society, 1961), 2, 10.

3. [John Evelyn], *A Character of England, As it was lately presented, in a Letter, to a Noble Man of France* (London: J. Crooke, 1659), 34–5.

4. James Howell, 'To Judge *Rumsey*', in [Walter Rumsey], *Organon Salutis. An Instrument to Cleanse the Stomach. As also divers new Experiments of the virtue of Tobacco and Coffee* (London: R. Hodgkinsonne for D. Pakeman, 1657), xxi.

5. *Coffee-Houses Vindicated in Answer To the late Published Character of a Coffee-House* (London: J. Lock for J. Clarke, 1675), 3.

6. John Aubrey, *Brief Lives: with, an Apparatus for the Lives of our English Mathematical Writers*, ed. Kate Bennett (Oxford: Oxford University Press, 2016), 37.

7. See Jeremy Boulton, 'The Poor among the Rich: Paupers and the Parish in the West End, 1600–1724', in P. Griffiths and M. S. R. Jenner, eds, *Londinopolis: Essays on the Cultural and Social History of Early Modern London* (Manchester: Manchester University Press, 2000), 197–223 (p. 197).

8. John Owen, *Bradshaw's Ultimum Vale* (Oxford: [n.p.], 1659), 12.

9. M. P., *A Character of Coffee and Coffee-Houses* (London: John Starkey, 1661), 4; The *Maiden's Complain[t] Against Coffee* (London: J. Jones, 1663), 3.

10. *Observator in Dialogue* (30 September 1682), 1.

11. A Lady, *An Essay In Defence of the Female Sex* (London: A. Roper, E. Wilkinson . . . and R. Clavel, 1696), 87–8.

12. OBP (8 July 1696), trial of William Alcock (t16960708-40).

13. Aubrey, *Brief Lives*, 320.

14. Edward Ward, *The London Spy*, ed. Paul Hyland (East Lansing: Colleagues Press, 1993), 18.

15. Ibid., 11, 30.

16. Ibid., 31.

17. Tom Brown, *Amusements Serious and Comical Calculated for the Meridian of London* (London: John Nutt, 1700), 115–16.

18. SP diary, V, 50 (17 February 1664).

19. Francis Kirkman, *The Counterfeit Lady Unveiled* (London: Peter Parker, 1673), 100.

20. See Miles Ogborn, *Spaces of Modernity: London's Geographies, 1680–1780* (New York and London: Guilford Press, 1998), 91.

21. Matthew Beaumont, *Nightwalking: A Nocturnal History of London* (London: Verso, 2015), 37.

22. Kevin Williams, *Read All About It! A History of the British Newspaper* (Abingdon: Routledge, 2010), 5.

23. Robert Hooke, *The Diary of Robert Hooke, 1672–1680*, eds Henry W. Robinson and Walter Adams (London: Taylor and Francis, 1935), 65.

24. Ibid., 77.

25. OBP (4 May 1698), trial of F - P (t16980504-53).

26. Joseph Addison, *The Spectator*, ed. Donald F. Bond, 5 vols (Oxford: Clarendon Press, 1965), 44 (12 March 1711).

27. *The Character of a Coffee-House* (London: Jonathan Edwin, 1673), 1.

28. M. P., *A Character of Coffee and Coffee-Houses*, 7.

29. *A Proclamation for the Suppression of Coffee-Houses* (London: John Bill and Christopher Barker, 1675), dated 29 December 1675.

30. Andrew Marvell?, 'A Dialogue between the Two Horses' (1676), in George de F. Lord, *Poems on Affairs of State: Augustan Satirical Verse 1660–1714*, 7 vols (New Haven and London: Yale University Press, 1963), I, 283.

31. [Thomas Flatman], *Heraclitus Ridens, or, A Discourse Between Jest and Earnest* (London: Benjamin Tooke, 1713), 26 (no. 5, 1 March 1681).

32. Brown, *Amusements*, 156–7.

33. JE diary, III, 224 (22 November 1658).

12 RESTORATION AND A LICENTIOUS COURT

1. *The Diurnall of Thomas Rugg, 1659–1661*, ed. William L. Sachse, Camden 3rd series, vol. 91 (London: Offices of the Royal Historical Society, 1961), 90.
2. J. Evelyn, *Sculptura: or the History, and Art of Chalcography* (London: J. C. for G. Beedle and T. Collins, 1662), 25.
3. SP diary, I, 265 (13 October 1660).
4. *Diurnall of Thomas Rugg*, 145.
5. Ibid., 176.
6. Katharine Gibson, '"Best Belov'd of Kings": The Iconography of King Charles II' (PhD thesis, Courtauld Institute, University of London, 2004), 63.
7. Jeaffreson, III, 309 (10 January 1661).
8. JE diary, III, 464–5 (18 October 1666).
9. Gibson, '"Best Belov'd of Kings"', 54.
10. LMA CLC/509/MS05106/001 (22 August–1 September and 21–30 November 1664).
11. www.historyofparliamentonline.org/volume/1690-1715/member/turner-sir-william-1615-93 (accessed 20 February 2019).
12. BL Add MS 36916 (9 November 1671).
13. CSPD 1676–7, 24 (11 March 1676).
14. Jeaffreson, III, 316 (5 December 1661).
15. BL Add MS 36916 (20 January 1669).
16. Manuel Eisner, 'Long-Term Historical Trends in Violent Crime', *Crime and Justice*, 30 (2003), 83–142 (pp. 85, 99).
17. Jeaffreson, III, 326 (18 August 1662).
18. OBP Advertisements, 28 August 1700 (a17000828-1).
19. SP diary, VIII, 145–6 (3 April 1667).
20. *News from Hide-Park* (1663–74), University of Glasgow Library, Euing Ballads 250, EBBA 31799, ll. 43, 83.
21. *Diurnall of Thomas Rugg*, 127.
22. See Warren Chernaik, 'Pepys and the Restoration Theatre', in Margarette Lincoln, ed., *Samuel Pepys: Plague, Fire and Revolution* (London: Thames and Hudson, 2015), 81–9.
23. CSPD 1660–1, 423 (24 December 1660).
24. BL Add MS 36916 (18 November 1671).
25. Allan Richard Botica, 'Audience, Playhouse and Play in Restoration Theatre 1660–1710' (DPhil thesis, University of Oxford, 1986), Summary.
26. Bridget Orr, *British Enlightenment Theatre: Dramatizing Difference* (Cambridge: Cambridge University Press, 2020), 191.
27. BL Add MS 36916 (30 May 1668).
28. SP diary, IV, 128 (8 May 1663).
29. OBP (10 December 1684), trial of George Porter (t16841210-12).
30. Edward Ward, *The London Spy*, ed. Paul Hyland (East Lansing: Colleagues Press, 1993), 121.
31. JE, diary, IV, 75 (29 November 1675).
32. Jane Cox, *Hatred Pursued Beyond the Grave: Tales of our Ancestors from the London Church Courts* (London: HMSO, 1993), 64.
33. *The New Courtier* (1678–80), Pepys Library, Pepys Ballads 2.222, EBBA 20834.
34. *A New Satyricall BALLAD OF THE Licentiousness of the Times* (1679), Huntington Library HEH 479689, EBBA 32564, ll. 83–4.

13 PLAGUE, FIRE AND WAR

1. BL Add MS 10117 f. 139.
2. [John Evelyn], *A Character of England, As it was lately presented, in a Letter, to a Noble Man of France* (London: J. Crooke, 1659), 10, 29.

3. BL Sloane MS 1471 f. 19.
4. LMA ACC/1093/145.
5. LMA COL/SJ/12/048 f. 58.
6. *Londons Lord Have Mercy Upon Us* (1665), National Library of Scotland, RB.I.262(121), EBBA 34219, ll. 9–10.
7. *The Kings Majesties Love to London* (1665), National Library of Scotland, RB.I.262 (008), EBBA 34146, ll. 55–6.
8. LMA COL/SJ/12/048 f. 58.
9. *Intelligencer Published for the Satisfaction and Information of the People* (5 July 1665), 527.
10. William Boghurst, *Loimographia*, ed. Joseph Frank Payne (London: Shaw and Sons, 1894), 28–9.
11. LMA ACC/0262/043/051 (2 August 1665).
12. LMA CLC/509/MS05106/001 (10–20 August and 28 September 1665).
13. Ibid. (13–23 November 1665).
14. CSPV 1664–6, 182 (18 August 1665), enclosure dated 7 August 1665.
15. BL Add MS 10117 f. 147.
16. Ibid., f. 147.
17. SP diary, VII, 274 (4 September 1666).
18. Jeaffreson, III, 373.
19. Rebecca Rideal, *1666: Plague, War and Hellfire* (London: John Murray, 2016), 208.
20. JE diary, III, 457 (4 September 1666).
21. *The Londoners Lamentation* (1666), University of Glasgow Library, Euing Ballads 170, EBBA 31925.
22. Edward Atkyns, 'XV. Copy of a Letter to Sir Robert Atkyns ... from his brother ...', *Archaeologia: Or, Miscellaneous Tracts Relating to Antiquity* 19 (1821), 105–8 (p. 106).
23. CSPV 1666–8, 76 (28 September 1666).
24. William Taswell, 'Autobiography and Anecdotes by William Taswell, D.D.', *The Camden Miscellany*, vol. I (London: J. B. Nichols and Son, 1853), 13.
25. E. McKellar, *The Birth of Modern London: The Development and Design of the City 1660–1720* (Manchester: Manchester University Press, 1999).
26. K. Downes, *Hawksmoor* (London: Zwemmer, 1979; first published 1959), 242.
27. CSPD 1665–6, 227 (January? 1666).
28. SP diary, VII, 200 (10 July 1666).
29. Quoted by J. R. Tanner, *Samuel Pepys and the Royal Navy* (Cambridge: Cambridge University Press, 2013; first published 1920), 45–6.
30. CSPD 1665–6, 516 (10 July 1666).
31. SP diary, VII, 190 (1 July 1666).
32. CSPD 1665–6, 538 (15 July 1666?).
33. JE diary, III, 448 (25 August 1666).
34. CSPD 1665–6, 553 (19 July 1666).
35. Hazel Forsyth, *Butcher, Baker, Candlestick Maker: Surviving the Great Fire of London* (London: I. B. Tauris and Co. Ltd., 2016), 63; Jeremy Boulton and John Black, '"Those, that die by reason of their madness": Dying Insane in London, 1629–1830', *History of Psychiatry* 23, no. 1 (2012), 27–39 (p. 27).
36. SP diary, IX, 132 (25 March 1668).

14 THE SPIRIT OF DISCOVERY: CURIOSITY AND EXPERIMENT

1. BL Add MS 4441 f. 1.
2. Adrian Tinniswood, *The Royal Society and the Invention of Modern Science* (London: Apollo Library, 2019), 9.

3. James Howell, *Londinopolis: An Historicall Discourse or Perlustration of the City of London, the Imperial Chamber, and chief Emporium of Great Britain* (London: J. Streater for Henry Twiford et al., 1657), 396.
4. Stephen Wren, *Parentalia: Or, Memoirs of the Family of the Wrens* (London: T. Osborn and R. Dodsley, 1750), 206.
5. Ibid., 206.
6. BL Sloane MS 244 f. 61v.
7. Thomas Birch, *The History of the Royal Society of London for Improving of Natural Knowledge from its First Rise*, 4 vols (New York and London: Johnson Reprint Corporation, 1968), II, 42–3; SP diary, VI, 96 (3 May 1665).
8. Thomas Sprat, *History of the Royal Society* (London: T. R. for J. Martyn, 1667), 86.
9. JE diary, IV, 195 (26 February 1680).
10. Sprat, *History*, 113.
11. SP diary, V, 240 (13 August 1664).
12. Ibid., VI, 18 (21 January 1665).
13. D. V. Glass, 'John Graunt and his *Natural and Political Observations*', *Notes and Records of the Royal Society of London* 19, no. 1 (1964), 63–100.
14. CSPD 1675–6, 7 (4 March 1675).
15. [Arthur T. Bolton and H. Duncan Hendry, eds], *The Fifth Volume of the Wren Society 1928: Designs of Sir Chr. Wren for Oxford, Cambridge, London, Windsor, etc* (Oxford: The Wren Society at the University Press, 1928), 21.
16. John Aubrey, *Brief Lives: with, an Apparatus for the Lives of our English Mathematical Writers*, ed. Kate Bennett (Oxford: Oxford University Press, 2016), 305.
17. John Flamsteed, *An Account of the Revd. John Flamsteed, the First Astronomer Royal*, ed. Francis Baily (London: William Clowes and Sons, 1835), 246.
18. JE diary, III, 482–3 (30 May 1667).
19. Thomas Shadwell, *The Virtuoso*, eds M. H. Nicolson and D. S. Rhodes (London: Edward Arnold Ltd., 1966), 22 (I. ii. 7–10).
20. Robert Hooke, *The Diary of Robert Hooke, 1672–1680*, ed. Henry W. Robinson and Walter Adams (London: Taylor and Francis, 1935), 235.
21. Flamsteed, *An Account*, 215, to A. Sharp (18 December 1703).
22. Rebekah F. Higgett, ' "Greenwich near London": The Royal Observatory and its London Networks in the Seventeenth and Eighteenth Centuries', *British Journal for the History of Science* 52, no. 2 (2019), 297–322.
23. JE diary, IV, 277 (5 April 1682).
24. Michael Hunter, 'The Royal Society and the Decline of Magic', *Notes and Records of the Royal Society of London* 65, no. 2 (2011), 103–19 (p. 110).
25. *Annus Mirabilis*, 1,170 and 641–56 in John Dryden, *The Major Works*, ed. Keith Walker (Oxford: Oxford University Press, 2003), 69, 52–3.
26. John Locke, *An Essay Concerning Human Understanding*, ed. Peter H. Nidditch (Oxford: Clarendon Press, 1975), 44.
27. Isaac Newton, *The Correspondence of Isaac Newton Volume I, 1661–1675*, ed. H. W. Turnbull (Cambridge: Cambridge University Press, 1959), 416, to R. Hooke (5 February 1676).

15 DOMESTIC ANXIETIES: HOME IMPROVEMENTS

1. BL Add MS 80766 f. 2 (1676–7); 78432 f. 38v (28 March 1693); LMA DL/C/B/030/MS09174/001/011 (1659).
2. LMA DL/C/B/030/MS09174/001/008 (1661).

3. Sara Pennell, *The Birth of the English Kitchen, 1660–1850* (London: Bloomsbury Publishing, 2016), 62; William M. Cavert, 'Industrial Coal Consumption in Early Modern London', *Urban History* 44, no. 3 (2017), 424–43 (p. 427).

4. SP diary, II, 106 (25 May 1661).

5. Ibid., II, 238 (25 December 1661).

6. Hannah Woolley, *The Queen-Like Closet; Or, Rich Cabinet* (London: R. Lowndes, 1670), iv.

7. Gervase Markham, *The English House-wife*, 7th edn (London: W. Wilson for E. Brewster and George Sawbridge, 1660), title page.

8. Ibid., 29, 30.

9. E.g. *Strange News from Shadwell, Being a True and Just Relation of the Death of Alice Fowler, Who had for many years been accounted a Witch* (London: E. Mallet, 1685).

10. W. M., *The Queens Closet Opened* (London: Nathaniel Brook, 1655), 14.

11. BM 1896,0501.934.1-49.

12. Tim Reinke-Williams, 'Female Attractiveness and the Female Life-Cycle in Seventeenth-Century England', *Cultural and Social History* 15, no. 4 (2018), 469–85 (p. 474).

13. Patricia Crawford and Laura Gowing, eds, *Women's Worlds in Seventeenth-Century England* (London and New York: Routledge, 2000), 71.

14. Peter Earle, *The Making of the English Middle Class: Business, Society, and Family Life in London, 1660–1730* (London: Methuen, 1989), 181–5.

15. BL Add Ms 78439 f. 4v (1664?).

16. BL Add MS 78431 f. 70.

17. BL Add MS 78430 f. 25v (1647).

18. BL Add MS 78431 f. 48 (Easter Monday 1660); W. M., *Queens Closet Opened*, 43.

19. LMA MJ/SP/1689/A/009; MJ/SP/1698/A/008; MJ/SP/1698/A/003.

20. Crawford and Gowing, *Women's Worlds*, 15.

21. R. Shoemaker, 'Gendered Spaces: Patterns of Mobility and Perceptions of London's Geography, 1660–1750', in J. F. Merritt, ed., *Imagining Early Modern London: Perceptions and Portrayals of the City from Stow to Strype, 1598–1720* (Cambridge: Cambridge University Press, 2001), 155.

22. Laura Gowing, *Domestic Dangers: Women, Words, and Sex in Early Modern London* (Oxford: Clarendon Press, 1996), 205.

23. Mark Merry and Philip Baker, ' "For the house her self and one servant": Family and Household in Late Seventeenth-Century London', *The London Journal* 34, no. 3 (2009), 205–32 (pp. 229, fn 21, and pp. 212ff).

24. BL Add MS 80766 f. 1.

25. BL Add MS 78440 f. 27 (9 April 1680); 80766 f. 2 (1676–7).

26. BL Add MS 78437 f. 51 (29 November 1685).

27. Paula Humfrey, ed., *The Experience of Domestic Service for Women in Early Modern London* (London: Routledge, 2016; first published 2011), 1–2.

28. *The Post Boy* (8–10 September 1696), 2.

29. BL Add MS 78539 f. 95v, M. Evelyn to R. Bohun (19 May 1693).

30. BL Add MS 78433 f. 100v, S. Draper to M. Evelyn (13 March 1696); 78539 f. 23, M. Evelyn to R. Bohun (1673).

31. BL Add MS 78539 f. 86, M. Evelyn to R. Bohun (26 December 1687); f. 84v, M. Evelyn to R. Bohun (20 September 1687).

32. BL Add MS 78433 f. 96 (28 February 1696).

33. Leonie Hannan, *Women of Letters: Gender, Writing and the Life of the Mind in Early Modern England* (Manchester: Manchester University Press, 2016), 3; Susan Whyman, 'Advice to Letter-Writers: Evidence from Four Generations of Evelyns', in Frances Harris and Michael Hunter, eds, *John Evelyn and his Milieu* (London: The British Library, 2003), 255–66 (p. 256); David Cressy, *Literacy and the Social Order: Reading and Writing in Tudor and Stuart England* (Cambridge: Cambridge University Press, 1990), 129.

34. BL Add MS 78439 f. 14.

35. BL Add MS 78434 f. 53, W. Glanville to M. Evelyn (14 December 1685); f. 81, S. Hungerford to M. Evelyn (11 May 1660).

36. BL Add MS 78539 f. 7, M. Evelyn to R. Bohun (3 February 1668).
37. LMA CLC/427/MS03041/004 f. 10 (1696?).
38. BL Add MS 78435 f. 187 (1668?); 78539 f. 20 (27 February 1671).
39. BL Add MS 78539 f. 27 (7 January 1674?).
40. BL Add MS 78539 f. 5, M. Evelyn to R. Bohun (1667?).
41. BL Harley MS 6828 f. 510v, M. Evelyn to Mrs Elizabeth Tillotson (9 March 1666).
42. BL Add MS 78432 f. 105 (22 July 1697).
43. W. M., *Queens Closet Opened*, 294.
44. George Hartman, *The Family Physitian* (London: H. Hills for the author, 1696), 511, 517, 522, 524.
45. BL Add MS 78435 f. 60, to Sir S. Tuke (*c.* December 1669).
46. LMA CLC/427/MS03041/009 (iii), Anne Celdyton to T. Bowrey (4 January 1704).
47. *The History and Proceedings of the House of Commons: Volume 1, 1660*–1680 (London: Richard Chandler, 1742), 86.
48. BL Add MS 78341 f. 89.
49. LMA CLC/427/MS03041/009 (iii).
50. Rosemary Weinstein, 'Kitchen Chattels: The Evolution of Familiar Objects 1200–1700', in *Oxford Symposium on Food & Cookery, 1988: The Cooking Pot: Proceedings*, ed. Tom Jaine (London: Prospect Books, 1989), 168–83 (p. 169).
51. A Lady, *An Essay In Defence of the Female Sex* (London: A. Roper, E. Wilkinson . . . and R. Clavel, 1696), 85–6.
52. Hannah Woolley, *The Gentlewomans Companion* (London: A. Maxwell for Dorman Newman, 1673), 1, 29.
53. *Advice to the Women & Maidens of London* (London: Benjamin Billingsley, 1678), 2.
54. Mary Evelyn, *Mundus Muliebris: Or, the Ladies Dressing-Room Unlock'd* (London: R. Bentley, 1690); *Mundus Foppensis: Or, the Fop Display'd* (London: John Harris, 1691).

16 IMMIGRANTS, OR 'STRANGERS'

1. Alfred Plummer, *The London Weavers' Company, 1600–1970* (Abingdon: Routledge, 2006; first published 1972), 162.
2. Ibid., 163–7.
3. Elizabeth Randall, 'A Special Case? London's French Protestants', in Debra Kelly and Martyn Cornick, eds, *A History of the French in London: Liberty, Equality, Opportunity* (London: Institute of Historical Research, 2013), 13–43 (p. 27).
4. BL Add MSS 36916 (2 May 1668).
5. CSPD Addenda 1660–85, 18 (1660?); TNA SP 29/274 no. 205, in Dan Cruickshank, *Spitalfields: The History of a Nation in a Handful of Streets* (London: Random House, 2016), 138.
6. Count Lorenzo Magalotti, *Travels of Cosmo the third, Grand Duke of Tuscany, through England during the reign of King Charles the second (1669)* (London: J. Mawman, 1821), 397–8.
7. Vanessa Harding, 'The Population of London, 1550–1700: A Review of the Published Evidence', *London Journal* 15 (1990), 111–28 (p. 112); Francis Sheppard, *London: A History* (London: Oxford University Press, 1998), 362.
8. *The Post Man: and the Historical Account* (11–13 June 1702), 2; (6–8 January 1702), 2.
9. Arthur P. Arnold, 'A List of Jews and their Households in London', *Miscellanies of the Jewish Historical Society of England* 6 (1962), 73–141 (p. 74).
10. *Domestick Intelligence, or News both from City and Country* (29 August 1679), 1.
11. CSPD 1673–5, 436 (29 November 1674).
12. CSPD 1683 (January–June), 389 (June?).
13. CSPD 1682, 9 (4 January 1682).
14. Howard L. Blackmore, *A Dictionary of London Gunmakers 1350–1850* (Oxford: Phaidon Christie's, 1986), 19.

15. Carl Ricketts, *Pewterers of London 1600–1900* ([n.p.]: The Pewter Society, 2001), 210.
16. Plummer, *The London Weavers' Company, 1600–1970*, 156.
17. Jeaffreson, IV, 227.
18. F. H. W. Sheppard, ed., *Survey of London, Vol. XXVII, Spitalfields and Mile End New Town* (London: The Athlone Press for the London County Council, 1957), 2.
19. Bernard Cottrett, *The Huguenots in England: Immigration and Settlement, c. 1550–1700* (Cambridge: Cambridge University Press, 1991; first published 1985), 190.
20. *The Post Man: and the Historical Account* (26–29 October 1700), 2; (17–19 November 1696), 2.
21. *The Flying Post: or, The Post-Master* (4–6 August 1698), 2; *The Post Boy* (18–20 November 1697), 2.
22. R. Turner Wilcox, *The Mode in Hats and Headdress, Including Hair Styles, Cosmetics and Jewelry* (New York: C. Scribner's Sons, 1945), 117–18.
23. Robin D. Gwynn, *The Huguenots of London* (Brighton: Alpha Press, 1998), 48, 49.
24. See Paul Boucher and Tessa Murdoch, 'Montagu House, Bloomsbury: A French Household in London, 1673–1733', in Kelly and Cornick, eds, *A History of the French in London*, 43–69.
25. Thomas Otway, *The Complete Works of Thomas Otway*, ed. Montague Summers, 3 vols (London: The Nonesuch Press, 1927), III, 103.
26. A. L. Beier, 'Engine of Manufacture: The Trades of London', in A. L. Beier and Roger Finlay, eds, *London 1500–1700: The Making of the Metropolis* (London and New York: Longman, 1986), 141–67 (p. 147).
27. William Robert Scott, *The Constitution and Finance of English, Scottish and Irish Joint-Stock Companies to 1720*, 3 vols (Cambridge: Cambridge University Press, 1910–12), I, 327–9.
28. *The Flying Post: or, The Post-Master* (23–26 April 1698), 2.
29. Anne J. Kershen, *Strangers, Aliens and Asians: Huguenots, Jews and Bangladeshis in Spitalfields 1660–2000* (Abingdon: Routledge, 2005), 170.
30. William Maitland, *The History of London, From its Foundation by the Romans, to the Present Time* (London: Samuel Richardson, 1739), 665.
31. CSPD 1686–7, 106 (21 April 1686).
32. *The London Post with Intelligence Foreign and Domestick* (25–28 April 1701), 2; *The Flying Post: or, The Post-Master* (14–17 June 1701), 2; *The Post Boy* (1–3 October 1696), 2.
33. Marchamont Nedham, *Christianissimus Christianandus, Or, Reason for the Reduction of France to a more Christian State in Europe* (London: Jonathan Edwin, 1678), 37.
34. Lien Bich Luu, *Immigrants and the Industries of London 1500–1700* (Aldershot: Ashgate, 2005), 245.
35. Magalotti, *Travels of Cosmo*, 398.
36. SP diary, II, 188 (30 September 1661).
37. George Reginald Balleine, *The Story of St. Mary Matfelon, the Parish Church of Whitechapel* (London: Free School Press, 1898), 22.
38. Irène Scouloudi, 'L'aide apportée aux réfugiés protestants français par l'Eglise de Threadneedle Street: l'Eglise de Londres 1681–1687', *Bulletin de la Société de l'Histoire du Protestantisme Français (1903–2015)* 115 (1969), 429–44 (p. 433).
39. *The London Gazette* (6–9 October 1701), 2.
40. Greig Parker, *Probate Inventories of French Immigrants in Early Modern London* (Farnham: Ashgate, 2014), 28, 122.
41. Mary Evelyn, *Mundus Muliebris: Or, the Ladies Dressing-Room Unlock'd* (London: R. Bentley, 1690), Preface.

17 INSURRECTION: JAMES II LOSES HIS WAY

1. JE diary, IV, 172 (6 July 1679).
2. Robert O. Bucholz and Joseph P. Ward, *London: A Social and Cultural History, 1550–1750* (Cambridge: Cambridge University Press, 2012), 25.
3. JE diary, IV, 479 (2 October 1685).

4. Ibid., IV, 320 (18 June 1683).
5. Henry Hyde, Earl of Clarendon, *The Correspondence of Henry Hyde, Earl of Clarendon and of his Brother Laurence Hyde, Earl of Rochester; with the Diary of Lord Clarendon from 1687 to 1690*, ed. Samuel Weller Singer, 2 vols (London: Henry Colburn, 1828), I, 129.
6. Jeaffreson, IV, 284–5 (2 and 18 March 1685).
7. Mark Knights, 'London's "Monster" Petition of 1680', *The Historical Journal* 36, no. 1 (1993), 39–67 (pp. 56–7).
8. Roger Morrice, *The Entring Book of Roger Morrice 1677–1691. Volume III, The Reign of James II 1685–1686*, ed. Tim Harris (Woodbridge: Boydell Press, 2007), 46–7.
9. *An Account of what passed at the execution of the late Duke of Monmouth* (London: Robert Horne, John Baker, Benjamin Tooke, 1685), 3.
10. *Tower Hill, c.* 1685. LMA, Collage: the London Picture Archive, 24831.
11. *The Countreys Advice to the Late Duke of Monmouth, And Those in Rebellion with Him* (London: T. M. for the author), vol. 2.
12. Tim Harris, *Revolution: The Great Crisis of the British Monarchy, 1685–1720* (London: Allen Lane, 2006), 96; John Childs, *The Army, James II, and the Glorious Revolution* (Manchester: Manchester University Press, 1980), 1.
13. JE diary, IV, 582 (13 June 1688).
14. Morrice, *Entring Book*, III, 213 (7 August 1686).
15. BL Add MS 72595 f. 109 (3 May 1687).
16. BL Harley MS 4182 f. 62.
17. BL Harley MS 4182 f. 68 (26 April 1687),
18. BL Add MS 72595 ff. 139, 141, 143.
19. BL Add MS 72595 f. 1v.
20. Tim Harris, *Restoration: Charles II and his Kingdoms* (London: Allen Lane, 2005), 28.
21. JE diary, IV, 524 (8 October 1686).
22. BL Add MS Sloane MS 3929 f. 39v.
23. Mark Goldie, *Roger Morrice and the Puritan Whigs: The Entring Book, 1677–1691* (Woodbridge: Boydell Press, 2016; first published 2007), 10.
24. Randall Monier-Williams, *The Tallow Chandlers of London Vol. 4* (London: Kay and Ward, 1977), 222.
25. Mark Knights, 'The Remodelling of the London Livery Companies in the 1680s', *English Historical Review* 112, no. 449 (1997), 1,141–78 (pp. 1,159, 1,162).
26. BL Add MS 72596 f. 7; 72595 f. 144.
27. BL Add MS 34487 f. 5 (4 May 1687).
28. JE diary, IV, 562–3 (29 October 87).
29. William Gibson, *James II and the Trial of the Seven Bishops* (London: Palgrave Macmillan, 2009), 71.
30. Hyde, *Correspondence*, II, 156 (18 January 1688).
31. BL Add MS Sloane MS 3929 f. 59v.
32. Roger Morrice, *The Entring Book of Roger Morrice 1677–1691. Volume IV, The Reign of James II 1687–1689*, ed. Stephen Taylor (Woodbridge: Boydell Press, 2007), 277.
33. BL Sloane MS 3929 f. 79v.
34. Ibid., f. 63v.
35. LMA COL/SD/01/054.
36. BL Sloane MS 3929 f. 69v.
37. Goldie, *Roger Morrice and the Puritan Whigs*, 8.
38. BL Harley MS 4182, f. 64; TNA SP 94/72 f. 95v.
39. Morrice, *Entring Book*, III, 295.
40. NPG D10694.
41. BL Sloane MS 3929 f. 79v.
42. BL Add MS 34487 f. 30.
43. BL Add MS 34510 f. 160v.
44. BL Sloane MS 3929 f. 105.

18 TAKING SIDES: THE DUTCH INVASION, 1688

1. John Miller, *James II* (New Haven and London: Yale University Press, 2000; first published 1978), 202.
2. BL Sloane MS 3939 f. 105.
3. Ibid., f. 107.
4. Roger Morrice, *The Entring Book of Roger Morrice 1677–1691. Volume IV, The Reign of James II 1687–1689*, ed. Stephen Taylor (Woodbridge: Boydell Press, 2007), 346.
5. JE diary, IV, 609 (2 December 1688).
6. BL Add MS 34510 ff. 182, 182v.
7. Morrice, *Entring Book*, IV, 443.
8. Guy de la Bédoyère, *Particular Friends: The Correspondence of Samuel Pepys and John Evelyn* (Woodbridge: Boydell Press, 1997), 186, Evelyn to Pepys (12 December 1688).
9. Morrice, *Entring Book*, IV, 383.
10. Cristina Bravo Lozano, 'Popular Protests, the Public Sphere and Court Catholicism: The Insults to the Chapel of the Spanish Embassy in London, 1685–1688', *Culture & History Digital Journal* 6, no. 1 (2017), 1–16 (p. 9).
11. Morrice, *Entring Book*, IV, 416.
12. Ibid., 399.
13. BL Harley MS 4182 f. 76.
14. *A Compleat Collection of Papers, in Twelve Parts: Relating to the Great Revolutions in England and Scotland From the Time of the Seven Bishops Petitioning K. James II. against the Dispensing Power, June 8. 1688 to the Coronation of King William and Queen Mary, April 11. 1689* (London: J. D., 1689), Collection XII, 14.
15. BL Sloane MS 3929 f. 129v.
16. Robert Kirk, 'London in 1689–90', *Transactions of the London and Middlesex Archaeological Society*, n.s. 6 (1929–32), 487–98 (p. 494).
17. Ibid., 491.
18. Morrice, *Entring Book*, IV, 530.
19. BM G3, FD.257.
20. BM 1902, 1011, 6934.
21. Lois G. Schwoerer, 'Women and the Glorious Revolution', *Albion: A Quarterly Journal Concerned with British Studies* 18, no. 2 (1986), 195–218 (p. 202); BM 1902, 1011, 6926.
22. Narcissus Luttrell, *A Brief Historical Relation of State Affairs from September 1678, to April 1714*, 6 vols (Oxford: Oxford University Press, 1857), I, 606–7.
23. Robert Kirk, 'London in 1689–90', *Transactions of the London and Middlesex Archaeological Society*, n.s. 7 (1933–7), 304–19 (p. 306).
24. BM 1932, 1112, 4. See Mark Knights, 'Pepys's England: Revolutions and Transformations', in Margarette Lincoln, ed., *Samuel Pepys: Plague, Fire and Revolution* (London: Thames and Hudson, 2015), 20–31 (pp. 28–9).
25. JE diary, IV, 612 (18 December 1688).
26. George Savile, Marquis of Halifax, *The Lady's New-Year's Gift. Or, Advice to a Daughter* (London: M. Gillyflower and J. Partridge, 1688), 32.
27. *A Compleat Collection of Papers*, Collection III, 36.
28. J. Strype, *A Survey of the Cities of London and Westminster . . . by John Stow . . . brought down to the present Time*, 2 vols (London: A. Churchill et al., 1720), II, V, 30.

19 A NEW REGIME: WILLIAM AND MARY'S TOWN

1. 'Diary of Dr. Edward Lake . . . Chaplain and Tutor to the Princesses Mary and Anne . . . 1677–1678', ed. George Percy Elliott, *The Camden Miscellany*, vol. II (London: Camden Society, 1847), 1–32 (p. 10).

2. Tim Hitchcock and Robert Shoemaker, *London Lives: Poverty, Crime and the Making of a Modern City, 1690–1800* (Cambridge: Cambridge University Press, 2015), 30.
3. LMA ACC/1302/075, D. Wood to her husband, undated but before 1704.
4. Agnes Strickland, *Lives of the Queens of England, from the Norman Conquest*, 6 vols (London: Bell and Daldy, 1865), VI, 21.
5. Sir William Dalrymple, *Memoirs of Great Britain and Ireland, from the Dissolution of the last Parliament of Charles II until the Sea-Battle off La Hogue*, 4 vols (Dublin: David Hay, 1773–88), III, 90 (Book IV).
6. Angela McShane and Clare Backhouse, 'Top Knots and Lower Sorts: Print and Promiscuous Consumption in the 1690s', *Printed Images in Early Modern Britain: Essays in Interpretation*, ed. Michael Hunter (London: Routledge, 2010), 337–57.
7. SP diary, VII, 32 (31 January 1666).
8. Celia Fiennes, *The Journeys of Celia Fiennes*, intro. by John Hillaby (London and Sydney: Macdonald, 1983), 332–3.
9. Todd Longstaffe-Gowan, *The London Square: Gardens in the Midst of Town* (New Haven and London: Yale University Press, 2012), 37.
10. N. G. Brett-James, 'A Speculative Builder in the Seventeenth Century: Dr. Nicholas Barbon', *Transactions of the London and Middlesex Archaeological Society*, n.s. 6 (1929–32), 110–46 (pp. 119–20).
11. TNA LC 5/42 f. 344.
12. Robert Kirk, 'London in 1689–90', *Transactions of the London and Middlesex Archaeological Society*, n.s. 6 (1929–32), 322–43, 487–98 (p. 327).
13. LMA ACC/1183/001.
14. Daniel Defoe, *A Tour Through the Whole Island of Great Britain*, eds P. N. Furbank and W. R. Owens with A. J. Coulson (New Haven and London: Yale University Press, 1991; first published 1724–6), 65.
15. JE diary, VI, 146 (13 July 1693).
16. LMA MJ/SP/1699/01/039; MJ/SP/1699/01/040.
17. Defoe, *A Tour Through the Whole Island of Great Britain*, 72.
18. LMA ACC/1302/073.
19. *A Collection for Improvement of Husbandry and Trade* (23 October 1696), 3.
20. Ibid. (5 April 1695), 4; *The London Post with Intelligence Foreign and Domestick* (20–22 March 1700), 2.
21. *A Collection for Improvement of Husbandry and Trade* (30 August 1695), 4.
22. Ibid. (25 May 1692), 1; (1 March 1695), 1.
23. Thomas Fairchild, *The City Gardener* (London: T. Woodward, 1722), 8–9.
24. Ibid., 6.
25. Ibid., 7, 64.
26. Guy Miège, *The New State of England Under Their Majesties K[ing] William and Q[ueen] Mary* (London: R. Clavel, H. Mortlock and J. Robinson, 1694), 231.
27. Kirk, 'London in 1689–90', 491–2.
28. Dalrymple, *Memoirs*, III, 196 (Book V), Mary to William (5 September/20 August 1690).
29. Arthur Mainwaring, 'Tarquin and Tullia', in *Restoration Literature: An Anthology*, ed. Paul Hammond (Oxford: Oxford University Press, 2002), 76, l. 107.
30. *Proposals for a National Reformation of Manners* (London: John Dunton, 1694), 15.
31. LMA ACC/1302/058, R. Wood to T. Wood (5 January 1695).
32. LMA COL/SD/01/063.
33. Thomas D'Urfey, *Gloriana: A Funeral Pindarique Poem* (London: Samuel Briscoe, 1695), l. 58.
34. Anthony Ray, 'Delftware in England', in *The Age of William III and Mary II: Power, Politics and Patronage, 1688–1702*, eds Robert P. Maccubin and Martha Hamilton-Phillips (Williamsburg: College of William and Mary, 1989), 301–7 (p. 305).

20 NO TIME FOR CYNICS: TOWARDS A NEW CENTURY

1. Narcissus Luttrell, *A Brief Historical Relation of State Affairs from September 1678 to April 1714*, 6 vols (Oxford: Oxford University Press, 1857), III, 174.
2. Natasha Glaisyer, *The Culture of Commerce in England, 1660–1720* (Woodbridge: The Royal Historical Society in association with The Boydell Press, 2006), 49.
3. Luttrell, *A Brief Historical Relation*, IV, 204.
4. Daniel Defoe, *The Anatomy of Exchange Alley: Or, a System of Stock-Jobbing* (London: E. Smith, 1719), 3. Cf. *The Villany of Stock-Jobbers Detected* (London: [n.p.], 1701), 13.
5. P. G. M. Dickson, *The Financial Revolution in England: A Study in the Development of Public Credit 1688–1756* (London: Macmillan, 1967), 46.
6. LMA MJ/SP/1696/024 and 025.
7. Luttrell, *A Brief Historical Relation*, III, 495.
8. LMA MJ/SP/1690/07/023.
9. Luttrell, *A Brief Historical Relation*, II, 630, 642; III, 1, 7, 85.
10. N. A. M. Rodger, *The Command of the Ocean: A Naval History of Britain 1649–1815* (London: Allen Lane, 2004), 206.
11. LMA MJ/SP/1691/04/017.
12. Luttrell, *A Brief Historical Relation*, III, 174,
13. Robert Kirk, 'London in 1689–90', *Transactions of the London and Middlesex Archaeological Society*, n.s. 6 (1929–32), 322–43, 487–97 (pp. 493–4).
14. *Antimoixeia: or the Honest and Joynt-Design of the Tower-Hamblets for the General Suppression of Bawdy-Houses* (London: n.p., 1691).
15. Luttrell, *A Brief Historical Relation*, II, 646.
16. John Ehrman, *The Navy in the War of William III 1689–1697: Its State and Direction* (Cambridge: Cambridge University Press, 1953), 637.
17. Luttrell, *A Brief Historical Relation*, II, 607.
18. *The Post Boy* (2–4 January 1700), 2.
19. Luttrell, *A Brief Historical Relation*, II, 210.
20. Rodger, *Command of the Ocean*, 158; Kirk, 'London in 1689–90', 495.
21. *The Letters of Samuel Pepys*, ed. Guy de la Bédoyère (Woodbridge: Boydell Press, 2006), 225.
22. Luttrell, *A Brief Historical Relation*, II, 163.
23. Ralph Davis, *The Rise of the English Shipping Industry in the Seventeenth and Eighteenth Centuries* (Newton Abbot: David and Charles, 1962), 136.
24. David Abulafia, *The Boundless Sea: A Human History of the Oceans* (London: Allen Lane, 2019), 768.
25. JE diary, V, 284, fn 5.
26. *A Brief History of Trade in England* (London: E. Baldwin, 1702), 23–4.
27. Peter Earle, *The Making of the English Middle Class: Business, Society, and Family Life in London, 1660–1730* (London: Methuen, 1989), 3–16.
28. Daniel Defoe, *An Essay on Projects* (London: R. R. for Tho. Cockerill, 1697), 1.
29. Ian W. Archer, 'Government in Early Modern London: The Challenge of the Suburbs', in P. Clark and R. Gillespie, eds, *Two Capitals: London and Dublin 1500–1840*, Proceedings of the British Academy, vol. 107 (Oxford: Oxford University Press, 2001), 133–47 (p. 146); Laura Gowing, *Domestic Dangers: Women, Words and Sex in Early Modern London* (Oxford: Clarendon Press, 1996), 36.
30. Tim Hitchcock and Robert Shoemaker, *London Lives: Poverty, Crime and the Making of a Modern City, 1690–1800* (Cambridge: Cambridge University Press, 2015), 27–8.
31. William C. Baer, 'Landlords and Tenants in London, 1550–1700', *Urban History* 38, no. 2 (2011), 234–55 (p. 247); Craig Spence, *London in the 1690s: A Social Atlas* (London: Institute of Historical Research, 2000), 66–8.

32. Jeremy Boulton, 'The Poor among the Rich: Paupers and the Parish in the West End, 1600–1724', in P. Griffiths and M. S. R. Jenner, eds, *Londinopolis: Essays on the Cultural and Social History of Early Modern London* (Manchester: Manchester University Press, 2000), 197–223 (p. 213).

33. WJ/SP/1695/03/002 (1695), 'Petitions to the Westminster Quarter Sessions: 1690s', in *Petitions to the Westminster Quarter Sessions, 1620–1799*, ed. Brodie Waddell, *British History Online*, http://www.british-history.ac.uk/petitions/westminster/1690s (accessed 18 April 2020).

34. LMA MJ/SP/1690/A/009.

35. Thomas Tryon, *Thomas Tryon's Letters upon Several Occasions* (London: Geo. Conyers and Eliz. Harris, 1700), 29.

36. Kirk, 'London in 1689–90', 493.

37. Glaisyer, *The Culture of Commerce in England*, 58.

38. LMA MJ/SP/1695/07/047.

39. Boulton, 'The Poor among the Rich', 201.

40. Brodie Waddell, *God, Duty and Community in English Economic Life 1660–1720* (Woodbridge: Boydell Press, 2012), 61–2.

41. G. S. De Krey, *A Fractured Society: The Politics of London in the First Age of Party, 1688–1715* (Oxford: Clarendon Press, 1985).

42. Luttrell, *A Brief Historical Relation*, II, 108.

43. Kirk, 'London in 1689–90', 334; Celia Fiennes, *The Journeys of Celia Fiennes*, intro. by John Hillaby (London and Sydney: Macdonald, 1983), 151.

44. BL Add MS 78436 f. 102 and 102v, E. Packer to Mary Evelyn (21 February 1696).

45. Fiennes, *Journeys*, 355–6.

46. Tony Claydon, *William III and the Godly Revolution* (Cambridge: Cambridge University Press, 1996), 128.

47. James Wright, *Three Poems of St. Paul's Cathedral: viz. The Ruins, The Rebuilding, The Choire* (London: Ben. Griffin for Sam. Keble, 1697), 11.

FURTHER READING

This list is for those interested in a broader guide to the material covered in this book. It is not exhaustive, and there is some overlap between categories.

GENERAL

Beier, A. L., and Roger Finlay, eds, *London 1500–1700: The Making of the Metropolis*. London and New York: Longman, 1986

Brimblecombe, Peter, *The Big Smoke: A History of Air Pollution in London since Medieval Times*. London: Routledge, 1987

Clark P., and R. Gillespie, eds, *Two Capitals: London and Dublin 1500–1840*, Proceedings of the British Academy, vol. 107. Oxford: Oxford University Press, 2001

Cockayne, Emily, *Hubbub: Filth, Noise and Stench in England 1600–1770*. New Haven and London: Yale University Press, 2007

Forsyth, Hazel, *Butcher, Baker, Candlestick Maker: Surviving the Great Fire of London*. London: I. B. Tauris and Co. Ltd., 2016

Harding, Vanessa, 'The Population of London, 1550–1700: A Review of the Published Evidence', *London Journal* 15 (1990), 111–28

Harris, Tim, *Rebellion: Britain's First Stuart Kings, 1567–1642*. Oxford: Oxford University Press, 2014

—— *Restoration: Charles II and his Kingdoms*. London: Allen Lane, 2005

—— *Revolution: The Great Crisis of the British Monarchy, 1685–1720*. London: Allen Lane, 2006

Jordan, Don, *The King's City: London Under Charles II*. London: Little, Brown, 2017

Merritt, J. F., ed., *Imagining Early Modern London: Perceptions and Portrayals of the City from Stow to Strype, 1598–1720*. Cambridge: Cambridge University Press, 2001

Orlin, Lena Cowen, ed., *Material London, ca. 1600*. Philadelphia: University of Pennsylvania Press, 2000

Pennell, Sara, *The Birth of the English Kitchen, 1660–1850*. London: Bloomsbury Publishing, 2016

Pincus, Steve, *1688: The First Modern Revolution*. New Haven and London: Yale University Press, 2009

Rideal, Rebecca, *1666: Plague, War and Hellfire*. London: John Murray, 2016

Sharpe, Kevin, *Image Wars: Promoting Kings and Commonwealths in England, 1603–1660*. New Haven and London: Yale University Press, 2018; first published 2010

—— *Rebranding Rule: The Restoration and Revolution Monarchy, 1660–1714*. New Haven and London, Yale University Press, 2013

Sheppard, Francis, *London: A History*. London: Oxford University Press, 1998

FURTHER READING

BUILT ENVIRONMENT

Borsay, Peter, *The English Urban Renaissance: Culture and Society in the Provincial Town, 1660–1770*. Oxford: Clarendon Press, 1989 (for context)

Cruickshank, Dan, *Spitalfields: The History of a Nation in a Handful of Streets*. London: Random House, 2016

Longstaffe-Gowan, Todd, *The London Square: Gardens in the Midst of Town*. New Haven and London: Yale University Press, 2012

McKellar, E., *The Birth of Modern London: The Development and Design of the City 1660–1720*. Manchester: Manchester University Press, 1999

Merritt, J. F., *Westminster 1640–60: A Royal City in a Time of Revolution*. Manchester and New York: Manchester University Press, 2013

Ogborn, Miles, *Spaces of Modernity: London's Geographies, 1680–1780*. New York and London: Guilford Press, 1998

Power, M. J., 'East London Housing in the Seventeenth Century', in Peter Clark and Paul Slack, eds, *Crisis and Order in English Towns 1500–1700: Essays in Urban History*. London: Routledge and Kegan Paul, 1972, pp. 237–62

Sheppard, F. H. W., ed., *Survey of London, Vol. XXVII, Spitalfields and Mile End New Town*. London: The Athlone Press for the London County Council, 1957

—— *Survey of London, Vol. XXXVI, The Parish of St Paul, Covent Garden*. London: The Athlone Press for the Greater London Council, 1970

Stevenson, Christine, *The City and the King: Architecture and Politics in Restoration London*. New Haven and London: Yale University Press, 2013

Thurley, Simon, *Whitehall Palace: An Architectural History of the Royal Apartments, 1240–1698*. New Haven and London: Yale University Press in association with Historic Royal Palaces, 1999

CIVIL WARS

Ackroyd, Peter, *The History of England, Volume III: Civil War*. London: Macmillan, 2014

Coates, Ben, *The Impact of the English Civil War on the Economy of London 1642–50*. Aldershot: Ashgate, 2004

Flintham, David, *The English Civil War Defences of London*. Bristol: Stuart Press, 2014

Lindley, Keith, *Popular Politics and Religion in Civil War London*. Aldershot: Scolar Press, 1997

White, Michelle Anne, *Henrietta Maria and the English Civil Wars*. Aldershot: Ashgate, 2006

Worden, Blair, *The English Civil Wars*. London: Weidenfeld and Nicolson, 2009

CRIME

Hitchcock, Tim, and Robert Shoemaker, *London Lives: Poverty, Crime and the Making of a Modern City, 1690–1800*. Cambridge: Cambridge University Press, 2015

Old Bailey Proceedings Online, www.oldbaileyonline.org

Shoemaker, Robert, *Prosecution and Punishment: Petty Crime and the Law in London and Rural Middlesex, c.1660–1725*. Cambridge: Cambridge University Press, 1991

CULTURE AND SOCIETY

Boulton, Jeremy, *Neighbourhood and Society: A London Suburb in the Seventeenth Century*. Cambridge: Cambridge University Press, 1987 (on Southwark)

Bucholz, Robert O., and Joseph P. Ward, *London: A Social and Cultural History, 1550–1750*. Cambridge: Cambridge University Press, 2012

Butler, Martin, *The Stuart Court Masque and Political Culture*. Cambridge: Cambridge University Press, 2008

Cressy, David, *Birth, Marriage and Death: Ritual, Religion, and the Life-Cycle in Tudor and Stuart England*. Oxford: Oxford University Press, 1997

Earle, Peter, *A City Full of People: Men and Women of London, 1650–1750*. London: Methuen, 1994

—— *The Making of the English Middle Class: Business, Society, and Family Life in London, 1660–1730*. London: Methuen, 1989

Ellis, Markman, *The Coffee House: A Cultural History*. London: Weidenfeld and Nicolson, 2004

Griffiths, Paul, and M. S. R. Jenner, eds, *Londinopolis: Essays on the Cultural and Social History of Early Modern London*. Manchester: Manchester University Press, 2000

Laird, Mark, *A Natural History of English Gardening*. New Haven and London: Yale University Press, 2015

Peck, Linda Levy, *Consuming Splendour: Society and Culture in Seventeenth-Century England*. Cambridge: Cambridge University Press, 2005

Picard, Liza, *Restoration London: Everyday Life in London, 1660–1670*. London: Phoenix, 2003; first published 1997

Porter, Stephen, *Shakespeare's London: Everyday Life in London 1580–1616*. Chalford: Amberley, 2009

Spence, Craig, *London in the 1690s: A Social Atlas*. London: Institute of Historical Research, 2000

Waller, Maureen, *1700: Scenes from London Life*. London: Hodder and Stoughton, 2000

IMMIGRATION

Arnold, Arthur P., 'A List of Jews and their Households in London', *Miscellanies of the Jewish Historical Society of England* 6 (1962), 73–141

Cottrett, Bernard, *The Huguenots in England: Immigration and Settlement, c. 1550–1700*. Cambridge: Cambridge University Press, 1991; first published 1985

Gwynn, Robin D., *The Huguenots of London*. Brighton: Alpha Press, 1998

Habib, Imtiaz, *Black Lives in the English Archives, 1500–1677: Imprints of the Invisible*. Aldershot: Ashgate, 2008

Kelly, Debra, and Martyn Cornick, eds, *A History of the French in London: Liberty, Equality, Opportunity*. London: Institute of Historical Research, 2013

Kershen, Anne J., *Strangers, Aliens and Asians: Huguenots, Jews and Bangladeshis in Spitalfields 1660–2000*. Abingdon: Routledge, 2005

Luu, Lien Bich, *Immigrants and the Industries of London 1500–1700*. Aldershot: Ashgate, 2005

Parker, Greig, *Probate Inventories of French Immigrants in Early Modern London*. Farnham: Ashgate, 2014

MARITIME, COMMERCE

Banbury, Philip, *Shipbuilders of the Thames and Medway*. Newton Abbot: David and Charles, 1971

Brenner, Robert, *Merchants and Revolution: Commercial Change, Political Conflict, and London's Overseas Traders, 1550–1653*. Cambridge: Cambridge University Press, 1993

Capp, Bernard, *Cromwell's Navy: The Fleet and the English Revolution, 1648–1660*. Oxford: Clarendon Press, 1989

Chaudhuri, K. N., *The English East India Company: The Study of an Early Joint-Stock Company*. London: Frank Cass and Co. Ltd., 1965

Davies, J. D., *Kings of the Sea: Charles II, James II and the Royal Navy*. Barnsley: Seaforth, 2017

Davis, Ralph, *The Rise of the English Shipping Industry in the Seventeenth and Eighteenth Centuries*. Newton Abbot: David and Charles, 1962

Dickson, P. G. M., *The Financial Revolution in England: A Study in the Development of Public Credit 1688–1756*. London: Macmillan, 1967

Farrington, Antony, *Trading Places: The East India Company and Asia 1600–1834*. London: The British Library, 2002

Glaisyer, Natasha, *The Culture of Commerce in England, 1660–1720*. Woodbridge: The Royal Historical Society in association with The Boydell Press, 2006

Morris, Derek, and Ken Cozens, *Wapping 1600–1800: A Social History of an Early Modern London Maritime Suburb*. London: East London History Society, 2009

Rodger, N. A. M., *The Command of the Ocean: A Naval History of Britain 1649–1815*. London: Allen Lane, 2004

MONARCHS (AND CROMWELL)

James VI and I

Cogswell, Thomas, *James I: The Phoenix King*. London: Allen Lane, 2017

Croft, Pauline, *King James*. London: Palgrave Macmillan, 2003

James I, *Letters of James VI and I*, ed. G. P. V. Akrigg. Berkeley, Los Angeles and London: University of California Press, 1984

Charles I

Brotton, Jerry, *The Sale of the Late King's Goods: Charles I and his Art Collection*. London: Macmillan, 2006

Corns, Thomas N., ed., *The Royal Image: Representations of Charles I*. Cambridge: Cambridge University Press, 1999

Cust, Richard, *Charles I: A Political Life*. New York: Longman, 2005

De Lisle, Leanda, *White King: Traitor, Murderer, Martyr*. London: Chatto and Windus, 2018

Sharpe, Kevin, *The Personal Rule of Charles I*. New Haven and London: Yale University Press, 1992

Oliver Cromwell

Coward, Barry, *Oliver Cromwell*. London: Routledge, 2013; first published 1991

Holberton, Edward, *Poetry and the Cromwellian Protectorate: Culture, Politics, and Institutions*. Oxford: Oxford University Press, 2008

Lay, Paul, *Providence Lost: The Rise and Fall of Cromwell's Protectorate*. London: Head of Zeus, 2020

Morrill, John, *Oliver Cromwell*. Oxford: Oxford University Press, 2007

Charles II

Hutton, Ronald, *Charles II: King of England, Scotland, and Ireland*. Oxford: Clarendon Press, 1989

Jackson, Clare, *Charles II: The Star King*. London: Allen Lane, 2016

Uglow, Jenny, *A Gambling Man: Charles II and the Restoration, 1660–1670*. London: Faber and Faber, 2009

James II

Childs, John, *The Army, James II, and the Glorious Revolution*. Manchester: Manchester University Press, 1980

Gibson, William, *James II and the Trial of the Seven Bishops*. London: Palgrave Macmillan, 2009

Miller, John, *James II*. New Haven and London: Yale University Press, 2000; first published 1978

William III and Mary II

Claydon, Tony, *William III*. London: Longman, 2002

—— *William III and the Godly Revolution*. Cambridge: Cambridge University Press, 1996

Keates, Jonathan, *William III and Mary II: Partners in Revolution*. London: Allen Lane, 2015

PEPYS AND EVELYN

Bédoyère, Guy de la, *Particular Friends: The Correspondence of Samuel Pepys and John Evelyn*. Woodbridge: Boydell Press, 1997

Darley, Gillian, *John Evelyn: Living for Ingenuity*. New Haven and London: Yale University Press, 2006

Evelyn, John, *The Diary of John Evelyn*, ed. E. S. De Beer, 6 vols. Oxford: Clarendon Press, 1955 (JE diary)

Harris, Frances, and Michael Hunter, eds, *John Evelyn and his Milieu*. London: The British Library, 2003

Lincoln, Margarette, ed., *Samuel Pepys: Plague, Fire and Revolution*. London: Thames and Hudson, 2015

Pepys, Samuel, *The Diary of Samuel Pepys*, ed. Robert Latham and William Matthews, 11 vols. London: G. Bell and Hyman, 1970–83 (SP diary)

—— *The Letters of Samuel Pepys*, ed. Guy de la Bédoyère. Woodbridge: Boydell Press, 2006

Tanner, J. R., *Samuel Pepys and the Royal Navy*. Cambridge: Cambridge University Press, 2013; first published 1920

Tomalin, Claire, *Samuel Pepys: The Unequalled Self*. London: Viking, 2002

Willes, Margaret, *The Curious World of Samuel Pepys and John Evelyn*. New Haven and London: Yale University Press, 2017

POLITICS, RELIGION

Cogswell, Thomas, Richard Cust and Peter Lake, eds, *Politics, Religion and Popularity in Early Stuart Britain*. Cambridge: Cambridge University Press, 2002

De Krey, G. S., *A Fractured Society: The Politics of London in the First Age of Party, 1688–1715*. Oxford: Clarendon Press, 1985

Goldie, Mark, *Roger Morrice and the Puritan Whigs: The Entring Book, 1677–1691*. Woodbridge: Boydell Press, 2016; first published 2007

Lake, Peter, and Steven Pincus, eds, *The Politics of the Public Sphere in Early Modern England*. Manchester and New York: Manchester University Press, 2007

Liu, Tai, *Puritan London: A Study of Religion and Society in the City*. Newark: University of Delaware Press; London: Associated University Presses, 1986

Morrice, Roger, *The Entring Book of Roger Morrice 1677–1691. Volume III, The Reign of James II 1685–1686*, ed. Tim Harris. Woodbridge: Boydell Press, 2007

—— *The Entring Book of Roger Morrice 1677–1691. Volume IV, The Reign of James II 1687–1689*, ed. Stephen Taylor. Woodbridge: Boydell Press, 2007

Pearl, Valerie, *London and the Outbreak of the Puritan Revolution: City Government and National Politics, 1625–43*. London: Oxford University Press, 1961

Seaver, Paul S., *Wallington's World: A Puritan Artisan in Seventeenth-Century London*. Stanford: Stanford University Press, 1985

Waddell, Brodie, *God, Duty and Community in English Economic Life 1660–1720*. Woodbridge: Boydell Press, 2012

Wallington, Nehemiah, *The Notebooks of Nehemiah Wallington, 1618–1654: A Selection*, ed. David Booy. Aldershot: Ashgate, 2007

Walter, John, *Covenanting Citizens: The Protestation Oath and Popular Political Culture in the English Revolution*. Oxford: Oxford University Press, 2017

SCIENCE, MEDICINE, HEALTH

Greenberg, Stephen, 'Plague, the Printing Press, and Public Health in Seventeenth-Century London', *The Huntington Library Quarterly* 67, no. 4 (2004), 508–27

Hunter, Michael, *Boyle: Between God and Science*. New Haven and London: Yale University Press, 2009

—— *Science and Society*. Cambridge: Cambridge University Press, 1981

North, Susan, *Sweet and Clean? Bodies and Clothes in Early Modern England*. Oxford: Oxford University Press, 2020

Porter, Roy, ed., *Patients and Practitioners: Lay Perceptions of Medicine in Pre-Industrial Society*. Cambridge: Cambridge University Press, 1985

Tinniswood, Adrian, *The Royal Society and the Invention of Modern Science*. London: Apollo Library, 2019

Wear, Andrew, *Knowledge and Practice in English Medicine 1550–1680*. Cambridge: Cambridge University Press, 2000

WITCHCRAFT, MAGIC

Davies, Owen, *Cunning-Folk: Popular Magic in English History*. London: Hambledon, 2003

Elmer, Peter, *Witchcraft, Witch-Hunting, and Politics in Early Modern England*. Oxford: Oxford University Press, 2016

Gibson, Marion, *Early Modern Witches: Witchcraft Cases in Contemporary Writing*. London and New York: Routledge, 2000

Hunter, Michael, 'The Royal Society and the Decline of Magic', *Notes and Records of the Royal Society of London* 65, no. 2 (2011), 103–19

Thomas, Keith, *Religion and the Decline of Magic: Studies in Popular Beliefs in Sixteenth- and Seventeenth-Century England*, rev. edn. London: Weidenfeld and Nicolson, 1973

WOMEN

Barroll, J. Leeds, *Anna of Denmark, Queen of England: A Cultural Biography*. Philadelphia: University of Pennsylvania Press, 2001

Crawford, Patricia, and Laura Gowing, eds, *Women's Worlds in Seventeenth-Century England*. London and New York: Routledge, 2000

Dunn-Hensley, Susan, *Anna of Denmark and Henrietta Maria: Virgins, Witches, and Catholic Queens*. London: Palgrave Macmillan, 2017

Gowing, Laura, *Domestic Dangers: Women, Words, and Sex in Early Modern London*. Oxford: Clarendon Press, 1996

Griffey, Erin, ed., *Sartorial Politics in Early Modern Europe: Fashioning Women*. Amsterdam: Amsterdam University Press, 2019

Hannan, Leonie, *Women of Letters: Gender, Writing and the Life of the Mind in Early Modern England*. Manchester: Manchester University Press, 2016

Humfrey, Paula, ed., *The Experience of Domestic Service for Women in Early Modern London*. London: Routledge, 2016; first published 2011

INDEX

INDEX

Newgate Street 12

Newport Street 147

newspapers 93, 116, 168, 169, 174, 179, 311, 322; advertisements in 173, 251, 302, 305, 310; *London Gazette* 168, 174, 213, 229, 254, 289

Newton, Isaac, mathematician, physicist, astronomer 231, 314, 322; interest in alchemy 219; *Principia Mathematica* 219, 225; and Mint 230, 314–15

Newton, William, builder 70–1

night watchmen 5, 56, 172, 173, 205, 315

Nonconformists 169, 200, 214, 254, 262, 265, 286, 298, 300, 301, 325; persecution of 87, 187; *see also* Dissenters; Quakers

North American colonies 12, 52, 53, 150, 151, 153, 154, 245, 304, 318, 319, 320

North Road 2

North Sea 49, 84, 318

Nottingham, Daniel Finch, 2nd Earl of 299

Ogilby, John, cartographer 174, 230

Old Artillery Ground 11, 254

Old Bailey 12, 26, 183, 314, 319

Old Jewry 168

Old Slaughter's coffee house 260

opera 144, 242

Orange Street 256

Otway, Thomas, dramatist 259

Owen, Hugh, Catholic agent 16, 20

Owen, John, Nonconformist 169

Oxinden, Henry, letter writer and poet 101, 142

Page, Damaris, brothel keeper 214

Pall Mall 175, 190, 226, 243

Palladio, Antonio, architect 66

pamphleteering 89, 90, 91, 93, 115, 117, 118, 120, 123, 168, 180, 269, 287

Papin, Denis, Huguenot 258

Paris, comparisons with 70, 172, 222

Paris Garden Stairs 6, 7

Park Street (Mayfair) 14

parks 46, 110, 143, 147, 190 *see also* individual parks

Parliament 4, 50, 82, 327; 'Long' (1640–60) 93, 145; 'Rump' (1648–53, 1659) 126, 127, 132, 133, 138, 149, 152; 'Short' (1640) 92; and Buckingham 67; and Charles I 51, 65, 68, Chapter 6 *passim*, 98, 125; and Charles II 182, 183, 187, 214, 251; and Civil Wars 99, 100, 102–14, 118, 119, 121, 122, 138; and

Commonwealth 131, 132–3, 139, 142, 143, 151, 153; and James I 14, 15, 16, 29, 30; and James II, 267, 271, 278, 282; and London demonstrations 97, 99, 101, 121, 287; and Protectorate 133–4, 140, 141–2; and Scotland 93, 119–20, 125; and William III (Convention Parliament) 286–7, 288, 290–1, 308, 320, 326; *see also* Commons; Lords; Members of Parliament

Parliament Square 145

Penington, Sir Isaac, politician and Lord Mayor 105, 112

Pepys, Elizabeth, wife of Samuel 170, 171, 172, 201, 222, 226, 233, 235

Pepys, Samuel, diarist 9, 34, 44, 60, 166, 172, 177, 238, 255, 262, 274, 297; at executions 129, 183–4; bladder operation 79; Fellow of the Royal Society 220, 226, 227, 228; home improvements 233, 239; marriage 235, 236; member of Rota Club 171; naval administrator 212–13, 240, 281; scientific curiosity 222; theatre-going 194, 195, 238; and fashion 188–9; and Mathematical School 228; and plague 199, 201, 202, 203, 204; and Fire 207, 209

Percy, Thomas, conspirator 17, 18, 19, 20

pesthouses 72, 200, 203, 204, 260

Peter I (the Great), Tsar of Russia 225, 227, 321

petitions and petitioning 18, 37, 38, 40, 72, 79, 92, 96, 97, 99, 109, 112, 120, 182, 188, 211, 213, 265, 287, 290, 318; 'Petition of the Citizens of London' 94; 'root and branch' 93; *The Poor-Whores Petition* 214; Seven Bishops' 272; Women's 101, 116, 123–4, 139, 212, 236

Petre, Father Edward, Jesuit 271, 277, 289

Pett, Christopher, master shipwright 160

Petty, Sir William, economist, physician, philosopher 75, 219, 222; dual-hulled ship design 220; *Political Arithmetic* 231

Petty France 249

philanthropy *see* charity

Philip III, King of Spain 18

Piccadilly 214, 258, 271, 297

Pierce, Edward, sculptor 300

piracy 12, 57, 84, 155, 319, 325 *see also* corsairs